Henry W. Grady

SPOKESMAN
OF THE NEW SOUTH

From a photograph taken soon after "The New South" speech

HENRY W. GRADY

Spokesman of the

New South

BY

RAYMOND B. NIXON

NEW YORK / RUSSELL & RUSSELL

TO THE PRESENT EDITOR

OF THE *ATLANTA CONSTITUTION*

Ralph McGill

IN WHOSE LIBERAL AND CONSTRUCTIVE LEADERSHIP

THE SPIRIT OF HENRY W. GRADY

LIVES ON

Preface

IN the fifty-four years since the death of Grady, the facts of his brief but remarkable career have become obscured by a haze of myth and legend. Although thousands of schoolboys still declaim his famous oration on "The New South," too many persons today think of him merely as a gifted public speaker, when oratory was never more than a side-line to his lifelong profession of journalism. Even those who recall that he was a newspaperman who "never held nor sought public office" probably regard him primarily as an editorial-writer, whereas except for the last two or three years of his life he actually devoted far less attention to the editorial page than to the news columns. Most ironical of all is the fact that a few recent writers, seeking to find in the past a scapegoat for the South's present ills, have painted Grady as a "front" for predatory economic interests and even have implied that he exploited the race issue for personal and party gain — a view which hardly seems tenable when his actions are considered in the light of the social forces that he articulated.

One reason for these misconceptions is that up to this time Grady's life and work have never been the subject of a critical study. The usual source of information has been Joel Chandler Harris's *Life of Henry W. Grady, Including His Writings and Speeches* (New York, 1890), a memorial volume compiled by so many hands that it contains three conflicting birth-dates, to say nothing of other errors and an inevitable lack of historical perspective. Valuable though Harris's introductory sketch always will be as the testimony of one of Grady's closest friends, it is necessarily too much a eulogy of the orator who died "literally loving a nation into peace" to be an adequate picture of the editor who made the weekly edition of the *Atlanta Constitution* the most widely circulated paper of its kind in America.

The late Dr. Willard Grosvenor Bleyer, professor of journalism at the University of Wisconsin and a pioneer in the field of journalistic history, first urged me to undertake to fill this gap in biographical literature. At the outset I was encouraged beyond measure by the editor's daughter and son, Mrs. Augusta Grady Black and the late Henry W. Grady, Jr., who placed at my disposal without any reservations whatsoever all the personal papers and other memorabilia of their father in their possession. Mrs. Black and Mr. Grady continued to be helpful throughout the entire period of my study and at my request eventually checked most of the manuscript for factual errors. It is to their credit that neither of them sought to influence my interpretation in the least. The same may be said of the present president and publisher of the *Constitution,* Brigadier General Clark Howell, and the editor, Ralph McGill, both of whom facilitated research without in any sense standing as sponsors of the work. The conclusions reached in this volume, therefore, together with the responsibility for any errors therein, are my own.

I would be ungrateful, however, if I did not acknowledge my especial indebtedness to Dr. Marvin G. Bauer, assistant professor of speech at Brooklyn College, with whom I frequently exchanged ideas while Dr. Bauer was engaged in the analysis of Grady's speaking which he summarizes in his article in *A History and Criticism of American Public Address* (New York, 1943) . Since each read the other's work in manuscript, it is no coincidence that we both should have selected, as the most appropriate of all the phrases applied to Grady following his death, the subtitle "Spokesman of the New South." It is not extraordinary, either, that our interpretations of Grady's national significance should be in substantial agreement.

To mention individually all the others from whom I have received assistance would be a hopeless task, for the list is so large that some surely would be omitted; but I do, nevertheless, express to them my sincere thanks. Special note should be made of the fruitful hours I spent in conversation with Mr. James R. Holliday, of Atlanta, who was Grady's private secretary. I am particularly grateful, too, for the initial help of four residents of Athens — Mr. and Mrs. Madison G. Nicholson, Mrs. Roby Redwine, and Mr. Thomas W. Reed — in running down facts about Grady's ancestry and early life. The chapters dealing with those matters were read by Dr. E. Merton Coulter, professor of history at the University of Georgia, who also kindly permitted the use of quotations from his *College Life in the Old South*. For permission to quote from Professor Coulter's *Short History of Georgia* and from Josephus Daniels's *Tar Heel Editor*, I am indebted to the University of North Carolina Press. I appreciate also the encouragement of Dr. Paul H. Buck, professor of history at Harvard University, who granted the privilege of quoting from his book *The Road to Reunion*, which is the best general work on the reconciliation period. And in my search for illustrative material I should have been handicapped indeed without the aid rendered by Mr. Gentry Dugat, of Dallas, Texas; by Miss Grace M. Mayer, of the Museum of the City of New York; by Miss Ruth Blair, executive secretary of the Atlanta Historical Society; and by Colonel Telamon Cuyler, whose memory today of people and events in the eighties is no less remarkable than was his photographic skill at that time.

This biography was written in part on the campus of the University of Minnesota, where the first draft was criticized by Professors Ralph D. Casey and Mitchell V. Charnley of the Department of Journalism, Professors William Anderson and Harold S. Quigley of the Department of Political Science, and Professor George M. Stephenson of the Department of History, all of whom made valuable suggestions. The bulk of the work has been done, however, in the Asa Griggs Candler Library at Emory University, where the Grady Collection now is permanently housed and where files of the *Constitution* for most of the Grady period also are available. To three of my colleagues at Emory — Professors Floyd K. Baskette, Thomas H. English, and Ward Pafford — and to my wife, Amy Quillian Nixon, I am indebted more than even they probably realize.

Preface

A final word of appreciation goes to Dr. Theodore Henley Jack, president of Randolph-Macon Woman's College, who as professor of history at Emory in my undergraduate days did much to interest me in the Grady period. Dr. Jack kindly read the proofs of the entire book, and for that assistance as well as for his earlier inspiration I am most grateful.

RAYMOND B. NIXON

Department of Journalism
Emory University
July 1943

Contents

Illustrations

Henry W. Grady

SPOKESMAN
OF THE NEW SOUTH

CHAPTER ONE

Earthquake in Charleston

ON the night of August 31, 1886, the eastern seaboard of the United States was rocked by the worst earthquake in its history. The disturbance centered on the South Carolina coast, but tremors were felt all the way from Maine to Florida and as far west as Terre Haute, Indiana. Buttressed three hundred miles inland by the Georgia hills, the city of Atlanta suffered little actual damage; yet it, too, was shaken sufficiently to cause many persons a sleepless night.

One Atlantan who stayed up most of the night was Henry W. Grady, the thirty-six-year-old managing editor of the *Atlanta Constitution*. When the first and most severe shock occurred on that Tuesday evening in late summer, Grady was working in the living-room of his Peachtree Street home. A few minutes before nine he and his family were startled out of their seats by the rattling of windows, the swinging of the gas chandeliers, and "a noise like a streetcar running through the house." The Gradys rushed outdoors just as a tall brick chimney crashed through the slate roof of a neighboring residence.

After ascertaining that no other damage of consequence had been done near by, Grady grabbed his hat and hurried down the dusty, unpaved streets to the *Constitution* office, a mile away. Here he found more confusion, for the five-story building had swayed perceptibly and the workers in the editorial and composing rooms had scurried from the upper floors, fully expecting the structure to collapse.

The arrival of the managing editor quickly restored order, and the staff turned its attention to the news dispatches which by now were trickling into the office from the Associated Press and the *Constitution's* special correspondents throughout the

South. Within a half-hour reports had been received from all the important cities in the earthquake area except Charleston. The telegraph lines to that point were broken and before long the wildest rumors were afloat, one story having it that the ocean was running riot where once the city had been.

It was ten o'clock Wednesday morning before communication with Charleston was restored. When Grady learned from the first dispatches that at least forty persons had been killed and hundreds injured, that damage would run into millions of dollars, and that "three-fourths of the city would have to be rebuilt," he determined to go to the scene at once. Accompanied by his editor-in-chief, Evan P. Howell, and three other Atlantans who desired to "render assistance," he caught the first train for Augusta, the half-point between Atlanta and Charleston.

Grady started out in a spirit of high adventure, but the tone of his first article became much more serious when, in the early hours of Thursday morning, he reached Augusta. Here he found the wide downtown streets filled with packing boxes and mattresses on which terrified townspeople had spent the two previous nights. This was "the outer edge of the region" where the earthquake was "altogether the most awful experience of the century." He soon learned, too, that he would have difficulty in proceeding farther. The railroad tracks had been washed out by the breaking of the dam at Langley Pond, ten miles to the east, and all train service from Augusta to Charleston was paralyzed.

The *Constitution's* managing editor immediately wired the superintendent of the South Carolina Railroad and arranged to have a special engine meet him on the other side of the washout. Then, at a livery stable, he found a venturesome driver who was persuaded to take the five Atlantans by carriage over the cracked road to Langley. Arriving there two hours later, they discovered that the breaking of the dam had flooded such a large area that travel either by carriage or on foot was impossible. But Grady spied a small boat drifting on the pond and induced a native to strip and swim for it. Soon he and his companions were rowing to the other side, where the locomotive was fired and waiting.

As the engine backed out toward Charleston, Grady perched himself on the wood-tender and began to write a running description of what he saw. Every mile held something of interest — "families living under trees . . . an immense hole vomiting sand and water . . . at Ridgeville not a chimney left standing . . . hundreds of Negroes and whites gathered, singing and praying . . . women and children with tears streaming down their faces, begging us to take them with us." Since the twisted condition of the tracks necessitated slow speed and frequent stops, it was ten o'clock Thursday night before the "earthquake hunters" reached their destination.

Riding over the city, inspecting ruined buildings, and interviewing refugees and authorities, Grady within four hours after his arrival had completed a comprehensive story of four thousand words. This he telegraphed at two o'clock Friday morning to the *Constitution,* the New York *World,* and other papers requesting it. Without undressing he slept a few hours and then rose at sunrise to write ten thousand words more. To his mind, the earthquake was the most important news event in the South since the surrender of the Confederate armies. He remained in Charleston through Friday night, not only reporting the local angles but obtaining from scientists throughout the country their explanations of the disturbance. The *Cincinnati Enquirer,* one of the many prominent dailies carrying his stories, termed the articles "the most brilliant and accurate description of the earthquake . . . that had appeared in print." The *Constitution* claimed that it had published more news on the disaster than any other paper in the country and that its circulation for the week had bounded to new heights.

After his return to Atlanta on Saturday, Grady wrote a detailed review of the disaster for the Sunday papers. He drew a graphic picture of the havoc in the stricken city: "When Sherman put the torch to Atlanta and Columbia, he did not inflict on both cities one-tenth the damage that has been done to Charleston. . . . If the brick houses of Charleston were in New York today, seven out of nine of them would be condemned and torn down. . . . No American city was ever in such straits." He closed with an urgent appeal for nation-wide contributions to be sent for the relief of a city which before the war had been "the wealthiest of its size in America, if not in the world."

Since Grady had a theory that the rich who have become poor by accident or misfortune suffer more keenly than those who always have been poor, he sympathized particularly with the plight of the ante-bellum aristocrats whose homes had been damaged or destroyed. Many of them, he said, had been "impoverished to a pitiful degree" before the quake and now appeared unable "either to rebuild or to recuperate." Less than any other Southern city, he thought, had Charleston, "the last citadel of the old regime," adapted itself to the "social and business revolution" brought about by the war. It stood in particularly striking contrast to Atlanta, which had been leveled by Sherman's army but had found a new spirit of enterprise and was now the booming industrial and commercial center of the New South.

Grady was in a position to make such observations, for by his own admission he had written "more than any man living" about the changes epitomized in the term "New South." For nearly a decade it had been the dominant theme of his writing, and the *Constitution* had become the most important organ of the movement, just as Atlanta was its center. To Grady, the New South meant the utilization of the dormant natural resources of the region and the diversification of its agriculture. It meant the development of manufacturing to supplement the once almost exclusively agrarian economy. It meant a logical adjustment of the Negro question. And since sectional animosities retarded the attainment of these goals, the New South implied, first of all, complete fraternity with the North. Hence it was to be expected, following an outpouring of sympathy from all sections of the country for the earthquake sufferers, that Grady would exclaim with enthusiastic gratification: "We are one people, after all!" [1]

Published in the New York *World* and elsewhere in the

---

[1] *Atlanta Constitution* and New York *World*, September 1–9, 1886; Joel Chandler Harris: *Life of Henry W. Grady, Including His Writings and Speeches* (New York, 1890), pp. 34, 63. (Hereafter, in citing the *Atlanta Constitution* and Harris's *Life*, the short forms *Constitution* and Harris will be used.)

North over his full name, the earthquake stories placed their author "suddenly and conspicuously before the whole American people." A few weeks later he was invited to make his now celebrated address before the New England Society of New York City on "The New South." That one brief talk, described by Champ Clark a generation later as "the most famous after-dinner speech within the memory of any living man," [2] established Henry W. Grady as the acknowledged spokesman of the Southern spirit of progress and goodwill.

2

"What a radiant and charming and accomplished man he was!" exclaimed Josephus Daniels, who met Grady in this period of his mounting fame. "His countenance irradiated the charm that won all to him. . . . He wore a slouch hat, overcoat turned up at the collar, nothing that looked like being tailor-made, and yet he wore his clothes with distinction. You could not look at him without feeling that you were in the presence of a real person with an individuality and a flavor of rare quality." [3] The little souvenir bust by Orion Frazee, an Atlanta sculptor who saw Grady almost daily and who made the editor's death mask, shows the soft hat and upturned collar of which Daniels speaks. It also reveals a quizzical smile — an expression which, according to Grady's closest friends, conveys "the real spirit and genius of the man."

Grady's boyish appearance and manner usually impressed those who saw him for the first time. He stood only five feet eight, his erect figure ranging from slenderness in his youth to an athletic trimness in his twenties and a growing plumpness in his late thirties. A Memphis reporter who visited the *Constitution* office soon after "The New South" speech described him as having "the appearance of a man whose stomach never gets left." His round head was topped by a short growth of black hair, with a faint glint of brown. His clean-shaven, olive-skinned face was lighted by piercing brown eyes, one of which strayed slightly "off center" in moments of concentration. But

[2] Champ Clark: *My Quarter Century of American Politics* (New York, 1920) , p. 190.
[3] Josephus Daniels: *Tar Heel Editor* (Chapel Hill, 1938) , p. 382.

even this peculiarity, acquaintances declare, added to his charm: his eyes "could speak fire, enthusiasm, conviction, tenderness, pathos, persuasion, humor, seriousness when no spoken word was heard." [4]

His voice was well-modulated and pleasing, but high-pitched and penetrating. Usually "a jolly laugh or the cheerful but fragmentary whistling of some sentimental ditty" announced his coming. As a rule he wore a blue serge suit, with a white handkerchief extending from the pocket under the lapel of his sack coat. When more formal occasions required a frock coat or a dress suit, the buttonhole of his lapel invariably contained a flower. He wore a wing collar with his white shirts, a moonstone pin adorned the center of his full silk cravat, and his stiff detachable cuffs frequently proved convenient for note-taking when no paper was at hand.

Joel Chandler Harris once said that if the art of conversation was dead before Grady's time, Grady resurrected it. "When he had the incentive of sympathetic friends and surroundings, he was the most fascinating talker I have ever heard." He sometimes boasted to his intimate acquaintances that he could bring laughter or tears to any person's face at will, and on this point he never was known to lose a wager. He had "the greatest knack in the world of unexpectedly turning corners; and while tears were coursing down one street smiles were speeding up another; and they sometimes collided." [5]

His mental capacity, according to Dr. T. DeWitt Talmage, the eminent Presbyterian clergyman, was "so wonderful it was almost startling." Talmage told of being in active conversation with Grady while the editor was dictating an editorial to his stenographer.[6] Others have testified that he could repeat a page of print from an ordinary book "almost word for word" after one reading.

A frequent visitor to his home relates that occasionally Grady would be sitting in his living-room with a group of friends when he would remember he had a book to review.

[4] T. W. Reed: *Henry W. Grady* (Athens, 1934) , p. 11.

[5] Harris, pp. 26–7; Lucian Lamar Knight: *Reminiscences of Famous Georgians* (Atlanta, 1908) , II, 343.

[6] *Constitution*, February 23, 1890.

BUST OF GRADY BY ORION FRAZEE

It conveys "the real spirit and genius of the man"

A SHEET OF HIS NEWSPAPER "COPY"

From a manuscript in the Grady Collection

"He would go into his study and we would not see him for an hour; then he would reappear, his work apparently accomplished. The next morning we would be amazed to read the full and ample review, beautifully done." Grady once explained that he reviewed books in this short order by "reading down the middle of the page."

Although Grady occasionally dictated a news story or an editorial, he did most of his writing in his own hand. In his office was an old-fashioned, high-backed wooden chair. Here he sat, with his legs crossed or his feet upon the desk, and wrote with a heavy pencil on a pad of copy paper held upon his knee. He held the paper close to his face on account of the astigmatism and near-sightedness from which he suffered and his aversion to wearing glasses. In the living-room of his home was another favorite chair — a large, leather-upholstered affair upon a pedestal, in which he would lean back and write or read in the evenings. Even when those around him were carrying on a lively conversation he could continue his work, apparently lost in thought, but never missing a word. Frequently he would interpose a comment of his own, or, if something was said that he did not understand, would look up from his paper with a quick "What's that?" Some of his best work was done under these conditions, the office boy from the *Constitution* calling for the articles at the Grady home between eleven and twelve o'clock at night.

Grady could write legibly when he tried, as in his letters to President Grover Cleveland, but his mind worked so much faster than his pen that ordinarily his handwriting was almost as undecipherable as Horace Greeley's. Once the Atlanta post office received a letter addressed to "Mr. H. W. Crookedmark, Atlanta." It was delivered promptly to Grady's desk. Unless he attached great importance to a letter, he always wrote with a pencil — never with a pen, because the latter necessitated dipping in ink. To intimate friends and members of the family he scribbled on scraps of copy paper, the back of an envelope, a telegraph blank, or whatever happened to be handy. Though his name usually appeared in print as "Henry W. Grady," he seldom took time to sign more than "H. W. Grady," with the final "y" hastily and incompletely formed. In most of his newspaper copy, as in his letters, he used ampersands and numerous abbreviations, which the *Constitution's* compositors obligingly translated into complete words.

Writing came easily for him, and he could transmute even the most unpromising subjects into vivid word pictures that lived and pulsated with human interest. His famous story of the "Pickens County funeral," for example, probably did more to call attention to the potential wealth of the South than any set of cold facts he could have produced. Grady used the story in numerous speeches and articles, the best version in print being that taken down by a shorthand reporter at Boston in 1889:

I attended a funeral once in Pickens county in my State. A funeral is not usually a cheerful object to me unless I could select the subject. I think I could, perhaps, without going a hundred miles from here, find the material for one or two cheerful funerals. Still, this funeral was peculiarly sad. It was a poor "one gallus" fellow, whose breeches struck him under the armpits and hit him at the other end about the knee. . . . They buried him in the midst of a marble quarry: they cut through solid marble to make his grave; and yet a little tombstone they put above him was from Vermont. They buried him in the heart of a pine forest, and yet the pine coffin was imported from Cincinnati. They buried him within touch of an iron mine, and yet the nails in his coffin and the iron in the shovel that dug his grave were imported from Pittsburgh. They buried him by the side of the best sheep-grazing country on the earth, and yet the wool in the coffin bands and the coffin bands themselves were brought from the North. The South didn't furnish a thing on earth for that funeral but the corpse and the hole in the ground. There they put him away and the clods rattled down on his coffin, and they buried him in a New York coat and a Boston pair of shoes and a pair of breeches from Chicago and a shirt from Cincinnati, leaving him nothing to carry into the next world with him to remind him of the country in which he lived, and for which he fought for four years, but the chill of blood in his veins and the marrow in his bones.[7]

If anyone chose to question the accuracy of an incident thus embellished by the writer's imagination for illustrative pur-

[7] Harris, pp. 204–5.

poses, Grady always had a ready answer. "Why be hampered by facts?" he said. "It *could* be so!"

Never did Grady use a manuscript on the platform. His important speeches he wrote out in advance, as a means of fixing his thoughts in mind, but once the talk was composed he spoke without referring to a note. Almost invariably the oral presentation was more vivid than what he had written. In all his prepared speeches he departed widely from the original composition, the departure being prompted by the inspiration of the moment or the need he felt of adapting his material to specific circumstances.

The ringing quality of his high-pitched voice made it most effective in large outdoor gatherings. He spoke rapidly, using frequent gestures which were more expressive than emphatic. He professed that his knees shook whenever he rose to address an audience, but a reporter who heard him at Dallas, Texas, in 1888 observed that his nervousness seemed to vanish when he heard the audience's cheers. His favorite position while speaking, according to this eyewitness, was with "his right hand in his trousers' pocket, his left hand resting on the table, and his body tipped gently to the left." His sentences were as well arranged as those of Robert G. Ingersoll, the critic said, and the quality of his voice was "not unlike Ingersoll's" in the latter's younger days. A contemporary who claimed to have heard "every great American orator" since Webster and Clay, including Ingersoll, Henry Ward Beecher, James G. Blaine, L. Q. C. Lamar, and Chauncey M. Depew, asserted that none of them surpassed Grady in eloquence.[8]

Grady began speaking in a conversational tone, grew more dramatic as he progressed, and gradually worked up to a climax such as the peroration of his widely quoted address at Dallas:

I see a South, the home of fifty millions of people, who rise up every day to call from blessed cities vast hives of industry and thrift; her country-sides the treasures from which their resources are drawn; her streams vocal with whirring spindles; her valleys tranquil in the white and gold of the harvest; her mountains show-

[8] Isaac W. Avery: "Henry W. Grady," in *National Cyclopedia of American Biography* (New York, 1892), I, 527.

ering down the music of bells, as her slow-moving flocks and herds go forth from their folds; her rulers honest and her people loving, and her homes happy and their hearthstones bright, and their waters still, and their pastures green, and her consciences clear; her wealth diffused and poor-houses empty, her churches earnest and all creeds lost in the gospel, Peace and sobriety walking hand in hand through her borders; honor in her homes; uprightness in her midst; plenty in her fields . . . her two races walking together in peace and contentment; sunshine everywhere and all the time. . . .[9]

To the modern reader, these rhetorical flourishes may seem artificial and excessively ornate, like the bustles which characterized the fashionable women's dresses of Grady's day, but there can be no doubt of their effectiveness upon audiences accustomed to such spellbinding.

In most of his speaking, as in his writing, Grady used a more informal style, illustrated by his Pickens County funeral story. Humor brightened his speeches, but his anecdotes always formed an integral part of his talk, never being of the "that reminds me" variety. In delivering a speech, he tried to get what he called the "swing." He said that "whenever he rose to address an audience he felt the same sensations he had felt as a child trying to 'jump' in a swing," and that "if he could succeed in moving off easily and gracefully, gradually increasing in length and sweep the 'back and forth,' he always felt secure and knew the warning symptoms of a great speech." [10] This "swing" is reflected in the rhythmic quality of his oratorical prose, some of which can be scanned almost as easily as blank verse.

Grady liked excitement, whether in delivering a stirring oration, managing a political or civic campaign, or reporting a big news story such as the Charleston earthquake. He was happiest when he was in the thick of affairs. "Newspapers, like men," he once declared, "prove themselves in emergencies." While he insisted that his paper should be evenly good from day to day, he took boyish delight in the occasions that justified a "big spread." His mind and hand were never surer, said

[9] Harris, p. 120.
[10] W. T. Turnbull: "Grady as an Orator," MS., Harris Collection.

a close associate, than "when the huge press of the *Constitution* was waiting his orders; when the forms were waiting to be closed; when the compositors were fretting and fuming for copy, and when, perhaps, an express train was waiting ten minutes over its time to carry the *Constitution* to its subscribers. . . . He seemed to infuse something of his fire and enthusiasm into every member of his staff, and each man seemed to feel that it was incumbent upon him to be at his best." Besides being "able to tell news when he saw it," wrote still another associate, "he was equally able to tell in advance when it was going to happen, and he could usually manipulate things so as to make it happen." [11]

"There is no sense of editorial dignity about me," Grady explained. "I hold that the editor of a newspaper or anybody else about the establishment ought to do anything that comes to his hand, for news is the feature and opinions are of secondary importance. If I see a dog fight and think I can hit it off to suit the reader, I am going to do it." Later, when he was compelled by his growing prominence to devote more time to the editorial page and less to the outside exploits in which he so delighted, he wrote: "A good reporter who subsides into an able editor marks a loss to journalism." [12]

Grady believed that reader interest alone should determine the length of a newspaper article. He did not insist on short sentences or condensation if he had something interesting to say, but he frowned upon "padding." One of his former reporters, T. W. Reed, recalls that during his own "cub" days on the *Constitution* he was assigned, in Grady's absence, to write a story on Atlanta preachers who were spending their vacations in Europe. Reed turned in two columns of copy, much of which was an imaginary description of places in Europe which might have been viewed by the vacationing ministers. The next Sunday he wrote another two-column article on how preachers were spending their vacations in Atlanta. As soon as Grady returned to the office, he inquired as to the authorship of those articles and called Reed into his office.

[11] Harris, p. 20; Thomas H. Martin: *Atlanta and Its Builders* (New York, 1902), II, 652.
[12] MS., Grady Collection.

"Now Tom," he said, "I want to talk to you just as I would to my own boy. I want to show you how much space you should have taken to cover those subjects."

Grady took his blue pencil, ran rapidly over the four printed columns, and handed the paper back to Reed. The articles had been reduced to four inches of type. The imagination had vanished and only the unclothed facts remained. "What was left was so bare that it might have been sent to jail for public indecency."

"He was kind and patted me on the back," said Reed. "Not even a young stripling like myself could ever get mad at Henry Grady. But I learned the lesson all right and it stood me well in hand for twenty years in newspaper work." [18]

Another member of the staff, in criticizing a dramatic performance, used the expression: "The audience was well pleased." The next morning he received a reprimand from the managing editor.

"If one is pleased, he is well pleased," said Grady. "He cannot be badly pleased. And besides, where is any authority for its use?"

"I can cite the highest usage," the reporter replied. "Did not God say, 'This is my beloved Son, in whom I am well pleased?' "

Grady laughed and admitted that the reporter for once had the best of him.[14]

His sympathetic nature prompted Grady many times to suppress unimportant stories which would have wounded someone without serving any legitimate public purpose, but he was not squeamish about publishing the details of crime or scandal to which he thought his readers were entitled.

An Atlanta woman called on him one day to inquire indignantly why he had printed a certain article.

"Did you read it?" Grady asked.

"Yes, I did," was the reply.

"Well," said the editor, "that's why I put it there."

It was this constant emphasis upon reader interest and terse writing that caused Amos J. Cummings, managing editor of

18 T. W. Reed, op. cit., pp. 7–8.
14 *Life and Labors of Henry W. Grady* (Atlanta, 1890) , pp. 61–2.

the New York *Sun,* to describe the *Constitution* of Grady's day
as "a summer sky in journalism. It was as cheery as the man
himself." [15]

The secret of Grady's success as an executive, T. W. Reed
thought, lay in his genius as an organizer. "He first determined in his own mind just what he wanted his paper to ac-
complish. Then he picked out with unerring judgment the
men who could best carry out his plans, and he looked after
each worker as he proceeded with his task. The successful and
satisfying result was inevitable." [16]

Both as a writer and as a speaker Grady exhibited a flair for
showmanship, but his feeling for the art was not confined to its
rhetorical aspects. Of the three expositions held in Atlanta
during the eighties, he helped to promote the first and personally managed the other two. For the 1889 exposition he signed
up the "Combined Wild West Show of Comanche Bill and
Pawnee Bill." A month before the opening date, however, he
received a telegram saying that the Wild West aggregation was
being disbanded in New Jersey because of a flood. Dispatching
an agent immediately to the North, Grady "bought the entire
show" and brought the three cars of Indians and cowboys,
with their stock and equipment, to Atlanta, where they were
placed in guarded quarters until the fair opened.[17]

Whenever a circus or a minstrel show played in Atlanta,
Grady was in evidence. On one occasion he came to the relief
of a circus-owner whom he had never seen before. The Sells
Shows were exhibiting in Atlanta, and just as the afternoon
performance was about to begin, an attachment was served.
Grady was sitting in the audience with his family and a group
of schoolgirls. When news of the trouble reached him, he went
immediately to the sheriff and signed Sells's bond so that the
show could start.[18] And how Grady did love the brass band!

One of the most worn books in the Grady library — and
one of the most frequently consulted by the editor, according
to his son — is the autobiography of P. T. Barnum. In this

[15] Clipping, Grady Scrapbooks.
[16] T. W. Reed, op. cit., p. 12.
[17] *Constitution,* September 14, 1889.
[18] Peter Sells in *Constitution,* December 28, 1889.

work, so popular that it went through seven editions, the greatest showman of the age takes his machine apart and shows how it turned the wheels of human credulity. Grady, like Mark Twain, found in Barnum's story "the root of the human matter — the inner revelation of the human being at first hand." The essential difference between Barnum and Grady is that the latter used his knowledge of human nature not simply for private profit, but for the promotion of great public enterprises in which his sole reward was the thrill of accomplishment.[19]

Grady as a rule was so interested in making a success of an undertaking that money seemed to "melt right out of" his hands. Once he gave $5,000 to his secretary, J. R. Holliday, and asked that it be placed in a safe-deposit vault so that he could not spend it. Within a short time, however, he had asked Holliday to return the money for various purposes, one of which was to lend $2,000 to a friend. The loan was never repaid.

Joel Chandler Harris has told about the rainy Christmas Eve when he and Grady were walking down the street. They saw a seedy-looking old man who once had been a leading citizen, but who had been dragged down by drink.

"Yonder is the judge," said Grady. "Let's go and see what he is going to have for Christmas."

Although the judge had been receiving "loans" from Grady for a number of years, his manner did not betray his indebtedness.

"It isn't too early to wish you a merry Christmas, I hope," said Grady, as they shook hands.

"No, no," replied the judge. "Not at all. The same to you, my boy."

When Grady suggested to the old man that he should be fixing up for the occasion, the judge relaxed his pompousness and asked to have a word in private. After a whispered conversation, during which the judge confided that he had no money with which to buy food, Grady turned to Harris and said: "Come with us. The judge here has found a family in distress, and we are going to send them something substantial for Christmas."

By the time the three had entered a near-by grocery store, the judge had recovered his decorum, even to the point of haughtiness, much to Grady's delight.

"We must get what you think this suffering family most needs," Grady began, with a sly twinkle in his eye. "You call off the articles, the clerk here will check them off, and I will have them sent to the house."

Leaning against the counter, the judge named a long list of articles which he had enjoyed in his more prosperous days — chowchow pickles, strawberry jelly, mincemeat, dates, deviled ham.

"The whole episode was like a scene from one of Dickens's novels, and I have never seen Mr. Grady more delighted," wrote Harris. "He dwelt on it then and afterwards, and often said that he envied the broken-down old man the enjoyment of the luxuries of which he had so long been deprived." [20]

Grady claimed no special virtue for such acts of philanthropy. He simply explained that every man was entitled to some form of selfishness, and that his particular form of self-indulgence was the pleasure he experienced in helping persons like the "old judge."

"I don't know how it is," he wrote, "but I have a mania for looking into cases of this sort. It is not philanthropy with me; it is a disease.

"At the editorial desk, I sit opposite a young man of a high order of mind. He makes it a point to compass the problems of nations. I dodge them. His hero is Bismarck, that phlegmatic miracle that has yoked impulse to an ox, and having made a chess-board of Europe, plays a quiet game with the Pope. My hero is a blear-eyed sot, that having for four years waged a gigantic battle with drink, and alternated between watery Reform and positive Tremens, is now playing a vague and losing game with Spontaneous Combustion." [21]

[20] Harris, pp. 35–7.   [21] Ibid., p. 212.

3

Grady ordinarily rode back and forth between his home and office on the horse-drawn streetcar which ran from Five Points, the business center, out Peachtree Street and thence to Ponce de Leon Springs, a favorite recreation park. In fair weather he always stood on the front platform, talking to the driver, chatting with other passengers, or whistling softly to himself.

He left for his office about eight thirty in the morning, came home for dinner in the middle of the day, and then returned to the house at night around six. In the evening he would jump off the car at Merritts Avenue, the corner nearest his residence, and whistle to his big St. Bernard, King. Giving the dog a friendly pat, he would go through the iron gate and enter the large frame house. Tossing his coat and hat on a V-shaped corner chair just inside the door, he would push open the sliding door to his living-room and call out a cheery greeting to each member of the family. Besides his wife and two children, the household much of the time included his mother, his maiden sister, and his brother. After kissing his wife and mother and passing on some lively bit of pleasantry heard during the day, he would retire to the small adjoining study to glance over the newspapers from which he was forever clipping items and stuffing them into his pocket. But he seldom remained long by himself. He preferred to do both his reading and his writing in the big pedestal chair in the living-room, where he could enjoy the general conversation.

An out-of-town friend who visited him in the eighties observed that "his children play all around him, and often ask him questions, which he answers with some playful remarks, yet he continues at work."

"I abhor as the most terrible curse ever issued by tyrant that sentence 'children should be seen and not heard,' " Grady once said. "You might as well say birds should be seen and not heard." [22] The excitement and pleasure of the children at Christmas-time delighted him so much that on one Fourth of July he brought home an armful of packages and told his young daughter, Gussie, and his son, Henry, Jr., to hang up

[22] MS., Grady Collection.

their stockings. "I've decided the Gradys will have two Christmases this year," he announced.

While Gussie was attending a kindergarten about half-way between the home and his office, Grady made a practice of walking to school with her each morning. One day he had to leave the house before Gussie was ready. He could see that the little girl was disappointed. By the time he reached his office the matter preyed upon his mind so much that he bought a bag of candy and sent it to her by special messenger with this note:

Jan. 31, 1884

My Dear Little Girl

Did you get mad with "old Pop" this morning because he wouldn't wait for you? I wanted to wait & walk with you, but I had so much work that I could not wait.

Papa loves his baby with all his whole heart and it makes him happy to walk with her, but he has so much work that he has to hurry all the time.

I send my darling little "warm-mouth" some candy. Give it to your little friends & eat some yourself. Good bye. Love your old "pater," who loves his little "filia." With love,

Your old "Pop"

That letter became one of the most cherished possessions of the daughter, who today is the widow of the late Eugene R. Black, one-time Governor of the Federal Reserve Bank. On the back the note bears in childish handwriting this memorandum: "I was not mad with Pop."

In writing to Clark Howell, son of Evan P. Howell, on the occasion of the young man's twenty-first birthday, Grady noted that "my son will be just about your age when you are about mine." He then gave Howell the advice which he said he wished given to his own son:

Never Gamble. Of all the vices that enthrall men, this is the worst, the strongest, and the most insidious. Outside of the morality of it, it is the poorest investment, the poorest business, and the poorest fun. No man is safe who plays at all. It is easiest *never* to play. I never knew a man, a gentleman and man of business, who did not regret the time and money he had wasted in it. . . .

Never Drink. I love liquor and I love the fellowship involved in drinking. My safety has been that I never drink at all. It is much easier not to drink at all than to drink a little. If I had to attribute what I have done in life to any one thing, I should attribute it to the fact that I am a teetotaler. . . .

Marry Early. There is nothing that steadies a young fellow like marrying a good girl and raising a family. By marrying young your children grow up when they are a pleasure to you. You feel the responsibility of life, the sweetness of life, and you avoid bad habits.

If you never drink, never gamble, and marry early, there is no limit to the useful and distinguished life you may live. You will be the pride of your father's heart, and the joy of your mother's.

I don't know that there is any happiness on earth worth having outside of the happiness of knowing that you have done your duty and that you have tried to do good. You try to build up, — there are always plenty others who will do all the tearing down that is necessary. You try to live in the sunshine, — men who stay in the shade always get mildewed.[23]

Grady himself married early, and after a few youthful experimentations with poker-playing and liquor he followed his own advice about gambling and drinking. He refrained from the use of tobacco as well as of hard liquor, not on moral grounds, but simply because "they make me sick." Champagne and cigars were always available in his home, however, for those who cared for them. There was nothing of the kill-joy about him.

He satisfied his own gambling instincts by performing a major if not decisive role in the election of every Georgia governor and senator in the eighties. And he never could resist the temptation to play the market. Several times he was fortunate, but one speculation in cotton futures, particularly, cost him heavily.

An Atlantan who knew of Grady's ventures in the market called one day to present him with an array of statistics on the production, consumption, and export of cotton. Each time the visitor made a point he would ask: "Ain't that true?" Each time Grady would assent. Finally the interviewer asked: "If all

[23] Harris, p. 41.

these things are true, is it not clear that the price of cotton must go up, and I will make a killing if I buy futures on this set of facts? "

"Yes," replied Grady, "except for one thing."

"What is that?" inquired his visitor.

"Cotton is a damned fool!" [24]

No one enjoyed a good story more than Grady. Before getting down to serious work in the morning, he almost invariably sat on Joel Chandler Harris's desk for a few minutes and traded jokes with the members of the editorial staff. He would laugh at an amusing story until he became red in the face, and sometimes he literally doubled up with mirth.

One evening a "mind-reader" who was performing in Atlanta was invited to a party at the Grady home. Among the other guests was a notoriously thick-headed social leader, who asked the seer for a reading. The "mind-reader" looked at the man, hesitated, and seemed lost for something to say. Grady became so amused that he retired to his back porch to give vent to his laughter. "He couldn't find it!" he shouted.[25]

From his family and intimate friends Grady's interest in people radiated to all classes, races, and creeds. His servants — Charley Moon, the butler; "Aunt" Sarah, the cook; and Lizzie, the maid — were devoted to him. He enjoyed attending services at a Negro church or talking to a street beggar just as he did moving among the great of the business and political world.

The editor knew most of the *"Constitution* family," down to the newsboys, by their first names. He was in his glory presiding at a Christmas dinner during the holiday season for the paper's employees and out-of-town correspondents. One of his dinners for his "newsies" attracted so much attention among his readers that Atlantans made the affair virtually a civic testimonial.

Grady's religious nature expressed itself in such deeds rather than in creeds. His tolerance was evident in the fact that his own secretary and several of his closest friends were Catholics. One of his most trusted co-workers was a Jew.

[24] Daniels, op. cit., p. 158.
[25] Mrs. W. L. Peel in *Constitution,* May 24, 1921.

He himself was a member of the Methodist church, but after getting out from under the parental wing he became somewhat irregular in his attendance at services. In his three years as a member of the official board of the First Methodist Church of Atlanta, the minutes reveal that he answered the roll-call only once. Nevertheless, his article on "The Atheistic Tide," written from New York during the heyday of the agnostic Ingersoll's influence, shows clearly the importance he attached to religion as a stabilizing influence in society:

The practical effects of the growth of atheism are too terrible to contemplate. A vessel on an unknown sea that has lost its rudder, and is tossed in a storm — that's the picture. It will not do for Mr. Ingersoll to say that a purely human code of right and wrong can be established to which the passions of men can be anchored and from which they can swing with safety. It will not do for him to cite his own correct life or the correct lives of the skeptical scientists, or of leading skeptics, as proof that unbelief does not bring license. These men are held to decency by pride of position and by a sense of special responsibility. It is the masses that atheism will demoralize and debauch. It is thousands of simple men and women who, loosed of the one restraint that is absolute and imperious, will drift upon the current of their passions, colliding everywhere, and bringing confusion and ruin.[26]

Despite his religious convictions, Grady never could bring himself to talk from the pulpit. He was invited to do so by a prominent New York minister following the publication of his article on "The Atheistic Tide," but he promptly refused. A friend once persuaded him to drop in on the mid-week prayer service at the First Methodist Church. The pastor, spotting Grady in the congregation, called on the editor to lead in prayer. Grady complied, but later said he was "scared for a week afterward."

Ministers were drawn to Grady, however, and he numbered many of them among his friends. Besides his own pastors, his clerical acquaintances and admirers included such nationally known figures as Dr. T. DeWitt Talmage; Dwight L. Moody

26 *Constitution*, January 30, 1881.

and Ira D. Sankey, the famous evangelistic team; and Dr. James W. Lee, pastor of the Trinity Methodist Church in Atlanta and a gifted author and lecturer. Dr. Lee, the father of Ivy L. Lee, wrote one of the most unreserved of all the eulogies of Grady's character.[27] Although Ivy Lee was only thirteen years old when Grady died, he said later, after he had become America's leading expert in public relations, that in his boyhood he idolized Henry W. Grady and acquired from his own father a great admiration for the editor-orator's facility in influencing people.

Another ministerial friend of Grady was the Georgia evangelist and prohibition leader Sam Jones of Cartersville, who had "shifted from the law to a drunkard's gutter," then to the pulpit. Jones had revolutionized Southern preaching by the use of humor and ridicule in his sermons. "It was believed that he had received his first revealing vision of hell while drunk and looking into the glow of a blast furnace. . . . He made vivid comments on drinking, card-playing, Sabbath-breaking, dancing, and low-neck dresses. In rural eyes he had no equal, either for religion or for entertainment." [28] Any man who had demonstrated such marked ability in arousing the masses was bound to be of interest to Grady, though the latter's techniques never included the sarcasm, ridicule, and caustic comments for which Jones was noted.

Grady had a positive distaste for denunciation and personal controversy. That is why the legends which attempt to cast him in the same mold as Horace Greeley, the most familiar prototype of the personal journalist, fail to fit. Silas Bent once classified Grady along with Greeley and a long line of other "personal journalists, old style," who resorted to duelings and horsewhippings, and who "went about armed as a matter of course." [29] Grady began his journalistic career at a time when such happenings were common, but he never took part in a duel or a whipping in his life, and if he ever carried a gun, no one recalls it. Whenever the *Constitution* became involved in

<hr>

[27] *Henry W. Grady: the Editor, the Orator, the Man* (St. Louis, 1896) .

[28] H. C. Nixon: *Possum Trot* (Norman, Okla., 1914) , p. 39.

[29] "Personal Journalists," in *Saturday Review of Literature,* December 12, 1936, pp. 4–5.

an acrimonious dispute, some other writer was delegated to handle it. Grady had more effective methods of getting things done.

His approach to complexities was constructive. In Atlanta, in Georgia and the South, and finally in the nation at large he continually was urging discordant groups to "come together, talk together, and work together." He displayed much more in common with the first great American journalist, the placid Benjamin Franklin, who urged his fellow colonists to hang together lest they hang separately, than with the petulant Greeley, who "attacked, scolded, and everywhere aroused antagonism." [30] Thus he became in the popular mind the logical successor to Henry Clay and Daniel Webster, who were making their dying pleas for national unity in the year he was born.

But Grady lived through War and Reconstruction, through bitter personal disappointments and disillusionments, and even through a few flings of his own with the journalistic fireworks before he learned that tolerance and understanding are the way of progress. The story of how he eventually came to be cast in the role of "loving a nation into peace" is one of family heritage and environmental conditioning, interwoven with historical circumstances and other coincidences almost as remarkable as the earthquake which helped to bring him the opportunity to become the "Spokesman of the New South."

[30] Don C. Seitz: *Horace Greeley* (Indianapolis, 1926), p. 28.

CHAPTER TWO

From O'Grady to Grady

GRADY delighted in astounding his friends with feats and pranks of memory. One evening the conversation in his living-room drifted to the question of how far back each person present could remember. After various guests had told of incidents occurring in their early childhood, Grady solemnly declared that the earliest event in his own recollection was hearing somebody say: "It's a boy!" He added that he had been ashamed all his life of his inability to recall just who made the announcement. "I was so swaddled," he explained, "that I could not see him."

Only in this humorous vein did Grady ever refer to his family history. "My father was an Irishman and my mother a woman," he sometimes said, in accounting for his glibness of speech. To the suggestion that he attempt to trace his ancestry, however, he laughingly replied: "I once studied my family tree and gave it up when I found several ancestors hanging from the limbs."

The Irish emigrant was William O'Grady, who left County Donegal, Ireland, about 1700, dropped the "O" from his name en route, and settled in Bertie County, North Carolina. O'Grady is the Irish form for "a descendant of Grady," and McGrady or MacGrady, another variation, signifies "a son of Grady." The name, originally Gradha, is allied to the Latin *gradus*, a "step" or "stairway," and means "noble" or "ambitious." Since the Irish Gradys pronounced the name with a short "a," colonial officials with a bent for phonetic spelling usually entered it on the records as "Graddy."

Aside from the fact that the emigrant William gave service in colonial days, and that at least three of his descendants became Revolutionary soldiers, there is little of definite record about the activities of the family during the first four generations in America. The Gradys were mostly farmers and tradesmen, in religion Protestants, whose blood mingled by marriage with the Scotch-Irish stream that flowed during the eighteenth century into Virginia, the Carolinas, Tennessee, and Georgia.[1] Perhaps the most interesting family tradition, so far as its possible bearing upon the character of Henry W. Grady is concerned, is that one of these early Gradys planned and actually began the construction of a chain of inns, each a day's journey apart, for the convenience of stagecoach travelers between Boston and Charleston. Although this story cannot be fully verified, it is a fact that a later Grady owned a number of hotels in upper South Carolina and was quite proud of his ancestor's reputed enterprise in facilitating travel between North and South.

Beginning with the fifth generation of the family in America and with Henry Grady, the grandfather of Henry W. Grady, the records become more plentiful. This first Henry Grady, born in 1788, was the son of Jonathan and Harriet Sammons Grady, of Halifax County, Virginia. His mother dying in his infancy, he was reared in the home of his maternal grandfather, William Sammons, near Greenville, South Carolina. Faced at the age of fifteen with the prospect of being apprenticed to a blacksmith, he fled to Asheville, North Carolina, and made his home with his older sister, Mary, and her wealthy and influential husband, John Woodfin. With the aid of this friendly brother-in-law Henry soon became a success as a farmer and acquired several large tracts of land in the Mills River district, south of Asheville. In 1812 he married Leah King, daughter of a hospitable Mills River family whose ancestry, like his own, was traceable directly to Ireland. The couple had five children, the first of whom they named, quite logically, John Woodfin.

Soon after the birth of their fourth child, William Sammons, in 1821, Henry Grady was elected high sheriff of Bun-

---

[1] Benjamin Grady, *John Grady of Dobbs and Duplin, with Some of His Descendants* (Wilson, N. C., 1930), pp. 9–11; Orville A. Park: "The Georgia Scotch Irish," in *Georgia Historical Quarterly*, XII (June 1928), 131.

combe County. This office he held for only a brief period, however, because the infliction of certain forms of punishment was more than his sensitive nature could bear. The penalty for larceny in North Carolina at that time was "thirty-nine lashes well laid on the bare back with keen switches in the hands of the sheriff," while the penalty for manslaughter was "branding by the sheriff in the palm of the right hand with a red-hot iron shaped to the letter M." The duration of the branding was determined, according to the law, by the speed with which the prisoner could repeat three times the words "God save the state." The story is told of one iron-nerved victim who, while being branded by a sheriff named Dave Tate, quickly added: "And God damn old Dave Tate!" [2] The administration of such legalized torture was extremely trying to Sheriff Grady, and when it became necessary for him to officiate at a double hanging, he resigned forthwith.

Devoted to his young wife, Grady vowed at her deathbed in 1829 that he would never marry again — a promise he faithfully kept. Lonely and restless, he disposed of his Mills River lands shortly thereafter and moved southward to Cherokee County to engage with his two sons in the mercantile business. Early in the 1840's the three men again set forth and traveled into the wild, mountainous region of northwest Georgia, which was being opened for settlement following the eviction of the Cherokee Indians.

Building a home five miles northwest of Ellijay, the seat of Gilmer County, Henry Grady helped to found a community which took the name of Mountaintown. In addition to farming, he operated a general store and was postmaster of the village. He died there in 1879 and is buried in the local cemetery. He is remembered even today by a few old residents of the county as a rather small man, with dark brown hair and blue eyes, who usually dressed in black broadcloth and wore a tall "churn" hat. Known in the neighborhood as "the captain," he is reputed to have been gracious in manner, precise in language, and generous to a fault.

Two other traits of Grandfather Grady which made a deep

[2] John Preston Arthur: *Western North Carolina: A History from 1730–1913* (Raleigh, 1914) , pp. 389–90.

impression upon his neighbors were his hatred of strong drink and his views on religion. He is said to have been a Universalist, a faith sometimes described by wits of the period as that of "those who believed that God was too good to damn them, in contrast to the Unitarian conceit that they were too good to be damned." He read many books, and his keen, active mind could not except religion from the field of its inquiry, even though he soon came to realize that the staunch Baptists and Methodists of Mountaintown unjustly suspected him of being an atheist. One youngster, to whom Grady expressed a desire to give certain religious volumes in his library, was forbidden by his parents to accept such heretical literature. Tradition has it that, following the old man's death, the books were burned.[3]

Following their arrival in Georgia, the two sons of Henry Grady went into business for themselves. John pushed on forty-five miles southeast of Ellijay to Dahlonega, opened a general store, and by 1850 had become a member of the town council. William remained with his brother for a short while, but by 1846 had moved sixty miles farther southeast to Athens, which he selected as a strategic trading center because it was the terminus of the only railroad connecting the mountain region with Augusta and the coast. Soon the Grady store in Athens was shipping merchandise by stagecoach and wagon to Dahlonega, Mountaintown, and all the surrounding country.

Gold had been discovered near Dahlonega in 1828 and was, indeed, the principal reason for the opening of the mountain counties and the removal of the Indians. Lumpkin County, of which Dahlonega is the seat, was organized in 1832, although the final treaty extinguishing the Cherokee claims was not signed until 1835 and the majority of the Indians were not removed until 1838. By the late forties the lure of gold and free land had brought into the county more than eight thousand inhabitants, less than ten per cent of whom were slaves. The mining frontier, with its almost exclusively white population, developed a lusty, earthy democracy in Dahlonega. Something

[3] G. G. Ward: "History of Gilmer County," MS. in his possession, Atlanta.

of the frontier spirit still survives in its quaint newspaper, the *Dahlonega Nugget.*

On a visit to Dahlonega in the summer of 1848 William S. Grady passed a house where a bright-eyed, dark-haired girl stood on the porch, polishing steel knives with sand and ashes. The flashing brown eyes found a mark in Grady's heart, and he contrived as quickly as possible to be introduced to their attractive possessor.[4] The upshot was that on September 26, 1848 he married the brown-eyed girl, Ann Eliza Gartrell.

2

The Gartrells were of French Huguenot descent, the name, according to family tradition, having been originally "de Gartrelle." In the colonial records of Maryland, where the earliest entries are found, the name is spelled variously Gatril, Gartril, Gartrill, Gartrell, Garterill, Gatherell, Gatterell, and Gattrell. The first members of the family in America are revealed by wills on file in the Maryland Archives to have been tobacco planters, evidently much richer in their religious faith than in their worldly possessions. The records in the Land Office of Maryland tend to support the theory that the original emigrant came to Virginia during the Huguenot exodus which followed the revocation of the Edict of Nantes by Louis XVI in 1685. The documentary evidence begins in 1697, by which time one John Gartril had moved into Maryland, married Jane Johnson, and acquired lands some thirteen miles south of Annapolis. These lands he transferred in 1718 to his son Francis, who became the forebear of the Georgia branch of the family.

Francis Gartrell's son John, of the third generation in America, had three sons, Francis, Joseph, and John, all of whom were listed as militiamen during the Revolution. At the close of the war the three brothers abandoned their impoverished tobacco plantations in Maryland and joined the exodus to Wilkes County, Georgia, where free land awaited settlers un-

4 Andrew W. Cain: *History of Lumpkin County, 1832–1932* (Atlanta, 1932), pp. 18–19, 39, 92, 400–1.

der a legislative act of 1783. Francis and Joseph acquired adjoining plantation sites about eleven miles southeast of Washington, the county seat. John, the youngest of the three, moved
on farther and settled in what subsequently became Columbia
County. Here he married Elizabeth Jones, and here was born
their seventh child, Jeremiah.

Jeremiah Gartrell married Julia Ann Thompson, of Columbia County. In 1831 — just before the family moved to
Dahlonega for Jeremiah to take up gold mining — Ann Eliza,
the bride-to-be of William S. Grady, was born. On her mother's side Ann's great-great-grandfather was the venerable
Thomas Cobbs, of English and Welsh descent, who died in
1835 at the almost unbelievable age of 111. Cobbs's only
daughter, Sarah, had married John Benning, and one of their
daughters had married a Thompson, another a Moore, and
still another Colonel Peter Lamar, a cousin of Associate Justice L. Q. C. Lamar of the United States Supreme Court.[5]
Thus the Gartrells, and through them the Gradys, were linked
with four other families of eminence in Georgia history — the
Cobbs, the Bennings, the Lamars, and the Moores.

Following the death of her mother and the subsequent re-
marriage of her father, Ann lived in Dahlonega at the home of
one of her mother's relatives, Robert Hughes Moore. It was
in the parlor of the Moore home, before a fireplace almost
large enough to hold the wedding party, that the marriage of
Ann to William S. Grady took place.[6]

3

Returning to Athens, William took his bride to a little four-
room cottage at the southeast corner of Hoyt and Jackson
Streets. On May 24, 1850, in this vine-covered dwelling, occurred the event to which Henry W. Grady later jokingly referred as the earliest in his recollection. Ann Grady bore her
husband a son, who was named Henry Woodfin in honor of
the grandfather, Henry Grady, and the grandfather's brother-
in-law, John Woodfin.

[5] Knight: *Reminiscences,* I, 196–9.
[6] Cain, op. cit., pp. 418–19.

WILLIAM SAMMONS GRADY
Grady's father

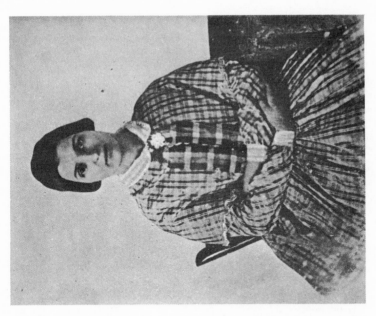

ANN GARTRELL GRADY
Grady's mother

BIRTHPLACE OF GRADY IN ATHENS
His mother is standing in front of the fence

Both in his facial features and in his sunny disposition, the boy resembled his mother rather than his father. William S. Grady was described by those who knew him in Athens as "an unusually quiet man, courteous and brave, but given to the formulas of business rather than to the bonmots of conversational banter." [7] The only touch of humor discovered in thirty-two letters from husband to wife is a closing remark about "the Baby — I suppose it is hardly worthwhile for me to advise him to be good." But these same intimate letters reveal a strength of will, a love of family, and a religious and patriotic fervor which Henry W. Grady did hold in common with his father.

William S. Grady was idealistic almost to the point of zealotry; for example, his firm at first sold whisky, as did nearly all general stores of that day, but so strong was the owner's hatred of alcohol that he eventually eliminated his entire stock of liquor. Much of the father's idealism was passed down to the son, but in Henry W. Grady it was tempered happily by the humor, the tolerance, and the imagination of the mother.

Although Ann Grady, like her husband, was an active member of the Methodist church, her religion was of the cheerful sort traditionally associated with her Huguenot forebears. According to one who spent many evenings in the home, the mother was the merriest member of the household. Playing cards she outlawed, but at games such as checkers, backgammon, and "animal whist" she was adept. "If she had ever acquired the art of playing poker," wrote a friend, "she could have bankrupted any steamboat captain on the Mississippi River." Ann Grady loved people, and only darkness or urgent family responsibilities could bring her home from a visiting expedition. It was said that "she could beat any doctor in Athens in furnishing tonic for the sick-room" and that "even the most hopeless case of rheumatism wore an aspect of cheerfulness when she was near." [8]

If the joyous spirit that buoyed Henry W. Grady throughout his life came from the gay, gentle, magnetic woman by whom he was reared, then the shrewd determination that

[7] Knight: *Reminiscences*, II, 348.
[8] Ibid., pp. 348–50.

made of his light-heartedness something more than shallow optimism can be seen in the face of the father, whose high fore-head, piercing eyes, and firmly set mouth suggest force and perseverance.

The contrast between the Grady and Gartrell temperaments was brought out by an incident occurring in Henry's early boyhood. Soon after the discovery of gold in California, Grand-father Jeremiah Gartrell and a son, Homer, together with several hundred of the mining population of Dahlonega, set out for the new El Dorado on the west coast. While in Cali-fornia, Jeremiah slipped from a foot-log over a swollen stream and was drowned. This tragedy led William S. Grady to make a trip to the West, but nothing he saw there could induce him to give up a growing mercantile business for the uncer-tainties of a prospector's life. True to his foresight, the Cali-fornia fever soon began to subside, and by 1856 many of the rainbow-chasers had returned to Georgia without their pot of gold. Grady, on the other hand, had become by this time one of the most successful merchants of northeast Georgia.

Early in the fifties Grady took into partnership John W. Nicholson, who married a sister of Ann Grady in 1852. In this same year the firm of Grady and Nicholson built a plant to supply the town of Athens with gas made from pine wood.⁹ With this profitable new venture and a sawmill added to the thriving wholesale and retail trade of the store, the tax digests of Clarke County each year reflected a steady growth in the wealth of the firm and its senior partner.

⁹ H. J. Rowe: *History of Athens and Clarke County* (Athens, 1923), p. 7.

CHAPTER THREE

Athens, the War, and the University

AROUND the little college town where Henry W. Grady was born and spent his first eighteen years were to be clustered some of the most poignant feelings of his life. Carved out of the wilderness in 1801 by those looking for a sufficiently isolated and sinless site for the new University of Georgia, Athens had grown until in 1850, the year of Grady's birth, it had a population of 3,500, approximately half whites and half slaves. The town was a trading center for the thriving plantations of the surrounding country, and already on the banks of the Oconee River were three cotton factories. Athens, however, "had no ambition to become an industrial metropolis; it was . . . a cultured community, was born so, grew up so, and profited much from its cultured immigrants," who had come chiefly from Virginia and the Carolinas, with a sprinkling direct from Europe. "People with money and a love for respectable and intellectual leisure moved here, built their white-columned homes among the green groves, and . . . helped make the finest product of the civilization of the Old South." [1]

The white-columned mansions on Prince and Milledge Avenues contrasted sharply with the little cottage in which Henry was born, but as his business prospered, William S. Grady provided his family with surroundings in keeping with his improved financial circumstances. Soon after the birth of their second child, William Sammons, Jr., in 1851, the Gradys moved into a two-story house on Broad Street, in the same block with the store and within sight of the university campus.

[1] E. M. Coulter: *College Life in the Old South* (New York, 1928) , pp. 1–14, 264–9.

Here the third child, Martha Nicholson, known as Mattie, was born in 1855, and here the family resided until Henry's fifteenth year.

Living only a few steps from the busy store, the Grady children came into contact with all classes of society and had an opportunity to learn much about human nature. Even toward the slaves they acquired an attitude somewhat different from that which might have been developed by plantation life such as was being experienced at Eatonton, forty miles away, by Joel Chandler Harris. The five Negroes owned by William S. Grady were household servants, who under the customs of the pre-war South enjoyed a status somewhat above that of the ordinary field hand. In the group, for example, was a Negro boy of Henry's own age with whom the children played in their early years. Henry called the little slave "Brother Isaac" until an older person corrected him.[2]

Under the influence of their parents, the Grady children attended the Methodist Sunday school. Here they received copies of the *Visitor,* a religious weekly for boys and girls. Observing that this periodical invited letters from its readers, Henry at the age of seven wrote to it the contribution that first gave him the thrill of seeing his name in print. Oddly enough, his pride in this accomplishment was accompanied by humiliation of a sort that he also was to know frequently in later years: the printer made an error in setting his letter in type!

Inasmuch as files of the *Visitor* for this period have been destroyed, the earliest extant composition of the boy is a letter written at the age of eight to an uncle in Augusta. Printed neatly with pen, this missive contains in its closing reference to Henry's younger brother a suggestion of the humor to be found in Grady's later writing. "Brother sends his love to you," Henry wrote, "and says he will print you a letter if he ever learns to print." [3]

By this time Henry's education had begun under his mother's tutelage. A year later, when he was nine, he was sent to a private school conducted by Mrs. Elvira Lee, the widowed

---

[2] Harris, p. 22.

[3] T. R. Crawford: "Early Home of Henry W. Grady," in *New England Magazine,* II (June 1890) , 427, 434.

ATHINS OCt 28TH 1858

MY DEAR UNCLE

I RECEIVED YOUR KIND L-
ETTER AND WAS VERY GLAD to HEAR FROM YOU
AND to SEE that YOU HAD Not FORGOttEN ME.
I SHOULD LIKE VERY MUCH INDEED to GO HOME
WItH YOU. I HAVE MADE UP MY MIND that
A GUSTA IS A GREAT PLACE AND I WOULD ENJOY
the VISIt VERY MUCH INDEED. tHE ATHENS GAUR-
DS LOOK VERY PREttY BUt I EXPECt YOUR MILITARY
COMPANIES LOOK A GREAt DEAL PREttIER WE HAVE
two FIRE COMPANIES AND A HOOK AND LADDER CO-
MPANIES tHEY CAME OUt LAST WEEK AND I thought
tHEY LOOKED VERY PRETTY. BROTHER AND I WENt
OUt to UNCLE GRAHAMS AND WE SPENt It PRETTY
MUCH IN the WOODS HUNtING NUtS FANNY AND
KATE MAWNE WERE THERE WE ENJOYED OURS-
ELVES VERY MUCH INDEED. BROtHER SENDS HIS LOVE to
YOU AND SAYS HE WILL PRINT YOU A LETTER IR HE
EVER LEARNS to PRINt GIVE MY LOVE to COUSIN
WILBY AND COUSIN GUS TELL tHEM I WOULD LIKE
VERY MUCH to SEE tHEM PLEASE WRItE SOON to YOUR
AFFECTIONATE NEPHEW   HENRY W GRADY

GRADY'S EARLIEST PRESERVED LETTER

Reduced in size from a facsimile in the "New England
Magazine," June 1890.

daughter of Dr. Alonzo Church, president of the university. Even in these spelling-book days he impressed at least one of his schoolmates with his "tact and expertness in telling all he knew about his lessons." Another fellow pupil remembered him as "a saucy boy, whose mind was as bright as his eye." All the reminiscences of his boyhood friends agree that he "always was the leader," that he excelled in athletic sports, and that he usually came out victor in the few fights in which he engaged.[4] Henry never forgot, however, a "fearful thrashing" that was inflicted upon him on one occasion by Emory Speer. "After my suspenders broke, and he had reduced me to a condition of squalling despair, he committed the further indignity of pouring sand in my mouth, which I had incautiously opened for the purpose of sounding a truce." [5] The two combatants eventually became such close friends that in later years Grady, a Democrat, supported Speer for Congress on an Independent ticket.

Unlike many active children, Grady also had a passion for reading. When he had gone through all the books in the Grady library, he exchanged with other boys and borrowed from friends of the family. At the age of eleven he clerked for a few months in a bookstore, the only compensation he asked being the privilege of reading when there was no work to be done. "There was a Dickens worship abroad in the land," and no worshipper was more devoted than young Henry, who eagerly devoured each new novel as it appeared and soon could claim an acquaintance with the whole fascinating galaxy of Dickens's characters. But his interest went far beyond this popular fiction of the day. A contemporary described it by declaring that "he read every book in Athens," even including the legal tomes of Blackstone.[6]

Wide reading soon kindled his own genius for writing. Not long before the war he conceived and carried out the idea of publishing an amateur newspaper, "The Monthly Skedaddle." In form it was merely a sheet of paper ruled off and lettered by hand, but Henry stipulated that its columns should contain

[4] Clippings, Grady Scrapbooks.
[5] *Constitution*, November 13, 1878.
[6] Harris, p. 43.

nothing but original matter, most of which came from his own
pen. The idea for the newspaper probably originated in a visit
at this period with his uncle, Henry A. Gartrell, who was publishing the weekly *Southerner* in Rome, Georgia, some hundred and twenty miles northwest of Athens. Stout, jolly Uncle
Henry, who served as Mayor of Rome in 1859–60, was well informed on politics and literature, and extremely witty. But irrespective of the uncle's influence, "The Skedaddle" bore ample evidence that its young editor possessed both a sense of
humor and a "nose for news." [7]

The stirring events of the late fifties and early sixties were
enough to stimulate a "nose for news" in any wide-awake
youngster with an active imagination. Though Henry was too
young to comprehend the full significance of the issues that
were being discussed by his elders, he must have sensed some
of the tension created by a series of incidents which, superim-
posed upon the fundamental conflict between an industrial
and an agrarian economy, were straining the emotions of
North and South to the breaking-point. The sensational circulation of *Uncle Tom's Cabin* from 1852 on, the passage of
the Kansas-Nebraska Act in 1854, Representative Preston
Brooks's attack on Senator Charles Sumner in 1856, the Dred
Scott decision of 1857, John Brown's raid at Harper's Ferry
in 1859, and the fatal split in the Democratic Party preceding
the national campaign of 1860 — all these were happenings
which conditioned the very atmosphere that Grady breathed.

Following Lincoln's election, excitement ran high in Athens. A servile insurrection was feared, and a Vigilance Committee was formed, with Henry's father as one of twenty members, "to investigate all alleged attempts at insurrection among
our slaves and to deal out summary punishment." [8] Rumors
filled the whole countryside with "spies, abolitionists, and Lincoln incendiaries." The fears were groundless, of course, for
there were few Negroes in Athens, or in the whole South, for
that matter, who did not remain loyal to their masters, but
reason seldom prevails when talk of war is in the air.

[7] Interview with C. M. Goodwin in *Constitution*, December 29, 1889;
George M. Battey, Jr.: *History of Rome and Floyd County, Georgia* (Atlanta,
1922) , p. 246.
[8] *Southern Watchman*, Athens, November 15, 1860.

Shrewdly anticipating difficulties that would disrupt business, William S. Grady, within three weeks after the election in November, sold his interest in the firm of Grady and Nicholson. Retaining half-ownership of the three-story brick store building, the gas works, and the sawmill, he invested heavily in real estate. So successfully did he manage his affairs that even in war his taxable possessions increased.

2

Public opinion in Georgia was opposed to secession. Indeed, the strength of the moderates in 1855 had been a factor in inducing L. Q. C. Lamar, an ardent Democrat, to return to Mississippi.[9] Especially in educational centers like Athens was the sentiment against drastic action, for the bulk of the students came from Whig families, and the leading Whigs had consistently denounced secession as inopportune, if not unconstitutional. In the presidential election of 1860 Henry Grady's father supported Bell, the Union Democratic candidate, and Georgia clearly showed a preference for Bell and Douglas, the two candidates advocating moderation. But division had crept into the ranks of the peace-loving majority, and the will of a minority prevailed, both in the election of Lincoln and in the subsequent secession of the Southern states. South Carolina seceded in December, Georgia did likewise in January, and on February 4, 1861 Jefferson Davis took office as President of the Confederate States of America.

After the firing of the first shot at Fort Sumter, differences of opinion among Southerners rapidly disappeared. Like many others who had striven earnestly to preserve the Union, William S. Grady was convinced that the Southern states had a constitutional right to be independent if they chose. At his own expense he organized and equipped a company of "Highland Guards" in the upper counties of Georgia and the neighboring counties of North Carolina. By the end of July he was on his way to Virginia as a captain in the Twenty-fifth North Carolina Regiment.

⁹ Wirt A. Cate: *Lucius Q. C. Lamar: Secession and Reunion* (Chapel Hill, 1935) , p. 47.

Accompanying Captain Grady were two of the family slaves, Tom and Milas. It was the faithfulness of servants like these to which the son later referred when he declared that "history has no parallel to the faith kept by the negro in the South during the war." He often mentioned another "trusty slave, who for four years while my father fought with the armies that barred his freedom, slept every night at my mother's chamber door, holding her and her children as safe as if her husband stood guard." This was the picture that Henry had in mind years after the war, when he finally saw *Uncle Tom's Cabin* on the stage and characterized it as an unfair and yet vivid . . . picture of a system that, wrong in itself, had been made tolerable by the people on whom it was saddled." [10]

The family left behind by the soldier-father consisted of five children. In addition to Henry, Will, and Mattie, there were now two others — four-year-old Annie King and one-year-old Julia Kennon. Just a few days after the father's departure a sixth child, Elizabeth, was born and died. A still more severe shock came to the home in April 1862 when both Annie and Julia were stricken fatally by scarlet fever. This tragedy brought the father, now promoted to major, back home on a brief furlough.

While in Athens on a second furlough in July 1863, Major Grady bought from Richard D. B. Taylor the mansion on Prince Avenue, now known as the Grady home, which had been built some time before 1850 by Taylor's father. For the house and a 338-acre farm adjoining, he paid a total of $50,000 — in inflated Confederate currency, of course. Without moving his family, he hastened back to Virginia to rejoin his troops.

The formal schooling of the Grady children had come to a close with the outbreak of the war, but there was no end to excitement. By the summer of 1863 thirteen-year-old Henry was a captain in the Georgia Rangers, an organization in which Athens boys between the ages of twelve and sixteen drilled daily with mimic weapons. A favorite haunt of the Rangers was the university campus, where a Confederate hospital and supply depot had been established, and where for a

10 *Constitution,* January 12, 1881; Harris, p. 97.

while some six hundred Northern prisoners were corralled under a guard made up of the elderly men of the town. Henry's conversations with the soldiers, both Confederates and Federals, usually resulted in their receiving a share of any food or cash he might have about him.[11]

There was a new baby, too, in the Grady household — Minor Graham, born in January 1863, who demanded his share of attention. And in the large back yard was the usual establishment of cows, pigs, chickens, turkeys, and pigeons, the care of which involved many chores for Henry and Will, especially since two of the men slaves were at the front with Major Grady. With jeans selling at twenty-five dollars a yard, even a new suit for a member of the Georgia Rangers was an exciting event.[12]

Excitement faded into tragedy late in July 1864, when news came that Major Grady, commanding his regiment at Petersburg, had been wounded five times. At first his condition was not thought to be hopeless, but after two weeks Mrs. Grady received a telegram asking her to come to his bedside. She went to the Confederate hospital at Danville, Virginia, and with the aid of the faithful Tom brought her husband back to the home of his brother, John, in Greenville, South Carolina. Here he died on October 21. The body was placed in a vault in Greenville until it could be moved to the family lot in Athens after the war.

The death of his father was not the only tragedy experienced by Henry during these impressionable years. In the spring of 1864 his mother's younger brother, Adjutant J. Madison Gartrell, was fatally wounded in action near Atlanta. In December of this same year Henry Gartrell, a captain under General Nathan B. Forrest, was captured and thrown into a federal prison. Two months later Minor, Henry's baby brother, succumbed to pneumonia — the fourth of the Grady children to die in less than three years. If the deaths of two other Gartrell uncles just before the war are considered, there

11 Crawford, loc. cit., p. 428.
12 H. W. G. to Ann Grady, October 23, 1864. This letter is dated two days after the death of Major Grady, but apparently Henry did not know that his father had died.

was only one year between 1857 and 1865 when a life did not
begin or end in the Grady family circle. Such moving events
as these must have fostered in Henry that tenderness toward
the weak and unfortunate which invariably is mentioned by
his boyhood associates.

In the summer of 1865 Henry Gartrell moved temporarily
from Rome to Athens to help his sister with the administration of the estate. It was in this same period that the family
occupied the Prince Avenue residence — a large white board
house, with the roof of its two-story portico supported by thirteen columns, one for each of the original states. Set back from
the street among giant oaks, with acres of farm land extending
to the rear, the new place seemed to signalize the arrival of
the Gradys at that level of society on which the planter aristocrats of a previous era had moved.

Fortunately for Henry, however, the circumstances of the
family were neither so prosperous as to encourage idle self-
indulgence nor so poor as to cast a shadow over his youthful
spirits. The amount of the bond given by Uncle Henry, who
was appointed in 1868 as guardian of the two boys, indicates
that the value of the estate left to the widow and three children was approximately $60,000. In earlier years it would
have been worth more, but now it was impaired by the freeing
of eight slaves and the depreciation in the value of real estate.
Only the gradual sale of various pieces of property enabled the
family to live in comfort while the children completed their
education.

3

Having been outside the path of Sherman's march to the
sea, Athens emerged from the war still unscathed by the fire
of battle. Nevertheless the town was demoralized by the cas-
ualties among its citizens, the loss of a large part of its wealth,
and the closing of the university for more than a year. Immediate reopening upon the cessation of hostilities in April was
impossible because federal troops occupied the college buildings, and the state treasury lacked funds for educational pur-

poses. In the fall of 1865, however, Williams Rutherford and other returning members of the faculty opened a private school for young men planning to enter the university.[13] Among their students was fifteen-year-old Henry W. Grady.

In a debating society formed by the young men of this school and called Lipscomb's Lyceum, after the university's chancellor, Grady made his first public speech. Carlton Hillyer, an upperclassman, took a special interest in the boy. One day, on leaving the hall where Henry had spoken, Hillyer commented to a friend on his protégé's "keen originality." Grady overheard the compliment and later said that it made a deep impression upon him as to the value of being original in thought and expression.[14]

When the university proper reopened on January 5, 1866, Henry was admitted to the sophomore class. Among the seventy-eight students on the campus were many mature men who had taken part in the war: one-armed and one-legged veterans were a common sight. Notwithstanding the competition of men much older than himself, Grady quickly won recognition among both students and faculty for his humor, his facility in expressing himself, and his "easy and apparently unconscious leadership of others." [15]

It was in the Phi Kappa Literary Society, according to Henry's own testimony, that he received "the most valuable training" of his college life. The rules of the university required every student to join one of the two societies, Phi Kappa or Demosthenian, and to participate in the weekly meetings on Saturday mornings. That the organizations encouraged writing as well as speaking is indicated by Phi Kappa's order of business, which provided for original composition and letter-writing, as well as declamation and debate, on each program. Although the minutes of the society are extant for only the first two months of Grady's membership, even this short period is enough to reveal that Henry won his first debate and that "Brother Grady" was fined on one occasion

13 Coulter: *College Life,* p. 350.
14 Interview with Hillyer in *Constitution,* December 25, 1889.
15 A. L. Hull: *Historical Sketch of the University of Georgia* (Atlanta, 1894), p. 77; F. H. Richardson: *A Fruitful Life* (Albany, Ga., 1890), p. 7.

GRADY AS A SOPHOMORE

At the University of Georgia, with Carlton Hillyer,
who encouraged him in his speaking.

AS A NEWSPAPERMAN OF TWENTY-THREE

GRADY'S HOME IN ATHENS, 1865-8

for "talking without permission" and on another for "laughing aloud." [16]

Once the boys brought out an issue of a student newspaper, *The Cat,* which still is remembered for Henry's caricature of the chancellor, Dr. Andrew A. Lipscomb. The chancellor, a retired Methodist minister, was prone to use somewhat erudite language and also to explain the misconduct of his students in scientific terms. These failings led Grady to burlesque an alleged faculty trial of a student in these words: "When the other professors had expressed their views, one plainly declaring that he believed 'Mr. M. was *dwunk,*' Dr. Lipscomb said, 'I apprehend that the unconscious cerebration in Mr. McL—'s case, reacting through the nervous system, so excited the brain cells that the impulse given to muscular action became irresistible." [17]

Of the six men on the faculty, it is a rather strange coincidence that the two for whom Grady developed the strongest attachment were Chancellor Lipscomb, whom he caricatured, and Williams Rutherford, who taught the one subject he detested — mathematics. Perhaps the explanation is that both men were noted for their largeness of heart and for a genuine interest in their students. Henry also expressed particular admiration for Dr. Patrick H. Mell, professor of ethics and metaphysics, who later became chancellor. Dr. Mell had a theory that "governing should be done by influence, not by authority" — a sentence which Grady said would "do to frame."

Considering that he devoted so much of his time to outside reading and activities, Henry's scholastic standing was remarkable. His grades in mathematics and science, for which he had little interest, were only fair, but in history, literature, and rhetoric he excelled. He was chosen by the faculty as one of the eighteen sophomore orators at the 1866 commencement, an honor which was awarded in recognition of scholarship as well as speaking ability.[18]

But there was about him nothing of the bookworm or lit-

[16] *Minutes,* Phi Kappa Society, January–February 1866; Nat E. Harris: *Autobiography* (Macon, Ga., 1925) , p. 165; T. W. Reed, op. cit., p. 6.
[17] Hull: *Historical Sketch,* p. 58.
[18] *Minutes of the Faculty,* University of Georgia, 1866.

erary freak. Under the hand-hewn timbers of the Grady home was an improvised gymnasium where he and his friends practiced boxing and wrestling. This training sometimes proved useful, as it did on the night Henry and Emory Speer fought off a band of practical jokers armed with pistols and masquerading as outlaws. Grady's favorite sports were baseball and sprinting, and on a trip to Atlanta with one of the campus baseball clubs he staged a three-heat race with a youth who claimed to be "the fastest runner in Atlanta." It was a long time before Henry overcame the disappointment of discovering that there actually was someone who could run faster than he.[19]

Besides taking part in sports and in such student pranks as the nocturnal ringing of the chapel bell, Henry found ample time for social diversions. A favorite serenading spot with him and his friends was Lucy Cobb Institute, not far from the university. Once at this "select school for young ladies" the college boys were barred from the annual May Day celebration. Grady, however, sent word through a window that he was "starving," and a fair student smuggled out a large platter of refreshments. At oratorical contests and other special events on the university campus, the young women sometimes would be guests. Following the formal program there would be "promenading, and music, laughing and talking, and, mayhaps, a little love-making." Grady became so fond of reading the lilting lines of Owen Meredith's *Lucile* to the girls that he learned this delightful metrical romance "literally by heart." [20]

In spite of innumerable college flirtations, the one serious object of his attentions seems to have been his childhood sweetheart, Julia King. Their mutual affections dawned so early that Henry often said that he fell out of his baby-carriage while reaching into Julia's carriage for her hand. When he was fourteen and Julia twelve, he made his first proposal of marriage. Julia agreed that if her answer was yes, she would wear a yellow dress to a Sunday-school picnic the next day and wave a handkerchief at him. Grady never tired of teasing her by relating how frantically she waved. A convenient occasion for

[19] *Constitution*, December 29, 30, 1889.
[20] Coulter: *College Life*, p. 348; Harris, p. 72.

appearing together in public was going to and from church services on Sunday. Henry and Julia liked the custom so well that in 1865 they joined the Methodist church together.

Julia, or Jule, as Henry called her, had light-brown hair, dark-blue eyes, and radiantly fair skin. Her father, Dr. William King, was a homeopathic physician who owned a drugstore and later became Mayor of the town. Her mother was the daughter of Judge Augustin S. Clayton, a member of Congress in Jackson's time and one of the builders of the first cotton mill in Athens.[21] Julia attended Lucy Cobb Institute and then, in the fall of 1867, was sent by her parents to enter a seminary in Philadelphia.

In April 1867 a chapter of the Chi Phi fraternity was installed at the university. It was the second Greek-letter organization on the campus, Sigma Alpha Epsilon having made its appearance the previous year. Next to Peter W. Meldrim, who has been called the founder of Chi Phi in Georgia, Grady seems to have been the most active in organizing the chapter and later in introducing Chi Phi at Emory and Mercer colleges. The good judgment he and Meldrim displayed in selecting their associates is seen in the fact that out of nine members comprising the chapter in Henry's senior year, at least five besides himself rose to positions of high honor in the state. Walter B. Hill became chancellor of the University; John D. Hammond, president of Wesleyan College; Walter R. Hammond, judge of the Superior Court; Benjamin H. Hill, Jr., associate justice of the state Supreme Court; and Nathaniel E. Harris, Governor of Georgia.

Nat Harris was a veteran of the war and consequently somewhat of a hero to the other members of Chi Phi. When Harris found himself in the summer of 1867 without funds, Grady and Meldrim went to the home of Alexander H. Stephens at Crawfordville and obtained from the former Vice President of the Confederacy the aid that enabled the future Governor to complete his education. "Little Aleck," one of the most influential Georgians of his day, was resigned by his semi-invalidism to bachelorhood and hence found much satisfaction in helping young men like Harris. The sympathetic hearing

[21] Rowe, op. cit., pp. 6, 13, 16, 124.

that Stephens gave Meldrim and Grady made an impression which the latter never forgot.[22]

4

Commencement in August 1867 brought Grady for the first time into full view of the political storm that was bearing down upon the South from Washington. Until the spring of this year Athens had succeeded well in her efforts to put the war behind her. Federal troops for a time had been a forcible reminder of the late unpleasantness: a Southern lady would cross the muddiest street rather than encounter a Yankee soldier. There had been trouble, too, with the newly freed slaves, especially the hordes who descended upon the town from the surrounding countryside, believing that their "year of jubilee" had come and willing, consequently, to do almost anything except work. But Southern intelligence, aided by a generally reasonable attitude on the part of the Northern soldiers, was beginning to solve such problems as these.[23] It was not defeat but Radical Reconstruction that inaugurated the "Reign of Terror" in the South.

Under the moderate Reconstruction policy of Presidents Lincoln and Johnson, Georgia quickly had met all the prescribed conditions for readmission to the Union. These included the abolition of slavery, the repudiation of the state's war debt, and the ratification of the Thirteenth Amendment. In April 1866 President Johnson proclaimed the end of Reconstruction and the restoration of peace. But the congressional Radicals, led by Senator Charles Sumner and Representative Thaddeus Stevens, declared the President's course illegal. They denied seats to the Southern senators and representatives, and the election of November 1866 assured them of a Radical majority with which to pursue their vengeful way.

In March 1867 the storm broke. Over the President's veto Congress passed the first of its Reconstruction Acts, dividing the former Confederate states into five military districts. In reorganizing the state governments, the military governors of

22 Nat E. Harris, op. cit., p. 158; E. Ramsay Richardson: *Little Aleck: A Life of Alexander H. Stephens* (Indianapolis, 1932) , pp. 177–80.
23 Coulter: *College Life,* pp. 324–35.

these districts were instructed to extend the franchise to all male citizens who had not "engaged in insurrection or rebellion." Moreover, they were ordered to call conventions for the purpose of drafting new state constitutions which would provide for Negro suffrage. As a condition of readmission to the Union, the legislatures elected under these constitutions were required to ratify the Fourteenth Amendment, guaranteeing civil rights to the Negro, providing for reduction of representation in Congress if the former slaves were not allowed to vote, and disfranchising the former Confederates. The "ironclad" test oath imposed upon both voters and prospective office-holders required the affiant to swear that he had "never voluntarily participated in rebellion or given aid and comfort to the enemies of the United States." Thus most of the South's natural leaders were excluded from office, and the states were placed at the mercy of Negroes, "scalawags," and "carpetbaggers."

When General John Pope arrived in Atlanta on March 30 to take charge of the military district embracing Georgia, Florida, and Alabama, he began the registration of "qualified" voters. Of 4,223 residents in Athens, only 450 whites were allowed to register, while 657 Negroes were enrolled. "What a mockery!" commented the local *Southern Watchman*. "And all to gratify the malignity of grinning devils . . . who have denounced the Constitution and Bible as a 'covenant with death' and a 'league with hell.' " Along with the new military government came emissaries of the Northern Union League, who, together with many agents of the well-intentioned Freedmen's Bureau, set about inflaming Negroes against whites. The hopelessness of obtaining relief through legal channels inevitably led to the rise of vigilante organizations like the Ku-Klux Klan, with their equally inevitable abuses.[24]

Of the statesmen to whom Georgians were accustomed to look for leadership, only two had spoken prior to the university's commencement in August. Stephens, "ill and hopeless," was in temporary retirement at Crawfordville; Howell Cobb,

24 Ibid., pp. 335–9; Claude G. Bowers: *The Tragic Era* (Cambridge, 1929), pp. 198–203; C. Mildred Thompson: *Reconstruction in Georgia* (New York, 1915), pp. 171–3.

Secretary of the Treasury under Buchanan and a dominant figure in the pre-war South, was still hesitant to speak; and the never-to-be-reconstructed General Robert Toombs had just returned from his voluntary exile in Europe and could not attend the commencement exercises. But the shrewd and practical Joseph E. Brown, Georgia's war-time Governor, after a careful canvass of the situation, had startled the whole state in February by urging immediate acceptance of the Radical Reconstruction Acts as the only feasible way of averting even worse indignities. Georgians had followed Brown as their Governor for eight years — longer than any other man — but sentiment now was too inflamed for the native whites to see any wisdom in the canny statesman's bold suggestion. Instead most of them turned to Benjamin H. Hill, who in 1857 had made a brilliant but unsuccessful campaign against Brown for the governorship. Hill, a former member of the state Senate and House of Representatives, had fought secession to the last, but once war was decided upon, had become the leading spokesman of the Davis administration in the Confederate Senate.

Hill remained silent on Reconstruction until the summer of 1867, because he regarded the presidential plan as fair and wished to give it every chance to succeed. Now that the die had been cast by Congress, however, he felt under no further compulsion to restrain his voice. On July 16, before an Atlanta audience including the military staff of General Pope himself, he denounced the new Reconstruction Acts as being unconstitutional and motivated only by the desire of the Radicals to perpetuate themselves in power. "Ye hypocrites! Ye whited sepulchres!" he addressed the Radicals. "Ye mean in your hearts to deceive him, and buy up the negro vote for your own benefit!" This stirring speech he followed with a series of newspaper letters entitled "Notes on the Situation," which Grady subsequently described as "the profoundest and most eloquent political essays ever penned by an American." These brought an immediate rejoinder from Brown, who sent to the press his own vigorous "Review of Notes on the Situation." [25]

[25] Haywood J. Pearce, Jr.: *Benjamin H. Hill: Secession and Reconstruction* (Chicago, 1928) , pp. 142–52.

At this juncture the commencement exercises of the university were held, and Athens enjoyed "a wild thrill, unequaled in intensity since the days of Confederate victories." The two opponents, Hill and Brown, together with Howell Cobb and other trustees of the university, were seated on the platform. In such a setting it was only natural for the pent-up resentment of students and townspeople to seek an outlet. This is exactly what happened when Albert H. Cox, a classmate of Grady, spoke on "The Vital Principle of Nations." Cox reached his climax in a subtle but none the less pointed reference to the situation in the South. By gesture and intonation he clearly indicated his opinion that Brown was a traitor to his people. As he concluded, the audience burst into wild applause, the band played *Dixie,* and Hill rose and shook the young speaker's hand.

That night the students serenaded Cobb and Hill, and the latter responded in a half-hour talk that sent his auditors away with rising hopes for the redemption of Georgia from Radical rule. Some of the students immediately decided to do their part by driving the former Governor's son, Julius L. Brown, from the university, but they were dissuaded by those who, like Grady, thought it unfair to blame the younger Brown for his father's seeming apostasy.

Athenians were quite carried away by the appearance of Benjamin H. Hill as their champion, but General Pope, already incensed by Hill's Atlanta speech and by his "Notes on the Situation," was enraged upon learning of the commencement incident. He ordered the university closed and all state funds withheld. Although Chancellor Lipscomb and a committee of trustees hastened to inform the military commander that the institution itself had done nothing to justify such a drastic penalty, the General was obdurate. Not until Hill himself made a trip to Washington and obtained the sympathy of General Grant did Pope rescind his order and permit the university to reopen for Grady's senior year.[26]

As a result of his association in Chi Phi with Ben Hill, Jr., Grady was invited during the Christmas holidays of 1867 to

[26] Ibid., pp. 158–60; Coulter: *College Life,* pp. 339–47; Bowers, op. cit., p. 210.

visit the Hills at their beautiful Ionic-columned home in La-
Grange. Here he came to admire the senior Hill as much for
his playfulness and gentle nature as for his statesmanship and
earnest concern over the Reconstruction problem. Hill had
just returned from Macon, where he had been elected president of a convention at which Democrats, Whigs, Know-
Nothings, and all other native white factions had joined hands
in the effort to restore home rule in Georgia. To emphasize
their common ground of opposition to the Radicals, who were
opening their Constitutional Convention in Atlanta in this
same month, Hill and his followers called themselves "Conservatives." There was nothing conservative, however, about
the grim determination that the great Georgian displayed in
his conversations with Ben, Jr., and his guest.

Throughout the remainder of his senior year at Georgia,
Grady followed closely the political developments in which
Hill was such a prominent figure. The Constitutional Convention ended in March, producing a document which, thanks
to former Governor Brown, was much less objectionable than
the carpetbag constitutions of most Southern states. Along
with such congressionally stipulated provisions as Negro suffrage, the convention had to its credit the beginning of Georgia's system of free education and the removal of the state
capital from Milledgeville to Atlanta. But to the Conservatives the whole Radical Reconstruction program was a "usur-
pation." Hill campaigned vigorously against the new constitution and even more bitterly against the Radical nominee for
governor, Rufus B. Bullock. To oppose the latter in the special April election the Conservatives nominated General John
B. Gordon, who was ruled eligible since he had not held office
before serving in the Confederate Army.

But, with the polls under military supervision and with so
many whites disfranchised, Bullock, an express agent with no
political experience, was elected Governor, and the new constitution was ratified by a large majority. The Radicals also se-
cured a majority in the General Assembly of the state, twenty-
eight legislative seats going to Negroes. Even Clarke County,
home of Athens and the state university, was represented by
two of her former slaves.

Frustrated within the borders of Georgia, the Conservatives now looked to the national Democratic Party, which at its convention in July nominated Horatio Seymour for the presidency and denounced Radical Reconstruction as "unconstitutional, revolutionary, and void." Presidential amnesty on July 4 assured most of the whites who had been disfranchised in April of a chance to vote in November. "Conservative" and "Democratic" became synonymous terms, and a great rally was called to meet in Atlanta on July 23, the day after Bullock's inauguration, to muster strength behind the Democratic national ticket.[27]

Meanwhile Grady had been doing the best speaking of his career at the university, and as the date of his graduation approached he was elected unanimously as Phi Kappa's commencement orator, the society's highest honor. Seeking inspiration for this task, or simply intrigued by the excitement of the occasion, he took time out from classes to make the trip to Atlanta, seventy miles west of Athens, for the Conservative-Democratic gathering.

Known as the "Bush Arbor Meeting" because of the immense bush arbor erected to shade the speakers' platform from the heat, the rally brought together a crowd of more than ten thousand persons, who sweltered in the sun for five hours while three of Georgia's political darlings — Toombs, Cobb, and Hill — excoriated the Radicals.

Of Hill, the last speaker, Grady wrote:

I don't think I was ever so much impressed by any human being as by Mr. Hill that day. He lacked the superb presence of Mr. Toombs, who preceded, for in personal majesty I never saw the man that equaled the unpardoned Georgian. He lacked the prestige of Mr. Cobb, for that statesman made a larger national figure than any Georgian since Crawford, but in fervid eloquence, in the stirring invective and appeal demanded just then to arouse the people to a true understanding of the situation, Mr. Hill walked like a god for hours at heights to which the others did not soar. . . . Such a speech, of such a compass, pitched upon such a key, was never made in this State before or since.

[27] Pearce, op. cit., pp. 16–76; Thompson, op. cit., pp. 193–8.

At its close General Toombs rose, moved by impulse more significant than deliberation could have been, and, throwing his hat into the air, called for "three cheers for Ben Hill." I picked up his hat, and I remember how my heart swelled to think I had done even that much to help on the deafening applause that followed.

From that moment, a student of politics told Grady, the redemption of Georgia from military rule was assured. "All the bayonets in the United States could not have awed, nor all the wealth of the government debauched, a people who had listened to that speech." [28]

Despite his enthusiasm over the fight against the Radicals, Henry determined to strike a happier note in the speech then taking form in his own mind. Even if he had been inclined to controversy, the university trustees, after their experience with Cox the previous year, had voted that politics should be excluded from the commencement orations. Grady therefore selected as his subject "Castles in the Air," a topic which enabled him to paint his vision for the future of the South. He showed his manuscript in advance to Hill and obtained the advice of the orator he now admired above all others.

Grady's "Castles in the Air" was delivered in the university chapel on the night of Monday, August 3. According to the Athens newspaper, it was "a masterly address, which for sound sense, smoothness and eloquence of diction is rarely equalled by one of his age." Beginning with the words: "In the spring time of life, in the glorious flush of young manhood," he attempted to demonstrate the practical utility of dreams and lofty ideals as sources of genuine happiness.[29] Although the manuscript of this speech has not been preserved, there remain scraps of early notes which represent the manner if not the exact words in which the young orator voiced his praises of "dream castles":

How they fire the heart of the dreamer . . . how they stir his impulses. These are the forerunners of action, these the plans drawn by the subtlest architect that ever worked. . . . Why, Napoleon long before he ever fought a battle caught his inspiration

28 H. W. G. in *Constitution,* August 20, 1882.
29 *Southern Watchman,* August 12, 1868; W. W. Adams, roommate of Grady at University of Virginia, in *Charleston Daily Star,* December 28, 1889.

from the clouds. In rapt and ecstatic revery, he saw phantom le-
gions swept across the sky; he saw airy navies grappling in the far-
off blue; bugle notes sounded from shadowy lips dropped from
the cloudland upon his listening ears; the thunder of cannon,
whose fire sprang from the hand of no human artillerists, put
tumult in his soul. . . . Our forefathers — our Jefferson and our
Patrick Henry — dreamed through their young lives of a perfect
Republic. They saw a government as unsubstantial as Utopia,
stretching through the infinite azure of the sky, long before they
sought to lay its cornerstone on earth. . . . And so of our smaller
affairs. . . . What man ever builded a Palace out of the Impossible, but amid some summer sunset had seen an ideal cottage,
raising its humble head amid the glories of the sky . . . that gave
shape to his purpose, and emphasis to his passion? [30]

These must have been typical of the thoughts that poured,
with somewhat reckless rhetoric, from the lips of the eighteen-
year-old speaker of Phi Kappa. Full of pathos, wit, and eloquence, Grady's speech was "the hit of the commencement.
. . . Instead of the usual tittering and inattention, there was
profound attention and silence. . . . In full possession of
himself . . . he won the mastery of listless spectators and po-
lite auditors alike." [31]

On Commencement Day, two days later, the thirty-one
members of the class of 1868 sat around a giant oak on the
campus and smoked a calumet, "after an ancient and respectable custom." Their days at the University of Georgia had come
to a close. And though Henry may not have realized it at the
time, his years in the town of Athens also were nearing an end.

[30] MS., Grady Collection.
[31] Clipping of article by Dr. A. A. Lipscomb, Grady Scrapbooks.

CHAPTER FOUR

Deciding a Career

LIKE many other Southerners of the rising middle class, William S. Grady had planned a career in law and politics for his elder son. So strong was the mother's confidence in Henry's ability to decide for himself, however, that she did not attempt to influence him in his choice of a profession. In the summer of 1868 there was some talk of his going to Rome with Henry Gartrell to operate a gas plant, but this idea was so distasteful to Grady that he rejoiced when the uncle's plans were changed. Although law held little attraction for him, the possibility of entering public life was becoming more and more fascinating now that he had seen the influence wielded by Hill and had tasted the thrill of applause for his own commencement oration. He therefore determined to spend another year in college to develop his powers as a public speaker.

Chancellor Lipscomb urged him to remain in Athens and take a master's degree at the University of Georgia, but the college that appealed to him above all others was the University of Virginia, at Charlottesville. He was eager to go to Virginia for several reasons. One was his admiration for Thomas Jefferson, the founder of that historic institution. Another was the university's reputation as the principal training ground for Southern leaders and their sons. And "perhaps the chief reason," as he wrote Julia King, was "that I am obliged to see you before a whole year." [1] Julia was planning to remain another year at the seminary in Philadelphia, where during the previous winter she had heard Henry's literary idol, Dickens, on his second tour of America. Henry longed not only to be nearer Julia, but also to be closer to the main current of important national affairs.

[1] [July 1868], Grady Collection.

As usual, Henry's wishes prevailed with his mother and uncle. When the University of Virginia opened for the fall term on October 1, 1868, he and an Athens college-mate, Hamilton Yancey, were among the 452 students registering. Every state in the South was represented in the enrollment, Georgia alone by thirty-four.

This latter fact was unquestionably due to the high esteem in which the Charlottesville institution was held throughout the South as "the center of higher thought and knowledge." Its faculty of fifteen members generally was believed to be "without a superior" in the United States. The professors were not only "masters of the ground they trod," but well educated in the arts and sciences generally. Virginia, consequently, had a serious atmosphere and an inspirational quality which were lacking in most Southern institutions of that day.[2]

Registering as a post-graduate student, Henry enrolled for courses in modern languages, history, literature, and rhetoric. His first letter to his sister described the room he and Yancey occupied in Winnville Hall as "the nicest in College":

It is a nicely plastered room — has two windows and two closets. Wednesday we got us a carpet and stove, a bureau and book case, some green window shades, a nice crimson table cover, and two good chairs. We fixed it all up nicely, and have got photographs and pictures hanging all around the wall, and over the mantle piece we have printed in large letters "Sunshine Hall," which is the name of our little room. In the center of the letters is a wreath of cypress from Jefferson's tomb. Then we have pins nailed up on the wall with our hats hanging on them and a bright gas light in the center of the room. The door to the stove is isinglass and you can see the bright flame jumping up and down inside, and when we let down our curtains and build a big fire and throw our blankets over our chairs and cock our feet upon our trunks we are as snug as a bug in a rug.

The achievement of which he seemed most proud, after two weeks on the campus, was his success in persuading a habitually drunken student to join the temperance society. "I joined

[2] David M. R. Culbreth: *The University of Virginia* (New York, 1908), pp. 366–70.

last Friday night," he wrote. "Not many in it, but we are all working." He added: "I am studying two times harder than I ever did in my life," and "I have learned more since I came here than I ever learned in my life." [3]

The mention of the cypress wreath revealed that Henry already had realized one of the earliest ambitions of all new students at the university, which was to make the four-mile journey to Jefferson's home and tomb. The Monticello of that day was a total wreck, and Grady was saddened to find that "no one, seemingly, was left with sufficient means, interest, or patriotism to stay the inroad of decay." Indeed, he became inspired with such a "thorough melancholy" that he refused to join in a dance in the ballroom of the house, preferring to roam the grounds instead. The wreath over the mantel of "Sunshine Hall" was his constant reminder of the man whom he considered to be "the greatest this country has ever produced." [4]

2

The one consuming ambition of Henry from the day he arrived on the Virginia campus was to be the final orator of the Washington Literary Society. This group and its rival organization, the Jefferson, met each Saturday night in their respective halls for public debates, which were the means of elimination for the societies' highest honors — intermediate orator, final orator, and medalist. The intermediate orator was chosen on the last Saturday before the Christmas recess, and the final orator and medalist were elected on the first Saturday in April, all by popular ballot of the members present. The final orators of the two societies were the principal student speakers during the commencement week late in June, each society being allotted one evening on the program. Soon after joining the Washington group Grady announced his candidacy for final orator, and nearly all the extant letters from Virginia to his family are devoted to incidents in his campaign for this coveted honor.

[3] October [15], 1868, Grady Collection.
[4] Culbreth, op. cit., pp. 216, 222; J. W. Lee, op. cit., p. 101.

Henry's confidence in his ability to win the orator's place was strengthened by a series of victories in his early debates. On October 24 he was victorious in upholding the affirmative side of the question: "Had the American savage a full right to the soil?" On November 7 he again took the affirmative and winning side in a general debate on the subject: "Was the execution of Mary Queen of Scots justifiable?" [5] His reputation as a speaker quickly spread, and soon whenever it was known that Grady was to speak in the Washington Society, there was not even standing room.[6]

By the latter part of November the political maneuvers for honors in the Washington Society were in full sway. Grady's only announced opponent, Richard Jeffries, offered to withdraw on condition that Henry support him for intermediate orator, which the latter agreed to do. But the other two candidates for the intermediate honor, by promising Jeffries the support of their "parties," persuaded him to re-enter the race against Grady. It was late one afternoon when Henry learned the news:

As soon as I heard it I sent out for some of my friends & they came & as soon as supper was over we put on our overcoats & overshoes & started out to meet the other party & talk against them. It was pouring down rain & dark as pitch. We all took a lantern & all went to different places. Oh! it was glorious — just going all around through mud and rain & moulding the sentiment of the college. . . . The first crowd I got with were at "Texan's Retreat." I talked awhile & brought up the Election gradually. Perkins had been talking to them already & at last Robison says "Well, Grady, old fellow we like you & think you are the best man in College & we'll go for you through thick & thin. So just count on Texas." This was luck! The Texans poll 13 votes & every man going for me against anything. That encouraged me a good deal and after promising Robison my party's support for Clerk of Moot Court I left. I then went on to the Billiard Saloon to see some fellows & thus knocked on up. You see I could only talk *about* the Election; couldn't ask them, if they were going to vote for me, but I could hint around & I found out four or five that

5 *Minutes*, Washington Society, October–November 1868.
6 W. W. Adams in Charleston *Daily Star*, December 28, 1889.

would vote for me that I did not know of before. . . . Well at last
I went back to my room where all my friends were to meet. It is
now just a few minutes after 12 & they have just gone — they have
been wading through the mire & mud & rain for 4 hours looking
up my claims for Orator — & yet they were as cheerful as they
could be. . . . I had a big fire & they all came in dripping from
their overcoats, yet as rosy as pinks — they pulled off the coats &
shoes. I got out some pipes & cigars & such things & we commenced.
Well *every man* had some good news. Nearly the *whole college* is
for me. . . . So that in the morning I expect to hear that Jeffries
is down again. I know he must come down. He can't run against
me, after the votes that I have heard from tonight.[7]

Jeffries did "come down again," and again Grady felt confident of success. One Peter Francisco Smith entered the race
against him, but Henry wrote: "I am certain I can beat him.
. . . He was the second fellow I met in debate, and I whipped
him like fury. I have made only three debates, each one against
medal or orator candidates, and I have whipped every crack
by big majorities." He could win the honor of medalist easier
than he could be elected final orator, he thought, but he
wanted "to make a good speech at commencement and make
a name and reputation." He enjoyed the "great crowds that
come out every time good speakers speak," many persons not
being able to get inside the hall. "Oh, it's jolly!" he beamed.
"I think I'll be a politician." [8]

After the Christmas holidays, however, his letters began to
take on a more somber tone. True to Grady's prediction, Smith
had been eliminated from the race, but a blind student, Noel
McHenry, of Greensboro, Georgia, was now running against
him.

"Oh, he is all the rage," wrote Henry. "Everybody is shouting 'Hurrah for McHenry' or 'Hurrah for Grady' — and our
debate which comes off next Saturday night is decidedly the
absorbing topic. . . . I am afraid McHenry will whip me.
He is 26 yrs old — is a graduate of Philadelphia, has been
to Europe &c and is the best educated man in College — &
then he has the good side of the question. I gave him his

[7] To Mattie Grady, [November 1868], Grady Collection.
[8] Ibid.

choice & he took the best side. It is the crisis of my life, I do believe." [9]

But this crisis, too, was resolved in his favor. The blind orator was stricken ill in the middle of his speech and had to be led from the stage.[10] Thus Grady again had the field to himself, though without any real test of his powers against the only rival he apparently feared.

Hard upon the heels of the debate with McHenry came midyear examinations, which necessitated a brief respite from oratorical and political activity. Grady now had a new roommate — another Chi Phi, W. W. Adams, of Charleston, South Carolina — whom he described as "a glorious fellow" and "the most prominent man in the Jefferson Society." Although he had confided to his sister in his concern over the blind orator that "a month ago I was the most popular man in the University & now I am not," the stream of visitors to his room was so steady that he had difficulty in preparing for his examinations.

"On last Friday men were in our room nearly all day, & at night from $7\frac{1}{2}$ till $1\frac{1}{2}$," he wrote. "Well, we couldn't study and something had to be done. Locking the door would do no good for men would see us thro' the windows & we'd have to let them in. So we locked the door — let down the windows, shut the blinds, drew the curtains & *lit a lamp* & went to studying. We lit our lamp at ten o'clock Saturday morning and studied by lamplight all day — & we will do that all thro' the week." Such sustained effort on his textbooks evidently came hard for him because, as he admitted, "I ain't used to it!" [11]

In March Henry went with a group of students to Washington for the inauguration of President Grant. There is no record of any serious thoughts that may have passed through his mind as he saw the new President, without Johnson, riding down Pennsylvania Avenue. It was simply a Southern college boy's first visit to the national capital, and he was eager to see the show. In his desire to obtain a good view of the procession, he climbed a tree in Capitol Square, where he sat, "blissfully perched, until ordered down by an unsympathizing police-

[9] To Mattie Grady, [January 1869], Grady Collection.
[10] Gentry Dugat: *Life of Henry W. Grady* (Edinburg, Texas, 1927) , p. 16.
[11] To Mattie Grady [December 1868, January 1869], Grady Collection.

man." News of this incident preceded him back to Charlottesville, with the result that he was greeted on his return to the
campus by a large caricature representing the procession, the
Capitol Square, "a calf in a tree and a policeman pulling it
down by the tail and larruping it with a billet." No one enjoyed the joke better than "the calf of the Grampian Hills,"
as his friends sometimes called Grady.[12]

3

Life proceeded in this care-free fashion until the last Saturday in March, one week before the election for final orator in
the Washington Society. Grady had routed every other aspir-
ant from the field and had reason to believe that he would be
chosen unanimously. But on the Saturday before his own
election, the society named its new president. For this office
Henry's party was supporting the Texan, Robison. A caucus
at three o'clock Saturday afternoon showed that Robison was
ten votes ahead. At six o'clock that night, however, Robison
came to the supper table with the news that the opposite party
was "going to bring in twenty-three new men." Forgetting
food, Grady went to work with his friends and "electioneered
for 2 hours as hard as I ever did in my life," but it was too late.
Robison lost by twenty-two votes.[13]

Henry now realized something he had been told but had
not quite believed: that under the method then employed in
awarding the honors of the two societies — a majority vote of
the members — the best speakers were not always the winners.
Any student could join either society at any time provided he
could pay the ten-dollar initiation fee, and it was not uncommon for an ambitious candidate with plenty of money at his
disposal to defray the initiation expenses of enough new members to swing the election in his favor.[14] It was in this way
that the rival party had defeated Robison for the presidency.

"We were not discouraged but somewhat astonished,"
Henry wrote his family on Thursday, April 1, two days before

---

[12] W. W. Adams in Charleston *Daily Star*, December 28, 1889.
[13] H. W. G. to Mattie Grady [January 1869], Grady Collection.
[14] Culbreth, op. cit., pp. 225-7.

the election in which he was a candidate. He was still "pretty confident" of success, although he saw some forebodings of failure in the fact that, "having beat our candidate by twenty-two votes, the opposition might find some man who would on the strength of this come out against me." [15]

Before he had a chance to mail that letter, two of the students upon whom he had counted most heavily for support — Peter Francisco Smith of Newnan, Georgia, and William Marshall of Vicksburg, Mississippi — sent him notes withdrawing their pledges. Both men up to this time had been candidates for the medalist's honor, but Marshall now had withdrawn from this race in favor of Smith and had come out against Grady for final orator.

Grady "did not get an hour's sleep" that Thursday night. A council of his supporters was held, and by the next evening they had decided upon the strategy of challenging Marshall to "speak it out" before the election on Saturday. Marshall, having been up to this time a candidate for another honor, had not competed with Grady during the year, but was reported to have been working three weeks on a speech for such a contest. Grady sat up all night again Friday composing his own oration, and by eight thirty Saturday morning was confident that he had "the best speech I had ever written." His friends were jubilant, and "went to work not trying to pledge any man but just asking everyone to go to the Hall & vote for the man who beat speaking."

At three o'clock Saturday afternoon Grady received a note from Marshall saying that he did not intend to speak and would not. Henry was "thunderstruck." The depth of his feeling was revealed by his almost pitiful entreaty to his rival:

Dear Marshall —

I do beg you for the sake of our past friendship to grant me this privilege. You know that you have more than half of the Hall pledged to you at present. They say that if we speak & if I beat you that they will go for me. Now if you want to run a fair race please give me a chance for my life. I am pleading for my salvation! If you do not give me a chance to speak I *must be beat,* & I

[15] Grady Collection.

beg for God's sake that you will give me *one* chance & if I must die, let me die in harness & in fight.

                                    Yrs   H. W. Grady

But Marshall replied:

Mr. Grady —,
  I decline to meet you —
                    Marshall [16]

Henry was defeated that night by eight votes, a much narrower margin than he had anticipated. Some of Marshall's "party" had revolted against their leader for his refusal to "speak it out." After the election there were shouts for "Grady," and he responded in a short speech. "Two men cried after I had finished," he wrote his mother.

It was clear from his fourteen-page letter to Ann Grady that the defeat "nearly broke his heart." On the last page he begged for permission to return to Virginia the following year and "take an honor," declaring: "I am certain of doing it — as far as man can be certain — & I don't want to come back to Athens at all this summer. I am nearly dead this evening with homesickness but I don't want to go home till I can go carrying the highest honor of the University — wch I know I can get next session & wch I deserved this session. I can't bear to come to Athens without it. So if you say so & Uncle Henry agrees I will stay in Virginia . . . till the summer after the coming one & then I'll come home with the brightest laurel of the University around my brow. May I do it?" [17]

In the light of the emotional crisis through which he was passing, it is not surprising that Henry shortly thereafter "slipped off" to Richmond with several of his friends for "a gentlemanly debauch." It was one of the few occasions in his life when he is known to have touched intoxicating liquor, and probably the only time he was ever really drunk. Of this particular occasion he wrote: "I was not simply drunk; I was sobby. For a full week we had been out of sight in champagne — a most mild but persistent beverage, by the way." Still un-

[16] H. W. G. to Ann Grady, [April 10, 1869], Grady Collection.
[17] Ibid.

der the influence of drink, he "staggered" into a hotel, picked up a paper, and began to read. His eyes fell upon a short story entitled "The Luck of Roaring Camp." As he described it, "The pure, breezy genius that swept through the story, chased away the fumes of the wine, and its splendid pathos, reaching down into the heart of that miserable debauch, lifted me like a feather up to a high moral plateau, where I was not only sobered, but reformed. It was the best sermon I ever heard or read." [18]

This was Grady's introduction to the writings of Bret Harte, who had been installed in 1868 as the first editor of the *Over-land Monthly* and had contributed "The Luck of Roaring Camp" to its second number. Harte had adapted "the tried and true formula of Dickens — the mingling of humor, sentiment, pathos, and whimsical character — to new material, the California mining country." In this he became a teacher not only of Grady, who was to use the same technique in his human-interest sketches of real life, but of many "local-color" fiction-writers. Among them were such gifted Southerners as George W. Cable, Joel Chandler Harris, and, later, O. Henry. Grady, with his fondness for Dickens, doubtless would have applied the human-interest formula in his newspaper writing if Harte had never lived, and the South was ripe for an outburst of local color in fiction, even if it had not appeared in the West.[19] But Grady followed Harte's work closely from this time forward, and his respect for "the prose-poet of California" was increased a few years later when the blond Westerner, on a lecture visit to Atlanta, asked Benjamin H. Hill not to introduce him as "The Dickens of America." The reason for this request, Harte explained, was that such an introduction would immediately "set every lover of Dickens in the audience against me." After the death of Dickens, Grady referred to Harte unreservedly as "the best writer of pure English on either side of the ocean." [20]

[18] Clipping dated Washington, February 7, 1877, Grady Scrapbooks.
[19] Fred L. Pattee: *A History of American Literature since 1870* (New York, 1915) , p. 297.
[20] Clipping, Grady Scrapbooks; *Atlanta Daily Herald*, March 18, 1875.

4

Grady's discovery of an "American Dickens" probably had much less to do with it than his political defeat, but soon after the Richmond trip his thoughts began to turn to journalism as a career. Perhaps writing for print rather than for platform delivery was his calling, after all? At least journalism would not bring the disappointments now inseparably associated in his mind with oratory and politics. And so he began to write — not speeches, as he had done up to this time, but a newsy letter, in the Dickens-Harte manner, for the *Atlanta Constitution*.

The *Constitution* was a natural choice, for one of its owners was W. A. Hemphill, whom Henry had known as superintendent of the Methodist Sunday school in Athens before Hemphill moved to Atlanta. Established to provide more vigorous journalistic leadership in Georgia's fight against Radical rule, the paper had made its first appearance on June 16, 1868. Its founder and first editor, Carey W. Styles, had visited Washington the preceding month to congratulate President Johnson upon the failure of the impeachment proceedings against him. On being told of Styles's plans, the President had recalled that prior to the war there was a Democratic daily in Washington named the *Constitution*. He suggested that this would be an excellent name for a paper seeking to restore constitutional government in the South. Styles liked the idea, carried it back to his associates, and the *Constitution* it became.[21]

Grady's letter, dated May 21, was mailed to Hemphill, who was the business manager. Hemphill turned it over to Isaac W. Avery, who only a few weeks earlier had succeeded to the editorship. Avery, a writer of considerable ability, was struck by the letter's "delicious humor," "descriptive verity," and "affluent diction," and published it in full.[22]

The first two paragraphs revealed that Henry was recovering from his April depression:

[21] Sam W. Small in *Constitution*, June 14, 1928. Small was connected with the paper intermittently from 1869 to his death in 1932.

[22] Isaac W. Avery: "Henry W. Grady," in *National Cyclopedia of American Biography* (New York, 1892), I, 526–7.

Virginia women are glorious creatures — buxom, blushing, beautiful. There is a delightful vigor in their action, a luscious fulness in their forms, and a rosy glory in their complexion that we find nowhere else. They are all healthy and glowing — all frank and merry; as plump as partridges, and as pretty as pearls. Could any man have witnessed the long procession that filed through the University grounds yesterday afternoon, and then fail to endorse the sentiment recorded above, he should be unanimously voted an ass.

The object of the procession alluded to was the decoration of the soldiers' graves, and the destination of the procession was the soldiers' cemetery. We followed them (how could we help it!) up and down hill, till we stood among the graves of our soldier dead. There was no lugubrious gloominess about the cemetery, but on the contrary, everybody was cheerful and happy, as this sincere tribute was paid to the memory of those immortal men who were buried in light and glory. Ere long every little mound had received its floral crown, and then a very squeaking-voiced man arose to address the crowd upon the "sad and solemn occasion which had called them together"; just then, by a most lucky dispensation of Providence, it began to rain. Squeaky had to suspend — the ladies became "frightened," you know — umbrellas were sought for and found — cloaks were jerked on, dresses looped up, ankles began to flash delightfully, and the whole thing grew exciting. Your correspondent, having procured an umbrella, made advances to a delicious little bundle of curls, cloaks, and calico, that stood close by trembling prettily. The arrangement was consummated — curls cuddled up affectionately under our arm, and — this is the way they dressed the soldiers' graves at the University of Virginia.

After devoting three paragraphs to a discussion of the political situation in Virginia, the writer reported, in a matter-of-fact fashion, that "H. W. Grady of Georgia" had been defeated in the race for final orator, and then concluded:

By the way, this system of college politics is a hard nut to crack. Boys, like apes, are imitative in their actions; hence you will find in every canvass within our college walls the same electioneering trickery, the same party combinations, and the same stump speaking which characterize the campaigns of older politicians. We have our caucuses — secret and open; we have our party issues and every candidate must define his platform and we have all the bluffings and villainies and chicanery that you will find in the outer world. And, in fact, so strongly are we tinctured with the mad spirit of the age that our elections are getting such affairs of importance, that an explosion is soon inevitable. And none of us would be surprised at the institution of a college "Imperialist," which should propose to give to the Faculty prerogatives in this department, and to utterly abolish our present republican form of government.[23]

The letter was signed "King Hans," a pseudonym coined from Henry's name and that of his sweetheart, Julia King. Avery ascertained from Hemphill the real name of the author and wrote to him, inviting further contributions. The result was a second letter, published June 19, in which Grady gave his impressions of Monticello and further observations on Virginia politics.

These two letters "turned his career." By the time he returned to Georgia, following the end of the session at Virginia, Henry had made up his mind to enter journalism. Hemphill approached his guardian with a proposal to sell him an interest in the *Constitution* and to make him the paper's managing editor,[24] but either the Grady estate could not afford the price or, more probably, Henry Gartrell's judgment told him that the boy was not yet ripe for such responsibility. Several weeks later, however, Grady accepted Avery's invitation to cover a fair at Marietta for the *Constitution* and, soon after that, to report a press excursion. On the latter assignment he made the contacts that resulted in his first regular newspaper position.[25]

[23] *Constitution*, May 28, 1869. As predicted by Grady, the faculty abolished popular elections of speakers the following year.

[24] Harris, p. 603.

[25] In his address at the University of Virginia twenty years later Grady referred to himself as a "scapegrace son" and mentioned the "charity" with which his Alma Mater "sealed in sorrow rather than in anger my brief but stormy career within these walls" (Harris, p. 142) . This latter remark has given some persons the impression that he left the university under a cloud. Actually he is listed in the *Records of the Faculty* among those "distinguished" in literature and rhetoric for the 1868–9 session. There is no record as to the quality of his work in history and modern languages, most likely because he was not sufficiently interested, after his defeat for orator, to take the final examinations.

5

Soon after his return to Georgia, Henry wrote in Julia
King's album of "Mental Photographs" [26] the answers to a list
of questions, some of which afford additional insight into the
mind of the budding journalist who had just passed his nine-
teenth birthday. His favorite prose author, as might be expected, was Dickens, with Thomas De Quincey second. His
favorite poet he listed as Owen Meredith (Edward Robert
Bulwer-Lytton), the author of *Lucile*. His favorite fictional
character was Becky Sharp, the shrewd and calculating heroine
of Thackeray's *Vanity Fair*. His favorite historical character
was the brave, affable, and quick-witted King Henry of Na-
varre, from whom his own Huguenot ancestors had received
their first charter of religious and political freedom.

The trait he most admired in a man, he revealed, was "Christian charity," and in a woman "pluck," while the traits he detested most were "selfishness" and "prudery." His own most
distinguishing characteristic, he frankly admitted, was his "im-
pudence." The epoch he would choose to have lived in, he
happily declared, was "that one just following my birth." His
idea of misery was "living in the house with my dear 'mother-
in-law,' " and the thing he dreaded most was "my wife's getting fat and flabby."

But perhaps we should not take these sentiments too seriously, for Grady's sense of humor was always with him in filling out these questionnaires by which the young women of
that day coyly exacted compliments from their male visitors.
Answering the question as to his favorite names, he wrote, for
Julia's special benefit: "Henry and J — ane." As his aim in life
he gave: "To die in the arms of J — esus."

[26] Grady Collection.

CHAPTER FIVE

Newspaper Apprenticeship

By his assignment to cover the press excursion of 1869 for the *Atlanta Constitution*, Grady was catapulted into the midst of a seething political caldron. Military rule in Georgia had come to an end the previous summer, following the Radical legislature's quick ratification of the Fourteenth Amendment, but Governor Bullock and his supporters continued to hold the offices to which they had been elected. The state, consequently, was being treated to an orgy of extravagance and corruption in government. Corruption was especially flagrant in the floating of bond issues and the voting of huge expense accounts. One legislative committee, for example, received reimbursement for such expenditures as "50 gallons of whiskey, 15 gallons of sherry, 7,000 cigars, and 57 dozen lemons."

Without military backing, however, all was not smooth sailing for Bullock and his Radical cohorts. First, in September 1868 enough white Republicans voted with the Conservatives in the legislature to oust the twenty-eight Negro members, whose right to hold office was left in doubt by the new constitution. Then the following November, by rolling up a majority of 45,000 for the Democratic national ticket of Seymour and Blair, the Conservatives demonstrated that they could carry an "unsupervised" election. Meeting again in January, the legislature not only ignored the Governor's request to reseat the Negro members but also failed to ratify the Fifteenth Amendment, the purpose of which was to prevent disfranchisement "on account of race, color, or previous condition of servitude." It was widely believed that Bullock himself had worked secretly against the amendment, in order that he might use its defeat to support his plea to Congress for the restoration of military rule. Be that as it may, he had hastened to Washington as soon as the legislature adjourned and had been told to bide his time until Congress met again in December.

Such was the condition of affairs in August 1869 when E. Hulbert, manager of the state-owned Western & Atlantic Railroad, invited the newspaper editors of Georgia to be his guests on an excursion over the road. Extending from Atlanta to Chattanooga and providing Georgia's only outlet to the West, the Western & Atlantic had been wrecked by Sherman's army during the war, but had been restored by the state during the period of Presidential Reconstruction. The road was now paying into the state treasury a net income of more than $25,000 a month under the administration of Hulbert, who apparently was a capable administrator in spite of being a Bullock appointee. The manager was enthusiastic over the coal and iron deposits of northwest Georgia and sought to enlist the support of the press in their further development.[1]

The excursion train, equipped with dining car, smoking car, writing car, and the usual accessories, including baskets piled high with champagne, left Atlanta on August 24. More than forty newspapers were represented, most of them by their editors. The *Constitution,* being bitterly opposed to the Radical administration, evidently chose to avoid political implications by sending a relatively unknown correspondent.

But Grady did not remain unknown for long. His daily news stories, describing the frequently amusing experiences of the excursionists in the coal mines and other places visited, were full of that same individuality which had characterized his letters from Virginia. "There was not much which was original or interesting in Georgia journalism at that time," wrote Joel Chandler Harris. "The state was in the hands of the carpetbaggers, and the newspapers reflected in a very large degree the gloom and hopelessness of that direful period." Grady's humor and descriptive power created a "lively diversion" among the editors, and he "eclipsed the entire press gang in his reports." [2]

[1] Walter G. Cooper: *The Story of Georgia* (New York, 1938), III, 139–43, 160, 168–75, 193.

[2] Isaac W. Avery: *History of the State of Georgia from 1850 to 1881* (New York, 1881), p. 615; Harris, p. 23.

From the first, Grady seems to have been suspicious of the presence of Governor Bullock on a trip which was avowedly non-political in purpose. Until the last day, however, he wrote in a semi-humorous vein. Then as the excursion drew to a close, the editors adopted a resolution thanking the Governor for accompanying them. Unable to restrain his indignation any longer, Grady gave vent to his feelings in an article declaring that "bribery" had been attempted on the excursion. When the *Atlanta Intelligencer* took up the charge and demanded that he either produce the facts or withdraw the insinuation, the young reporter replied: "Of course we will do no such thing." He reiterated that Bullock had gone with the editors solely for the purpose of "bartering patronage" for newspaper support. That statement, he asserted, would be confirmed by "every observant gentleman" on the trip.[3]

If Grady's humor had created a "lively diversion," his attack upon the Governor caused a mild sensation. It was reprinted widely over the state. At first the *Constitution* was careful not to assume editorial responsibility for its correspondent's "grave words," merely praising him as a "faithful, careful and honest" reporter. A little later, however, the paper itself was hurling similar charges at Bullock. As a result, it soon found itself defendant in a $25,000 libel suit. But by that time the opposition to the Governor was so strong that the suit "simply evoked derision and stimulated the paper to greater activity."[4]

2

Included in the itinerary of the press excursion was Rome, the seat of Floyd County, sixty miles northwest of Atlanta and fifteen miles east of the Alabama line. This attractive town on the banks of the Coosa River was the home of Henry Gartrell, who had returned there from Athens the previous year. Since Grady previously had visited his uncle in Rome, he was acquainted with Melville Dwinell, editor of the weekly and triweekly *Rome Courier*. Consequently, when the excursion train arrived at half past one o'clock Friday morning, Septem-

---

[3] *Constitution*, September 4–9, 1869.
[4] Avery, op. cit., p. 452.

ber 3, his first act was to rush to the *Courier* office with a col-
umn-and-a-half story, for which Dwinell was saving space in
his paper.

Besides describing the editors' trip in detail, the article
struck a note somewhat prophetic of Grady's later work by
urging the people of northwest Georgia to put political differences aside in the development of their natural resources —
"something more substantial than politics, and of infinitely
more advantage to our bankrupt people."

Before the excursion left Rome, Grady had been employed
as associate editor of the *Courier* at a salary of five hundred
dollars a year.[5] He reported for work on Monday, September
6. In the tri-weekly edition of the paper for the following day
appeared this announcement:

TO THE READERS OF THE COURIER

With this issue of our paper we present MR. HENRY W. GRADY
in the capacity of Associate Editor. The vigor, versatility and pol-
ish of his pen has recently been exhibited in his correspondence
for the Atlanta Constitution, over the *nom de plume* of "King
Hans"; and we may reasonably hope, with his assistance, to ma-
terially increase the interest of these columns.

Feeling confident that this effort to interest and please will be
successful, we let Mr. Grady make his own bow to the public.

M. Dwinell,
Proprietor.

The above notice renders necessary the infliction of a salutatory
upon you. We shall be as brief as possible. We are young, and
without editorial judgment or experience, yet we hope that the
enthusiasm with which we enter our new profession, and the constant labor with which we are determined to bend to our work,
may, partially at least, atone for these deficiencies.

The *Courier* shall be in the future, so far as our management
is concerned, devoted, as it has been in the past, to the dissemina-
tion of useful and interesting information, to the bold assertion
and maintenance of correct political opinions, and to the development of the best interests of the country. We enter the editorial
ranks of the State with ill-feeling towards none, but with kindness

[5] Battey, op. cit., p. 246; *Rome News-Tribune*, February 12, 1933.

towards all. We shall cheerfully, and with vigor co-operate with
the press in the furtherance of any project which tends toward
good, and we shall endeavor with courtesy and politeness, to ad-
just nicely any differences of opinion which may arise between us
and any of our contemporaries. Begging, in conclusion, that the
justice you render us may be tempered with mercy, we don our
harness and enter the lists.

> Most respectfully yours,
> Henry W. Grady.

In the same issue with this salutatory appeared Grady's first
editorial — an attack upon the editor of the *Talladega Sun*,
who had reported, following the press excursion, that he was
"delighted with Gov. Bullock — he is the right man in the
right place, and will do all that any man could do to restore
Georgia to her former condition of peace and prosperity." Replied the *Courier's* new associate editor:

> The truth of the matter is, that any man who knows nothing of
> Bullock's political filthiness, will inevitably become "delighted
> with him, etc." We have never in the whole course of our life,
> seen a man who was gifted with so great an amount of beguiling
> blarney as is this man. Present him to a Democrat, and the sweet-
> ness of his countenance is absolutely appalling — infinite smiles
> ripple over his cheeks, and break in soft laughter on his lips — a
> thousand little benevolent sparkles are beamed from his eyes —
> his nostrils play with kindly palpitation, and — believe me, for I
> tell ye the truth — his whiskers resolve themselves into a standing
> committee to invite you just to walk down into his heart, and take
> a place in that large and open receptacle. — Oh! his face is tre-
> mendously delusive.

Grady also continued his battle against the *Atlanta Intelligencer,* which he declared had been "bought out of the ranks."
He was reluctant to conduct a crusade against this "long established journal," he wrote, because he had "just entered the
editorial ranks" and desired "to crusade against nothing." Yet,
he asserted, it was "the duty of every Democratic paper in the
State to declare against it, and to let the people know that the
Intelligencer . . . is no longer worthy the confidence of Dem-

ocratic readers." Another paper he accused of selling out to the Bullock administration was the *Griffin Star,* to whose editor, F. S. Fitch, he referred with evident approval as having been called "a dirty little son of a Fitch."

Although Grady took time out in November to write another series of "King Hans" letters for the *Constitution* from a fair at Macon, his editorials in the *Courier* continued to deal mainly with Bullock's efforts to "rule or ruin." He particularly deplored the efforts of the Radicals to fasten the Fifteenth Amendment upon the country, terming it "the consummation of the Revolution." Later, when Governor Bullock's chief business agent, H. I. Kimball, closed a deal to sell the state his half-finished opera house as a capitol, Grady observed: "Mr. Osgood in the House wants a bill passed defining swindling and cheating. Let him examine the Opera House Bill and he'll not only have it defined, but illustrated." [6]

Just before Congress met, the Governor issued a carefully timed proclamation reciting outrages against "colored citizens and white Republicans" and charging "a concert of action and purpose on the part of certain organizations to defy the law." He ordered the proclamation to run as legal advertising for fourteen days in the daily newspapers of the state, paying scandalously large sums for the space in a rather obvious effort to obtain the support or at least the quiescence of these papers. The *Courier* described it as a "whining and false proclamation" which the Governor intended to use in urging Congress to authorize a new military reconstruction of Georgia. "Let the people stand firm to principle," the paper urged, "and we'll see the strategies of this traitor foiled."

For the time being, however, "the strategies of the traitor" were successful. Through lavish expenditure of state funds at the national capital, Bullock lobbied through both houses of Congress a new bill "to promote the reconstruction of Georgia." This measure directed the Governor to supervise the convening of the General Assembly and required all members thereof to take the iron-clad test oath before they could be seated. It also forbade the legislature to exclude any members because of race or color and authorized the Governor to call

[6] Clippings, Grady Scrapbooks.

upon the military to enforce its provisions. Georgia was required to ratify the Fifteenth Amendment before its representatives could be admitted to Congress.

As soon as President Grant signed the measure, Bullock summoned all qualified members of the General Assembly to meet at the Capitol in Atlanta on January 10, 1870. When the legislature convened, both houses were organized in arbitrary fashion by carpetbaggers appointed by the Governor for the purpose of seeing that his views were carried out. The Negro members were reseated, the Fifteenth Amendment was ratified, and, for good measure, the Fourteenth Amendment was approved for a second time.

The Governor, however, still was not satisfied. Although he could and did replace appointive officers like Hulbert, the manager of the state railroad, with tractable tools of his own choosing, he found that Georgia still had some constitutional officers who balked at looting the treasury. Even the Atlanta *New Era,* a daily founded by a Northerner to support the Republican cause, rebelled at Bullock's irregularities and exposed them so effectively that the Governor bought the paper for $25,000 to silence it. He also returned to Washington to seek the enactment of a measure which would declare Georgia's status provisional and thus give him the power to remove recalcitrant officials. But Congress, suspicious at last of Bullock's high-pressure lobbying, refused to comply with his request. A Senate investigating committee returned a report condemning him for "improper" methods, and Congress thereupon quickly passed a bill which, on July 15, 1870, readmitted Georgia to full statehood.[7]

3

Despite the *Courier's* emphasis on state politics in these months, the paper contained a number of editorials reflecting the embryonic journalistic ideals of its nineteen-year-old associate editor. Commenting, for example, on the courage and independence of the Democratic New York *World* in exposing corruption within its own party, the *Courier* said:

[7] Cooper: *Story of Georgia,* III, 160–1, 176–86.

No great journal can afford to be a mere party follower. No journal can become great, or remain great, as a party hack. The journalist has a grander function than to be merely a flag-bearer. He is, or ought to be, a General. We never hear reports and intimations and hints that this or that little clique of partisans are about to establish a paper or an "organ" without a feeling of supreme disgust. For what is a mere partisan organ worth to the public after all, or even to its party, for the matter of that? Does anybody expect an essentially partisan "organ" to tell the truth about any other party leaders than its own? The public have no confidence in it. It can never make converts because those whom it would convert do not believe it. A fig for your party organs! They are never self-sustaining, and always break their owners. Which is about the only good they serve.[8]

"The bravest editor," the *Courier* asserted, "is he who dares to tell his readers the truth."

Of all Grady's contributions to the *Courier* on non-political subjects, none is more beautiful than his editorial on the death of Dickens. It began: "There is great weeping to-day in the world of fiction. Charles Dickens is dead. And his multitude of children — the beings whom his kindly fancy brought into life — have come to a great sorrow." The editorial then went on to describe the imaginary reactions of a score or more of Dickens's most familiar characters to the news of their creator's death. These and "a thousand others," Grady wrote, would "gather around the grave of the greatest novelist the world has ever seen, or ever will see."

Grady was particularly active as a member of the Rome Library and Historical Association, which, spurred on by his editorials, soon began to plan for a new building. He also joined the Volunteer Fire Department, and once went so far as to insinuate editorially that certain merchants who refused to pay a dollar for a ticket to the firemen's benefit ball were "devoid of certain qualities that enter into the composition of a gentleman." In the next issue, however, he urged those who had been offended to visit their indignation upon him personally, explaining that the proprietor of the *Courier* "never saw or heard of the article until it was printed." He did not intend

[8] February 26, 1870.

his remarks, he said, for those whose "religious scruples" prevented them from lending "their presence or sanction to a
ball."

Other accounts tell of his playing baseball, of his fishing and
swimming in the Coosa River, of his going on picnics to near-
by Cave Springs, of his visiting a pretty girl cousin at "Mrs.
Smith's Select Seminary for Young Ladies," and of his giving
commencement addresses at near-by schools.[9]

The most significant influence upon Grady in Rome, however, was his contact with what he described as "a nest of the
raciest, keenest and pleasantest wits that chance ever threw together." In favorable weather some members of the group usually were to be found on the veranda of the Choice House, a
short distance from the *Courier* office and from Grady's own
rooming place. On other occasions they gathered in the establishment of "Big John" Underwood, the bartender, who,
Grady said, was "the funniest man in speech and manner I
ever knew." Most of them were lawyers, but "their fun-hunt-
ing was earnest and continuous," and "a new joke was of more
importance to them than a new case." A man who sat in their
midst "became humorous by absorption, just as the teetotaler
was made drunk by sleeping with a toper."

A prominent member of the group, of course, was Henry
Gartrell, the one-time Mayor, "whose laugh was infectious,"
and "whose relation of an anecdote was better than the anecdote itself." [10] An example of Gartrell's humor may be found
in a letter written while he was still in Athens. Reporting the
"death" of two horses belonging to the Hodgson family, he
wrote: "I did not see them die, nor did I hear that they were
dead, but I *know* they could not survive after the hard service
they performed while Miss Lizzie's beau from Charleston was
here — poor things!" In the same letter, referring to difficulties which caused Henry's younger brother, Will, to be
dropped from the university for "idleness and inattention,"
Gartrell said: "I am not uneasy on account of his injuring his
health by studying." [11]

9 H. W. G. to Mattie Grady, May 21, 1870, Grady Collection; Battery, op.
cit., p. 250.

10 H. W. G., clippings, Grady Scrapbooks.

11 To Ann Grady, June 28, 1867, Grady Collection.

Another member of the coterie was Dr. H. V. M. Miller, "the most brilliant talker," in Grady's opinion, that Georgia ever produced. Popularly known as the "Demosthenes of the Georgia Mountains," Miller had been elected to the United States Senate in 1868 but was being denied his seat by the Radicals. On one occasion he was said to have been greeted by a public gathering with such thunderous applause that some loose plastering dropped from the ceiling overhead. "Ladies and gentlemen," he observed, "I expected to bring down the house before I finished, but not before I commenced."

The best-known wit of them all, however, was Major Charles Henry Smith, another former Mayor of Rome, who already had published a volume of his newspaper letters under his pen name of "Bill Arp." The real Bill Arp was a local wag who had allowed his name to be signed to the first of Smith's letters, addressed in the early part of the war to "Mr. Abe Linkhorn." From that time forward "Bill Arp" rapidly had become one of America's "uneducated but wise, humorous, rustic philosophers," for whose sound common sense Grady developed much admiration.[12] Eventually he helped to introduce "Arp" to a much larger audience through the columns of the *Constitution,* and as a speaker he was to quote this friend of his Rome days more than any other humorist.

4

After ten months in Rome, Grady felt sufficiently well established to assert his independence of his employer, Melville Dwinell. A native of Vermont, Dwinell had established the *Courier* in 1843, had taken the Southern position in the slavery controversy, and had risen to the rank of captain in the Confederate Army. His inherent cautiousness, however, sometimes led other newspapermen to speak of him as "Grandmother Dwinell, from the land of the wooden nutmegs." It was this prudence that now led his youthful and impetuous associate editor to buy a paper of his own.

Although the town's population was less than 3,000, it had three newspapers. Oldest and largest of the three was the

[12] H. W. G., Clippings, Grady Scrapbooks.

Courier, which claimed 500 subscribers for the tri-weekly and 900 for the weekly. Next in size was another tri-weekly, the *Rome Commercial,* which had begun publication in 1865 and for a time had been edited by "Bill Arp." The *Commercial* had absorbed Henry Gartrell's old *Southerner* and thereby had taken the name of the *Southerner and Commercial* for its weekly edition, which had a circulation of 900 against 400 for the tri-weekly. The newest of the three papers was the *Rome Daily,* started in 1869, which managed somehow to exist with only 400 subscribers, with 750 more for its made-over *Rome Weekly.*[13]

The *Commercial* first appeared with Henry W. Grady's name as editor and proprietor on July 29, 1870. Henry invested his remaining patrimony in the venture over the protests of his uncle, who knew from experience that publishing a weekly newspaper had its griefs as well as its joys. Associated with the twenty-year-old editor as business manager was his brother, Will, to whom Henry was genuinely devoted in spite of the erratic temperament that usually made Will much more of a liability than an asset. The third member of the firm was the managing editor, J. F. Shanklin, "a first-rate political writer and practical printer," who fortunately for his less-experienced associates could get out the entire paper by himself when necessity arose, as it sometimes did.[14]

According to Joel Chandler Harris, Grady bought the *Commercial* "in the course of the few hours" after Dwinell refused to run in the *Courier* an editorial denouncing a political "ring" in Rome.[15] Evidently the change was made suddenly, as the masthead of the *Courier* for July 29 continued to list Henry W. Grady as associate editor. Dwinell's reference to this error in his next issue, however, indicated that he and Grady were still friends:

Overpowered with glory, our friend Grady thinks that two papers, both tri-weekly, is too much at once for his modesty to bear, and calls upon us to remedy it so far as the *Courier* is con-

13 *American Newspaper Directory,* 1869–70 (New York: Geo. P. Rowell & Co.).
14 Rome *Daily Commercial,* May 16, 1871; clippings, Grady Scrapbooks.
15 Harris, p. 24.

cerned. Not wishing to sail under false colors, we comply with his request, and this morning haul down his name from our mast-head, where it has so long floated with honor to himself, and profit to our paper.[16]

Apparently referring to the controversy that had caused Grady's departure, the *Courier* asserted that a meeting which had been called at the City Hall was not "the movement of a particular clique or ring," as had been intimated, but "a movement of the people of Floyd who are opposed to the prolongation of Radical rule." By "prolongation" was meant the latest scheme of Governor Bullock to retain control of the state. Although the bill readmitting Georgia to the Union was presumably in effect, Congress had adjourned without seating the state's senators and representatives. The Governor therefore insisted that military rule must continue until Congress met again in December, and that the legislature should call off the election scheduled for that fall. By thus depriving the people of the ballot, he hoped to extend the life of his administration for two more years.

Of course Grady was opposed to prolongation. He was opposed so strongly, in fact, that he lost patience with the cautious attitude of Dwinell and certain other Conservative Democrats. After Grady left the *Courier,* that paper urged its readers to "keep cool" and "not to allow our enemies to provoke us into a passion"; it likewise advocated the election of "old and conservative men to office." The *Commercial,* on the other hand, not only denounced Bullock and all his works but also demanded "bold opposition to the monstrous requirements of the test oath," which barred most of the ex-Confederates from office until Congress should remove their disqualifications.

Prolongation was defeated in the legislature on August 11, but the controversy between the *Courier* and the *Commercial* over the test oath continued. Reasoning that it was wiser "to take the best among those eligible, rather than by not choosing at all to have the very worst imposed upon us," Dwinell favored the renomination of General P. M. B. Young as Con-

[16] August 5, 1870.

gressman from the Seventh District. Grady, however, charged that Young was the "ring" candidate, and proclaimed that "some man of consummate talent and power" was needed "to rally the shattered forces of the Southern wing of the Democracy . . . and infuse life and energy into them." He unfurled from the masthead of the *Commercial* the name of "Dunlap Scott, Our Choice for Congress," as "the very man, and the only man," that the situation called for.[17]

Tall and erect, with black hair and flashing hazel eyes, the thirty-six-year-old Scott was the handsomest member of Rome's nest of wits. After graduating from the University of Georgia, he had become a successful lawyer, had risen to a captaincy in the Confederate Army, and had witnessed the surrender of Lee at Appomattox. Though "a trifle unwieldy in small talk," he fought his political opponents with piercing sarcasm and satire and was a leader of the anti-prolongation forces in the legislature.[18] The *Courier* regarded his opposition to the test oath as "somewhat biased," saying that he himself was clearly ineligible under this requirement. Grady, however, was captivated by the dashing young legislator and worked vigorously to send him to Congress.

But cooler heads prevailed, and General Young defeated Scott for the nomination in the Seventh District Democratic convention at Cartersville. Since the successful candidate's name was placed before the convention by Henry Gartrell, it is evident that Grady differed even with his uncle on this particular question. Once the party had made its choice, however, the *Commercial* editor hauled down Scott's name and joined in an active canvass for the Democratic nominee, who was successful. In fact, Democratic candidates won a sweeping victory throughout the state despite the desperate efforts of the Republicans to carry the election through the Negro vote.

5

More serious matters now caused the factions among the Democrats of Floyd County to put aside their differences for

17 *Rome Tri-Weekly Courier*, September 3, 1870; clippings, Grady Scrapbooks.

18 *Rome Tri-Weekly Courier*, September 16, 23, 1870.

the moment. Blocked in the attempt to prolong his power without benefit of an election, and overwhelmed by the avalanche of Democratic ballots, Governor Bullock speeded up the production of his "slander mill." Apparently realizing that he could retain control only so long as he could convince the North that Georgia was "seething with rebellion," he seized upon every incident that might be described as an "outrage" and loudly proclaimed to the world that loyal Republicans and innocent Negroes were at the absolute mercy of the Ku-Klux Klan. The newly elected Democratic legislature would not convene until November 1871; hence, the Governor had nearly an entire year in which to carry on his machinations.

Although the Ku-Klux Klan had been formally disbanded by its commander in the early part of 1869, the continuance of carpetbag rule inevitably led to further activities by bands of hooded night-riders. Floyd County having been "a center of Ku Klux activity from the time of the first appearance of the order in Georgia," it is not surprising that there should have been further outbreaks there.[19] On December 26, 1870, and on January 13 and February 6, 1871, occurred clashes of disputed severity between groups of whites and Negroes around Rome. As one result, Grady's name was drawn into the Ku-Klux investigation conducted by the joint committee of Congress a few months later.

The situation in Floyd County came to a head in January, when the grand jury for the first week of the spring term returned a presentment against "secret organizations of men who went about at night in disguise, and committed acts of lawless violence." Both the *Courier* and the *Commercial* criticized the report, and the grand juries of the second and third weeks subsequently attacked it as "gratuitous and uncalled for." But it was just such an opportunity as Governor Bullock had been waiting for. He immediately issued a proclamation calling attention to the "outrages" and offering $16,000 in rewards for the arrest and conviction of the persons responsible.[20]

[19] Stanley F. Horn: *Invisible Empire* (Boston, 1939), pp. 179, 356–9.

[20] *U. S. Congress, Testimony Taken by Joint Select Committee on Condition of Affairs in the Late Insurrectionary States* (Washington, 1872), VII, 625, 634–7, 879; Horn, op. cit., pp. 179–80.

Both the *Commercial* and the *Courier* refused to print the Governor's proclamation as paid advertising, declaring that the facts had been greatly exaggerated and that Bullock was actuated solely by political motives. Before the proclamation appeared, however, Grady and his successor as associate editor of the *Courier*, B. F. Sawyer, engaged in a bit of "pleasantry" over the happenings on the night of February 6. Grady printed in the *Commercial* a report that Sawyer had been caught by the Ku-Klux and made to dance to his own whistling. Sawyer retaliated by insinuating that Grady was in the Ku-Klux party. Grady's denial on February 17 told the story:

NOT A BIT OF IT

The venerable whistler of the *Courier* takes advantage of us in the following savage style:

MURDER WILL OUT

The amusing account given by our neighbor of the Ku-Klux adventure tells more perhaps than the writer intended. We suspected all the while that we were exerting ourselves to please the ghostly crew, that we knew the form and recognized the snigger of the little fellow in the spotted shirt, who rode the little mule, and since no one but those engaged knew what transpired, we are now convinced that our suspicions were correct, and that the tail end of the Ku-Klux was no one else than our facetious young friend, Henry W. Grady.

We deny the impeachment, but we do not blame the colonel for making the mistake. He was a little excited, and besides he always shuts his eyes when he whistles.[21]

Whether these exchanges were in truth merely "pleasantry," or whether both Grady and Sawyer had been involved in the incident, as their words seem to imply, is difficult to determine. When the seriousness of the situation became evident, how-

[21] Clipping, Grady Scrapbooks.

ever, Grady laid joking aside and came out with this sober warning:

THE KU–KLUX KLAN

AN ARTICLE IN WHICH THE EDITOR
SPEAKS HIS MIND VERY PLAINLY

A few words of soberness and truth with you, good friends, then we drop the subject.

It is a pretty well acknowledged fact that "Ku-Klux outrages" beat Seymour and Blair in the election of 1868. We do not mean by this that the actions of the Ku-Klux in themselves effected this disaster, but the construction and exaggeration put upon them by the scallawags in the South and scoundrels in the North did do it.

The radical party are evidently determined to make the next race upon the same basis. The sending out of the southern outrage committee, at an expense of $20,000, is the first step in the schedule.

It is absolutely necessary that these corpse-hunting, grave-yard ransackers be met and baffled. We should give them no grounds upon which to base a bloody report, or the campaign of '72 will duplicate the disaster of '68.

Hence, the *Commercial,* as a guardian of the good of the public, appeals to those of its friends who have any connection whatever with secret organizations, *to remain perfectly quiet and orderly, for the present at any rate.* Let there be no suspicion of disorder or lawlessness; let there be no parading of disguised men, no stopping of innocent men and forcing them to dance; this is all child's play and foolishness.

.   .   .   .

Above all, let there be no idle vaunting, no boasting about the country for mere buncombe. Remember, brothers, that *the strength and power of any secret organization rests in the attribute of mystery and hidden force, and in the fact that upon the thousand hills of our country a legion of brave hearts that are throbbing quietly can be called together by a tiny signal, and when the work is done, can melt away into shadowy nothing.* Every time you act you weaken your strength; *then be quiet.* If an inexorable necessity calls for action, act promptly, with decision, and do nothing more than is absolutely necessary.[22]

[22] Cited in *Testimony Taken by Joint Select Committee*, VII, 886.

Although such editorials prompted some persons to imply that the young editor of the *Commercial* knew more about the Klan than he was willing to admit, Grady was not subpœnaed to appear before the congressional committee at its hearing in Atlanta. Sawyer was summoned to testify, but, as he sarcastically described it, "the shearing of the pig" produced "little wool." Indeed, the committee found "little wool" on any of the Conservative witnesses. Even General Gordon, the reputed head of the Klan in Georgia, professed ignorance of "any Ku Klux organization, as the papers talk about it." Gordon admitted that there had been a "secret organization," but said that it was simply "a brotherhood of . . . peaceable, law-abiding citizens" who were seeking to protect white citizens against the carpetbag-inspired Union Leagues of the Negroes.

Latter-day historians have recognized considerable justification in the General's point of view. In spite of the barbaric abuses which eventually arose under the mask of the Klan, the order in its early days undoubtedly was "a knight in shining armor" to which the best elements in the South looked for relief from dangers to which open resistance, under the Radical regime, would have been utter folly. Before the Ku-Klux committee completed its hearings in Georgia, Governor Bullock resigned and fled the state to escape impeachment by the incoming Democratic legislature. With Georgians once more in control of their own affairs, the Klan soon faded out of the picture.[23]

6

The fun-loving spirit which caused Grady to relish the episode in which a rival editor was made to "whistle and dance" manifested itself in many other ways. He brought a skating rink to Rome and "went 'skeeting' around the rink like a streak of greased lightning chased by a Mississippi alligator." While the excitement over Bullock's proclamations was at its height, he sponsored a performance by a Mexican magician, who swallowed a sword and did "many other feats of legerde-

[23] *Testimony Taken by Special Joint Committee,* VI, 308; VII, 878–907; Horn, op. cit., pp. 376–7.

main, truly astounding." At the conclusion of the performance, the audience called for Grady, and he made "a talk, a
speech, an address, something," that was received with "up-
roarious applause." With somewhat prophetic insight his
partner Shanklin wrote: "Henry, my dear boy, thou art the
man, a showman for to be."

Grady's master stroke in entertainment, however, was an
invitation to the entire press of Georgia to come to Rome in
April 1871 for the opening of the new building of the Library
and Historical Association. After inspecting the library and
riding around the city, the visiting newspapermen were taken
by the Grady brothers down the Coosa River on a steamboat
excursion. Features of the trip were dancing to the music of a
brass band and distribution of a four-page newspaper entitled *The Rome Commercial, Jr.,* published "on the Bounding
Wave." On their return to Rome the guests were entertained
in the *Commercial* building at a supper which "loaded down
ten tables" and included "champagne, ice cream and strawberries, music and dancing." The final feature of the program was a memorial address by the Rev. Dr. W. Walkins
Hicks on "The Great Virginian," Lee.

Many of the newspapermen returned to their homes to
write anew of Rome's "infant editorial prodigy." One editor
termed Grady "one of the most happily constituted 'cusses' in
the world." The editor of the *Athens Banner* said Grady's
home town might well be proud of a native son who was so
"chuck full of that sparkling versatility which makes a popular journalist." The *Commercial* itself was praised as "unsur-
passed in the annals of Georgia for tact, ability, vim, professional elan, and other essentials of good journalism." [24]

His ambition fired, Grady now determined to have the
largest paper in Rome. On May 4, therefore, he announced
the purchase of the *Rome Daily* and its *Weekly,* the unex-
pired subscriptions and advertising contracts of which were
to be carried out by the *Commercial*. Henceforth his paper
claimed a circulation "greater than that of any journal now
published in the section of the country from which the business men and merchants of Rome derive their patronage."

[24] Clippings, Grady Scrapbooks.

On May 16, 1871, twelve days after the merger, the four-page *Daily Commercial* carried nineteen and one-half columns of advertising, with only eight and one-half columns of reading matter. This was a much heavier proportion of advertising than was to be found at that time in the *Courier,* or, for that matter, in the *Atlanta Constitution.*

The enterprise displayed by Grady in building up his local advertising is illustrated by a story that is still a favorite in Rome. It seems that he tried to sell space to a grocer named J. A. Rounsaville, who protested that he did not believe in advertising. The editor finally went away, but the next day the merchant was treated to "a deluge of cats." Nearly every small boy in town invaded the store with from one to six cats for sale. They revealed that they had come in response to an advertisement in the *Commercial.* Buying a copy of the paper, the grocer found a small want ad saying: "Will pay good cash price for cats — Rounsaville & Bro." Hastily he sent for Grady and demanded that the joke be called off. The editor agreed, but this time he carried away with him a half-page advertisement. In the center of it the Rounsaville firm notified the people of Rome that it was not in the market for cats.

The young editor's keen sense of responsibility is exemplified by another story which still persists in Rome. After an issue of the *Commercial* already had been printed, Grady discovered in it an item that would have offended a certain woman in the town. Buying "a dozen pairs of scissors," he set everyone in the office to clipping out the offensive article. He was determined that his paper should be "devoid of personal abuse." [25]

About this time Grady met Joel Chandler Harris, who had begun his newspaper career several years earlier on the *Forsyth Advertiser* and was now an editorial-writer on the *Savannah Morning News.* Some "foolish paragraphs" of Harris's appealed to Grady's sense of humor, and he wrote an appreciative letter to the Savannah journalist. The outcome of the correspondence was that in August 1871 Harris accompanied L. H. Estill, the proprietor of the Savannah paper, on a visit to Rome. Calling at the *Commercial* office, the visitors were in-

[25] Battey, op. cit., p. 252; clipping, Grady Scrapbooks.

formed that Grady might be found at a street carnival near by. There, sure enough, Harris got his first glimpse of his friend, riding on the merry-go-round. When the "flying jenny" stopped, Grady, covered with dust and perspiration, jumped off and bade him welcome.

Always ready for fun, Grady joined Harris and Estill on a trip to Lookout Mountain, Tennessee, some fifty miles away. From Chattanooga the trio proceeded to Atlanta to see the plays at DeGive's Opera House. Grady was "the life of the party," Harris said. "He was its body, its spirit, its essence. We found in our journey a dissipated person who could play a zither. . . . The man with the zither took the shape of a minstrel, and in that guise he went with us, always prepared to make music, which he had often to do in response to Mr. Grady's demands." Of the "spicy letters" which Harris sent back to the Savannah paper, Grady wrote: "They are filled with quaint 'Twainities,' and go right to a man's heart. He is a genius." [26]

A photograph of Grady, Harris, Estill, and a companion, taken "under a shelving rock somewhere in the fastnesses of Lookout Mountain," was sent to the *Constitution*. Acknowledging the picture editorially, the Atlanta paper referred to Grady as "leaning against a rock in a sort of demoralized abandon . . . a slender, youthful figure, with a wretched smile upon his face seemingly anticipatory of some early event that would make him in his happiness love Rome 'not less.' " That event, as the writer doubtless knew, was Grady's approaching marriage to his boyhood sweetheart, Julia King, of Athens.

7

That Henry would marry Julia when he reached the age of twenty-one seems to have been taken for granted ever since the courtship of his college days in Athens. He corresponded with her while she was attending school in Philadelphia, and after moving to Rome he made frequent trips back to Athens — partly to visit his mother and sister, of course, but also to see the one to whom he wrote: "If you were to die, my dar-

ling, I would want God to take life from me, too." His family
evidently approved the match, for, as he told Julia in the same
letter: "Mother . . . thinks there is nobody like you — She
would kill me if I was to marry anybody else." Their marriage,
he declared, was the "one grand course that I have determined
on, & that schedule I will run in spite of the world, the flesh &
the devil." That this determination was a restraining influence upon his conduct is indicated by his statement in the
same letter that he and his brother had "made a solemn
pledge that we would not take another drink of spirituous or
malt liquors, play a single game of billiards or any other game
of chance, or do certain other things (that I need not mention) for the space of one year from date. . . . I have commenced and I'll go on if it kills me, for I'd cut off my right
arm before I'd break my word. . . . I did not know what a
hold certain sins had upon me until I tried to quit." [27]

The wedding of Henry and Julia took place on the night
of Thursday, October 5, at the Methodist Church in Athens.
The marriage ceremony was performed by the Rev. E. W.
Speer, father of Emory Speer, Henry's boyhood chum. The
couple remained in Athens several days for a round of parties.
Then, on October 9, Henry sold to his uncle, John W. Nicholson, the remainder of his interest in his father's estate, consisting mainly of real estate in Athens, for $4,000. With this
sum to tide them over the financial stringency caused by
Grady's purchase of the two Rome papers, the couple left on
a wedding trip to Philadelphia and New York.

In Philadelphia the Gradys visited the home of Laura Hart,
who had been second bridesmaid at the wedding and with
whom Julia had lived during her two years in that city. In a
joyous letter to the *Commercial,* Grady wrote that "I meet no
one, high or low who does not at once (they all recognize
Southerners at a glance) ask about the Ku Klux. I answer
them according to my mood — some I horrify, others I soothe;
all I find perfectly saturated with false prejudices, and scarcely
think it worth the while to squeeze them out." [28]

Just as this article reflected Grady's interest in the Ku-Klux

[27] [June 1870], Grady Collection.
[28] Clipping, Grady Scrapbooks.

hearing then being held in Atlanta, so did his other writings in these months follow closely his personal experiences. Soon after the honeymoon there was added to his Rome scrapbook an amusing sketch in the Bret Harte manner, entitled "How I Had Some Fun in New York" and describing an alleged flirtation on his first trip to Manhattan. On a subsequent page is to be found an article on "Wives," mirroring the marital bliss that is still more clearly revealed in the young husband's intimate letters to his wife. Then, toward the end of the book, appears a tribute to "Babies," indicating that his thoughts were turning toward an event which, as he joyously confided to his mother in a letter of September 30, 1872, was anticipated for the following year. In answer to the complaints of readers who thought that matter of this type had no place in newspapers, Grady announced his intention, "even in defiance of these thickheads," to continue "sprinkling a little gold dust" through his columns.

In a speech made about this time to a graduating class of girls, Grady indicated the part that Julia was playing and was to play to the end of his days in his own happiness. "In ninety cases out of a hundred," he said, "the wife makes the man. There are just enough exceptions to prove the rule. The wife should comfort her husband. She should win his secrets — she should guide his footsteps — she should share his troubles — she should strengthen him when he is weak, and humble him when he is strong. She should fill his life for him, and leave him nothing to desire. . . . She should make herself precious to him in little things. It is little things that win men's hearts." [29] A similar thought is continued in a letter to his sister, Mattie, telling of the room he and Julia were fitting up for his library, to which he was adding new books every day. "The secret of life after all, Mattie," he wrote, "is to be happy over little things. Did you ever see me discontented with what God had given me? I will be happier, I will bet, with my plain little library room that cost only a few dollars than many a millionaire with his magnificent suites of rooms costing thousands." [30]

[29] MS., Grady Collection.
[30] [September 1872], Grady Collection.

Following his marriage, Grady left his rooming place on Broad Street and moved with his bride into a house located at the southeast corner of Third Avenue and East First Street, opposite the Presbyterian Church. The location is worth noting, for it was chiefly responsible for a friendship that developed between the Gradys and the young daughter of the Presbyterian minister. This round-faced, brown-eyed, curly-haired girl, Ellen Louisa Axson, afterward became Mrs. Woodrow Wilson.[31]

An even more noteworthy friendship growing out of the Gradys' married life in Rome was with Henry Hunter Smith and his attractive wife, the former Estelle Cuyler. "Miss Tellie," as Grady came to call her, was the daughter of Colonel Telamon Cuyler, one of the founders of the old Rome *Southerner*. Her mother, who was Ann Frances Hamilton before her marriage, was a novelist of ability. Quick, witty, and lively, "Miss Tellie" seemed to have inherited the literary interests of both parents; she provided a companionship which Henry and Julia found most agreeable. Her husband, a successful cotton merchant, was frequently consulted by the young editor on business and financial matters. The two families continued to visit each other after the Gradys left Rome, and later they acquired homes in the same block on Atlanta's Peachtree Street.[32]

8

In the early fall of 1872 Grady and Dunlap Scott enlisted the support of General Robert Toombs in an effort to buy a half interest in the *Atlanta Constitution*. Although Grady frequently had opposed the policies of the "Burly Bob" in his editorial columns, he had a great personal admiration for the "unreconstructed" General. Toombs, in turn, had taken a fancy to the "boy editor," possibly as a result of a widely quoted interview which Grady had obtained from him. The

---

31 Battey, op. cit., pp. 290–4; information from records of First Presbyterian Church, Rome, and from Telamon Cuyler.

32 Information from Telamon Cuyler, son of Mr. and Mrs. Henry Hunter Smith. Originally named Telamon Cruger Smith, Mr. Cuyler in 1905 legally adopted the family name of his mother.

deal of the three men for the *Constitution* stock fell through when the price was advanced, but the negotiations whetted in Grady an intense desire to try his journalistic talents in the much larger field of Atlanta.

Soon after this, while returning to Rome from Athens, Grady missed railroad connections in Atlanta and stopped for the night at the Kimball House. At the registration desk he was approached by the tall, military figure of Robert A. Alston — the same Alston who some months earlier had likened Grady's courage in fighting the Radicals to that of a "monkey who runs riot over a powder magazine with a red hot poker in his hand." Alston told the young editor that he had been thinking of telegraphing him to come to Atlanta and buy an interest in the *Atlanta Daily Herald*. What then happened was described by Grady himself:

In an hour after I had met Alston the trade was closed. No papers were drawn up that night, and the details were fixed over a bowl of oysters in Thompson's. Alston and I returned to the Kimball at midnight and took the same room. After arranging to make about one hundred thousand dollars the first week we dropped to sleep. During the night I was awakened by Alston's calling me. I remember so well the tones of that soft quizzical voice as it came through the darkness: "Grady, is there any insanity in your family?"

"None at all! Why do you ask me?"

"Well, I've been thinking over this *Herald* trade for a week. You've only known of it a few hours. Now, I know that a man that's quicker on a trade than I am must be crazy, and I was afraid I'd gone in partnership with a lunatic!" [33]

Grady became a co-proprietor of the *Herald* on October 21, 1872, paying $5,000 for a one-third interest. Of this amount, $1,800 was cash which he and Shanklin had saved from the *Commercial*, and the remainder was obtained as a bank loan on security borrowed from his mother. His partners in the enterprise were Alston and Alexander St. Clair-Abrams, the paper's founder, each of whom also owned a one-third interest. Returning to Rome, Grady sold the *Commercial* to Dwinell,

[33] H. W. G. in *Constitution*, April 18, 1880.

the proprietor of the *Courier,* on terms which he thought would enable him to repay the loan and to return his mother's security within thirty days.[34]

On November 11 the editor and his wife moved to Atlanta. In his valedictory to the readers of the *Commercial,* Grady recalled that he had come to Rome "three years ago a foolish boy, filled with the conceits of college, puffed with the pride of youth." That, he said, was before "tough experience" had knocked the "extravagant juices" out of his soul. He referred to the days when "collections were dull" and he had "scoured the streets in search of the wherewithal" to meet his obligations. Now, he proudly declared, the *Commercial* was "on a paying basis" and was "one of the best circulated, best patronized, and handsomest papers in Georgia." Of his feelings toward the people of Rome, he wrote:

. . . I have fought some, allied with others; frolicked with some, prayed with others; loafed with some and caucussed with others; dunned by some and dunning some others; but knowing *all* well and truly; and in leaving I feel a joy in saying that towards no man of all your clever population is there the least bit of dislike or resentment in my soul — not even towards SAM JOHNSON [the bailiff]. God rest his patient bones.[35]

It was probably such humorous references as this that led to the circulation of reports that Grady, on departing from Rome, had been able to elude "a battery of bill collectors" only by leaving his trunk behind and entrusting his wedding silver to a friend. These rumors, he wrote his mother shortly thereafter, were "absolute lies in every particular." Explaining that he did not owe a cent in Rome or anywhere else except two hundred dollars which was "satisfactorily arranged," he continued:

I am square with the world at last! & so help me God I will keep so. I have more friends in Rome than any man ever had. Alston went there a day or two & just got every man in town to take my

[34] H. W. G. to Ann Gartrell Grady, October 21, 1871, Grady Collection.
[35] Clipping, Grady Scrapbooks.

paper. . . . So there isn't a shadow of truth in any of these stories.[36]

Will Grady, who despite his shortcomings was praised by Henry as "the noblest boy that ever lived or died," came to Atlanta at this same time and was employed by Alston "selling cotton." Will had left the business managership of the *Commercial* some months earlier and, according to Henry, had been "doing nothing" in Rome. In December Henry wrote his mother that the younger brother had gone to Savannah to take a job on a ship. "I sold my watch to get him $70 the day before he left," he confided. "I had taken $300 out of the *Herald* office to pay Shanklin and couldn't take any more."

The new paper's business was "remarkable," he added. There had been "no blue Mondays" since coming to Atlanta.[37]

[36] [November 1872], Grady Collection; Battey, op. cit., pp. 251, 489.
[37] Grady Collection.

CHAPTER SIX

"*The* Atlanta Herald"

SINCE the founding of the *Constitution* in 1868, there had been a number of changes in Atlanta journalism. The *Sun*, a Democratic daily bearing the name of Alexander H. Stephens as editor, appeared on the horizon in 1870. In this same year a new Republican sheet, the *Daily True Georgian*, was launched, but, following the overthrow of the Bullock regime in October 1871, both the *True Georgian* and its older Republican rival, the *Daily New Era*, collapsed. The city's oldest daily, the *Intelligencer*, also passed from the scene, unable to withstand the competition of two other Democratic papers in the face of suspicions as to its own loyalty. By the summer of 1872, therefore, Atlanta had only the two morning newspapers, the *Constitution* and the *Sun*, both Democratic.

Atlanta at this time had all the characteristics of a booming frontier town. The city was only a few years older than Henry W. Grady, for there had been little more than an Indian cross-trails at the spot when it was staked off in 1837 as the southern terminus of the W. & A. Railroad. Even before the community's name was changed from Marthasville to Atlanta in 1845, John C. Calhoun had predicted that its location — at the convergence of openings in the mountain ranges to the west with ridges from the north, east, and south — would make it the great inland city of the Southeast. The strategic advantages which had caused General Sherman to burn the business section in 1864, together with the added attraction of its now being the state capital, had brought thousands of settlers since the war to assist in the rebuilding. Stores and residences had sprung up far beyond the original burned area, and horse-drawn streetcars were operating in three directions from the heart of the city. The population, which had jumped from 14,000 at the time of Sherman's visit to 30,000 in 1872, was a human mélange. Few persons bothered to ask where the other fellow came from: all were much too busy making money.

Thus the stage was set for the entry of Alexander St. Clair-Abrams, "a brisk young fellow full of bustle and excitement, spiced with a foreign flavor," to start a new newspaper. Abrams, a talented but warm-blooded Spanish Creole, had worked before the war on papers in several Southern cities. Serving the Confederacy as a captain of artillery, he had been wounded five times. After the war he had become an editorial-writer on the *New York Herald*. His wife, however, inherited from her father a one-third interest in the building formerly occupied by the defunct *Daily New Era*. This circumstance, coupled with a desire to live in a less rigorous climate, led the tawny-skinned, goateed editor to resign his position in New York and come to Atlanta. With a cash capital of less than two hundred dollars, he gained use of the equipment as well as the building of the old *New Era* and, assisted by General John B. Gordon, brought out the first issue of the *Atlanta Daily Herald* on August 22, 1872.[1]

By a coincidence, the leading position on page 1 of the *Herald's* first issue was devoted to the reprint of an article from Grady's Rome *Daily Commercial* entitled "CRIME — Outrageous Attempt to Ruin a Girl at Rome — A Lascivious Beast Employs the Services of a Procuress." Other crime stories in this same number were headed "A Horrible Wife Murder," "Negro Murderers Respited," "The Atlanta Murderers," and "A Spicy Scandal," the last being a case of miscegenation. The *Herald* continued to give similar stories equal prominence except on Sundays, when the "CRIME" column was replaced by one headed "RELIGIOUS." In striving to publish "the livest, raciest, newsiest and most interesting paper in Georgia," Abrams obviously was following the same pattern of sensationalism that had enabled his former employer, James Gordon Bennett, to make such a success of the *New York Herald* in its early days.

[1] *Atlanta Daily Herald*, May 23, July 16, 1873; H. W. G. in *Constitution*, August 18, 1880; letter from Abrams in *Constitution*, June 14, 1928.

The *Constitution* was quick to denounce the *Herald* for its "slavish imitation of the vices" that had made Bennett's paper "notorious," but Abrams denied that he was imitating any journal's "vices." To attack a newspaper for printing crime news was as ridiculous as to "charge Dickens or Thackeray with possessing prurient minds," he wrote, "because in painting the world as it exists they depicted the base, the mean, the immoral and the criminal" along with "the good and the virtuous." He continued: "If . . . anybody desires a newspaper which publishes nothing but the good that is done in the world . . . let that person seek some other paper than the *Herald*. We give both pictures . . . and endeavor to make the coloring perfect." Evidently the paper's contents made a hit with Atlanta readers, for when it appeared on October 19 with "the only full and reliable account" of a duel between J. H. Townsend and Houston T. Force, it sold a "second edition" of 1,500 copies — "a feat then unprecedented in Atlanta."

The rivalry between the two papers was intensified by the fact that their offices were located almost opposite each other — the *Herald* at the northwest corner of Broad and Alabama Streets, and the *Constitution* in a slender brick building which still stands at 30 Broad Street, S.W. The two buildings literally were less than a stone's throw apart, for the street between was full of loose rocks with which the rival newsboys bombarded each other's windows until the police put a stop to it.

Barred at first from obtaining the dispatches of the co-operative press associations, Abrams hit upon the plan of delaying publication each morning until the *Herald* could "lift" important telegraphic items from the *Constitution*. To work this scheme, he would start his presses as a blind. The *Constitution* staff, thinking the *Herald* had gone to press, also would begin printing. Abrams then would stop his presses, obtain a copy of the rival paper, and have compositors quickly set the wire news into type.[2]

After two weeks of obtaining telegraph news through such devious devices, the *Herald* announced that it henceforth

[2] *Life and Labors,* p. 49.

would receive the dispatches of the New York Associated Press and would appear "at an earlier hour" each morning, through the "kindness" of the *Constitution* and the *Sun*. Later, however, Abrams charged that the two older papers had "blackmailed" him into giving them notes of two hundred and fifty dollars each for the right to obtain the service. Neither the *Constitution* nor the *Sun*, he declared, had ever paid a dollar for the same privilege.

These two notes and other obligations were beginning to cast some doubts upon the ability of the *Herald* to survive when Abrams succeeded in interesting Robert A. Alston, who in turn brought Henry W. Grady into the enterprise. When first approached by the fiery Creole, Alston was said to have offered Abrams "one hundred dollars a week to edit a paper if he would allow himself to be put in an iron cage." The pertinence of this suggestion became evident several months later when Abrams, gun in hand, set out to fight a duel with Carey W. Styles, founder of the *Constitution* and then editor of the *Albany News*. Although Abrams was arrested before any shots were fired, Grady and Alston realized as never before that they had a firebrand on their hands.

As one of their associates observed, however, it would have done little good to "cage Abrams" while Alston was "running around loose." For Grady's second partner was scarcely less impetuous than the fiery Abrams himself. He was descended from the Alstons of South Carolina, who were "duellists born and men who rated life as a bubble in combat for a principle." Courageous to the point of recklessness, he had risen to distinction in the war as a captain with Morgan's Raiders and had "survived a hundred fights" without receiving a wound. Although his peace-time experience was limited chiefly to farming, law, and politics, he brought to the *Herald* considerable business ability and a reputation for daring that added to the paper's fame.[8] But neither he nor his senior partner was of a disposition such as to restrain Grady's own youthful impulse to "run riot over a powder magazine with a red hot poker in his hand."

[8] H. W. G. in *Constitution*, March 12–14, 1879.

2

Two days after Grady and Alston closed their deal with Abrams, the *Herald* appeared with the names of all three men as "Editors and Managers." Apparently this gave each member of the trio coequal authority, and indeed they did announce that they would consult on "all important issues," but actually the more experienced Abrams continued to dominate. He soon was reiterating editorially that "nothing could swerve the *Herald*" from "its old habit of saying just what it pleases, just when it pleases, and just as it pleases" — a habit which kept the paper in a continual controversy. It was not surprising, therefore, that a few months later Abrams again assumed the title of editor, and Grady became known only as business manager. Even so, the younger partner was drawn by loyalty into the paper's editorial disputes, sometimes on a side different from that of his own inclinations.

Since the redemption of Georgia from Radical rule in 1871, Grady had grown gradually less belligerent toward those who advised acquiescence in the results of Reconstruction. In the light of events, this was a change logically to be expected in a Georgian who had been too young to take part in the war. A Conservative-Democrat, James M. Smith, had been inaugurated Governor in January 1872. The Negroes, who two years before had been reported "almost in a state of mutiny," were now said by the same observer to be "behaving like lambs." The General Amnesty Act, passed by Congress in May 1872, had removed the disabilities of most of the leaders who had been excluded from office by the Fourteenth Amendment. What was even more important, so far as Grady was concerned, Benjamin H. Hill in 1870 had made peace with former Governor Brown and had urged Southerners to accept the Fourteenth and Fifteenth Amendments as accomplished facts. Revolutionary "usurpations" though the amendments were, said Hill, they were now the law of the land, and they did not change the right of a state to regulate its own affairs except to forbid discrimination against the Negro on account of color. Hill had followed this "change" by making in 1871 a brilliant plea for better educational facilities, especially technical schools; for diversification of agriculture and development of long-neglected natural resources; for construction of "furnaces and foundries, studios and workshops"; and for education of the Negro. And so Grady, although at first opposed to the 1872 coalition of Democrats and Liberal Republicans, soon followed the lead of both Hill and Brown by advocating the election of the "New Departure" candidate, Horace Greeley. Most likely he would have explained his change simply by quoting what Hill had said in 1870: "I have not changed . . . but times change; circumstances change; issues change; necessities change; and we should adapt ourselves to them if we expect to prosper." [4]

Abrams, on the other hand, while professing in the news columns of the *Herald* to steer a middle course between the pro-Greeley *Constitution* and Alexander Stephens's anti-Greeley *Sun,* openly fought Greeley and the New Departure on his editorial page. In this he was aligned with the irreconcilable General Toombs, who still delighted in "clanking the chains of an alleged unpardoned rebel in the face of the government." It was Toombs who egged on his friend and life-long admirer, Stephens, and who eventually paid off many debts of the latter's ill-fated *Sun.*[5]

Before Grady began work on the *Herald,* the Democratic and Liberal Republican ticket had gone down to national defeat, though the New Departure won a striking victory in Georgia, one of the six states carried by Greeley. Not all the controversies in which Abrams involved the paper, however, were so happily settled. Almost from the first issue he had been condemning the lease of the state-owned Western & Atlantic Railroad to a company headed by former Governor Brown. One of Grady's closest friends, Dunlap Scott, had introduced the legislative bill authorizing the lease, and Hill was a member of the company with Brown, as was Stephens also until Toombs exploded. The former Governor's company had made the best offer of any responsible bidder for the lease, and Brown was a logical man to be president of the

[4] Pearce, op. cit., pp. 231, 240–2, 254.
[5] H. W. G. in *Constitution,* November 27, 1881; E. R. Richardson, op. cit., p. 315.

group, since as Governor he had put the road on a paying basis for the first time. Moreover, the new Democratic legislature, after full investigation and vigorous debate, had voted in July 1872 to sustain the lease, thus confirming its fairness and validity. But Abrams insisted upon continuing the fight, and eventually Grady was dragged into it by "reckless inexperience." [6]

In assailing Brown and the state-road lease, Abrams undoubtedly had hit upon a popular issue. The doughty ex-Governor, despite his proved business and political ability, was still anathema to most Georgians, who regarded his early acceptance of Reconstruction as a betrayal. It now should have been obvious that Brown in 1867 merely had anticipated the stand taken by Hill in 1870 and by the Democratic Party itself in 1872, but the masses of the voters were slow to forgive such acts as the former Governor's acceptance of an appointment from Bullock as Chief Justice of the Supreme Court, a position he had resigned in order to head the railroad-leasing group. Even Hill's tremendous popularity of a few years earlier had declined because of his association with this man he once had denounced, as his defeat for the Senate by General John B. Gordon proved. Accordingly, when Abrams opposed a lease obtained by Brown's company under a Radical administration, he was certain of drawing applause.

As the controversy waxed furious, Abrams accused Brown, as president of the road, of withholding a pass from an agent of the *Herald* because of the paper's "war" upon the lease. Not long afterward he charged Brown's "gross mismanagement" with being responsible for frequent accidents, delays in the forwarding of freight, and fostering of a "coal monopoly" designed to hold up prices for the benefit of the former Governor's coal mines. Declaring it to be a scandal for the president of a state-owned railroad to promote his own private enterprises by discriminations in freight rates, the *Herald* editor raged on:

If Governor Brown is to own coal mines and force manufacturers to buy his coal or allow their shops to stand idle, and citizens to

6 H. W. G. in *Constitution,* April 18, 1880; Pearce, op. cit., pp. 217–30.

burn it or suffer with cold . . . if he is . . . in truth to use a public highway, worth ten millions of dollars, of which he obtained the control without paying one cent for it, as an engine of oppression, then he becomes the most mighty potentate of modern times, and can force the people of an entire state to knuckle to his will or suffer for their temerity.[7]

Grady was drawn into the dispute when Brown submitted a four-column reply to two questions which, the *Herald* said, "could have been intelligently and fully answered in twenty lines." As business manager, Grady ruled that the lengthy contribution was unwarranted "puffing" for the former Governor's coal mines. "It would find an apt parallel," he explained, "in the case of a merchant, who, on being asked if he were guilty of some peculation, replied, 'No, but I have a choice lot of hams, vegetables, and canned goods,' and then proceed in a column of laudation to prove that he could outsell and outsatisfy any rival merchant in the city." The *Herald* ran the letter in full, but sent the writer a bill for twenty-five dollars to cover the "actual cost of composition." When Brown refused to pay and accused Grady of attempting "blackmail," the latter replied in a signed editorial which showed that he, too, could lose his temper under fire: "How natural it is for a man who knows that he would steal if he had the chance, to conclude that everybody does steal, who, he supposes, has the opportunity!" [8]

Throughout this period the *Herald* also was in conflict with Brown over the "bawdy bonds" issued or endorsed by the state under the Bullock administration, mostly for the building of railroads. The General Assembly in 1872 had declared more than $9,000,000 worth of these bonds to be fraudulent and void, but in the early part of 1873 it received a compromise proposal whereby all the discredited bonds would have been surrendered in exchange for a new issue of $1,600,000. Despite the questionable circumstances under which the bonds were issued, some railroad mileage had been constructed and the proposed settlement probably represented a fair estimate of the value received by the state. Brown and many others

[7] May 14, 1873.   [8] May 20, 1873.

advocated the compromise as the best means of restoring the state's credit and of doing justice to all concerned. The *Herald* insisted, however, that if the bonds were fraudulent, "we ought not to pay one cent of them."

Since the *Constitution* was supporting Brown with reference to the state-road lease and the bond compromise, it came in for its share of the fire. It was accused by the *Herald* of "prostituting the profession of journalism to the basest of ends" and of being "the avowed harlot" of Georgia journalism. The *Herald* declared that the older paper never took sides until everybody else had decided, then always went with "the biggest crowd and the 'leading men.' " The *Constitution* was the "Brown organ," the "municipal ring organ," the organ of whatever the *Herald* happened to be attacking.

By June 1873 the *Herald* claimed that its circulation of 3,400 was the largest in Atlanta, and "probably the largest in the state," although the *Constitution* may have been right in saying that this growth was due in part to its extending credit "right and left." For no matter how fast it grew, the income of the paper never seemed to keep pace with the expenditures. Its receipts undoubtedly were nearer the $1,000 to $1,200 a week mentioned on January 19, 1873, than the $5,000 a week claimed by Grady seven years later,[9] and this was not enough to operate on the scale to which Abrams was accustomed. On May 31, 1873 the paper was forced to borrow another $5,000 from Grady's mother, and a few months later Grady was seeking her endorsement on a note of Alston's to the Citizens Bank for a similar amount.

On June 24 the suspension of the *Atlanta Sun* was announced by Stephens, whose election to Congress had provided a fortunate way out of an unprofitable journalistic venture. "Mr. Stephens is a man of great ability," commented the *Herald*, "but he is not a journalist and never will be one." Employing William H. Moore, former city editor of the *Sun*, as its own city editor, the *Herald* again announced plans to make itself the "best newspaper south of New York."

The *Herald* now launched one of the boldest and most foolish ventures of its career. The departure of the night mail

[9] *Constitution*, April 18, 1880.

train between Atlanta and Opelika, Alabama, had been changed to eleven o'clock, making it impossible for the train to carry morning papers with a full telegraphic report. The *Herald* therefore announced the chartering of "a special mail train for the carrying of its paper and nothing else . . . leaving Atlanta at 4 a.m. and making all points between this city and Opelika on the liveliest schedule that can be made." The train, consisting of an engine and a mail car, made its maiden trip on July 24, with Abrams, Alston, Grady, Moore, and Will Grady, who was now back in Atlanta, all aboard to "watch things."

The trip was "a perfect ovation." Apprised by telegrams of the unusual event, crowds met the train at nearly every crossing. There was a breakfast in Grantville, a barbecue at West Point, all "in compliment to the special train." The *Herald* staff reciprocated by distributing "a bottle of champagne to the Mayor of every station along the route and to every newspaperman."

When the special train to Opelika was announced, the *Constitution* ridiculed the idea. Ten days later, however, upon the discontinuance of the night train to Macon, the *Constitution* proposed that the two papers jointly operate a special to that city. The *Herald* replied by announcing that it already had made its own arrangements for an engine to Macon at $2,000 a month, with members of the staff again carrying an "ample supply of champagne, cigars and other necessaries of life" on the initial trip. Not to be outdone, the *Constitution* also put on a special, so that by August 5 two engines were running 104 miles to Macon each day to carry "not over one thousand papers."

"Both papers went to press at four o'clock, and it was a race to the depot every morning. The paper which got there first was given the main line first, and the day's sales depended largely on the quickness of the cart-boys." But the sales yielded only a fraction of the $150 a day the *Herald* was paying for its two engines, or the $75 a day the *Constitution* was spending for one.

Outside circumstances soon forced an end to this extravagance. On September 18 began the financial convulsions now known as the Panic of 1873, and on this same day the *Herald* announced the discontinuance of its special trains. Two days later the *Constitution* still was running its special to Macon, but it "had to publish a little four-page paper to do it." The *Herald* had increased its own size from four pages of eight columns each to eight pages of six columns each just before the crash. Within a week, however, an Atlanta savings bank temporarily closed its doors, and the *Constitution,* too, discontinued its special train. On November 11 the *Herald* again was reduced to four pages "because of the terrible disasters which day after day startle and paralyze the commercial world."

This retrenchment was preceded, two days earlier, by the retirement of Alexander St. Clair-Abrams. Denying that there was any "want of harmony" among the partners on matters of editorial policy, Abrams stated that his withdrawal was due solely to "irreconcilable differences as to the business management." He later revealed, however, that the Citizens Bank, under the control of former Governor Brown, had threatened to foreclose a mortgage given as security for Alston's $5,000 loan unless the *Herald* ceased its attacks on the state road. Since Abrams had started the "war" and had been chiefly responsible for continuing it after Grady and Alston joined the paper, the only solution was for him to withdraw. The other two partners gave him their notes for his one-third interest in the paper, and he left for New York.[10]

Long after his departure the *Herald* continued to pay for Abrams's metropolitan ideas. For example, he apparently had been responsible for launching an elaborate circulation-building contest, by which more than $7,000 in prizes was to be given away to the paper's subscribers in January 1874. Alston and Grady carried out the scheme because "it was a matter in which their good faith was involved," but they pledged that henceforth they would devote their entire energies and capital "to the legitimate improvement of the *Herald* as a newspaper." In pursuance of this pledge, the next time an important mail train was changed they started an evening edition

[10] *Atlanta Daily Herald,* November 9, 1873; Abrams in *Constitution,* June 14, 1928.

instead of hiring a special engine. "It may not be quite so showy," they admitted, "but it is vastly safer."

Meanwhile a much anticipated event had taken place in the Grady family — the arrival of their first child, Henry King,[11] who was born June 6, 1873, in Athens, where Julia had gone to be with her parents. Soon afterward, the Gradys moved from the little cottage on Harris Street, where they had lived since coming to Atlanta, into a somewhat larger one-story house at the southeast corner of Spring and Baker Streets. This afforded more room not only for their own growing family but also for Will, who now was living with them. There were more frequent visits than ever, too, from Julia's parents and from Henry's mother and sister in Athens, now that the baby had come.

Grady's love for children was reflected in his editorial of the following Christmas Eve on "The Little Ones and Their Stockings." Although his own first-born was too young to have been the toddler referred to, Grady must have had little Henry in mind when he wrote for the *Herald*:

We know of a home, an humble one, too, where tonight while the pillow of a cradle is being warmed, a darling little rascal, barely able to toddle, and with just four teeth in his busy mouth, will work his way to the mantle piece and hang Grandma's woolen stocking — too big by half for his meager gifts — on the nail therein imbedded! And happy will he be! Noble will he be! Great will he be, if in all the life stretching out before him, his heart is filled and his impulses started by no meaner motives, than the sturdy faith, the honest hope, the abiding confidence that inspires him, as he pins the wrinkled old leggin to the chimney-board tonight. God bless the children all and fill their stockings full!

Editorials and feature stories in this human-interest vein were far more characteristic of Grady's contributions to the *Herald* during the period of Abrams's editorship than was his heated reply to former Governor Brown.

[11] The name was changed to Henry Woodfin, Jr., after the father's death.

3

After Abrams left the paper, Alston took over the business management and Grady became editor — a position much more to his liking. From this time forward, the editorial page of the *Herald* reflected in increasing measure the ideas and ideals to be associated with Grady in the period of his greatest fame. The political leaders backed by the paper, likewise, were now men of his own choosing, with whom he continued for the most part to be identified.

One of the men whom he backed most enthusiastically was General John B. Gordon. Although the *Herald's* support of Gordon's successful race for the Senate in January 1873 might be attributed in part to the aid he had given Abrams in starting the paper, there is ample evidence that Grady himself considered Gordon to be "the most beloved and distinguished Southerner living." Without any previous military experience, Gordon had entered the war in his twenties as captain of a company of "Raccoon Roughs" from the mountains of northwest Georgia. He had distinguished himself repeatedly and had survived numerous wounds to rise to the rank of major, colonel, brigadier general, and finally lieutenant general. He had participated in Lee's last council of war, had led the final Confederate charge at Appomattox, and had returned to Georgia the state's most illustrious hero. A Minié-ball scar upon his face seemed only to enhance the charm of his handsome bearing.[12]

Grady found in Gordon qualities of personal magnetism that exercised an almost hypnotic influence. "It is impossible that after talking to the man and looking squarely into his eyes, one can fail to be affected in his favor," he wrote. Even if the hyperbole in this statement be discounted, the fact remains that Gordon's political instincts did seem to be as unerring as his military genius. He probably would have won his first political race — his campaign against Bullock for the governorship, at the age of only thirty-four — if the votes had been fairly counted. Grady praised him as a progressive who

12 Knight: *Reminiscences,* I, 319–49.

perceived "the folly of attempting to restore our liberties by retracing our steps."

With Gordon ensconced in the Senate, the *Herald* launched a campaign to restore Benjamin H. Hill to office by sending him to Congress from the Ninth District. Grady urged that Hill's "superb ability, his matchless eloquence, his absolute mastery of the philosophy of government" would make him a congressman "second to none in this broad land." Pointing out that every position taken by Hill now had been "solemnly endorsed" by the Democratic Party of Georgia and of the Union, the young editor praised his idol as "the peer in intellect of the most gifted among America's statesmen." When an opposition paper insinuated that the candidate had "bought up" the *Herald's* influence, Grady quoted Hill's own words: "If I could buy the influence of every paper in the United States for fifty cents, I would not pay the price. . . . I would not give ten cents a million for empty newspaper puffs." In December 1875 Hill took his seat in Congress.

In 1875 the *Herald* also endorsed General Alfred H. Colquitt for governor. Colquitt had been a member of Congress before the war and had served the Confederacy with distinction as a brigadier general, becoming popularly known as the "hero of Olustee." Despite his background as the son of a wealthy pre-war planter, which might have been expected to align him with Toombs and Stephens, Colquitt had kept abreast of the times and favored the New Departure. To the *Constitution's* charge that the *Herald* was "the mouth-piece and organ" of Colquitt, Grady replied: "If it is intended to mean that we are outspoken and earnest in advocating his claim to public favor, we admit the charge. In any other meaning, it is untrue, for General Colquitt has never dictated or inspired a line in the *Herald* since his name has been before the people."

A fourth name, that of Lucius Q. C. Lamar, should be mentioned at this point, for he definitely was one of the statesmen whose liberal and conciliatory views influenced Grady's thinking. Lamar, a native of Georgia and a distant kinsman of Grady, was at this time a member of Congress from Mississippi. In April 1874 he delivered in the House of Representatives his eulogy of the dead abolitionist Charles Sumner — a speech described by one historian as "the first and loftiest plea" for reunion of the sections. Closing with the plea: "My countrymen, *know* one another, and you will *love* one another," Lamar dwelt on the theme that North and South were estranged simply because each was ignorant of the inner mind of the other, and that it was the policy of the Radical Republicans to inflame this misunderstanding. In subsequent months he again demonstrated his statesmanship by his fight against the obnoxious "force bill," which would have placed election machinery in four Southern states under federal control.

When Lamar passed through Atlanta in the spring of 1875 Grady interviewed him at length and wrote: "There are few men in the country to whom the appellation of 'statesman' can be more justly applied, and none to whom the much-abused adjective of 'eloquent' more properly belongs." The Mississippi leader was, in Grady's opinion, "the pattern of a true Southern man who has accepted the situation . . . and turned his whole attention to a resuscitated and rehabilitated country." He particularly admired the way in which Lamar, "when passion ran high, . . . curbed the rage of his strong nature and counseled moderation." He admonished certain other Southern congressmen, notably the hot-headed John Brown Young of Kentucky, to emulate Lamar's example.[13]

The extent to which Grady himself was learning to "counsel moderation" was revealed by his willingness to give an impartial hearing even to H. I. Kimball, who had antagonized Georgians far more than Brown had done by his business dealings with the Radical regime of 1868–71. The financial structure of Kimball's numerous enterprises, which included seven railroads and Atlanta's largest hotel, the Kimball House, had collapsed along with the Bullock administration. At that time Kimball had left the state, broken in health as well as in fortune. But on February 6, 1874, his health restored, he returned to Atlanta, denouncing the charges against him and declaring he could "triumphantly defend" the legality of all his deeds. In an editorial in the *Herald* the next morning,

[13] Cate, op. cit., pp. 1–7, 164–99; *Atlanta Daily Herald,* March 24, 1875.

Grady said that while in Rome he had opposed all Kimball's works "from the sale of the opera house to the end of the chapter," but that he now thought the New Englander should be given an opportunity to prove his innocence of crime. The editorial stressed particularly the fact that Kimball had come back voluntarily and placed himself within the jurisdiction of the state.

Perhaps Atlantans were more inclined than other Georgians to be lenient with Kimball because their city held many tangible benefits of his promotive genius — some at the cost only of the repudiated bonds held by Northern and European investors! But no grounds for prosecuting the promoter could be found either by Linton Stephens, who made a thorough investigation at the request of Governor Smith, or by a Fulton County grand jury, which investigated the whole Bullock administration and indicted Bullock but not Kimball. The foreman of the grand jury which conducted the investigation was one of the leading citizens tendering Kimball a "vindication banquet" at the hotel named in his honor.

The representative Atlantans making this gesture regarded Kimball "preeminently as a builder," whose "talent as an organizer" was unquestioned and whose "ability to handle men" was conceded by all. A "steam engine in breeches" the *Constitution* called him several years later, after he had missed election as mayor of Atlanta by only fifty-four votes. Tall, handsome, and energetic, Kimball possessed such rare persuasive powers that it was said the only way to resist doing what he asked was to refuse to see him. Bullock, too, eventually rehabilitated himself and became a respected citizen of Atlanta, but he never was accepted by Grady as enthusiastically as was Kimball.[14]

"The New South," as Grady called it in an editorial as early as March 14, 1874, needed men with ability and enterprise, even though they might have been associated with the carpetbaggers of Reconstruction days. Proclaiming that factories as

[14] Eugene Muse Mitchell: "H. I. Kimball: His Career and Defense," in *Atlanta Historical Bulletin*, III (October 1938), 349–83; E. M. Coulter: *A Short History of Georgia* (Chapel Hill, 1933), pp. 332, 385–8. Cf. Thompson, op. cit., pp. 226–38.

well as farms were essential to prosperity, the *Herald* endorsed
a plan to build Atlanta's first cotton mill by public subscription and favored the proposal to make Kimball its first president. Declaring that "a wholesale immigration of good capitalists to Georgia" could be brought about by publicizing "her
unparalleled resources," the paper proceeded to tell the state's
story through special "trade editions," which were distributed widely in the North. At the same time it emphasized the
need for diversified agriculture, declaring that the South was
bankrupt because "we have devoted our entire energies to one
staple, and, to do this, we have been compelled to go into debt
for everything which entered into its cultivation."

Here, as in Hill's speeches, was the unmistakable outline
of Grady's program for the economic regeneration of the
South, the details of which were to be filled in by his work in
the eighties. But in the seventies, as in the decade that followed, the chief obstacles were political. Not all the Southern
states had been freed from carpetbag control, and the Radicals in Congress, seeing power slipping from their grasp with
the election of a Democratic House in the fall of 1874, strove
desperately to retain the advantages they had gained through
the Negro vote. They sought to make capital out of the war
by "bloody-shirt waving" and "rebel-baiting," all of which in-
cited Southern politicians and newspapers into spirited and
frequently ill-tempered replies. This "miserable sectional
strife," as Grady saw it, was the greatest bar to Southern
progress.

Thanks chiefly to the brilliant efforts of Lamar, the "force
bill" was defeated by the "lame-duck" Congress of 1874-5.
Toward the end of the same session, however, another coer-
cive measure — the long-debated Civil Rights Bill of Charles
Sumner — was passed in modified form. The purpose of this
measure was to break down the barriers erected in the South
to prevent mingling of the races in hotels, saloons, restaurants, public conveyances, and places of entertainment. Grady
urged the Southern people to be "cautious and prudent"
while waiting for the Supreme Court to pass upon the consti-
tutionality of the bill. While holding that "social equality"
was an "utter and eternally impossible condition," he declared

that the South could defend itself best by giving the Negro "equal and even-handed justice." Commenting on "A Brace of Civil Rights Cases" resulting from the inferior coaches provided for Negroes on the railroads, he wrote: "Let the Georgia Railroad and all other Roads, which have not done so already, provide equal accommodations for the negro . . . and then the Civil Rights Bill will become practically a nullity."

In state and local affairs, as well as in national politics, the *Herald* advocated "clear-headed, sensible statesmanship." Noting that 134 out of 143 acts passed by the General Assembly of Georgia at one session were "purely local in character, many ridiculously trivial," the paper favored "home rule" for counties and cities so that the legislature could devote its time to more important matters. On another occasion the *Herald* expressed itself as "heartily tired of having small men in the Atlanta City Council" and advocated the abolition of the system of ward nominations then in effect.

Grady took an active interest in his Alma Mater, the University of Georgia. When a movement developed to elect Jefferson Davis, former President of the Confederacy, as chancellor of the university, he was "utterly and absolutely opposed." He asserted: "There is no profession that demands more thorough and arduous preparation than that of the educator. The chancellor of the University of Georgia should be a scholar, of technical as well as general attainments. Sentiment should never interfere with so great an institution as our State College, and so serious a matter as our higher education." Later, when he condemned certain "unwise and unpopular" policies fastened upon the university by its "unwieldy" board of thirty-two trustees and suggested the appointment of a smaller board, one trustee sarcastically replied that perhaps the best idea would be for all to resign and to turn the management of the university over to the editor of the *Herald.*

The editor's interest in education, however, went much deeper than his concern for his own Alma Mater. When the City Council threatened to abolish the public high school "in the interest of economy," the *Herald* launched an intensive campaign to arouse citizens to the need for a full system of tax-supported education. Other editorials urged the South to "get out of its lazy way of living," and through gymnasiums, athletic clubs, and public contests of skill, to make the average Southerner "a sturdy, broad-shouldered young giant; full of glow and health and ruddiness; able to push himself through life and assert his rights in any crowd."

On matters of public morality and charity Grady had pronounced views. The *Herald* opposed a "foul and monstrous measure" to license houses of prostitution in Atlanta, citing as one argument for the new cotton factory that it would "relieve poverty and suppress vice among women and children who cry for aid." When the paper revealed that a mother and baby had been found dying from starvation, and that a corpse had been allowed to remain in a house for nearly three days, the Mayor called the *Herald* a "popinjay juvenile squirt gun," and the *Constitution* denied that such conditions existed. The *Herald* came back, however, with such "incontrovertible testimony" that within ten days a group of citizens organized the Atlanta Benevolent Association to operate "a home for the destitute and helpless."

The *Herald's* protests against "intemperate efforts to promote temperance" are particularly interesting in the light of Grady's later connection with the prohibition movement in Atlanta. When the General Conference of the Methodist Episcopal Church, South, adopted a rule that "making, buying, selling, or using liquor as beverage would be grounds for expulsion from the church," Grady, speaking as a Methodist, set forth these views:

Whenever you educate the public mind to look upon drinking, no matter how moderate, as an evil *per se,* and make a Christian lady feel that it is a sin to keep it in the house, that moment you add a stimulus to the craving, and make every child as he grows to his freedom, anxious to indulge it.

. . . We regret this step on the part of the great church, which the writer loves above all other churches. We fear that it will add hypocrisy to the vice of intemperance. We admit . . . that intemperance is the monster vice of the land. We confidently believe that it has caused more crime, more poverty, more sorrow, than all other vices combined. God knows we would rejoice to see it banished from the world, and would cheerfully lend our aid to do it, if it were possible — but is it possible? We have no hesitation in stating from what has been accomplished in the past, that it is not.[15]

As he had done in Rome, Grady frequently expressed his ideas as to what newspapers should and should not be. In an editorial on "Southern Newspaper Writers" he observed that the greatest fault of Southern journalism was "its lack of first-class editorial writers." The average Southern newspaper depended upon one editorial-writer to fill some three columns daily, he said, whereas "no editor who hopes to make an impression upon his age" should write more than one editorial a day, and preferably "not more than three a week." He regarded Henry Watterson of the Louisville *Courier-Journal* as "perhaps the smartest writer of the Southern press," but attributed a "slouchiness and slanginess" in Watterson's writing to overwork. The best editorial-writer in the South, he thought, was John Forsyth, of the *Mobile Register*, and the best in Georgia since Albert Lamar left the *Columbus Enquirer* was John H. Martin, of the same paper. "The secret of his power is earnestness and purpose," said Grady. "He never writes unless he has something to write about, a good but neglected rule."

In these same months Grady reiterated his conviction that a newspaper, to serve its purpose in a democratic society, "must be free." The *Herald's* most spectacular act in the direction of maintaining its independence was the announcement, after Abrams's departure, that it would "totally abolish, as far as it is concerned, the miserable deadhead system, which is the bane and the disgrace of Southern journalism." Whereas Abrams had complained of the state road's refusal to issue a pass to one of his agents, the paper now printed under its masthead that "any man in its employ who asks any Hotel, Theater, or Railroad for a deadhead pass, or deadbeat privileges, forfeits his situation." In an editorial explaining the reasons for this policy, it declared:

[15] May 31, 1874.

Above all human agencies, the press should be independent, fearless, truthful. It is the great director of public opinion, the guide of the people, and hence there rests upon it a fearful responsibility. It should, therefore, be above all temptation, so far, at least, as it is possible to place it on that elevated ground.

We have often thought it a great misfortune that newspapermen have to depend upon business for a living. No man, however pure, with any protracted experience in journalism can look back without recurring to a time when the demands of pecuniary interest influenced him either to suppress the truth, or to say what in his heart he did not believe to be strictly true. And it will be so just so long as the press consents to receive favors, and the human heart is alive to emotions and gratitude.[16]

A public official or a journalist, the paper declared, should "regard the offer of a free ticket by anybody upon whose rights he may by any possibility be called to pass, as an insult and indignity."

4

When Grady wrote of the difficulty of maintaining an independent newspaper in the face of "the demands of pecuniary interests," he knew whereof he spoke. Although there is no evidence that the *Herald* "suppressed the truth" when it abandoned the sensational and unreasonable attacks of Abrams on former Governor Brown, there is ample proof that the paper had increasing difficulty in obtaining adequate funds without strings attached, and that it was the pursuit of policies distasteful to its creditors that finally led to its demise. By a not so strange coincidence, it was Brown himself who dealt the fatal blow.

After the loan of $5,000 which Grady's mother made to the paper in May 1873, there was little she could do except to assign her mortgage on the Herald Publishing Company to the Citizens Bank as security for a new loan obtained by Grady and Alston in February 1874. By this time Ann Grady had sold every piece of her property, including the Prince Avenue home and the store building, from which funds could be re-

16 January 7, 1874.

alized to help the paper. It therefore became necessary for the partners to look elsewhere for financial aid.

Shortly before the withdrawal of Abrams, Alston obtained a $4,000 loan for the *Herald* on a $5,000 letter of credit from the irascible General Toombs. According to Abrams, Toombs told Alston that he was making the loan because of his satisfaction with the policies followed by the paper under Abrams's editorship, and that he expected those policies to be continued. According to Grady, Alston definitely warned the General that the *Herald* might be called upon frequently to differ with him "as a public man." Probably each man took more for granted than was put in writing; the undisputed point is that, as soon as Grady succeeded Abrams as editor and the paper modified its attitude toward former Governor Brown, Toombs began to demand his money. Finally, in August 1874, Alston obtained a loan from another source and repaid the General.

Several months later, word reached Grady and Alston that Toombs had accused the *Herald* of "robbing him of five thousand dollars." Grady immediately jumped to the defense with another of his rare personal "cards," in which he recited Alston's version of the transaction and summed up Toombs's "generosity" in the sentence: "He loaned the money like a prince and collected like a Shylock." Abrams, who had returned to Atlanta in the spring of 1874 and commenced publication of the *Daily News,* took up the cudgel with an editorial accusing Grady and Alston of "treachery" to Toombs in that they had changed the policy of the *Herald* after accepting the loan. Toombs, however, made no public reply to Grady's account of the affair, and Abrams, after struggling for eleven months to make a success of the *News* through such sensationalism, suspended publication in May 1875 and moved to Florida. But while it lasted, the verbal slugging was furious, with Abrams exchanging for the *Herald* editor's epigrams such names as "H. Wiggler" and "H. Whippoorwill" Grady.[17]

At times during the 1874–5 period the *Herald* gave hopes of getting on its feet. Throughout these two years the paper

[17] Atlanta *Daily News,* July 18, 1874; January 22, 1875.

was doing either the city or the state printing, and for several months it had both contracts, much to the discomfort of the *Constitution*. When Alston wrote H. I. Kimball in March 1874 for assistance in obtaining a loan, he revealed that the paper had paid off $17,000 of a $27,000 indebtedness and had "bonded" $6,000 of the remainder. It still owed "several thousand dollars" in smaller amounts, however, and these unpaid bills were resulting in troublesome lawsuits.

In his reply to Alston, Kimball suggested that if the *Herald* believed "in the folly of repudiation and the wisdom of 'state aid' and would devote its columns to advocating such a policy and such *special* enterprises as met its favor," he could "consistently promise" his support "in procuring such aid as would make the *Herald* financially strong and independent." Judging from the letters that followed, Alston was unwilling to make any such bargain.[18] Although the *Herald's* endorsement of Kimball for the presidency of the cotton mill in subsequent months might have led to the suspicion that it was repaying him for favors received, there is no evidence that he gave the paper any financial assistance. Certainly nothing occurred to make the *Herald* "financially strong and independent," as Kimball had offered to do if his terms were met.

The pressure of debt was relieved temporarily a few weeks later by the sale of a one-third interest to I. W. Avery, who resigned the editorship of the *Constitution* to become a partner of Grady and Alston. Since Avery was a capable, experienced, and well-informed journalist, his association of nearly a year with the paper doubtless had considerable influence upon Grady. Indeed, the older man probably was responsible for most of the editorials which cannot be traced to the young editor himself in the period from April 24, 1874, to April 8, 1875. On the latter date the *Herald* announced Avery's resignation on account of ill health, and the retiring partner expressed his regrets at leaving such a "brave, independent and virtuous newspaper."

Avery's one-third interest was bought by Alston, thus giving the second of the "uncaged" partners, for the first time,

18 Alston-Kimball correspondence, published in *Constitution*, February 26–9, 1876.

undisputed control of the paper. The ominous nature of this circumstance was lessened only slightly on May 1 when the *Herald* announced that the partners had agreed to form a stock company with an authorized capital of $60,000. At this time James A. Burns, formerly connected with the Western & Atlantic Railroad and more recently with Kimball, bought $5,000 in stock and became secretary-manager of the corporation. Grady and Alston were careful to state, however, that they controlled a majority of the stock and would be responsible for the paper's policies. Under the reorganization Alston became president and Grady managing editor.

But this arrangement, too, afforded only temporary relief. Financial conditions still were stringent in Atlanta, as elsewhere, and in spite of economies the paper's outgo continued to exceed its income. By August 16, 1875, when Grady's second child, Augusta King, was born, his personal finances had reached such a low ebb that he was forced to write his mother for a loan of forty dollars to tide him over the emergency. By the middle of November the Herald Publishing Company was involved in new legal difficulties, resulting in the withdrawal of Burns, the secretary-manager. To make matters worse, Grady fell seriously ill with pneumonia and Alston once more was left in full control.[19]

That Alston had lost none of his propensity for fighting is shown by the fact that only a few months previously he had engaged in a "near duel" with E. Y. Clarke, editor of the *Constitution*. Since the laws of Georgia forbade sending or accepting a challenge under severe penalty, the two men agreed to meet across the Alabama line. Only the intervention of Alabama officers prevented the duel.[20]

But it required more than duels to stop the *Herald*. The real crisis started on November 17 with the publication of a letter charging that the *Constitution* "took bribes from Kimball" and "was started with money stolen from the State

[19] *Atlanta Daily Herald*, November 12, December 24, 1875; correspondence in Grady Collection.

[20] *Atlanta Daily Herald*, July 2, 1875. Alston was killed in March 1879 as the result of a pistol encounter growing partly out of a "bold and horrifying report" he had made, as chairman of the legislature's Penitentiary Committee, on the convict lease system.

Road." A few weeks later the *Herald* published another sensational story exposing a "pool" by which the railroads of the
Southeast, under the leadership of former Governor Brown,
had "parceled out the carrying of cotton crops, thereby effect-
ing a monopoly that enabled them to raise rates." According
to Alston, he immediately was notified that what he had written "about railroad pools and rates" would lead to the foreclosure of the mortgage held by the Brown-controlled Citizens
Bank. His reply was to print further attacks on Brown, including the charge that $70,000 had been expended on the
legislature of 1871 to secure the endorsement of the Western
& Atlantic lease. Simultaneously the *Herald* launched a campaign against the system by which the state of Georgia leased
its convicts to private individuals and corporations. Brown in
his coal mines was one of the largest users of convict labor,
although even his critics admitted he also was one of the most
humane.

The inevitable outcome was that Brown, as Grady described
it, "sat down" on the *Herald* "with a vigor and emphasis only
equaled by that with which Humpty Dumpty sat down on the
inflated baby." [21] On February 6, 1876 a legal advertisement
in the *Constitution* announced a sheriff's sale of the Herald
Publishing Company to satisfy the mortgage held by the Citizens Bank. Another advertisement in the same issue told of a
levy on the property of Alston and Company to satisfy the
mortgage given to one D. E. Scannell, from whom Alston had
borrowed to repay General Toombs. Thus, ironically enough,
a paper which had tried to assert its independence of both
Brown and Toombs was smashed between forces originating
with two leaders who stood at the opposite poles of Georgia
politics in the Reconstruction era.

At the time of the foreclosure, Alston was re-airing his accusations against Brown and the *Constitution* before the Joint
Special Committee appointed by the General Assembly to investigate the endorsement of the state-road lease by the legislature of 1871–2. To the specific charge that the *Constitution*
"got $5,000 for favoring the lease," W. A. Hemphill, the busi-
ness manager, explained that the paper had received approx-

21 *Constitution*, December 8, 1876.

imately $5,000 from Brown and others for printing communi-
cations favoring the lease, and that it was paid approximately
$2,000 by the other side for publishing contributions oppos-
ing the lease. This was confirmed by Brown and the treasurer
of the road, who testified that all together some twenty to
twenty-five thousand dollars was paid "by direction of the
president" to newspapers in various places for printing "favorable communications." Reprehensible though this may
seem by present-day standards, it must be remembered that
until the passage of the Postal Act of 1912 it was a common
practice for newspapers to accept payment for publishing matter of this kind. As for Alston's charge that money had been
used to buy the legislators themselves, Brown admitted only
that "several thousand dollars" had been paid to lawyers in
different parts of the state "as retaining fees in the event of
litigation."

The legislative committee finally rendered a report declaring that Alston's charges were based entirely on "hearsay,"
and that there was "no evidence to establish the charge that
any sum of money was paid to a member of the legislature of
1871 and 1872 to influence his vote upon the passage of the
resolution to ratify the lease of the Western and Atlantic railroad." Thus ended the *Herald's* "war" upon the state road,
which two years later was described by Grady as being operated so successfully that the Brown lease would have been endorsed "almost unanimously" if put before the people.[22]

A casualty incidental to the collapse of the *Herald* was the
abandonment of plans for the publication of a "History of Atlanta" by Henry W. Grady, which had been announced in the
paper for some weeks previously. The author explained that
"when over one hundred pages had been completed, Mr. Per-
kerson, the Sheriff, and a man of much literary acumen,
showed signs of dissatisfaction at the way in which the work
had been done. This dissatisfaction increased until at length,
with the fall of the *Herald*, he seized the unfinished work, evidently being determined to finish it himself." [23]

Soon afterward the *Constitution* acquired the "books and

[22] Ibid., February 22, 26–9, 1876; May 14, 1878.
[23] Clipping, Grady Scrapbooks.

subscription accounts" of the *Herald*. It was, for the first time since its founding, "without a rival and the only morning daily in Atlanta." [24] The *Commonwealth*, an afternoon paper established the previous year by B. F. Sawyer, Grady's onetime rival in Rome, apparently offered no serious competition.

5

Disheartening though the death of the *Herald* must have been, Grady did not easily admit defeat. Even while the paper was breathing its last, he and Alston were making plans with their business manager, A. P. Woodward, to bring out a new daily named the *Atlanta Courier*. But where the *Herald* had succumbed at the tender age of three and a half years for want of financial nourishment, the *Courier* "died a-borning" for the same reason.

Of the issues of the *Courier* actually published between February 22 and March 24, 1876, only a few clippings remain. Of these, one dated February 20 from Philadelphia gives Grady's description of his first ocean voyage, which he made on his trip north to buy type and material for the new paper. A few passages from this article suffice to show the recovery of the author's buoyant spirits:

I never saw the ocean until the trip that results in this letter: I shall never forget the impression it made upon me.

I had imagined that it would be a moment of ecstasy. I had believed that my soul, in the glad recognition of something as infinite, as illimitable as itself, would laugh with joy, and leap to my lips, and burn in my fingers, and tingle in my veins. I wisely reserved the first sight until we had steamed out beyond the land, and then with the air of one who enchains himself, I raised my head and looked out to the future. There, as far as the eye could reach, aye, and way beyond, as if mocking the finiteness of sight, stretched the blue waters. Ah! how my fine-spun fancies crumbled and came tumbling back on me in dire confusion! . . . My soul didn't leap to my lips. . . . I regret to say that my breakfast did. . . . I do believe that if I had tied a cannon-ball to a crumb of bread and swallowed them both, the crumb would have come

24 *Constitution*, February 15, March 26, 1876.

prancing to the front again, and brought the cannon-ball with it. . . . For three days I lay like an old volcano, still, desolate and haggard; but with an exceedingly active crater. . . .

. . . The ocean is meant to be looked at and enjoyed — from the shore, or through books. You may see more of it by going on board a ship. It is pretty apt to see more of you, though, than you do of it. There are moments during the first day or two, when, leaning over the taffrail, you yawn into its face, that it can see you clear through to your boots.[25]

Returning from Philadelphia to Atlanta, Grady stopped in Washington and "penetrated" the Capitol for the first time in the company of his friend Benjamin H. Hill, Jr. The reflections of the young Georgian on his first visit to the Senate chamber are contained in another amusing *Courier* article, which began:

The American Senate is the baldest-headed body of men on earth — or in the heavens above or the waters beneath, for that matter. . . . I have heard that women have no beard because they keep their jaws wagging so perpetually that the whisker has no time to bloom; so I suppose the constant turmoil of the brains beneath the skulls of these seigniors have worn their hair off, just as volcanoes with any vim in their craters have no shrubbery about their summit. The best explanation, however, that I ever had of bald-headedness, came from an old fellow that I once accosted with the question, "How come you bald-headed?" "My son," said he, leaning paternizingly [*sic*] over me, "I was born so." [26]

After the suspension of the *Courier,* Grady picked up a few dollars each month as Atlanta correspondent of the *Augusta Constitutionalist.* Eventually he found sufficient backing to bring out five issues of a small weekly, the *Sunday Telegram,* which, he promised, would be "full of sensations, stories, letters, gossip, and humor." A regular feature was a review of "The Daily Press During the Week," in which the editor good-humoredly expressed his opinions of the *Constitution,* the *Commonwealth,* and a newly started Atlanta daily, the

[25] Clipping, Grady Scrapbooks.
[26] Clipping dated Washington, February 23, Grady Scrapbooks.

Times. One Sunday late in June, however, he announced through the columns of the *Times* that the *Telegram* "does not appear this morning for a number of reasons, the principal one being that there are no funds to bring it out with."

These were familiar words to readers who now had seen the failure of three Grady-edited newspapers in less than five months. They found an equally familiar note of light-heartedness in the editor's concluding words:

> Arrangements have been made to refund at once all subscriptions paid in advance. This being the case, the public has little right to grumble, much less, perhaps, than the publisher.
>
> HENRY W. GRADY
>
> Good-bye, little Whid! Ta, ta, old boy! — H. W. G.[27]

<hr>

[27] Clipping, Grady Scrapbooks. "Whid" was a columnist on the *Constitution* named Whidby, who sometimes wrote "naughty paragraphs" about the *Telegram*.

CHAPTER SEVEN

A Scoop for Mr. Bennett

FOLLOWING his three successive newspaper failures in Atlanta, Grady was left, for the first time, entirely dependent upon his own earnings. The last dollar that could be obtained from his father's estate was gone. To use his own words, "starting life ready-made," he had "speedily unmade himself and was now hopefully rambling along the road to regeneration."

In July 1876 he received a letter from Senator Zebulon Vance, of North Carolina, offering him the editorship of a Raleigh paper in which Vance was interested. The North Carolina leader had become acquainted with Grady during several speaking engagements in Atlanta, one under the auspices of the Young Men's Library Association. Grady was on the verge of accepting this offer when, yielding to a sudden impulse, he decided to "strike high." Borrowing fifty dollars, he packed his grip and took the train for New York.[1]

Grady did not know a soul in the metropolis, but he was eager to make a connection with the *New York Herald,* which he long had admired for its political independence, its friendliness toward the South, and its unprecedented enterprise in getting the news. Some of this admiration he doubtless had absorbed from his one-time partner Abrams, who under the direction of James Gordon Bennett himself had written editorials denouncing the Radicals for their treatment of President Johnson. The *Herald* now had passed under the control of the younger Bennett, but it still was "probably the most profitable and potentially the most powerful newspaper in the world." Its sensational exploits, such as the expeditions of

[1] H. W. G. in *Constitution,* August 15, 1880, and in undated interview, Grady Scrapbooks; Harris, pp. 75–6.

Henry M. Stanley to Africa, had attracted the attention of the entire country.[2]

Landing in New York with three dollars and seventy-five cents in his pocket, Grady registered at the Astor House, which was located on Broadway, diagonally across from the *Herald* building. After a hasty breakfast he stepped out on the sidewalk in front of the hotel. Here he gave a bootblack twenty-five cents, "one-fifth of which was to pay for shining my shoes, and the balance . . . for the privilege of talking with him. I felt that I would die if I did not talk to somebody." [3] His nerves thus steadied, he walked across the street and entered the *Herald* building.

Grady's impression, after climbing the winding iron staircase to the editorial quarters on the second floor, must have been one of disappointment. The imposing exterior of the building was of marble, but the rooms occupied by the editorial staff on either side of the narrow second-floor hallway were "dark, dingy, dismal, and ill-ventilated." At the end of this hall, fronting on Broadway, he found the office of the managing editor, Thomas B. Connery, "the *alter ego* of young Jim Bennett" and the "absolute arbiter" of the paper's fate during the editor's frequent sojourns abroad. From Connery's office a door on the left led into the workroom of the editorial writers, and on the right into the sanctum of Bennett himself.[4]

Finally Grady obtained an audience with Connery, "a tall, angular, red-necked Irishman," whom the *Atlanta Herald* once had described as "the best newspaperman in America." When informed of Grady's desire to write for the *Herald,* the managing editor inquired if his visitor knew anything about Georgia politics.

"I know more about that than anything else," Grady replied.

Connery then suggested the writing of a trial article on the subject. Explaining that it would be necessary for him to be

2 Don C. Seitz: *The James Gordon Bennetts* (Indianapolis, 1928) , p. 340.
3 Harris, p. 76.
4 Undated clipping from *Philadelphia Times,* Grady Scrapbooks.

out of the office for an hour or two, he tossed Grady a stack of copy paper and left the room.

Grady rapidly wrote out a 2,000-word article on the political campaign in Georgia. He could do this easily, for he had completed a series of letters on the same subject for the *Augusta Constitutionalist* a few weeks earlier. By the time Connery returned, the visitor from Georgia was leaning back in a chair with his feet on the desk.

"What's the matter?" asked the *Herald* executive.

"Nothing," replied Grady, "except that I'm through."

"Very well," said Connery, "leave your copy on the desk, and if it amounts to anything, you will hear from me."

Such an abrupt dismissal was disheartening. Grady feared that the article might not be published for several weeks, if at all, and he knew that his scant funds would last hardly a day in New York.

"Early the next morning," he later told his friends, "before getting out of bed I rang for a hall-boy and ordered a copy of the *Herald*. I actually had not strength to get up and dress myself, until I could see whether my article had been used. I opened the *Herald* with a trembling hand, and when I saw my article, I fell back on the bed, buried my face in the pillow and cried like a child."

Grady was at the *Herald* office that morning much too early, but he waited patiently until the managing editor arrived. This time the brusque Irishman received him cordially. After complimenting Grady on the trial article, Connery offered him the post of Georgia correspondent for the *Herald* at space rates. Grady accepted and departed, much too proud to say anything about payment for the article already published.[5]

The trip back to Atlanta was marked by an incident Grady loved to relate. "I had so little money," he said, "that when I got to Washington I had nothing left except fifty cents and my ticket to Atlanta. I asked myself, 'Shall I spend all this

[5] Harris, pp. 76–7, 512. Grady's trial article filled one and one-fourth columns in the *Herald* of July 25, 1876, headed "The Georgia Campaign." It bears no signature, but may be identified by the clipping and the record of payment in the Grady Scrapbooks.

money now on one good meal, or shall I spend it in bits on the way down?' I finally concluded that I had better spend the whole fifty cents for the biggest meal I could get, and then hold out as best I could. . . . I never ate so much in all my life before or since. On the strength of that meal I went on all right until we got to Danville, where we were delayed for three or four hours beyond the schedule time. This delay I had not reasoned on. . . . I remember that an old woman got on near Danville with a big old-fashioned cheese box in her arms. By and by, just as the hunger began to take a good grip on me, she took off the lid. It was her lunch box. She drew out all sorts of eatables one after the other, and ate of each sparingly, throwing the remnant out of the car window. I remember most distinctly a deliciously browned chicken and a deep-dark old-fashioned pumpkin pie. That wretched old woman just tasted that chicken, just nibbled at that pie, and then threw the rest away, while I sat starving in the next seat." [6]

Several weeks later the new correspondent's reportorial ability was put to a crucial test by a telegram from Connery asking him to ascertain whether a certain man was registered at any Atlanta hotel. Grady quickly searched every hotel register in the city, but without success. He then began to speculate why Connery wished to find this particular person. In a recent issue of the *Herald* he discovered the answer. The stranger was implicated in some difficulties in Cuba, had fled from Havana, and had landed two weeks previously in Charleston. Reasoning that the fugitive would be more inclined to go to New Orleans than to Atlanta, Grady telegraphed a friend in New Orleans and asked him to search the hotel registers there. The reply came back promptly that the man was registered at the St. Charles Hotel. From the moment Connery received this unexpected piece of information, he knew he had a Georgia correspondent who could be depended upon to get the news.[7]

[6] *Chicago Inter Ocean*, December 24, 1889.
[7] Clipping of article by Amos J. Cummings, Grady Scrapbooks.

Joseph E. Brown

Benjamin H. Hill

Alexander H. Stephens

Robert Toombs

Alfred H. Colquitt

Rufus B. Bullock

LEADERS OF RECONSTRUCTION DAYS

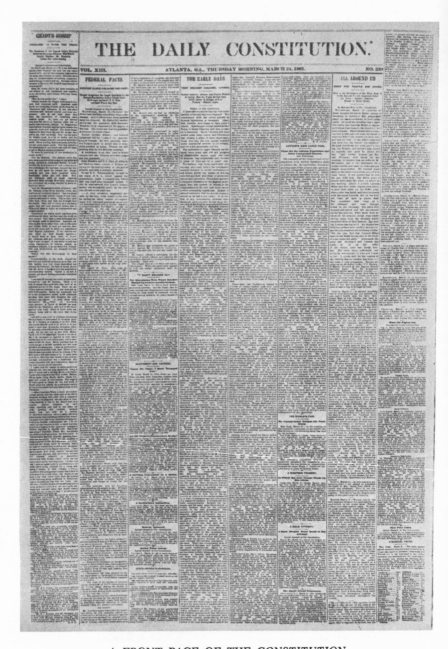

A FRONT PAGE OF THE *CONSTITUTION*

*When Grady went traveling, the first column usually carried
one or more articles signed "H. W. G."*

2

Even so, the news in Georgia was seldom of sufficient national interest to command much space in a New York newspaper. Grady's "string" for July, including the trial article written in the *Herald* office, brought him only twenty-two dollars, and his checks for August and September were even smaller. Although an assignment in October to cover the pre-election race riots in South Carolina promised to yield him sixty dollars, he felt keenly the need for a regular income adequate to support his family. Accordingly, when he called at the office of the *Augusta Constitutionalist* on his way back from South Carolina and was offered the editorship of that paper, he agreed to begin work as soon as he could make a brief trip home.

Overcoat on his arm and valise in hand, Grady was on his way to the railroad station in Atlanta several days later when he met Evan P. Howell, who inquired where he was going. Grady replied that he had accepted the editorship of the *Constitutionalist* and was leaving for Augusta to take up his new duties.

"I asked him what he was to get as a salary in Augusta and he said one hundred dollars a month," Howell later recalled. "I asked him why he did not remain in Atlanta. He said there was no opening. . . . I said, 'Why not work on the *Constitution?*' He said they would never hire him, because he had abused and belabored them so. I told him that I controlled the matter now and that I would give him what the Augusta paper had promised him if he would report to me the next morning at 10 o'clock." [8]

It developed that Howell had bought a half interest in the *Constitution* a day earlier and had been looking for Grady to offer him a position. Therefore, on the next day — October 19, 1876 — the paper carried this brief but significant notice:

From this date Capt. Evan P. Howell and Mr. Henry W. Grady are part and parcel of the *Constitution's* editorial staff. These gentlemen are well known in Georgia and need no introduction.

[8] Interview with Howell in *Atlanta Daily News*, September 12, 1901.

A lawyer by profession, Grady's new employer was known as Captain Howell because of his military rank in the Confederate Army. He was a native of Georgia and had been educated at the Georgia Military Institute at Marietta and Lumpkin Law School in Athens. At the outbreak of the war he had enlisted in the First Georgia Regiment, eventually becoming a captain of artillery in command of a battery defending Atlanta against Sherman's siege. Emerging from the war with only five dollars to his name, he had spent two years clearing and selling lumber from his father's land near Atlanta. Next he had been employed for a year as reporter and city editor on the *Intelligencer,* the city's first daily. Resuming the practice of law in 1869, he had served at various times as chairman of the Fulton County Democratic Executive Committee, member of the City Council, member of the state Senate, and solicitor-general of the Atlanta circuit. In his legal practice he was employed as counsel for the *Constitution,* and in this capacity he had discovered the willingness of E. Y. Clarke, the editor, to sell his half interest in the paper. Paying $10,000 cash and assuming half of a $27,000 indebtedness, Howell had reached an agreement with the other stockholders giving him complete control.

Howell was eleven years older than Grady and much more experienced in business and politics, but he freely acknowledged the superior talents of the younger man as a newspaper writer. When he announced his intention to give the *Constitution* "the best staff of any newspaper in the South," Grady urged the employment of his red-haired friend Joel Chandler Harris, who at that time was a refugee in Atlanta from a yellow-fever epidemic in Savannah. Howell assented, with the result that one of Grady's first duties on the *Constitution* was to carry to Harris an offer of twenty-five dollars a week as an editorial paragrapher.[9]

It would have been difficult to find three men whose talents were more complementary. Howell possessed the financial sa-

9 "Evan P. Howell," in *Georgia Historical Quarterly,* I (1917), 52–7; Julia C. Harris: *Life and Letters of Joel Chandler Harris* (Boston, 1918), pp. 131–2. Referring to the fact that Harris had been "temporarily engaged upon the *Constitution* for some weeks past," the paper on November 21 announced that "henceforth he will be a fixture on the editorial staff."

gacity and political experience that the two younger men
lacked, while Harris and Grady were writers who differed from
each other as much as from their employer. The quiet and un-
obtrusive Harris soon added to the duties of paragrapher those
of telegraph editor and eventually became a full-time editorial-writer, but it was not until the beginnings of his "Uncle
Remus" stories in 1878 that he attracted national attention.
The ebullient and irrepressible Grady, on the other hand,
was engaged within three weeks on his first big reportorial assignment — the Florida election frauds, which form part of
the sordid episode in which the presidency of the United
States, for the first and only time in history, was stolen from
the rightful winner and given to another.

3

The accession of Rutherford B. Hayes to the presidency has
been described as "the crowning crime of the tragic era" of
Reconstruction. On the night of the election, November 7,
the victory of Tilden was celebrated everywhere, and the next
morning all the New York newspapers except the *Herald* and
the *Times* conceded the defeat of Hayes. The *Herald* asked:
"Who is elected President? As we go to press the question is
nearly as much of a mystery as it was Tuesday morning." Just
what happened in the *Times* office has been sharply disputed.
The story now generally accepted by historians is that the
Times presses were running with an edition virtually announcing the election of Tilden when telegrams were received from several prominent Democrats asking for election
figures on South Carolina, Florida, and Louisiana. Discovering that the electoral votes of these three states would give
Hayes a majority of one, the managing editor of the *Times,*
which was supporting Hayes, stopped the presses and claimed
victory.

When Zachariah Chandler, the Republican national chairman, was apprised of the situation, he flashed telegrams to
"good men and true" in South Carolina, Florida, and Louisiana, telling each in turn that victory for the Republicans depended upon the vote in that state. Later in the day he boldly

announced that Hayes had carried these three states and therefore had won the presidency by a majority of one electoral
vote.

Since carpetbag governments still were in control of the
election machinery in these states, the Republican leaders had
good reason to believe that the returns could be manipulated
to produce the desired majority. Their gravest fears apparently
concerned Florida, where the powers of the state Canvassing
Board were prescribed by law as "purely ministerial." But
President Grant ordered the sending of troops to supervise
the count in the capitals of all three disputed states. Armed
with the less conspicuous but scarcely less effective induce-
ments of patronage and funds, Chairman Zach Chandler hurried to Tallahassee along with the soldiers.[10]

As official "visiting statesmen" in the Florida contest, the
Republicans designated William E. Chandler of New Hampshire and General Lew Wallace of Indiana. To protect their
interests, the Democrats appointed Manton Marble, editor of
the New York *World,* and former Governor Brown of Georgia. As soon as the portentousness of the situation became
known, the *New York Herald* wired Grady to go to Tallahassee, and he left for Florida with Governor Brown to cover the
developments for both the *Herald* and the *Constitution.*

When Grady boarded the Florida-bound train at Macon,
he found himself in the midst of three companies of the troops,
who were headed for Tallahassee on the same train. The Atlanta correspondent enjoyed listening to the lively political
discussion of the bluecoats, among whom, he reported, "the
democratic disputants had much the best of the fight as well
as the lion's share of the applause. . . . As a pretty general
thing, the soldiers were disgusted with the business in which
they were engaged and did not hesitate to show their disgust
in open terms."

The political situation in Tallahassee itself Grady found to
be "fairly indescribable":

Everything is overstrained and unnatural. It is all a whisper
and a wink. There is nothing frank or easy. One is carried off into

10 Bowers, op. cit., pp. 522–3.

a remote corner to receive in utter secrecy the most casual information. There are lips to your ear all day long. The most atrocious rumors poison the air hour after hour. Every stranger here is something or other. This one (really a stationery drummer) is a New York detective; that one (really a corn doctor) is a professional mail robber; yonder fellow (really a young student making for the coast to fish) is a telegraph wire tapper, and that box he carries with him (really his tackle) is the dire machinery with which he is to break the wire and intercept messages. Venice in her palmiest days never had half so much of delightful mystery about her. "That barber," whispers one politician to another, "is our friend. He is with us. You may rely on this — Sh-h-h!" And, with his finger to his lip and a suppressed wink trembling on his cautious left eyelid, he is off, leaving us to wonder what tonsorial art has to do with politics, and his friend to rejoice in the knowledge that he can at last secure a reliably democratic shave. The truth of the matter is that both parties are at sea. Neither knows exactly what to do, and yet is bewildered by the fear that the other will do it first. . . .[11]

After two weeks of preliminary court skirmishes between the opposing forces, the state Canvassing Board began its work on November 26. The board consisted of three members: one Democrat, Attorney General William A. Cocke, and two Republicans, Comptroller C. A. Cowgill and Secretary of State Samuel B. McLin. The last served as chairman. The Democrats pinned their hopes on Cocke and Cowgill, said Grady later, for no one accused McLin of "being gentleman enough to do right, scoundrel enough to do wrong, or social enough to be approached." [12]

Although it was Grady's first experience in handling a political story of such magnitude, the ease in personal contacts that he had gained from reporting state and local affairs now stood him in good stead. Indeed, the son of a Florida official who was in daily attendance at the proceedings reported that his father, in discussing each night the events of the day, "dwelt less and less upon the count, and more and more upon the presence of a young Georgian representing the *New York Herald,* and his doings." Grady's fun-loving disposition usu-

[11] *New York Herald,* November 20, 1876.
[12] Clipping, Grady Scrapbooks.

ally placed him in the midst of "a gaping, roaring circle, and he left a trail of mirth and comment in his wake." In the courtroom, at the Canvassing Board hearings, and in the hotel lobbies — he seemingly was everywhere.

That political differences did not prejudice Grady in his associations is indicated by the fact that he soon made a warm friend of General Lew Wallace, one of the Republican "visiting statesmen." The forty-nine-year-old Hoosier, a veteran of two wars and already the author of one novel, was then practicing law and grooming himself for political appointment. Since neither he nor Grady cared for the diversions of the bar and the gaming table, they spent some of their free hours together on a lake near the town. Here the young newspaperman concentrated upon fishing, while Wallace paddled his hands in the lake, revolving in his mind, as he subsequently told Grady, the plot of *Ben Hur*.[13]

One secret of the attraction between the two men may have been revealed by the later explanation that, in its dramatized form, "*Ben Hur* could never fail; if you mix a horse race, a ballet dance, and the Holy Spirit, you are bound to catch the American public." [14] Grady never tried his hand at a novel or a drama, but in his writings and speeches he displayed that same understanding of the popular mind which made *Ben Hur* a best-seller.

An even more important result of Grady's contacts in Tallahassee was an increasing respect for the man who had smashed his *Atlanta Herald* out of existence. In his first dispatch to the *Constitution* he told how "rapidly and skillfully" former Governor Brown was organizing for the contest. At the conclusion his tribute was unreserved: the bewhiskered Georgia leader was "the hero at the homeward march." During a threatened attack of pneumonia Brown had revealed a side of his character that Grady had overlooked up to this time:

> Although I have had a great deal to do with the ex-Governor
> . . . I never knew until he was sick what mental power the man

13 W. T. Turnbull in *Constitution*, February 23, 1890.

14 Quoted in F. Fraser Bond: *Breaking into Print* (New York, 1933), pp. 30–1.

had. He lay there on the bed, with two fly-blisters pulling torture out of his breast, and every breath he drew cutting his lungs like a knife, and surrounded by a pile of law books, which were being read to him, made up the skeleton of a legal argument on which the democrats will rest their case tomorrow. On Thursday night there was a ball in the dining room which is separated by a single wall from his room. The clamor was fearful. A brass band was blowing its brains out through some exceedingly noisy horns. A half dozen greased elbows were sawing across as many resonant fiddles, and the shouts and laughter were literally ear-splitting. I expressed the fear that it might make him worse by keeping him awake.

"Oh, no!" said he, "I can will myself to sleep at any time I want to."

And almost straightway he shut his eyes and did so. . . . I started out of the room on tip-toe, foolishly thinking of waking the sleeper. Jeff, his faithful attendant, laughed at my caution and said:

"You might shoot your pistol off right in the Governor's ear, and he wouldn't wake less he wanted to." [15]

But no amount of logic mustered by Brown or any other Democratic "visiting statesman" could have changed the Canvassing Board's verdict. The two Republican members, McLin and Cowgill, were both "predetermined, through either gall or greenbacks, on robbing the people of their choice for the presidency." Although the hearing brought out conclusive evidence of Republican frauds, including a particularly flagrant case of ballot-box stuffing and forgery in Alachua County, the board ruled that Hayes had carried Florida by 924 votes.

The result of the canvass was announced late in the afternoon. To the dismay of most of the newspaper correspondents, it was discovered that the telegraph wires had been cut. The nearest available telegraph office was at Drifton, nearly thirty miles away, and there would be no train until the next day.

Grady, however, had learned in advance that the wires were down and had prepared for the emergency. As soon as the

[15] *Constitution*, December 8, 1876.

decision was announced, he stepped from the Capitol into a light buggy drawn by a span of fast horses. By hard driving and a change of horses en route, he and a Negro driver reached Drifton in less than five hours. Just as they turned into the little station, a horse and rider dashed past them. Grady recognized the horseman as General Wallace. Leaping from the buggy, he ran down the station platform and reached the door of the telegraph office at the same moment as the General. Being friends, they had no difficulty in agreeing that Grady should have the wires immediately after Wallace sent brief messages to Governor Hayes and the Republican National Committee.

When the other correspondents arrived, they found Grady had taken possession of the office. Running out of copy, he had bought the telegraph operator's entire library — a well-thumbed volume of Webster's blue-back spelling book — and had torn from it enough matter to hold the wires until he could complete his story. Thus it happened that the *New York Herald* and the *Atlanta Constitution* received the news from Florida that night earlier than any other papers in the country.[16]

The Radical returning boards of Louisiana and South Carolina soon followed the lead of Florida in announcing a verdict for Hayes. In all three states, however, the Democrats set up rival groups of electors, who submitted to Congress certificates in favor of Tilden. To pass on these disputed returns, the Democratic House and Republican Senate appointed an Electoral Commission composed of five representatives, five senators, and five justices of the Supreme Court. Since the composition of the commission turned out to be eight Republicans and seven Democrats, the votes of the three contested Southern states, together with one disputed vote from Oregon, were all awarded to Hayes. He thus was declared the winner by an electoral vote of 185 to 184.

Before the Democratic leaders in Congress would agree to acquiesce in this decision, however, they exacted from the emissaries of Hayes a pledge that he would remove the remaining federal troops from the South and would allow the South-

16 Turnbull, loc. cit.; *New York Herald*, December 7–9, 1876.

ern states henceforth to control their own affairs. By a coincidence, the three Southern leaders who were most effective in reaching this bargain with Hayes were all political favorites of Grady: Gordon, Hill, and Lamar. Equally remarkable is the irony of the fact that former Governor Brown now joined the more rabid Democrats in advocating the use of force to seat Tilden. Incensed by the corruption he had seen in Florida, Brown thought the conciliators had "sold us too cheap."[17]

Grady stayed with the story to the finish, remaining in Florida until January and then going to Washington. During the Christmas holidays he was joined by his wife and three-year-old son for a brief outing. On an excursion up the St. Johns River he "revenged himself" on the author of *Uncle Tom's Cabin* by "turning up his nose" in passing the home of Harriet Beecher Stowe. From historic St. Augustine he wrote delightfully of the Seminole Indians, particularly one "handsome, athletic child" who was proudly identified by his pretty squaw mother as "part Injun — part Injuneer." The Indians were being taught to wear "coats, hats, boots, and breeches," he reported, "the only trouble being that they will only consent to wear one of these useful articles at a time." In a more serious vein he told of the "incredible" number of orange trees that were being set out and of the other attractions that were drawing Northern tourists and settlers to Florida in increasing numbers. Even on this casual pleasure trip he visualized with remarkable accuracy the major lines of the state's future development.[18]

Before leaving Florida, Grady for his own satisfaction made an affidavit to the effect that Tilden had carried the state. "That affidavit," he told his friends, "I shall keep and transmit to my son." In his opinion, the two Republicans on the state Canvassing Board "would have unhesitatingly voted" any majority required to elect their ticket.[19]

Grady's judgment at the time was essentially the same as

[17] James F. Rhodes: *History of the United States* (New York, 1893–1919), VII, 290; Coulter: *Short History*, pp. 358–9.

[18] *Constitution*, December 20, 21, 1876.

[19] Ibid., December 9, 1876; *Chicago Times*, December 24, 1889.

that of historical scholarship today. For example, the historian Rhodes, "never biased in favor of the Democracy," wrote in the early part of this century that "had the visiting statesmen stayed at home, both Louisiana and Florida would have gone to Tilden." A recent biographer of Hayes holds that while Hayes actually carried South Carolina, and in an absolutely fair election probably would have carried Louisiana, "there is no question that the Republicans far outdid the Democrats in the frauds practiced in Florida." Tilden carried Florida, and therefore should have been president by a vote of 188 to 181.[20]

4

Under further pressure from Lamar and other conciliatory Southern leaders,[21] President Hayes late in April removed the remaining federal troops from the Southern states. The *Constitution* greeted this event with an editorial on "The New South" in which it declared that henceforth the flag would wave over equal states, "not over a single province." The Democrats already had regained control of the state administration in Florida, and the withdrawal of the troops in Louisiana and South Carolina was followed quickly by the collapse of the carpetbag governments in those states. Whatever may have been Hayes's reasons for discontinuing the "ruinous policy of his predecessors," the *Constitution* said, his actions were such as to "invite and promote reconciliation" between the sections. "Freed from organized bands of robbers and bayonet rule," the South now had its "grand opportunity" for development.

The election frauds were too pregnant with issues for the next congressional campaign, however, to remain buried for long. In the spring of 1878 a bill was introduced in Congress seeking to bring about *quo warranto* proceedings in the Supreme Court to determine the validity of Hayes's title to his office. The *New York Herald* reported that out of 368 senators and representatives who had been interviewed, 256 defi-

20 Rhodes, op. cit., VII, 229; H. J. Eckenrode: *Rutherford B. Hayes* (New York, 1930) , pp. 189–93.
21 Cate, op. cit., pp. 288–92.

nitely were opposed to the revival of the controversy, as was the *Herald* editorially. Nevertheless, getting wind that additional evidence was being compiled in the effort to unseat Hayes, the New York paper asked Grady to investigate the rumors of "penitential spasms among the Florida republicans who managed the count."

Grady reached Tallahassee on April 21. The first few hours he spent in the "quiet pumping" of everyone whom he suspected of having any knowledge of developments in the case. Then he encountered in the Metropolitan Hotel a "reserved, leisurely gentleman" whom he recognized as Alfred Morton, a detective who had been employed by the Republicans in the contest of 1876. Considering it unlikely that Morton had returned to Florida "merely for health or pleasure," Grady had a long talk with him and soon learned that the detective now was working for the leaders of the movement to unseat Hayes.

Several months earlier Morton had discovered Samuel B. McLin, the former chairman of the state Canvassing Board, "starving in an attic" in Washington. As a reward for his services in delivering Florida's electoral vote to Hayes, McLin had been appointed by Hayes to a judgeship in New Mexico, but the appointment had failed of confirmation in the Senate. Embittered by this disappointment, broken by the tragic deaths of a son and a daughter, and confronted by the prospects of an early death himself from tuberculosis, McLin now desired to "make his peace with the world." Morton had carried this news to certain members of the anti-Hayes forces and had been commissioned to obtain confessions from McLin and any other penitents. He revealed to Grady that at Thomasville, Georgia, on March 23, McLin had given him a signed statement, fully confessing his part in the frauds.[22]

Morton's revelations provided material for a 2,600-word dispatch, which occupied the most important news position in the *Herald* of April 24. But the McLin confession was by no means the extent of the story. Morton had been with other participants in the frauds "just at the very time that a friend

[22] MS. Diary, Grady Collection; *New York Herald*, April 24, 27, 1878; H. W. G. in *Constitution*, October 7, 1879.

was needed to quicken their consciences or to guide the current of their remorse." The detective insisted that he had also a confession from L. G. Dennis, the chief "field man" for the Republicans in stuffing ballot boxes and forging returns. In this case, however, he could produce no signed statement such as he displayed for McLin. Some officials in Tallahassee supported Morton's contention that Dennis had confessed; others denied it. Whereas Grady wrote in his diary after his first interview with the detective that he was "happy with a big H," he confided on the next day that he was "very much troubled about Dennis."

Learning that Dennis was due at Jacksonville the next morning, Grady hastened by train to that city. "Dennis arrived early, but could not see him," he wrote in his diary. "Met him in front of Post Office. He dodged me. Finally treed him in Cheney's room. Had a long talk & satisfactory. He confessed to everything and gave me a good interview." There were two reasons why Dennis was willing to confess, Grady explained: first, he considered his appointment by the Republicans as a revenue agent at eight dollars a day to be an inadequate reward for his services, and, second, Democratic officials in Florida had promised not to prosecute seven criminal indictments then pending against him in the state courts.[23] The affidavit of Dennis formed the basis of another page-one story.

Summing up the exposures in a final article from Florida, Grady wrote: "The confessions follow right in the track of the democratic assault made during the sessions of the Returning Board; every prominent fraud attacked by the managing democrats is confessed to, and the very methods charged by the democrats were used." These methods were, first, to "stuff the ballot boxes by all known devices during the election "; second, "if the first did not suffice, to raise the returns, as was done in Alachua and elsewhere"; third, to hold back a certain county "until it was known precisely what was needed and then to count it into the returns"; fourth, to "throw out enough counties in the returning board canvass to give the state to Hayes."

"This was the program definitely arranged before the elec-

[23] MS. Diary, Grady Collection; *Constitution*, April 28, 1878.

tion came off, and faithfully carried out afterward," Grady declared. "Under the organization as it existed there was no possibility for the State to be carried for Tilden."

He was careful to add, however, that Florida Democrats were not "noisy" over the revelations, because, now that home rule had been restored in the South, they were satisfied to leave Hayes undisturbed. Furthermore, all those giving confessions were or had been indicted in the Florida courts, and this detracted from the value of their statements.[24]

This latter point obviously gave Grady no little concern. For several days after his return to Atlanta he continued to write in his diary that he was "worried! Worried! WOR-RIED!" His stories had gone exclusively to the *Herald* and the *Constitution,* and he feared that men of weak character like McLin and Dennis might be induced by rival newspapers to repudiate their confessions.

His apprehensions, however, were soon set at ease. Instead of a reprimand, there came from James Gordon Bennett as a reward for his work in Florida a check for $1,000.[25] A few weeks later the *Constitution* reported that Grady had received the offer of a position in New York "so attractive that he could hardly refuse it." Nevertheless, with his financial condition now greatly improved, he did refuse it.

5

The effect of the Florida experiences on Grady was unmistakable. In 1876 and again in 1878 he had outwitted some of the best special writers in the country, and the prominence given his stories by the *Herald* and the *Constitution,* over the signature "H. W. G.," did much to restore any of the poise and self-confidence he may have lost as a result of his earlier failures. Such a close-up view of political corruption in all its nakedness must have strengthened him, too, both in his preference for journalism to politics and in his contempt for certain leaders of the Republican Party — a contempt which, as a result of Radical Reconstruction, was now shared by most whites in the solidly Democratic South.

[24] *New York Herald,* April 27, 1878.   [25] Harris, p. 77.

Although the *Constitution* treated President Hayes most courteously when he visited Atlanta in the fall of 1877 on his goodwill tour of the South, Grady's attitude crept into the columns of the paper on many later occasions. He never could escape the conviction that Hayes, willingly and knowingly, had accepted a fraudulent title to office. Accordingly, when "His Fraudulency," as the *Constitution* called him, retired from office in 1881, a special story from Washington bore this typical headline:

LADEN WITH INFAMY

HAYES RETIRES AS HE CAME IN

THE WILLING TOOL OF DESIGNING KNAVES AND THE
CONSORT OF RINGSTERS AND THIMBLERIGGERS

"President Hayes goes out of office," the paper said, "the most neutral shade of greatness we have probably ever had." [26]

With his love for fun, Grady also was probably responsible for an idea used in decorating the residence of one of his friends, M. C. Kiser, in Atlanta. At least his associates gave him credit for it, and he always delighted in taking visitors to the Kiser home. On the wall over the stairway, in ascending order, were hung pictures of the Presidents of the United States. All the pictures were uniform in size and frame — that is, all save one. The picture of Hayes was most conspicuous by its smallness.

In the year following the President's retirement, Grady again wrote down his reflections on "the stealing of Florida for Hayes by the Republicans":

That was the ugliest chapter of American history. It was worse than war, and more odious than treason. As it was the first crime of its sort in the history of the republic it will be the last. Never again will the American people be in the temper to submit to so flagrant an outrage. It was inexorably proved before the case was decided that an Alachua county politician and a negro, by stuffing

[26] *Constitution*, March 4, 1881.

one ballot box, actually stifled the voice of fifty millions of people
and reversed the edicts of thirty-eight sovereign states. This jug-
gling was afterwards confessed to by the man who did it. And yet
the verdict stood for four years, and the dire stress for peace en-
forced submission to a fraud that fixed the character of one administration.

Truly it was an unholy swarm of strikers that infested Tallahassee during that period. Spies, false witnesses, bummers and
ballot thieves — more vicious than the flies that issued from her
sands — filthier than the buzzards that lolled on her chimney
tops! [27]

[27] Ibid., April 14, 1882.

CHAPTER EIGHT

"Just Human"

WHILE covering the final phases of the Hayes-Tilden dispute in Washington during February and early March 1877, Grady became acquainted with some of the country's ablest correspondents. One of these was George Alfred Townsend, better known as "Gath," who at various times had represented the New York *World,* the *Chicago Tribune,* the *Philadelphia Times,* and the *Cincinnati Enquirer,* and who was regarded by Grady as "the best letter writer in America." "Gath," like Grady, was a great admirer of Benjamin H. Hill, who recently had been elevated to the Senate and whose brilliant reply to James G. Blaine's "amnesty speech" in the House the year previous was still ringing in the ears of Washington newspapermen. Another capital reporter with whom Grady developed a warm friendship was Moses P. Handy, a Virginian whose "light touch" was brightening the columns of the new *Philadelphia Times.* With "Gath" and Handy to back him, it is not surprising that he soon was retained by both the *Times* and the *Cincinnati Enquirer* as their Atlanta correspondent.

Before returning to Georgia, Grady went to Philadelphia for a conference with A. K. McClure, the editor of the *Times.* In its weekly edition McClure's paper was starting a series of articles entitled "The Annals of the War." Leading actors in the struggle from both North and South were being invited to give their versions of events in which they had taken part. At Handy's suggestion, McClure enlisted Grady's aid in the undertaking and assigned him to make arrangements with Southerners from whom contributions were desired.[1]

On his way back to Atlanta, Grady stopped in Charlotte,

---

[1] H. W. G., clippings, Grady Scrapbooks. The articles later were published by McClure in book form as *The Annals of the War* (Philadelphia, 1879).

North Carolina, to arrange with the widow of General "Stonewall" Jackson to contribute to the series. He obtained Mrs. Jackson's consent, together with a brief interview for immediate publication in the *Times*. Unfortunately the interview quoted her as making several remarks which were regarded by certain of her friends as too critical of other Southern generals. After the story was printed, consequently, she wrote a letter to the newspapers, denying that she had said some things attributed to her. Later, upon learning from Grady that her action might cost him his connection with the *Times,* she admitted that she had spoken "too freely" and "incautiously." Absolving him of "intentional wrong," she offered to ask McClure not to penalize the correspondent for her own imprudence.[2] Evidently the *Times* editor was satisfied.

This was not the only reprimand received by Grady during a period when his ego otherwise might have been inflated by his successes in Florida. It appears that soon after his return to Georgia he was assigned to cover an unusually large number of hangings. His scrapbooks for the spring and summer of 1877 contain accounts of at least a dozen executions which he reported for the *Constitution* and other newspapers. With a temporary affection for puns and alliteration, Grady would give these stories captions such as "Jumping Jack," "Nicked in the Neck," "The Aerial Waltz," and "The Latest Noose."[3] These headlines proved extremely irritating to Williams Rutherford, his one-time mathematics professor at the University of Georgia, who wrote Grady as follows:

I . . . have been often pained at the apparent want of reverence, and the marked levity of your style, even when writing about the most serious matters. . . . When an account is to be given of the *awful* end of Meeks for murder, you head the column "Terrible Twist." Then again when an account is to be given of a hanging in South Carolina, you write under the head the "Swing in Carolina." These are specimens of numberless examples of the like levity on solemn occasions against which I enter my protest.[4]

[2] M. Anna Jackson to H. W. G., March 15, 24, May 3, 1877, Grady Collection; clippings, Grady Scrapbooks.
[3] Clippings, Grady Scrapbooks.
[4] May 9, 1877, Grady Collection.

But the dear old professor did not know the worst. According to a tradition in the *Constitution* office, one story of a hanging was already in type with the heading "Jerked to Jesus" when Grady, just before press-time, ordered the wording changed. This particular caption is said to have been the work of another member of the staff, who probably obtained the idea from the *Chicago Times*.[5] However, most of the headlines criticized by Rutherford did come from Grady's own pencil, if the editorial habits revealed by his manuscripts and clippings may be taken as an indication.

The most important event in Atlanta during the summer of 1877 was the state Constitutional Convention, which Grady also reported for various papers on his "string." This convention, he wrote, was "probably the most self-reliant body of men ever assembled. The day they met they declared themselves independent of the United States Government. The second day they declared themselves independent of the Governor by voting down a resolution requesting him to address the convention on the changes desirable in the present constitution. The third day they declared themselves independent of God Almighty by refusing to appoint a chaplain." The convention was dominated by General Toombs, who was so determined to undo the "carpetbag constitution" of 1868 that he advanced $30,000 out of his own pocket to defray the expenses of the gathering.

Under Toombs's influence, the new constitution decided the question of the repudiated bonds once and for all by declaring them to be "forever null and void." The convention also referred to the voters the matter of whether Atlanta should remain the capital — a question which was decided overwhelmingly in the affirmative, along with the adoption of the constitution, after a campaign in which the *Constitution* fought vigorously for both.[6]

What most attracted local attention to Grady in these months, however, was his crusade on behalf of Sallie, the girl

[5] The famous "Jerked to Jesus" headline appeared in the *Chicago Times* November 27, 1875, according to Frank L. Mott: *American Journalism* (New York, 1941), p. 467.

[6] Clippings, Grady Scrapbooks; Coulter: *Short History*, p. 362.

convict. While visiting a convict camp near the home of Evan P. Howell's father, Clark Howell, Sr., he was surprised to see a young white girl working side by side with the men prisoners, most of whom were Negroes. In response to his questions, the girl told him she was fourteen years old and had been sentenced to a year on the chain gang "for vagrancy — because I have no home." The incident so shocked Grady that he wrote for the *Constitution* a story which resulted in Governor Colquitt's promptly issuing a pardon for Sallie. Grady himself took the pardon to the girl and, after a dinner in her honor at the Howells', brought her into the city. Here she was given a room in the Benevolent Home, an institution his editorials in the old *Herald* had helped to establish. Soon he procured for her a position where she might earn an honest living.

Although Grady's charity was generally applauded and offers of aid for Sallie were received by the score, there were some who scoffed at the whole affair. A rival newspaper, the *Times,* interviewed the judge who had sentenced Sallie to the chain gang and printed his statement that the girl was not fourteen, as she had said, but at least sixteen. Furthermore, he asserted, she had not been sent to the chain gang merely for "having no home" but for repeated offenses as a streetwalker. In a "card" to the *Constitution,* the indignant jurist insinuated that Grady had transformed Sallie into an innocent girl by "a liberal use of the poet's fancy and license."

The *Constitution* replied editorially that "a reporter who could see a white girl — a mere child — half-naked and encased in dirt, sweltering in the midst of a gang of negro thieves and convicts, under a broiling sun, and not 'gush,' must be a very empty young man! Stoicism under such circumstances is little more than brutality." Grady reserved his own defense until a later occasion — an occasion which did much to establish him not only as Atlanta's favorite newspaper writer but also as her most popular lecturer.

2

The background of Grady's first appearance as a lecturer was the controversy over Sallie; the immediate cause of the speech, however, was an error in transmitting a telegram.

Grady at this time was a member of the Lecture Committee of the Young Men's Library Association. One of the association's speakers in the spring of 1877 was Samuel Sullivan ("Sunset") Cox, the Ohio Congressman, journalist, and orator. Cox owed his nickname to the fact that he had broken newspaper tradition in 1853 with a human-interest editorial on a sunset — a circumstance which probably caused Grady to suggest inviting him. Wishing to prepare advertising placards for the lecture, Grady wired Cox for his subject. The reply, written in longhand by the telegraph operator, Grady read as "Just Human." The placards were duly printed and distributed over the city. At last the lecturer came. What then happened was described by Grady himself: Cox was

a pleasant little gentleman, who beguiled the walk to the Hotel with the airiest of jokes and the brightest of comment. When he had registered his name, in the untutored chirography habitual with the great, he took me to one side and asked me in an undertone what those placards meant.

"That," I replied, looking at him in astonishment, "is the subject of your lecture."

"My lecture?" he shrieked. "Whose lecture? Whose subject? My subject, sir, is 'Irish Humor.' What is this 'Just Human'?"

And so it was the real subject, "Irish Humor," had become transferred by telegraph into "Just Human."

In introducing Cox that night, Grady announced that if the audience would listen to what the distinguished visitor had to say on "Irish Humor," he himself would make good his advertisement and lecture to them at a later date on "Just Human." [7]

Grady's lecture was delivered at DeGive's Opera House on the night of June 12, 1877, under the auspices of the Young Men's Christian Association. After saying a few words on his own behalf, in the manner of "the condemned man . . . upon the scaffold," the speaker launched into his ready-made title. "Just Human!" he repeated. "I like the subject. It is an earnest and sincere one. It holds a hundred sermons. . . . It

[7] MS., Grady Collection; Harris, p. 58.

is a rebuke for the aspiring — it is a promise to the despond-
ent — it is a plea for the erring."

"Just Human" was an appeal for "the inutilities of life —
for those trifling things that lie above and beyond the mere
making of money, and the winning of bread — for those
things that need not be, and yet should be." The speaker argued first for "the beautiful in life," then for "mercy in human judgments," and finally for "charity in all things." The
lecture alternated between descriptive passages and anecdotes, with unexpected twists of humor continually tempering the pathos. But when he had finished, Grady had made a
convincing reply to those who criticized his intercession on
behalf of Sallie. His views on punishment were typical of his
argument as a whole:

> . . . There is a reform needed in the method of punishment.
> It is not necessary that every man who is proven guilty of crime
> should be shut out from all hope of reclamation — that society
> should turn its hand against him — and that an eternal ukase of
> banishment should be issued against him. . . . If I had the power
> . . . I would invent and establish a system of law that would re-
> form while it punished — that would reclaim the criminal, while
> it avenged the crime — a system in which the punitive and the
> solvable elements might walk hand in hand — a system that would
> humanize its convicts while it protected society. . . . The first
> step . . . is that we shall cease to regard our criminals as brutes
> — that we shall remember that . . . they in their shackles and
> debasement and we in our assured spotlessness are creatures of the
> same mold — that the worst of them and the best of us and all that
> intervenes are "just human," nothing more or less.

As "the finest illustration of pure philanthropy that literature furnishes," Grady used the story of his favorite hero of
fiction, Jean Valjean of *Les Miserables*. Here was to be found
the key to his own views on charity:

> What we need is a full and abundant charity — a charity as
> penetrative and suffusive as God's sunlight. There is very little
> ever done by what is known as "a discriminating charity." Dis-
> crimination is another word for evasion. The Lord pity the pauper

that a discriminating man cannot find some reason for turning away empty-handed. . . .

If I were to dare to make a formula for almsgiving, I should say that we should let suffering be the touchstone, and capacity the limit. All question of desert or degree, of past or future, should be sunk in this one question: Is there suffering here, and can I relieve it? This answered, the alms should be measured only by the need of the subject and the capacity of the giver.

In urging the women of the city to take the lead in "tempering men's judgments" and "stirring philanthropy" to its depths, Grady quickly brought out the smiles by his references to "the mother, that sweet wielder of the punitive slipper, that lavish dispenser of the corrective paregoric," and to "the tender wife, who meets you at midnight at your front door with a rolling pin in her hand" and then "condemns you to an ignominious and uneasy rest outside of the mutual mosquito netting." He then shifted just as quickly from humor back to pathos, ending with a dramatic religious metaphor:

And where do we get the precedent for all this? Nearly twenty centuries ago, a new star was hung in the sky, a star that portended the coming of a Redeemer. And the wise men followed it and were led to a manger. They saw a miracle of the patience and goodness of the Lord. They saw omnipotence, imprisoned in the flesh of a babe — they saw omniscience gazing ineffably from the eyes of a child — they saw Divinity become "just human," that it might teach the world the lessons it should know.

Who can tell of the martyrdom that this great God endured, when He walked through Earth, as humble as the lowliest of us, His power shorn of its proportions, nothing infinite but the sense of pain? Did He not teach the lessons that I have spoken tonight? Was not His sense of forgiveness absolute? Did He not shield the Magdalen from her persecutors and take the crucified thief to His bosom? Was not His charity boundless, and perfect? Did He stop to consider whether any of the loaves and fishes with which He fed the multitude fell into guilty or ungrateful hands? In that pilgrimage, when God took on our poor habitat and became "just human," we may find the pattern for all life.[8]

8 MS., Grady Collection.

"Just Human" made a decided hit. Dr. H. V. M. Miller, the "Demosthenes" whose opinion Grady so highly prized, pronounced it "the best lecture he ever heard in Atlanta." Marion J. Verdery, a friend of the speaker's college days, was so entranced that he prevailed upon Grady to repeat it in Augusta to "the largest house that ever greeted a lecturer" in that city. The editor of the Macon *Telegraph and Messenger* arranged immediately for him to give the speech in Macon.[9]

The lecture in Macon was delivered for the benefit of the family of Asa R. Watson, a member of the *Telegraph* staff, who had died the preceding month. In his introduction Grady revealed something of his own journalistic idealism by referring to the dead newspaperman as one "who wrote always with a clear pen — with a pen that had no hint of gall or trace of bitterness — with a pen dipped in truth and impelled by sincerity. . . . He never wantonly stained a single reputation — never wilfully pained a single heart — never needlessly inflicted a single wound." The trait for which he praised Watson most highly was "an ineffable gracious sympathy that lies above all charity" [10] — the quality which Grady himself possessed in such a high degree.

A few days after the lecture, Grady received a petition signed by such distinguished citizens as Governor Colquitt, Senator Hill, and Dr. Miller, urging him to repeat "Just Human" in Atlanta. This he declined to do, on account of "indefinite absence from the city," but he did consent to give another lecture for the Y.M.C.A. in the fall. For this second appearance he selected as his subject "A Patchwork Palace — The Story of a Home."

The substance of the story upon which this second lecture is based — the struggle of one "Mortimer Pitts, Esq., a ragpicker," to build a home — is almost identical with that of a feature article published by Grady in the *Atlanta Herald* of November 9, 1875. The real "Patchwork Palace" was only a nondescript hut which a well-digger, Lewis Powell, had erected out of odd scraps of building material on a vacant lot at the northeast corner of Spring and James Streets. But un-

9 Clippings, Grady Scrapbooks.
10 MS., Grady Collection.

der Grady's touch this poor shanty, which to most passers-by was merely an eyesore, became the symbol of man's longing for a home and family. "Mr. Pitts wanted a home," the story-lecture related. "A man named Napoleon wanted universal empire. Mr. Pitts was vastly the more daring dreamer of the two."

The similarity between Grady's writing and his speaking is illustrated by these opening paragraphs from the two versions of the "Patchwork Palace":

THE FEATURE STORY	THE LECTURE
After a full and careful observation coupled with some personal experience, I am prepared to say Mr. Mortimer Pitts is the poorest man that ever existed!	Mr. Mortimer Pitts was a chiffonier. Ah! I see you skimming off to your French phrase books. Stop! I will translate — and confess. He was a rag-picker.
His larder could not be called empty, because he had no larder; his supper tonight is a crust; his breakfast for the morrow is a dream; and his dinner an unsolved problem. His whole earthly possessions, beyond the rags that covered him, was a cow, that, I believe gave both buttermilk and sweetmilk; a dog that gave neither, and a pocket knife that yielded him nothing but the luxury of an occasional whittle on a piece of borrowed wood. As an opposition to all this poverty he had: 1st, an aggravating wealth of children, that tumbled into the world as best they could, and were met with plenty of kisses but no crusts, and 2nd, a name — (Mortimer Pitts) — which his parents, whose noses were in the clouds when they christened him, had saddled upon	After a patient study of the responsibility that the statement carries, I do not hesitate to say that he was the poorest man that ever existed. He lived literally "from hand to mouth." His breakfast was a crust; his dinner a question; his supper a regret. His earthly wealth, beyond the rags that covered him, was a cow, that I believe gave both buttermilk and sweetmilk — a dog that gave neither — and a hand cart, in which he wheeled his wares about. His wife had a wash tub that she held in her own title, a scrubbing board similarly possessed, and two chairs that came to her as a dowry.
	In opposition to this poverty, my poor hero had, first, a name (Mortimer Pitts, Esq.) , that his parents whose noses were in the air when they christened him,

him aspiringly, but which fol- had saddled upon him aspir-
lows him now, his condition be- ingly, but that followed him
ing put in contrast with its rich through life, his condition be-
syllables, as an everlasting joke. ing put in contrast with its rich
syllables as a sort of standing
sarcasm — and, second, a perfect wealth of tow-headed children with shallow blue eyes.
These blonde brats came tumbling like April showers from
the perennial Mrs. Pitts, who,
withal she was a deprecating
woman, responded to her lord
with an enthusiasm that nothing could dampen and a
promptness of delivery that
nothing could check.

That Grady was fully conscious of the emotional quality in
his art is indicated by passages such as this from the same manuscript: "It is amusing to see how completely our emotions
master our will. How puny is the determination of the will before the flood of impulses that start at the subtlest suggestion!
It can no more control these swelling currents than the brit-
tle crust of Etna can constrain the molten lava when it surges
toward the light." And, in another place: "Talk of logic —
impulse is logic. Talk of will — emotion laughs at will. Talk
of law — sentiment overrides law. When public sentiment
finds no law, it makes one."

As for his reasons for writing and talking so much about
people in "the lower stratum of society," he declared: "It is
because here I find real human nature. Here passions and
sentiments, unsmothered by artificial conditions, unrestrained
by proprieties, unwarped by the small hypocrisies of society,
move with freedom and with power. Did you ever notice how
Dickens . . . points all his morals with actors taken from the
under crusts?" [11]

So enthusiastic was Atlanta's reception of the "Patchwork
Palace" that Grady, during the fall and winter of 1877–8, re-

[11] MS., Grady Collection.

peated the lecture in several other cities, including Augusta, Gainesville, and Athens. The *Augusta Chronicle* described his style as "rich, flowing, emotional, always ending with the intensely humorous." A Gainesville newspaper was equally lavish in its praise: "Strains of eloquence — the most beautiful word painting — touched the heart and welled up tears that had scarcely had time to fill the eyes, when an inimitable leap from the truly sublime to the irresistibly ridiculous shook the house with laughter." To Athens he was accompanied by "his wife, boy, and dog." It was his first speech in his old home town since his commencement oration ten years earlier, and the local newspaper reported: "He came! He spoke! He conquered!" A few people, the editor explained, "stayed at home to watch the fires and feed the baby. The rest went to hear Grady." [12]

In April Grady accepted an invitation to give the "principal address" before the South Carolina Press Association, but he was compelled to cancel this engagement on account of the assignment from the *New York Herald* to obtain the confessions in the Florida election frauds. In June he repeated the "Patchwork Palace" in Atlanta, the *Constitution* reporting that he had made "over five hundred dollars" from this lecture alone. Two weeks later, however, he announced that his next speech would be his "last appearance as a lecturer." [13]

There were two plausible reasons for Grady's decision to give up professional lecturing. The first and most likely, of course, was that his success in Florida and the thousand-dollar check from James Gordon Bennett had encouraged him to concentrate upon newspaper work. A second factor, however, may have been a realization that he had overdone the pathos in his somewhat sentimental glorification of Sallie and "Mortimer Pitts." For scarcely had the excitement over his crusade on behalf of the girl convict died down when the heroine of "Just Human" slipped back into her old life of vice.

"I was poked in the ribs facetiously," Grady later confessed. "A perfect shower of chuckles fell on my ear. It was

12 Clippings, Grady Scrapbooks; MS. Diary, 1878.
13 *Constitution*, July 2, 1878.

the joke of the season — this triumph of the Devil over the body of a girl. One mad young wag, who, with a keen nose for a joke, followed her into her haunts of crime, came back . . . bearing a statement from her to the literal effect that I was a d—d fool." [14]

But Sallie's downfall was not his only disillusioning experience. Just as the popularity of the "Patchwork Palace" reached a peak, Lewis Powell, the well-digger whom nearly everybody in Atlanta knew to be the original of "Mortimer Pitts," was haled into the police station after being thrown out of his romanticized home by a son-in-law for beating his wife. The *Constitution* reported that Powell had been "kicked off the same veranda where the ideal 'Mortimer' stood the picture of domestic felicity and contentment."

Grady was more "staggered and sickened" by the glee with which some of his friends greeted these events than he was by the fact that his efforts to help Sallie and "Mortimer" had come to naught. His faith in human nature was tempered but not destroyed; he continued to write of other heroes and heroines from the less fortunate classes. Indeed, his exaggerated pathos reflected the warm-heartedness which was a source of strength as well as weakness to the end of his days. But in his third human-interest lecture and in his later newspaper sketches he apparently was more fortunate in his choice of characters.

The last of Grady's three human-interest lectures was entitled "The Bright Side of Things" and expressed particularly well his philosophy of happiness. "Somebody has said," he asserted, "that the great danger of this age is the decay of seriousness. That's a lie. The decay of seriousness — yes, the seriousness of the Amminadab Slurk [15] and Company, the seriousness of the Puritans that objected to bull-baiting not because it hurt the bull but because it pleased the people."

[14] Harris, p. 211.

[15] Mr. Slurk was the editor of the "Eatanswill Independent," in Dickens's *Pickwick Papers:* "His aspect was pompous and threatening; his manner was peremptory; his eyes were sharp and restless; and his whole bearing bespoke a feeling of great confidence in himself, and a consciousness of immeasurable superiority over all other people." The use of the Biblical name "Amminadab" probably was due to Grady's sense of humor.

Confessing "an infinite tenderness for humor," he observed:
"I love anything that is soulful, bright, and cheerful, that
tries to dissipate the sombre clouds — to bring the sunshine
out — to make things happy and hearty."

"Happiness," he said, "is not a veneering that may be plastered over a man as a dauber or a wash. It is a glow that must
come from within — a fire that, lit upon the altars of the heart,
must burn brightly and serenely, and stream through the soul
and the brain until the whole man is luminous and full of
lambent joy." After pointing out "the amount of misery that
is self-inflicted," he declared: "I don't let people tell me
things. I know that life is good." [16]

This "philosophy of happiness" formed the theme of an
address delivered by Grady before the two literary societies at
Emory College (now Emory University) on July 17, 1878.
The president of Emory at this time was Dr. Atticus G. Haygood, whose views on the Negro question, on the relations between North and South, and on "standing by the good and
making it better" were very similar to Grady's.[17] In introducing his visitor, Dr. Haygood "publicly called his attention to the fact that it would be no legitimate cause of discour-
agement if, as soon as he commenced, certain ill-bred fellows
. . . should get up and stalk out with great noise and confusion. They had treated him so repeatedly and every other
speaker, so far as he knew, who had ever spoken there." But
this consoling introduction proved unnecessary in Grady's
case. "For once the animals in the gallery found good manners
comporting with inclination, and they never moved from
their seats."

Grady's appearance, according to an eyewitness account by
a member of the Emory class of 1878, was "boyish in face and
feature, but not disappointing in the least." He wore a business cutaway, and "defied the austerity of his surroundings
by a single rose dangling in his buttonhole. Upon being presented to the audience he advanced promptly, but with the
utmost composure, and with an impatient gesture simultaneously flung his handkerchief upon the speakers' table and

[16] MS., Grady Collection.
[17] Elam F. Dempsey: *Atticus Green Haygood* (Nashville, 1940) , p. 6.

launched the current of his utterance, which . . . never ceased for one moment during the two hours he held the audience." The writer of this account, W. T. Turnbull, was prepared by the end of the address to pronounce Grady "the most eloquent man I had ever seen." [18]

Although Grady's fame as a lecturer was spread widely by admirers such as this, he remained steadfast in his determination to retire from the lecture platform. Even when urged the following summer to address the alumni and the literary societies at the University of Georgia, he declined.[19] He was intent as never before upon his newspaper work.

3

By July 1878 Grady was doing so well as a free-lance writer that, in addition to giving up the profitable side-line of lecturing, he decided to relinquish his regular salary on the *Constitution* in favor of space rates. This allowed him greater freedom in covering assignments for a "string" which now included the Chicago *Inter Ocean* and the *Detroit Free Press,* as well as the *New York Herald,* the *Philadelphia Times,* and the *Cincinnati Enquirer.* Soon he added to this list the Louisville *Courier-Journal,* whose editor, Henry Watterson, he introduced to an Atlanta audience for a lecture during the winter of 1878–9. For "specials" to be published by it and three affiliated papers, the *Courier-Journal* paid him fifty dollars a month.[20]

In an article written for the *Constitution* in the summer of 1878, Grady expressed his views about writing and writers. He thought that "Jake" Harris, as he now affectionately called his "crimson-crest" friend, was "the most promising young writer" in Georgia. "Through his jagged and crude work of daily journalism," wrote Grady, "there shines the divine light of genius." The "foremost literary man" Georgia had produced so far, in his opinion, was William Tappan Thompson, editor of the *Savannah Morning News* and author of the hi-

---

[18] MS., Joel Chandler Harris Collection.
[19] *Constitution,* June 4, 1879.
[20] MS. Diaries, 1878–9, Grady Collection.

larious *Major Jones's Courtship*. Mrs. Mary E. Bryan, editor of the *Sunny South*, a literary weekly started in Atlanta in 1875, was "the most brilliant, fecund and versatile authoress" he had known; Paul Hamilton Hayne was the South's "sweetest singer," an "American Keats"; and Sidney Lanier was "the most artistic and cultivated poet this side of Swinburne and Tennyson."

In another article on this same topic, Grady deplored the fact that American fiction up to this time had created in the popular mind two false types of Southerners — "the long-haired, livid-faced slave-driver with uplifted whip and attendant bloodhounds, and the profligate planter whose passion rides in his blood and who spends money as easily as he spills blood." Observing that England had been brought closer to the heart of America by the writings of Dickens and Goldsmith than by all the history of her wars and conquests, he asked: "Is there no one among us who can send along to posterity with *Uncle Tom's Cabin* its fitting answer?" In this question he anticipated the benefits to accrue to the South from the work of writers like Harris, Thomas Nelson Page, and Mary Noailles Murfree, who were to give "the answer of Southern genius of the eighties to the Yankee genius of the fifties." [21]

Although he sensed accurately what a new creative literature could do for the South, Grady himself clearly preferred and always would prefer to write about actual events, such as the lively campaign between Democrats and Independents in two congressional districts of northwest Georgia during the summer of 1878. This was the first major assignment to which he turned his attention after his "retirement" from the lecture platform.

Since 1872 the Democrats had enjoyed undisputed sway over Georgia's political affairs except in the mountainous Seventh Congressional District. Here a population made up chiefly of white farmers, unmenaced by any danger from a large Negro vote and hard hit by falling prices even before the Panic of 1873, had revolted in 1874 by electing an Independent, Dr.

[21] *Constitution*, February 13, 1881; Paul H. Buck: *The Road to Reunion* (Boston, 1937), p. 211.

William H. Felton, to Congress.[22] Felton had been re-elected in 1876, when the spotlight was taken off his district by the presidential and gubernatorial campaigns, but now the Democrats were making a determined effort to oust him by electing the regular nominee, George Lester. To aid the party's cause, the leaders enlisted the services of Senator John B. Gordon, whose military glamour and platform eloquence brought out crowds such as Grady had not seen since Bush Arbor days.

The campaign was all the more interesting because Dr. Felton, a farmer-physician-preacher, was assisted by his politician-wife, Rebecca Latimer Felton. It was the first time a woman had figured prominently in Georgia politics. The Feltons obviously resented Gordon's participation in the campaign, recognizing in him a far more formidable opponent than Lester. When Mrs. Felton began to center her fire upon the character of Gordon, "simply because he chose to make a campaign against Dr. Felton's ambition for office," Grady asked: "What can Gordon say to Felton who is protected by a pulpit on one side and by a woman on the other?" Evidently even the mighty Gordon found this question too perplexing, for not only was Felton re-elected but another Independent, Emory Speer, was named Congressman from the neighboring Ninth District.

The campaign over, Grady launched a little weekly review called the *Sunday Gazette,* the first issue of which appeared on October 5, 1878. With the aid of Joel Chandler Harris, he continued this paper as a profitable side-line until the end of the following year, when he sold it because of the pressure of other duties. Although no complete issues have been preserved, there are sufficient clippings and comments of contemporaries to indicate that the *Gazette* was a sparkling sheet, devoted to feature articles, dramatic and literary criticism, and editorials. To it Grady contributed a regular column entitled "Gazette Gossip," as well as many human-interest stories which otherwise might have gone into the *Constitution.*[23]

22 C. Vann Woodward: *Tom Watson: Agrarian Rebel* (New York, 1938), pp. 68–9.

23 *Constitution,* October 12, 1878; MS. Diaries, 1878, 1879; Martin, op. cit., II, 273.

It was Harris who wrote for the first issue of the *Gazette* a paragraph which expressed the belief of the two friends that "an editor must have a purpose." Harris had voiced the same sentiments in his editorials in the *Constitution*. For example, following the death of Samuel Bowles, in January 1878, he had referred to the success of Bowles's *Springfield Republican* as being the result of "a singleness of purpose that was extraordinary." He had expressed his preference for the fame of Bowles to that of Greeley, declaring that Greeley was "a political writer who had political ambition," while Bowles was "nothing if not a journalist, utterly wrapped up in his profession, and having a supreme contempt for political preferment." In the *Gazette* paragraph Harris again referred to Bowles in the North and John Forsyth of the *Mobile Register* in the South as editors who made a "permanent impression" because their role in politics was subservient to their guiding purpose.

"I shudder when I think of the opportunities the editors of Georgia are allowing to slip by," Harris wrote. "It grieves me to see them harping steadily upon the same old prejudices and moving in the worn ruts of a period that was soul-destroying in its narrowness. . . . In the South today we sadly need the resurrecting hand of editors with a purpose; who will supply that need?"

"The answer to this question," comments the biographer of Harris, "was soon to be furnished by the editorial work . . . of Henry W. Grady and Joel Chandler Harris himself." [24]

Before the answer could be furnished by Grady, however, it was necessary for him to crystallize in his own mind the purpose that had been forming ever since his college days. He needed likewise to find a more satisfactory means of realizing his ambition to influence public opinion in accordance with that purpose. While in college he had decided against public office; he now had eliminated the professional lecture platform; only journalism remained. But free-lance writing did not afford the same satisfaction as editing a daily newspaper. That he became depressed at times by the ir-

[24] Clipping, Joel Chandler Harris Collection; Julia C. Harris: *Life and Letters*, p. 140.

regularity of his life was indicated by this entry in his diary for December 1, 1878:

Four times I have started a diary. Each time with the avowed purpose of keeping it up if it killed me. This time I propose that if I do not keep it I will kill myself. This may be taken as a joke but I mean it. I refer the doubting reader to this page, if I ever snuff myself out suddenly. Really I am determined to try this once to introduce some system into a life that is brilliant but rudderless. If I fail in this test the life itself will fail and death itself is the shortest and most agreeable way to meet a failure. There shall be four tests of my diary — 1st the amount of work done; 2nd the money received; work sent off; money spent carelessly and personally.[25]

This resolution was kept only until ten days later, when pages once more began to be left blank. Grady was no more suited to the systematic keeping of a diary than he was to any other merely routine task. He needed to center all his energies upon one impelling purpose; once he had done that, such matters as his diary and even money itself would fade into insignificance.

It was through his work as a reporter, especially as an interviewer of business and political leaders on both sides of the Mason and Dixon line, that Grady came to see his goal more clearly.

4

To interpret the views and activities of a leading Southerner to the people of the North was a new experience for Grady until he was assigned by the younger James Gordon Bennett to visit Jefferson Davis. Although the first article based on this interview was not published until the summer of 1879, Grady actually began work on the story two years earlier. In a letter from Bennett dated May 10, 1877,[26] he was informed that Davis had "nearly completed his memoirs," and he was assigned to interview the former President of the Confederacy with relation to the forthcoming work. Grady went immedi-

[25] MS. Diary, Grady Collection.
[26] Grady Collection.

ately to Memphis, Tennessee, Davis's nominal residence, only to find that the Confederate leader was not in that city and that his wife and daughter were in Europe. Finally he discovered that Davis's mail was being forwarded to Mississippi City, a little resort town on the Gulf coast. There he learned that Davis was a guest at Beauvoir, the home of Mrs. Sarah A. Dorsey.

As Grady's carriage drew up to the front gate of Beauvoir, he caught his first glimpse of the man he was seeking, seated on the broad veranda beside a large table covered with papers. Davis came down to the gate to meet him and, upon receiving his credentials, greeted him cordially. "A kind but grave voice, a tall, slender man, with brown hair and whiskers tipping out gray, clear eyes, calm brow, erect carriage, an indescribable air of dignity and sadness" — these were Grady's impressions of "the first and last President of the Confederate States of America." As they reached the veranda they were met by Mrs. Dorsey, who, in addition to being a connection of the Davis family by marriage, was an author of local renown. Grady spent the afternoon in the household circle, learning as much as possible about Davis and his forthcoming book.

Since the work was so far from publication, Grady deferred the use of the material obtained in the interview until a later date. The first article, entitled "Jeff Davis's Home," was published in July 1879, following the death of Mrs. Dorsey and the announcement that Davis had inherited Beauvoir. Later, as the date for the appearance of Davis's *Rise and Fall of the Confederacy* drew near, Grady wrote several more stories, the last being a five-and-one-half-column review of the book itself, prepared from "advance sheets."

The picture of Davis drawn in these articles was sympathetic, as one might expect from a writer of Grady's background, but it did not gloss over the blemishes. The writer praised Davis for maintaining a policy of dignified silence and seclusion after the war, and for not lowering himself, as Grant had done, to accept large sums of money raised by private subscription. At the same time he frankly mentioned the "general fear throughout the South" that Davis would "let his intolerant spirit get the better of him" and allow his book to "become a vehicle of personal opinions and prejudices." He gave full credit to the purity of Davis's motives and to "the caution and carefulness" with which the leader had prepared his version of the struggle. Grady recognized that the work, prejudiced though it might be, would be a document of great historical value.[27]

Never did Grady lavish upon Davis the unstinted praise that he bestowed upon General Robert E. Lee and Lee's Georgia confidant, Gordon. Grady had written the story of Gordon's life for the *Atlanta Herald* when the General first was sent to the Senate. He told it again in the *Constitution* when Gordon was re-elected without opposition in 1878. But in a six-column article written for the *Philadelphia Times* in the summer of 1879 he sang the praises of his friend to a much larger audience. "No man has accepted the situation with more heroism and sincerity than General Gordon," Grady wrote. "When he sheathed his sword at Appomattox, he quit fighting and devoted himself to the healing of the wounds of war and the building of his section. The men who did the least of the fighting during the war have done the most of the quarreling since; just as many of the bloody secessionists before the war were least valorous and devoted after the states had been plunged into war through their advice and appeals." [28]

In the same series of articles Grady interviewed another Georgia general who in popular esteem stood at the opposite end of the scale from Gordon. This was General James Longstreet, once regarded as one of the South's most accomplished soldiers, but more recently under fire from his fellow Southerners for his alleged delay in carrying out the orders of General Lee at the fateful Battle of Gettysburg — a delay to which some people even attributed the Confederate defeat. Grady felt that at least part of the suspicion directed at Longstreet was due to the fact that he, like Brown, had begun too soon to advocate the acceptance of congressional Reconstruction. He therefore went to Gainesville, Georgia, where Longstreet

[27] Clippings, Grady Scrapbooks.
[28] Reprinted in *Constitution*, August 31, 1879.

held a Republican appointment as postmaster, and persuaded the General to break his silence. This three-column interview, as reprinted from the *Times* by the *Constitution* and other Southern papers, did much to restore Longstreet to the good graces of his own people.

Grady also did the "ghost-writing" of two long articles, under the General's own name, for the "Annals of the War" series. In these articles, according to an editorial in the *Times,* Longstreet "quite effectually" disproved the charge of tardiness in carrying out Lee's orders at Gettysburg. "I regret most deeply that this discussion was not opened before the death of General Lee," Longstreet said. "General Lee would have answered them himself, and have set history right." [29]

From Longstreet, the too quickly reconstructed, Grady turned his attention once more to Toombs, "the great unreconstructed." In two articles for the *Times* — the first a long feature interview — Grady asserted that Toombs's reckless talk was "not an index of his character." He traced the fiery Georgian's distinguished career as legislator, Representative, Senator, and member of the Confederate Cabinet, ending with his flight to Europe at the end of the war. Unbeaten in a popular election throughout his public life, Toombs was to Grady "the most remarkable man in many respects that the South ever produced." Toombs was now sixty-nine, the article pointed out, and the "signs of his breaking down" had awakened "a tender interest in him."

In this interview Grady quoted Toombs as having remarked, with a laugh, that Alexander H. Stephens, after opposing secession, had written the resolution of secession adopted by the Georgia convention of 1861. Stephens, then in Washington, wrote to the *Philadelphia Times* denying that Toombs had made such a statement. Toombs, after having had time to hear from Stephens, also issued a denial.

Grady replied promptly in the *Constitution* that Toombs not only had consented to the interview but had made every statement attributed to him. In a letter to Stephens he offered to produce his original notes of the interview. He also appended a letter from Evan P. Howell, who certified that he

[29] Clippings, Grady Scrapbooks; Knight: *Reminiscences*, II, 221.

had been present and had heard Toombs make the remark as quoted. Moreover, Grady said, Toombs himself had confessed, in the presence of Governor Colquitt, that it was "the most correct interview" ever published with him.

"Mr. Stephens, I am a humble person & you are a great one," Grady's note concluded. "To a generous man this is all the more reason why you cannot afford to do me an injustice — or having unwittingly done one, to stand by it." [30]

There is no record of Stephens's reply. His own biographer reveals, however, that after the Georgia convention voted to secede, "Little Aleck" did serve on the committee drafting the ordinance of secession, though he did not introduce the resolution by which the committee was created.[31] Apparently Stephens was merely quibbling over words, as he was wont to do, while his friend Toombs was trying to clear himself of blame, as many another public man has done, by shifting to a newspaperman the responsibility for a statement he actually had made but had come to regret.

The Toombs and Stephens denials, and possibly the earlier experience with Mrs. "Stonewall" Jackson, were fresh in Grady's mind when he wrote for the *Constitution* a front-page article "On Interviewing." The interview, a relatively new journalistic device, was under fire at this time from numerous sources. Grady, as "one of the chief sinners, if there be any sin in the practice," defended it as "the neatest and handiest thing in journalism." Declaring that Socrates, "a thoroughly respectable person," had introduced the art on the streets of Athens, he explained why interviewing had become so popular:

The system of interviewing gave more dignity to a report. It brought the person interviewed and the public face to face. It enabled the correspondent to preserve the flavor of the great man's individuality, and carry his subtle characteristics into print. By leading him from the single thread of a narrative into suggestive by-ways and turn-outs, all the minor lights and shades of information could be brought out.

. . . A skillful journalist, fully acquainted with the specific

[30] September 3, 1879, Stephens Papers.
[31] E. R. Richardson, op. cit., p. 197.

points upon which the public desires to hear from a noted person, and knowing by instinct what will be of interest, can, by leading him into the deviable lines of discussion, and picking out of him exactly what is wanted, get up a much more interesting paper, and convey to the public more information, than would come from the great man . . . alone and unaided.

The great objection to interviews is that many persons consider them an unreliable way of putting things. On the contrary, they are the most reliable way. . . . I have always found that public men prefer them to any other method of communicating with the public; and it is only the fewest of them that are ever denied. I have interviewed nearly every prominent man in the South and many of the greatest men in the North and West. I have published interviews covering from one to three columns, and giving their words and peculiar expressions. And I have never had one single man to seriously deny the authenticity or correctness of the interview.[32]

Grady's statement that he had "interviewed many of the greatest men in the North and West," as well as in the South, indicates how he was using this journalistic device to carry out Lamar's injunction to *"know* one another, and you will *love* one another." For example, there was no Northerner who had been more hated in Atlanta than General William Tecumseh Sherman. Yet in 1879 the *Constitution* welcomed Sherman back to the city on behalf of "a people brave enough to bury their hatreds in the ruins his hands have made, and wise enough to turn their passion toward recuperation rather than revenge." On a visit to New York the following year Grady visited the General and gave his readers this revised estimate:

I doubt if there was a more conscientious soldier in the Northern army than General Sherman. There is no sentimentalism about him. To his notion war meant cruelty — it meant death — destruction — and the sooner this was realized the sooner there was a chance for peace. The heaviest, sharpest and most decisive blows, he contended, were the most merciful, and the real scourge, he held, was he who connived at the prolonging of the war with its inexorable desolation, by glossing its horrors over with a show

[32] *Constitution,* August 16, 1879.

of pity. This was his argument, severe and savage — but perhaps logical and just.[33]

Among the "weaker men" who had "overtopped" Sherman, Grady classified Grant. In November 1879 he reported to the *New York Herald* "a deep and strong undercurrent of non-partisan support" in the South in favor of re-electing Grant to the presidency in 1880 on a "peace and prosperity" platform. When certain newspapers suggested that he was trying to start a boom for the former President, however, Grady indignantly repudiated the idea and declared he "could never, under any circumstances, vote for Grant." Instead of "riding in the bandwagon, or driving one of the animal cages," he explained, "I am simply sitting on the fence, casually observing the procession as it passes."

The tolerant tone of the Grant article undoubtedly was due to Grady's growing desire to promote understanding between North and South. The paramount importance he now attached to this aim was indicated by these words from the same story:

The mass of the Southern people are heartily sick of sectionalism. They are tired of hearing of the solid South and the solid North. . . . The South is thrilling with a new growth and ambitious for material development. She needs peace, stability, capital, immigrants. Her people realize fully that as long as a sectional war is waged there must be a strife, and the suspicion of insecurity for investment; that capital will be withheld from her mines and forests; that immigrants will be directed westward from Castle Garden, and that her purposes and intention will be misrepresented by the evil and misunderstood by the indifferent. It was this very spirit, though then infinitely less developed, that led her people to give Horace Greeley a virtually unanimous vote eight years ago. She wanted peace and tranquility then; she is much more anxious about it now.[34]

Along with this growing zeal for "material development" and reconciliation there was coming into Grady's personal life a greater degree of order. This is shown by the fact that during 1879 he kept, for the first time, a month-by-month record of his receipts and expenditures. His income as a freelance writer for these twelve months totaled $3,841 — "a pretty good year's work," he wrote in his diary.

5

By 1880 Grady was convinced that economic betterment was the key to all the South's problems. He saw the North and West pressing forward with a speed which made the progress even of wide-awake Atlanta seem slow. He realized that, just as "waving of the bloody shirt" was frightening Northern investors and immigrants away from the South, the poverty of his native region was making it more susceptible to "the old prejudices." Hence, while he sought with one hand to allay political sectionalism, he worked with the other to promote the material progress that now was his chief aim.

In this material advancement he knew that railroads would play an important part. The capture and destruction of Atlanta during the war had emphasized the truth of what General Sherman reiterated on his visit in 1879: that this city, to the South, was like the palm of a hand with fingers extending to all the important ports on the Atlantic and Gulf coasts. Since the war the four railroads centering here had been burdened to the utmost. There was urgent need for unified systems with simplified tariffs and for new lines,[35] especially a proposed road westward to the coal and iron mines of eastern Alabama. The Louisville & Nashville Railroad already had been granted a charter for this project, which Atlantans hopefully called the "Georgia Western."

As early as 1878 Grady had written a series of articles on the Georgia Central Railroad, which extended from Atlanta to Savannah. The immediate occasion of these articles was the launching of a new steamer to enter the service of the Ocean Steamship Company, the road's subsidiary between Savannah and New York. In December 1879 Atlanta was visited by

[35] Allan Nevins: *The Emergence of Modern America 1865–78* (New York, 1927), pp. 50, 63–5.

E. W. Cole, president of the Nashville, Chattanooga & St. Louis Railroad, which connected with the Western & Atlantic from Chattanooga to Atlanta. Grady followed Cole's activities closely and soon broke the news that "King Cole" and President Brown of the W. & A. had made a contract whereby the lines and steamers of the Georgia Central would come under the joint control of the Cole-Brown companies. This arrangement would give Atlanta its first unified line from St. Louis to Savannah and thence by water to New York and Havana.

Convinced that the Cole-Brown deal was only the first in a series of "bombshells" which would affect Atlanta, Grady asked Howell for permission to make a trip to Nashville, Louisville, St. Louis, and other railroad centers. He obtained an advance on his expenses with the provision that the *Constitution* could take the amount out of his pay if the editor was not satisfied with the results. Evidently Grady's confidence was well founded, for, the day after leaving Atlanta, he wired from Nashville: "There is no doubt that the Louisville and Nashville Railroad has purchased a controlling interest in the Nashville and Chattanooga company. . . . I have this from Colonel Cole himself."

Moving on to Louisville, Grady obtained full details of the *coup d'état* by which L. & N. officials had quietly made contact with Cole's heaviest stockholders in New York, offering to buy their stock at a "handsome profit" and threatening to build a competing line from St. Louis to Atlanta unless they would sell. The "master mind" in the coup was H. Victor Newcomb, the L. & N.'s thirty-six-year-old first vice president, whom Grady described as "the Napoleon of the railroad world — the easy and assured master of the situation." He told how Newcomb's father, the founder of the L. & N., was facing ruin from the Panic of 1873 when young Victor went to London and sold a large block of bonds to save the road from the receiver's hands. Now managing "property worth $120,000,000," Newcomb, in Grady's opinion, had superseded James Gordon Bennett as "the most notable young man in America."

Grady impressed Newcomb so favorably that the railroad magnate offered the newspaperman a position as his private secretary at a salary of two hundred and fifty dollars a month.

Grady was unwilling to accept if it meant giving up newspaper work. After consulting with Howell, however, he agreed to accompany Newcomb for a time on condition that he should continue to write the railroad news for the *Constitution* and other papers on his string.[36]

As a result of this arrangement, Grady for the next few months obtained one exclusive story after another on the growth of "Newcomb's Octopus." First came the news of a five-year combination between the L. & N., the Georgia Railroad (from Atlanta to Augusta), and the Georgia Central, giving Newcomb's line access to "every important port from Charleston to New Orleans." Later there was a meeting of the L. & N. directors in Louisville, at which Newcomb was elected president. Finally, in April, the scene shifted to Savannah, where negotiations between Newcomb, Brown, and the Georgia Central resulted in the announcement that the freight rates on coal to Atlanta manufacturers would be reduced by two dollars a ton. "Victor Newcomb," Grady declared, "is the Moses that leads Atlanta out of bondage."

Grady traveled with Newcomb through thirteen states and finally ended his trip in Wall Street. Here he was fascinated by the Stock Exchange, where "brokers and operators rush to and fro in a perfect frenzy, with railroads as the cards and millions for stakes — putting fortune, future, home and often honor itself on the turn of a single chance." It was "a fearful scene," he wrote, that "kindles the blood of the looker-on as a battle would." With characteristic enthusiasm he repeated many stories of the fabulous fortunes that were being made both in "the Street" and in the gold mines of the West. Repeatedly, however, he cautioned inexperienced speculators against the dangers of falling into the clutches of bucket shops, sharpers, and thieves. He pointed out also the peril in the consolidation of enormous interests in individual hands, such as those of Jay Gould, who was said to own "one-fourth of the railroad property in the country."

While in New York City, Grady spent much time with Newcomb in the brokerage office of Cyrus W. Field. Having made

[36] *Constitution*, January 18–20, 1880; interview with Evan P. Howell in *Atlanta Daily News*, September 12, 1901; clippings, Grady Scrapbooks.

his fortune as a manufacturer of paper and his fame as the promoter of the first transatlantic cable, Field was now one of Wall Street's most successful operators. He soon came to share Newcomb's high regard for Grady's ability and signified his willingness to help the young Atlantan in acquiring an interest in a newspaper. A telegram to Howell brought the information that a one-quarter interest in the *Constitution,* then capitalized at $100,000, could be bought for $20,000. Field agreed to lend Grady this amount, while Newcomb offered to guide him in a stock speculation which would assist him in repaying the loan. The deal was closed, and on May 10 Grady returned to Atlanta with the funds to make him a one-fourth owner of the *Constitution.*[37]

An interested observer at the transaction in Field's office was the financier's brother, Dr. Henry M. Field, minister-editor of the *New York Evangelist* and later to be immortalized as the hero of *All This and Heaven Too.* Writing down his first impressions, Dr. Field said Grady's face was "almost boyish, round and ruddy with health, his eyes sparkling with intelligence, as well as with the wit and humor which he perhaps inherited from some ancestor of Irish blood. . . . We have seldom known a man who was so intensely alive — alive to the very tips of his fingers." [38]

With a newspaper that was partly his own, and with the fixed purpose of promoting the prosperity of the people he served — the only sure basis, after all, of his paper's prosperity — Grady was indeed "alive to the very tips of his fingers" from this time forward. The confidence with which he now assumed larger responsibilities on the *Constitution* was based upon a much more profound knowledge of people and of his own abilities than he had had at the time of his "Just Human" lectures.

[37] Cyrus W. Field to H. W. G., May 8, 1880, and promissory note of same date, Grady Collection.
[38] Clipping, Grady Scrapbooks.

CHAPTER NINE

"*Genius of the 'Constitution'* "

WHEN Grady returned from New York in May 1880, he brought not only the $20,000 with which to buy a quarter interest in the *Constitution,* but also the news that was to create the biggest political sensation of many a day in Georgia. General John B. Gordon, who only a year previously had begun his second term in the United States Senate, was resigning to accept a $14,000-a-year position with the L. & N. Railroad. Governor Colquitt had agreed to appoint former Governor Brown to fill the Senate vacancy, and Brown and Gordon were to support Colquitt for re-election. Grady confided these "inside facts" to some Athens friends who boarded his train as it neared Atlanta on May 10,[1] and ten days later the developments began to unfold, exactly as he had forecast.

Grady remained in Atlanta long enough only to complete the purchase of his stock and to reach an agreement with Howell whereby he became managing editor of the paper. He then hurried to Washington to send out the story of the Gordon resignation, which appeared in the *Constitution* on May 20. On the next day a second story revealed that Brown already had been appointed as Gordon's successor even before the Senator's resignation was announced. The *Constitution* praised Gordon's record and declared that Brown's selection was a "proper appointment" and "as good as could have been made."

To thousands of Georgians who still looked with disfavor upon Brown, however, the appointment was anything but "good" and "proper." Although no one ever had successfully impugned the former Governor's integrity, his one-time as-

[1] *Columbus Enquirer-Sun,* June 11, 1880; Rebecca L. Felton: *My Memoirs of Georgia Politics* (Atlanta, 1911) , p. 530.

sociation with the Radicals and his growing wealth had led to suspicions. A novelist of the period, portraying a character identified as Brown, said it was widely believed that, "if the mask could be torn off, this saint of the church . . . would be found to be the wiliest hypocrite, the most hardened, skillful, practiced, unconscionable knave on the face of the earth." [2] Immediately after his appointment was announced, therefore, an indignation meeting in Columbus adopted resolutions declaring that Brown was "not a Democrat" and that he was being "foisted upon the people." A newspaper in the same city hinted that the appointee had agreed to surrender the state-owned W. & A. Railroad to Victor Newcomb in exchange for the Senate seat. The L. & N. was to take over the W. & A. lease, so this story said, and was to make Gordon president of the state road. Not only that, but it was charged that "Victor Newcomb of the L. & N." had obtained "a heavy interest in the *Constitution* under the cover of the name of Henry W. Grady." [3]

Replying to the charges against Gordon, Grady said that the Senator had resigned his seat "simply because he was too poor to hold it." The managing editor explained that he had been with Gordon "a great deal" for the "last month or so," and that the General had told him six months earlier of his intention to resign in order to provide better for his family. Gordon himself asserted that the offer of a position with the L. & N. was "the consequence and not the cause" of his resignation, since he already had decided to leave the Senate to accept a railroad position in Oregon before Newcomb made him an offer. Brown and Colquitt likewise denied that there was any sinister "trade" or "bargain" among the three men, and the fact that Brown retained the presidency of the W. & A. effectually spiked the rumor that he had agreed to turn the road over to Newcomb. The report that the L. & N. was the real purchaser of Grady's one-fourth interest in the *Constitution* was attributed by the paper editorially to "adventurous liars." [4]

2 William Dugas Trammell: *Ça Ira* (New York, 1874) , pp. 30–5, 303.

3 *Columbus Enquirer-Sun,* June 15–18, 1880; *Macon Daily Telegraph and Messenger,* May 22, 1880; Felton, op. cit., pp. 79, 98, 117, 266.

4 *Constitution,* May 23–9, 1880.

The facts in the case, after weighing all the statements on both sides, appear simply to be these: Newcomb desired to make favorable connections in Georgia for his railroad. Gordon, being ambitious for wealth as well as for political preferment, was susceptible to a business offer. Brown, smarting under fifteen years of ostracism from public office, was eager to re-establish himself in Georgia politics. Colquitt, facing a difficult campaign for re-election, needed help particularly in the mountain districts where the Independent revolt had taken place and where Brown and Gordon were strongest. Grady, desiring to have a part in the ownership and control of the *Constitution,* borrowed the necessary funds from a friend of Newcomb. But after accepting this assistance he did not change his policies in any respect. Both he and the *Constitution* continued to follow the same course they previously had advocated as being in the public interest. Undoubtedly there were understandings of the kind that friends reach every day in business and politics, but on the basis of the available evidence the transaction must be described as "a deal, not a steal."

If Grady and the *Constitution* had "sold out" to the railroads, as their critics insinuated, they hardly would have been such outspoken supporters of the state Railroad Commission, which Evan P. Howell had fostered ever since the agency's establishment in 1879. The paper repeatedly insisted that "every step in the building equipment of a railroad, no matter under what condition, is in the nature of an obligation to the people." Unless the roads were regulated by state and federal agencies, it said, they would "cripple interests they ought to foster." And this was at a time when dailies like the *Savannah Morning News* were contending that government regulation would kill the roads, since "no capitalist would put his money into any such enterprise without liberty to manage it according to the dictates of his own experience." [5]

As for Cyrus W. Field's connection with the "deal," it is easy to believe that a man who had spent millions in promoting a supposedly fantastic scheme like the first transatlantic cable would have been willing to lend $20,000 to a promising

[5] *Savannah Morning News,* May 13, 1880.

young journalist like Grady. In addition, however, the Democratic National Convention was approaching, and Field's brother, Associate Justice Stephen J. Field of the United States Supreme Court, was being boomed as a possible successor to Samuel J. Tilden for the presidential nomination. Some weeks before Grady went to New York, the *Constitution* had expressed the hope that Tilden would retire in favor of a candidate who could harmonize conflicting factions in the party. Justice Field, a native of New England and a resident of California, was being heralded as such a man. His record on the Supreme Court bench and as a member of the Hayes-Tilden Electoral Commission of 1877 made him acceptable to the South. Brother Cyrus may have had in mind, therefore, that, with the support of Georgia and several other Southern states added to that of the Pacific coast, Stephen J. Field might have a chance of winning first place on the Democratic ticket.

There is no suggestion of a political obligation in the two letters extant from Field to Grady about the $20,000 loan. The young managing editor signed a twelve-month note, bearing interest at six per cent, and gave *Constitution* stock with a par value of $20,000 as security. But soon after Grady returned to Georgia, the *Constitution* began to give increasing prominence to suggestions that Stephen J. Field was "a man of pluck who can hold his own when the time comes." By early June, when Georgia Democrats met in Atlanta to select their delegates to the national convention, sentiment was strongly in favor of casting the state's votes for the Associate Justice. Howell, a Field man, was elected as a delegate, while Grady hurried back to New York to send out interviews with the state's favorite before going to Cincinnati to cover the convention. That Field did not "hold his own" when the time came was due to his failure to carry his own state of California, not Georgia.[6]

Once the convention had made its choice, the *Constitution* loyally supported the ticket of Hancock and English. When Howell and Grady returned home, however, they found that

6 *Constitution*, June 10–25, 1880; Frank R. Kent: *The Democratic Party* (New York, 1928), p. 367.

the dissension stirred up in their own state by the Brown-Gordon-Colquitt "deal" was not to be so quickly resolved. Indeed, the lines were being drawn for "the bitterest campaign ever known in Georgia."

Even before the Brown appointment, Governor Colquitt had antagonized many elements in that heterogeneous combination of factions known as the Georgia Democratic Party. For example, at the outset of his administration he had been besieged by some three thousand applicants for only thirty appointive offices. In addition to the disgruntled office-seekers, there were other critics, like Dr. Felton and his wife, who believed that the Brown-Gordon-Colquitt "ring" was in an unholy alliance with "big business." These insurgents attacked Colquitt for endorsing $260,000 worth of North-Eastern Railroad bonds, though he had acted in accordance with the law; they blamed him also for the evils of the convict lease system, though that system had been saddled upon the state by a Reconstruction legislature as an economy measure. At Colquitt's request, the General Assembly had investigated practically every branch of the executive department during his administration, and the fact that his opponents had been unable to pin anything corrupt upon him personally made them all the more eager to pounce upon him now for sending Brown to the Senate.

Despite the opposition, Colquitt succeeded in winning a majority of the county delegations. When the Democratic state convention met in August, however, he lacked the two-thirds majority necessary for the nomination. After sitting for six days and taking thirty-three ballots, during which Colquitt came within nine votes of the needed two-thirds, the convention still was unable to agree upon a nomination. The majority therefore adjourned by adopting a resolution simply "recommending" the Governor for re-election. A final effort to obtain the acquiescence of the minority had failed, partly as the result of a defiant speech by a slender, red-headed young delegate from McDuffie County — Thomas E. Watson.

After the minority had held a rump session and selected Thomas M. Norwood, former United States Senator, as its candidate, the majority leaders organized a Colquitt Central Committee, with Samuel M. Inman as chairman and Grady as campaign manager. The *Constitution's* managing editor soon was "in undisputed command." The Colquitt group systematically organized working subcommittees in every county and militia district of the state. Grady watched each locality, wrote hundreds of letters and dispatches, and sent help wherever it was needed to strengthen doubtful areas. When Colquitt replied to Norwood's attacks in a letter which was probably the strongest document of the campaign, the manager endeavored to mail a copy to every voter in the state. The opposition complained that Grady actually served as governor in the absence of Colquitt.[7]

In the *Constitution,* Grady's touch was to be found in the day-by-day news stories appearing on page one, usually in the first and second columns. Following his "lead-all" summary of the latest developments appeared brief signed reports from the paper's special correspondents throughout the state. Then came short paragraphs of news and comment headed "Campaign Straws," including one-sentence quotations of "What the People Say." Grady obviously was depending not upon editorial arguments, but upon thorough organization and adequate news coverage of the campaign itself.

The Norwood candidacy received its "death blow," in Grady's opinion, when it failed to obtain the endorsement of the Negro-dominated Republican state convention. The Norwood leaders attributed this set-back to Brown, who, they said, "having once been a Republican himself," knew how to "buy up the Negro votes." But Colquitt himself had no small influence with the Negroes, having preached to them frequently in his capacity as a Methodist minister, even while Governor. Brown, likewise, though not a minister, was a power among the Baptists, who were stronger numerically in Georgia than the Methodists. Referring to these facts and to the military record of Gordon, an opposition newspaper predicted: "Brown with his money, Gordon with his buttons,

7 Avery, op. cit., pp. 555–90; Felton, op. cit., pp. 288–310; Knight: *Reminiscences,* I, 405–16.

and Colquitt with his religion will make a combination that cannot be beaten." [8]

Toward the end of the campaign, Grady sent out return postal cards to the ordinary and the sheriff of each county, asking these officials to estimate their county's probable majority for Colquitt or Norwood. On the basis of this survey the *Constitution,* ten days before the election, forecast a Colquitt majority of 35,000. This turned out to be conservative, for the Governor actually was re-elected on October 6 by a margin of more than 54,000. The *Constitution's* headlines the next morning bore every earmark of having been written by Grady himself:

GRADY'S FACTS

FIRED FROM "HOWELL'S QUAKER GUN"

He Laughs Best Who Laughs Last

The People — the Whole People — Rise in Their Might

And Call Upon Uncle Alfred

To Occupy the Mansion Two Years Longer

The Prognathous Jaw in Motion, and the Eleven Able up to Their Necks in Colquitt Majorities!

The Constitution's Reply to Mr. Norwood's Little Jokes!

Majority Rolls in Upon Majority!

Rampart Captured After Rampart

And From the Throats of Thousands of Freemen

Come Plaudits for the Hero of Olustee

The People at the Ballot-Box Complete the Work That the Convention Left Unfinished

The avalanche of votes set in motion by the Colquitt victory also swept from office Dr. Felton, the Independent Congressman from the Seventh District. The only Georgia

[8] *Columbus Daily Times,* May 25, 1880.

Independent left in an important post was Grady's friend Congressman Emory Speer, who came so close to being a Democratic regular that some of the Felton group regarded him as one of "Brown's gang." [9]

Scarcely had the shouting died when the legislature added the final touch by re-electing Brown to the Senate. Grady interpreted this action as something far more significant than a further vindication of Governor Colquitt's administration. He saw the people of Georgia revolting against the dominion of the "obstructive prejudices" that had found expression for so long in General Toombs's "wild and reckless utterances." Brown was the symbol of the opposition to those prejudices, since he had been the first leader of prominence to set himself "against a narrow policy based upon . . . political abstractions" and for "a progressive and liberal treatment of the practical questions of government." His return to favor was, consequently, "the first substantial victory achieved by the New South over the Old South — the first breaking of the purely sectional passions and resentments that have repressed the best sentiments of the South for so long; the first turning from the past, with its terrible memories, to a hopeful and glorious future." [10]

2

As indicated by the article on Brown, Grady already was modulating from politics back into his major key of economic development. The South as a whole was shocked by the defeat of Hancock and English in November. In this "first full, and fair, and free presidential election" since the war, Southerners had looked forward to a Democratic victory in revenge for the theft of the presidency in 1876. But Grady, writing from New York shortly before the election, predicted that the victory of Garfield and Arthur was "inevitable," because of "the abundant prosperity that blesses all the land." When the "inevitable" happened and one prominent Southern leader declared he was "so depressed" that he did not "have the heart

9 W. H. Hidell to Mrs. Rebecca L. Felton, December 4, 1883, Felton Papers.
10 Clipping, Grady Scrapbooks.

to do anything," the *Constitution's* managing editor sounded a characteristic note of optimism:

The defeat of Hancock will be a blessing in disguise if it only tends to turn our people from politics to work. We have the best country in the world. The sun shines on us kindly, the soil yields us abundant crops, the earth gives us gold, iron and coal at every fissure. How grander a mission it is to develop this section into its full power and production than to win a share of public patronage. What we need is fewer stump-speakers and more stump-pullers — less talk and more work — fewer gin-mills and more gins — fewer men at the front and more men at the hoe. One plow is worth twenty politicians. In the old days of slavery it was a passion with us to lead in politics — in these days of close competition, he should be the best man who can lead in the corn row.[11]

"How immeasurably better it is for us to raise a ploughman than a politician!" This theme, reiterated many times by Grady, soon was swelled by other Southern newspapers into a loud chorus. Perhaps these other papers and their readers were simply reacting to the Democratic defeat in the same way that the managing editor of the *Constitution* had responded. Indeed, the "changed view" of some editors (not Grady) at first exhibited a tinge of "spitefulness": economic development would be another way of gaining revenge against the North, now that political revenge had failed once more. But only two days after Grady struck the keynote, the *News and Observer* of Raleigh, North Carolina, "which had been violently sectional and which for a few days after the election consoled its readers with hope of victory four years hence . . . changed front and gave expression to a new spirit that, suddenly and with compelling force, was sweeping the people." The Raleigh paper's closing words sounded too much like Grady's to be a mere coincidence: "We must have less politics and more work, fewer stump speakers and more stump pullers, less tinsel and show and boast, and more hard, earnest work." [12]

[11] *Constitution,* November 7, 1880.
[12] Raleigh *News and Observer,* November 9, 1880, cited in Broadus Mitchell: *The Rise of Cotton Mills in the South* (Baltimore, 1921) , p. 89.

The South was ripe for economic regeneration; the movement probably would have come in the late sixties but for the tragic interruption of Radical Reconstruction. Now that the hurts of that era were being forgotten and the country had recovered from the depression of 1873 (specie payments had been resumed in 1879), even a political defeat, when interpreted as Grady interpreted it, could become a "decisive accelerant" to the process of "real reconstruction." A leading historian of Southern industrialization testifies that nearly every stage of his study shows "the large extent to which such economic publicists [as Grady, and their newspapers] were responsible for economic growth." [13]

In an article written for *Harper's Magazine,* Grady summarized the central thought of his newspaper writings in these months and gave the background of the new movement. He showed how the poverty of the South and the high price of cotton following the war had stimulated a tremendous increase in the planting of this staple. At the same time the abolition of slavery had caused the breaking up of the large plantations into small farms. Other small farms had been started by the "poor whites" on lands which in earlier times had been considered unfit for cotton-growing. Nearly all these small farmers were men who "held too little land to command credit or justify investigation. And yet they were obliged to have money with which to start their work. Commission merchants therefore borrowed the money from banks, and loaned it to village brokers or storekeepers, who in turn loaned it to farmers in their neighborhood, usually in the form of advancing supplies. It thus came to the farmer after it had been through three principals, each of whom demanded a heavy percentage for the risk he assumed." In every case the farmer gave a lien upon his crops, and usually a mortgage also upon his farm and chattels. "Having once given such a paper to his merchant, his credit was of course gone, and he had to depend upon the man who held the mortgage for his supplies. To that man he must carry his crop when it was gathered, pay him commission for handling it, and accept the settlement that he offered." The result was that, according to the state

[13] Broadus Mitchell, op. cit., pp. 77–112.

Commissioner of Agriculture, Georgia farmers were paying for supplies at prices averaging 54 per cent interest on everything they bought. If ever they had had any chance of surviving such an oppressive system, it had been swept away by the fact that "cotton worth sixty-five cents in 1866 brought only forty cents in 1867. . . . In 1868, it declined to eleven and one-quarter cents, but ran up in a few weeks to thirty-six cents. After this, it went down steadily, involving thousands in ruin." The price had continued to go down steadily all through the seventies, except for a slight upswing in 1879. Consequently thousands of farms were passing into the hands of the lien-holders. The South was faced with the prospect of having a perpetual "host of croppers without money or credit . . . paying toll to usurers at home, and mortgaging their crops to speculators abroad even before it is planted."

One remedy for this situation was "the establishment of a proper system of credit," but this would do little good, Grady said, unless it was accompanied by a reform in the system of farming itself — not merely reform in the methods of cultivating cotton, but, first of all, diversification of crops. "The South must prepare to raise her own provisions, compost her own fertilizers, cure her own hay, and breed her own stock." The one-crop system, he declared, "never made any people prosperous." Farmers who "had the nerve to give up part of their land and labor to the raising of their own supplies and stock" had "but little need of credit."

Most important of all, Grady asserted, if the South was to reap the full benefits from its natural advantages as the "cotton kingdom," the region must produce the finished cotton goods as well as the raw material. "The cotton crop of 7,000-000 bales, when ready for the market, is worth in round numbers $300,000,000," he wrote. "The same crop when manufactured is worth over $900,000,000." Would the South "be content to see the whole of this added value realized by outsiders?" If not, "how much of the work necessary to create this value" would she be willing to do within her own borders? She had "abundant water-power . . . cheap labor, cheap lands, an unequaled climate, cheap fuel, and the conditions of cheap living." The doubling of the amount of cotton manufactured in the South between 1870 and 1880 "hardly indicated," in Grady's opinion, the progress that could be made during the next decade.[14]

The New South movement was far more than a movement for industrialization, as Grady's article revealed. But since manufacturing offered the most spectacular means of increasing the South's wealth, it naturally received the most attention from the public. Moreover, since factories promised to provide work for thousands of "poor whites" like Grady's Sallie and "Mortimer Pitts," the movement took on something of a humanitarian aspect. Otherwise it would be difficult to explain why the "Bring the Mills to the Cotton" slogan, with its dream of education and other benefits for the masses, "acted upon the South of the times as the sermons of Peter the Hermit acted upon Europe of the eleventh century." Southern pride, combined with this humanitarianism and the ever present economic impulse, was keen enough, indeed, to cause the great majority of the mills to be built as civic enterprises. Some of them actually were inspired by the exhortations of evangelists in revival meetings.[15]

The South itself had provided the original impetus for industrialization, and most of the capital down to 1880 had come from the Southern people. But there was a limit to what a region impoverished by war could do, even under the influence of mass emotion.[16] If the South was to develop its industries at the rate envisioned by Grady and others, the region needed Northern capital, and needed it urgently.

It was to help the South obtain this capital, as well as to look after the stock speculation which he hoped would bring him his own financial independence, that Grady decided to spend the winter of 1880–1 in New York City.

14 "Cotton and Its Kingdom," in *Harper's New Monthly Magazine,* LXIII (October 1881), 719–34. The figures on cotton prices are taken from Grady's article on "The New South" in the *New York Ledger,* November 23, 1889.

15 W. J. Cash: *The Mind of the South* (New York, 1941), pp. 176–7. This extremely readable book offers an excellent analysis of the changes in Southern attitudes throughout the years.

16 Broadus Mitchell, op. cit., pp. 232–5.

3

Grady went to New York twice in November, once before and once after the election. On December 1 he returned to the metropolis, accompanied by his wife and two children — seven-year-old Henry and five-year-old Gussie — and also by his mother and his sister, Mattie. The family stopped first at the St. James Hotel, a favorite haunt with Grady always because it was such "a great resort for the politicians." Later they moved to a boarding house near the Fifth Avenue Hotel, situated at the corner of Twenty-third Street.

In the North Grady found more interest in "the disposition of the South to subordinate politics to material development" than in anything else. "Fast mails, small farms, colonies of immigrants, internal improvements, new industries — these are the channels through which the south can command the respect and sympathy of the north — and through which she can best command her own self-respect," he wrote. "I am firmly convinced that as soon as the south is firmly planted on her platform of liberation and progressive development, and her position is well understood, we shall see northern capital seeking southern investment with eagerness and the stream of immigration turned toward Georgia." [17]

Articles in this vein predominated among the letters which Grady wrote for the *Constitution* several times a week during his five-and-a-half-month stay in New York. With the object of making the South's position "well understood" in the North, he continued also to write for the *New York Herald* and other Northern journals.

Much of Grady's interest in New York centered in Wall Street, where, under the guidance of Victor Newcomb, he was handling a sizable block of L. & N. stock on margin. Writing in December that he looked for "a break in the street" within the next six months, he observed that "behind all the dust and smoke and uproar . . . will be seen the livid and impressive face of Jay Gould." When stocks did tumble late in January, he referred to Gould as "the most baneful influence, personal or corporated, in America today." Later he expressed great

[17] *Constitution,* December 5, 1880.

concern over the "audacity" of Gould and Cyrus W. Field in attempting to gain control of the news reports of the nation's press associations. Gould already dominated the Western Union Telegraph Company, by which the news was gathered and disseminated, while he and Field together owned three of the seven newspapers in the New York Associated Press and needed but one more to control that agency. Although Field was a man of much higher moral repute than Gould, the belief that both men were engaged in a scheme to "prostitute" the press to "stock jobbery" was causing Grady to lose some of his admiration for the man from whom he had borrowed the money to buy an interest in the *Constitution.*

But Grady preferred to write of business leaders whose activities he regarded as constructive and helpful to the South, rather than to dwell continually on the "baneful influence" of men like Gould. As the result of his close association in the Colquitt campaign of the previous summer with Samuel M. Inman, an Atlanta cotton broker, he had come to regard Inman as Atlanta's "ideal citizen," one typical of the "self-made men" who were giving the city its "vitality, force, and power." In the North he became well acquainted with Inman's younger brother, John H. Inman, who had made a fortune since moving from Tennessee to New York and was planning to bring millions in Northern capital into the South. Writing to the *Constitution* about the younger Inman, Grady declared: "I should be charged with irreverence if I wrote down how many politicians, in my opinion, this one young merchant is worth."

His articles in this vein were not confined by any means to Southerners who had made their fortunes in the North. He again interviewed General Sherman. He wrote of ninety-year-old Peter Cooper, whose career had been "one of magnificence and philanthropy." He became an intimate of George I. Seney, a New York banker who, inspired by the liberal writings of President Haygood of Emory College, was making generous gifts to Emory and a Georgia college for women, Wesleyan. Referring to the benefactions of Cooper and Seney to education, Grady asked: "Which man leaves the best legacy to his children — the man who dies with the blessings of a people on his life and leaves a moderate fortune . . . or the man who leaves a mass of money and the taint of a selfish and miserly life?"

If Grady was inclined to glorify men who were using their wealth constructively, he was as sympathetic as ever in his treatment of the poorer classes. He continually was drawing human-interest vignettes of the people he saw as he moved about the city — in the streets, on the elevated railway, and in the parks. These sketches appeared in the *Constitution* under such headings as "Etchings," "Gradiana," and "Seated on a Bench." One "little boy in a balcony" whom Grady passed every day on the elevated intrigued him so much that he made the child's acquaintance and took him to Coney Island for a memorable outing.[18]

At DeGive's Opera House in Atlanta Grady had become acquainted with such stage favorites as Edwin Booth, Joseph Jefferson, Mrs. Lillie Langtry, and Madame Rhea. From Broadway he now wrote of Tommaso Salvini, the great Italian actor; of Mary Anderson, the "divine" Kentucky girl with "the slouching stride of a race horse"; and, most glowingly of all, of Sarah Bernhardt, who, although new to America, already was recognized as drama's first lady. When rumors about Bernhardt's private life reached Atlanta in advance of the French star's appearance there, Grady reminded the *Constitution's* readers that "outside of her love affairs it is claimed that Sarah's life is full of charm, charity and goodness." In any event, he added, "it might be well to remember that it was a magdalen on whom the Master poured the balm of forgiveness and mercy."

By the spring of 1881 much of Grady's time was being devoted to preparations for the First International Cotton Exposition to be held in Atlanta that fall. The idea of the exposition had been suggested in a letter to the *New York Herald* in August 1880 by Edward Atkinson, a Boston economist. The *Constitution* had reprinted the letter, and in October H. I. Kimball had brought Atkinson to Atlanta for an address. In December the first steps had been taken toward the formation of an exposition company with Senator Brown (later

[18] Harris, p. 310.

Governor Colquitt) as president, Samuel M. Inman·as treasurer, J. W. Ryckman, a veteran of the Philadelphia Centennial of 1876, as secretary, and Kimball as director-general.
After Atlanta had subscribed its allotted one-third of the capital stock in one day, the directors sent Kimball North to raise
the remainder. Although Grady held no official title in the
organization, he and John H. Inman enthusiastically aided
Kimball in New York, and Grady became the mainspring in
the exposition's publicity.

The opening news story in the highly successful campaign
for Northern subscriptions was one of which any publicity
man might have been proud: a $2,000 subscription from Gen-
eral Sherman, the man who once had burned the city in which
the exposition was to be held!

Grady's advance releases on the exposition in *Harper's
Weekly, Frank Leslie's Illustrated Newspaper,* and other
pictorial journals were illustrated by two artists — Horace
Bradley, a young Atlantan who then was studying in New
York, and James H. Moser, who already had a studio on
Peachtree and had drawn the illustrations for some of Har-
ris's "Uncle Remus" stories. Bradley and Moser accompanied
Grady to North Carolina in April to illustrate the articles
that he was writing for *Harper's* and the New York *Daily
Graphic* on the progress of the "Tar Heel" state.

While in Charlotte, Grady gave a reporter for the *Observer*
an interview which revealed the extent of his speculation in
L. & N. stock. The stock had advanced from $92\frac{3}{4}$ to $97\frac{7}{8}$ during
the two preceding days, according to press quotations, and
Grady stated flatly that this represented a profit to him of
$7,000.[19] By May 8, when his twelve-month note to Field fell
due, the stock had risen to 103, which in the same ratio would
have netted him another $7,000. On May 18, the last day he
is known to have been in New York, L. & N. was bringing 109,
its high for the year. Grady apparently did not sell at this
fancy figure, for his account book [20] shows that he borrowed
$10,000 in Atlanta to pay $10,000 on his note to Field. Soon

19 Clipping from *Charlotte Daily Observer,* April 24, 1881, Grady Scrapbooks.
20 Grady Collection.

after he returned home, however, he was able to pay all except $4,000 of the cost of building a new $16,000 residence — a fact which indicates that he may have realized as much as $12,000 on the transaction.

Yet actually he profited very little as a result of his tips from Victor Newcomb, for Albert Howell, brother of Evan P. Howell, later invested in L. & N. on Grady's advice and came out $10,000 the loser. Grady insisted on making good every dollar that his friend had lost. His account book reveals that by the end of 1881 he had paid $6,000 on this self-imposed debt and had given Howell a $4,000 note for the remainder.

Within two weeks after Grady's return to Atlanta, he was called upon to make two important speeches. The first was at a banquet in honor of E. W. Cole, who, undaunted by Newcomb's coup of the previous year, was building a new network of railroads extending through seven Southern states. The second talk was at a dinner tendered General Gordon to celebrate the beginning of work on the Georgia Pacific Railroad, which was to give Atlanta its coveted line to the Alabama coal mines and thence to the Mississippi. In the thirteen months since his resignation from the Senate the General had obtained the old "Georgia Western" charter from the L. & N. and had organized a new railroad 476 miles long with $10,000,000 capital, all of which was subscribed.[21]

Delighted though he was over the success of this enterprise of Gordon and the L. & N., Grady soon gave a convincing demonstration of his independence of the railroad which his critics once had said was the real owner of his stock in the *Constitution*. When the L. & N. sent "a parcel of lobbyists" to the legislature in a "bold attempt" to prevent the granting of charters to the new lines proposed by the Cole group, the *Constitution* exposed the scheme and condemned it vigorously. Voicing the opposition of the paper to monopoly, Grady said it favored "any and every enterprise" which would "develop the resources of the state, increase the facilities of transportation and give the people the benefit of competition."

[21] *Constitution,* June 8, 9, 1881.

4

After returning to Atlanta, Grady's first concern was to make his own newspaper an adequate instrument for reflecting and stimulating the progress that the approaching First International Cotton Exposition represented. Since 1876, when he joined the paper, the *Constitution's* circulation had grown from 2,400 to 5,200 daily and from 3,600 to 10,500 weekly. In number of subscribers it now claimed to be exceeded in the South only by the Louisville *Courier-Journal.* In size and appearance, however, the paper had changed little. It still was running only four pages of eight columns on weekdays, expanding occasionally to nine and ten columns on Sundays. Being now the only morning paper in growing Atlanta, and having eliminated all except one afternoon competitor, the *Post-Appeal,* it literally was bursting at the column rules with advertising. Grady therefore determined, with the approval of his partners, not only to enlarge the paper in size but also to introduce some of the methods with which he had become familiar in New York. On June 17, less than a month after he again took up his duties as managing editor, the *Constitution* announced that its size henceforth would be increased from four eight-column pages to eight six-column pages, and that it was acquiring an entirely new "type dress."

On September 6, 1881 the paper appeared for the first time in the new format — one which was to be maintained, with few modifications, throughout the eighties. Better organization was noticeable, along with improved typography and more extensive news coverage. The first page now was devoted to telegraph news, national and foreign, except for an occasional local story of unusual interest. State news from correspondents and exchanges was featured on page two, and the financial news on page three often filled as much as three columns. Editorials and editorial-page features occupied all of page four. Local news usually held the spotlight on page five, with a story by Grady himself frequently holding the top position. Page six was devoted to general news, page seven to "Local Tin-Types" (personals and bits of human interest), and page eight to general and local news. Advertising, as a rule, filled at least half of all inside pages except the editorial page. The Sunday paper was increased in size, first to twelve pages and later to sixteen, and carried an even larger proportion of advertising. Immediately preceding the exposition the paper brought out a thirty-two-page edition — the largest in its history.

In the same week that the *Constitution* donned its new dress, the Gradys moved into their new home at 353 Peachtree Street. In its jigsaw architecture the gray-colored house reflected the prevailing taste of the era, but in its interior arrangements it was ideal for the Grady family. Besides affording adequate space for entertaining — something the Baker Street cottage had lacked — it provided the additional rooms needed for Grady's mother, sister, and brother, all of whom now became regular members of the household. There were six bedrooms in all — four bedrooms and two baths on the second floor, and two bedrooms with one bath on the first floor. The guest room on the second floor was decorated by Grady's artist friend James H. Moser with a mural of "Uncle Remus" characters.

To the left of the entrance hall on the first floor was a large parlor, connected at the rear with the dining-room. At the right of the hall was the living-room, from which a door opened into a small wing containing Grady's study. Here a wall telephone — one of the first in Atlanta — gave him quick communication with his office. For entertaining, the sliding doors connecting the main rooms could be opened and the whole front part of the lower floor thrown into a space large enough to accommodate scores of guests.

On such occasions — and they were many during the exposition and afterward — refreshments flowed in the dining-room, an orchestra provided music for dancing in the parlor, and whiskered, frock-coated gentlemen sat in the living-room, smoking and talking of their plans for the New South.

The cotton exposition, scheduled for October 5 to December 31, was turning out to be a much more comprehensive affair than the originator of the idea had intended. As a representative of the New England Cotton Manufacturers' Association, Edward Atkinson had suggested only an exhibition to encourage more efficient methods in the raising, ginning, and packing of cotton for the use of factories in the North. In fact, in his letters and speeches he actually had endeavored to discourage the building of cotton mills in the South.[22] But as developed by Brown, Colquitt, the Inmans, Kimball, Grady, and others, the exposition set out to stimulate the development of all the "cotton kingdom's" resources, industrial as well as agricultural and mineral. Invitations went out to all the principal cotton-growing countries of the world and to all the leading manufacturers of textile machinery and cotton goods, both American and foreign, for exhibits.

For a city which had only 37,409 population by the 1880 census, such a "world's fair" was an ambitious undertaking. It was "the first time in the history of expositions" that a city of less than half a million inhabitants had undertaken an enterprise of this magnitude, the *Constitution* said. Furthermore, it was "the first time that any city of any size" had "conceived, organized and completed a world's fair in less than eight months."

Atlanta outdid herself in preparing to entertain the exposition visitors. New hotels, rooming houses, and restaurants sprang up like magic; old buildings received a fresh coat of paint; and the mourning colors occasioned by President Garfield's death in September turned everywhere into red, white, and blue decorations for the opening day.

The site of the exposition was Oglethorpe Park, two miles west of the city on the W. & A. Railroad. Here, almost filling the space enclosed by a circular race track, a huge cross-shaped building had been erected with auxiliary structures near by. Within these buildings 1,113 exhibits portrayed every chapter in the story of cotton "from seed to shimmering organdy." Carloads of the latest machinery for farm and factory were on hand, and three large steam engines were required to keep the industrial exhibits in operation. In an adjoining field cotton was blooming, while in the surrounding tents and pavilions were all the ordinary amusements of a large fair and some quite extraordinary for the South of that day.

Grady's services to the exposition were manifold, but his

22 Broadus Mitchell, op. cit., pp. 117–20.

most notable contribution was in enlisting the support of newspapers and magazines throughout the country and in helping to devise a program of such significance that the press could not afford to ignore it. Senators Zebulon Vance of North Carolina and Daniel W. Voorhees of Indiana spoke at the opening exercises; the governors of eight Southern states attended on Governors' Day. General Sherman and his staff were prominent visitors. Many large cities in the North as well as in the South sent special excursions, and the legislatures of three Southern states attended in a body. So great was the interest that twenty newspaper writers from leading American dailies were on hand to cover the opening — "the largest assembly of representative correspondents that ever visited Atlanta." [23]

One of the visiting correspondents was Charles R. Miller of the *New York Times,* who, the *Constitution* noted, had "entered journalism on the *Springfield Republican* under the elder Bowles." After Miller had been persuaded to accept the hospitality of the Grady home, a number of prominent Atlantans were invited to a dinner in his honor. The New Yorker informed his host, however, that he had not brought a dress suit with him. Grady assured the visitor that he would supply this deficiency immediately. Because of his increasing weight, he recently had discarded a dress suit of his own and given it to his Negro butler, Charley Moon. Grady hastily borrowed the suit and carried it to Miller, without telling his guest that it had been the butler's costume. The situation greatly amused Grady, and before the evening was over he had managed to reveal the joke to everyone present except the *Times* representative, who remained blissfully ignorant.[24]

The fair also marked the beginning of a friendship between Grady and Walter Hines Page, who visited the exposition as a correspondent of the New York *World.* Overwhelmed by the kindness of the *Constitution's* managing editor, Page applied to Grady for a position, but was told that there was no opening. The *World* reporter was eager to remain in Atlanta because he saw there "a southern spirit that was several dec-

---

[23] *Constitution,* October 7, 1881.
[24] Mrs. W. L. Peel in *Constitution,* May 23, 1921.

ades removed from the Civil War." One day Page himself was to be known as a "less lovable" but "equally sincere" successor of Grady in expounding the New South philosophy.[25]

The exposition came to a close on December 31 with a total attendance of 286,000 and a net profit of $20,000 to its credit. It had afforded great encouragement to the building of cotton mills and to industrialization generally; moreover, it had "opened the eyes of the North to the field of investment that lay in the South." The main exposition building became the home of the Exposition Cotton Mills, and most of the machinery on display was sold to Southerners. Indeed, it is said that Atlantans struck some rare bargains with Northern manufacturers for the "used" machinery. The *Constitution* itself acquired a small block of stock in the Exposition Cotton Mills, while Grady personally became interested in a new periodical known as the *Industrial Review and Textile Reporter*. Appearing for the first time in January 1882 at Atlanta and Philadelphia, this magazine continued publication for some thirteen years, though Grady sold his stock at the end of the first year to J. W. Ryckman, the former secretary of the exposition.[26]

Possibly because of a feeling that the exposition had been more successful in stimulating industry than in improving agriculture, the *Constitution* in the early months of 1882 gave increased emphasis to the problems of the farmer. The paper encouraged its rural readers to write letters on their experiences in diversifying crops and in making their farms self-sustaining. These letters were distributed by the thousands over the state. In Florida for a two weeks' vacation following the exposition, Grady issued a warning on the evils of "absentee landlordism," which he saw increasing month by month. "Nothing can be worse for the south than the tenant system," he wrote. "Under this system the south can only grow poorer, while alien greed insists that the land shall be robbed of the last possible yield." [27]

[25] Burton J. Hendrick: *The Life and Letters of Walter Hines Page* (New York, 1924), I, 34–7; John Donald Wade: "Old Wine in a New Bottle," in *Virginia Quarterly Review*, II (April 1935), 250–1.

[26] *Industrial Review and Textile Reporter*, January 1883.

[27] *Constitution*, January 17, 1882.

5

Meanwhile the elections of 1882 were approaching, and Grady was forced to turn his attention once more to political matters — if, indeed, he ever had forgotten them! With cotton prices still falling, the condition of agriculture described in his *Harper's* article had not improved, and both the Republican administration in Washington and the Independents in Georgia were seeking to utilize the agrarian unrest as a means of overthrowing the state's dominant Democratic leadership. Dr. Felton, the Independent leader, was particularly bitter against the *Constitution* and the Brown-Gordon-Colquitt triumvirate, whom he charged with "cheating" him out of his seat in Congress at the last election. He branded his opponents as "Bourbons" — a strange label for men who had accepted new ideas as quickly as Brown, their "chief boss," had done. The only authentic Bourbons in Georgia, actually, were a relatively small number of "die-hards" like Dr. Charles Colcock Jones, the historian, who thought that to accept industrialization was "to insult the graves of the Confederate dead and to abandon true civilization in favor of barbarism." [28]

In January Grady went to Washington and obtained an interview in which Senator Hill described the actions of the Republicans and the Independents as "a second attempt to Africanize the south." Hill pointed out that, since the ending of military rule in 1877, the race issue virtually had been eliminated in the South. This had resulted primarily from the fact that there had been little organized opposition to the Democratic candidates, except when disaffection had occurred among the Democrats themselves. But now the death of President Garfield had placed the "worst elements" in the Republican Party in the saddle, and the administration was determined to win back the Southern states through the votes of Negroes and malcontent Democrats. Thirty thousand disaffected Democrats, combined with the Negroes, could carry any state in the South, Hill explained.

Commenting on the Independents' "blatant pretenses of re-

[28] Interview with Felton in *Constitution*, December 22, 1880; Cash, op. cit., p. 181.

form, and still more blatant outcries against that mythical monster — the Bourbon Democracy of the South," Hill described the evidences of progress under the existing leadership:

Factories are springing up in all directions. Our industries are being multiplied as never before. Thousands of the best men of the north have gone home from the exposition enthused with the brightening prospects of all business in the state. Our taxes were scarcely ever so low. Our credit was never so high. Capital and people and machinery are flowing in, and everybody is brushing away the tears of war, and laughing with a new hope in a new era. All this, all this has been accomplished under the rule of the men who are denounced by trading politicians as narrow-minded, intolerant Bourbons.[29]

Felton replied with a tirade against Hill. He denied that he had made a trade with the Republicans and declared, so far as the charge of "Africanizing" the state was concerned, that he merely claimed "for every man, white and black, the right to vote a free ticket, and to have that vote counted." Mrs. Felton charged that Grady simply had "found a dull time on his hands" and had gone to Washington and "stirred up the beasties." [30]

Two circumstances, however, point to the genuineness of the fears expressed by Hill and reported by Grady. In the first place, no Southern state at that time had any of the present constitutional restrictions serving to limit Negro voting, so that a division among the whites in general elections did constitute a real and not an imaginary threat to "white supremacy." In the second place, the Georgia Republicans in March 1882 did endorse the Independent platform, and the very next year offered Felton the Atlanta postmastership,[31] thus indicating that they, at least, were seeking actively to form a coalition. In Virginia, the *Constitution* reminded its readers, such a coalition already had been partially successful.

29 *Constitution*, January 7, 1882.

30 Clippings, Grady Scrapbooks; Felton, op. cit., p. 399.

31 Correspondence between James Longstreet and W. H. Felton, Felton Papers.

The fears of Georgia Democratic leaders developed into grave alarm in April when it was learned that Alexander H. Stephens was cocking a receptive ear to the pleas of the Independents that he become their candidate for governor. Although the pale, bright-eyed statesman in the wheel-chair recently had announced his "retirement" from politics and even had corrected the proof of his obituary for the *Constitution,* he had a way of coming to life again under the stimulus of whisky, hypodermics, and political opportunity. His sympathy-arousing invalidism, his long record of public service, and his reputation for personal integrity and unselfishness made him a candidate to be reckoned with.[32] The hope of the coalition, said the *Constitution,* was "to use the honored name of Mr. Stephens to injure the democratic organization."

On the eve of the Independent convention in May, the *Constitution* announced that it would support Stephens for the governorship if he were nominated on the regular Democratic ticket, but not if he ran "in defiance of" the party. This should have served as warning to the insurgents that the regulars were flirting with their prospective candidate. Yet in spite of this omen the Independents went ahead and recommended "Little Aleck" for election. The Democratic state Executive Committee, of which Evan P. Howell was a member, immediately swung into action. A few days later Stephens denied that he had made any promises to the insurgents and announced instead that he was a candidate for the regular Democratic nomination — an announcement which the *Constitution* promptly endorsed.

In a further effort to strengthen the Democratic ticket, a movement now developed to "draft" Grady as a candidate for congressman-at-large. In less than a month more than fifty newspapers throughout the state gave the suggestion their endorsement. Democratic leaders in nearly a hundred counties wrote him offering their support. Finally he was presented with a petition signed by more than 1,200 Atlantans. "We feel that no journalist has done so much as yourself for the material progress of the south, and we wish to see the field of your work broadened," the petition recited. "We therefore ear-

32 Felton, op. cit., pp. 345–51; E. R. Richardson, op. cit., *passim.*

nestly ask that you allow us the use of your name in the coming canvass." [33]

In the light of all that Grady had written about his preference for business over politics, he hardly could have done anything with good grace except refuse. Only a few months earlier
he had observed: "With the state offices so belittled that they
offer scarcely a bare living, and the federal offices for two dec-
ades in adverse hands, there has been little temptation to sacrifice anything for the hope of leadership." Anyone with his
strong urge for influence and popular acclaim, however, could
not fail to be "flattered" and "strongly tempted" by a demand
so overwhelming that election seemed a foregone conclusion.
He toyed for three days with the idea of running, then issued
a formal statement in which he declined to permit the use of
his name. His refusal contains probably the finest expression
of his idealism as an editor:

When I was eighteen years of age I adopted journalism as my profession. After thirteen years of service, in which I have had various
fortunes, I can say that I have never seen a day when I regretted
my choice. On the contrary, I have seen the field of journalism so
enlarged, its possibilities so widened, and its influence so extended
that I have come to believe earnestly that no man — no matter
what his calling, his elevation or his opportunity — can equal in
dignity, honor and usefulness the journalist who comprehends his
position, fairly measures his duties and gives himself entirely and
unselfishly to his work. But journalism is a jealous profession, and
demands the fullest allegiance of those who seek its honors or its
emoluments. Least of all things can it be made the aid of the dema-
gogue, or the handmaid of the politician. The man who uses his
journal to subserve his political ambition or writes with a sinister
and personal purpose, soon loses his power and had best abandon
the profession he has betrayed. Within my memory there are frequent and striking examples of men who have sacrificed the one
profession, only to be sacrificed in the other. History has not recorded the name of a single man who has been great enough to
succeed in both. Therefore, devoted as I am to my profession —
believing, as I do, that there is more of honor and usefulness for
me along its way than in any other path, and that my duty is

[33] MS., Grady Collection.

clear and is unmistakable — I am constrained to reaffirm in my own mind and to declare to you the resolution I made when I entered journalism, viz: that as long as I remain in its ranks I would never become a candidate for any political office, or draw a dollar from any public treasury. This rule I have never broken, and I hope I never shall.

As a matter of course every young man of health and spirit must have ambition. I think it has been the curse of the south that our young men have considered little else than political preferment worthy of an ambitious thought. There is a fascination about the applause of the hustings that is hard to withstand. Really there is no career that brings so much of unhappiness and discontent — so much of subservience, sacrifice and uncertainty as that of the politician. Never did the south offer so little to her young men in the direction of politics as she does at present — never did she offer so much in other directions. As for me, my ambition is a simple one. I shall be satisfied with the labors of my life, if, when those labors are over my son, looking abroad upon a grander and better Georgia — a Georgia that has filled the destiny God intended her for — when her towns and cities are hives of industry, and her countrysides the exhaustless fields from which their stores are drawn — when every stream dances on its way to the music of spindles, and every forest echoes back the roar of a passing train — when her valleys smile with abundant harvests, and from her hillsides come the tinkling of bells as her herds and flocks go forth from their folds — when more than two million people proclaim her perfect independence, and bless her with their love, I shall be more than content, I say, if my son, looking upon such scenes as these can stand up and say, "My father bore a part in this work, and his name lives in the memory of this people." [84]

Such a disdain of political office was a novel thing. Newspapers as far away as the *Springfield Republican* praised Grady for his devotion to journalism, and more than a hundred editorial comments eventually found their way into his scrapbooks. Senator Brown congratulated him on gaining by this one act "as much distinction as almost any Congressman can gain in serving a single term." The Senator's son, Julius L. Brown, a friend of Grady's college days, wrote: "No one can hereafter charge you with doing or saying anything for

[84] *Constitution,* June 6, 1882.

the mere purpose of elevating yourself to political places. . . .
All will be compelled to admit that which your friends know
to be true, that you are working to build up the material interests of our grand old state. From the plane you now occupy
you can do that much better than if you had come to a different conclusion." [35]

A somewhat different attitude, however, was expressed by
the Macon *Telegraph and Messenger,* whose editor, Albert R.
Lamar, also was being boomed for the office of congressman-
at-large. The Macon paper published an editorial paragraph
insinuating that Grady himself actually had "introduced that
famous petition to the public, and solicited signatures to it." [36]
The *Constitution,* branding the *Telegraph's* charge as "mali-
cious misrepresentation," replied that Grady "had no knowledge of the petition until it was handed to him by his friends."

The Macon paper seemed to be most disturbed by the fact
that the "Atlanta ring," as it called the Brown-Gordon-Colquitt combination, was trying to deprive Macon's favorite
son, Augustus O. Bacon, of the gubernatorial nomination by
"forcing" Stephens upon the people. The *Constitution* could
afford to ridicule this charge, for the "ring candidate" swept
the field in the choice of county delegates to the Democratic
state convention and was nominated by acclamation. So certain was Grady of the little invalid's vote-getting power that
even during the campaign he went to Morehead City, North
Carolina, and Ocean City, Maryland, for a vacation.

Before leaving the state Grady had a farewell visit with
Benjamin H. Hill, who had come home from Washington to
die. The Senator was suffering from cancer of the tongue.
Following a third operation in March, his physicians had told
his family that the case was hopeless. At that time Grady had
written: "The greatest orator that this country has produced
since Clay or Webster comes home silent." With admiration
and tender feeling he now described the fortitude of a man
who, in spite of his intense suffering, desired to "make one
more speech . . . upon the relations between the white man
and the black man." These words of Hill "from the border of

[35] Letters in Grady Collection.
[36] June 11, 1882.

eternity" must have sunk deeply into Grady's mind and heart:
"I am in favor of giving the negro equal and exact justice;
nothing less and nothing more. My friend, we cannot have
good government or stable society when one party seeks to
dominate the other by the use of the negro vote." Recalling
Grady's interview with him in January, Hill told his visitor:
"I spoke from the sincerest convictions. I thought Georgia was
menaced, and I felt called upon to speak. I should have struck
the blow if it had fallen on my brother." [37]

Hill died on August 16. The next morning Grady's biographical sketch of the Senator filled the first and second pages
of the *Constitution*. It gives every indication of having been
prepared with the utmost care during the weeks in which
Grady had known of his friend's imminent death. Written
with admirable restraint and rare beauty, the obituary reveals
the writer's emotions in the loss of the man who probably
had influenced him more than any other: "I feel as one who
had seen the sun move down the western sky, and after it has
gone, stands gazing on the banks of clouds still luminous with
its glory, and finds that it lives in the quivering after-glow,
even after it has passed into the infinite."

During the summer and early fall of 1882 there were several other events worthy of note. First, Grady was elected a
trustee of the University of Georgia — a position which he
was to hold as long as he lived. Then, in September, the Chi
Phi fraternity held its convention in Atlanta and, following an
"eloquent and able" address by Grady, elected him as its
"Grand Alpha" or national president. He was the first Southerner to be honored with this office since the uniting of the
Northern and Southern orders of Chi Phi.[38]

Later in this same month President Arthur's Tariff Commission held a hearing in Atlanta, and Grady had another
visit with Walter Hines Page, of the New York *World*, who
was traveling with the commission. It was probably through
Page that Grady made the acquaintance of an obscure young
Atlanta lawyer who appeared at the hearing as an advocate of

[37] *Constitution*, July 22, 1882; Cate, op. cit., pp. 400–1.
[38] Information from Central Office of Chi Phi, based upon minutes of
Atlanta meeting.

free trade — Woodrow Wilson. The *Constitution* referred to Wilson's speech only as "lengthy" — perhaps a natural failing for one whom Grady is said to have regarded as "somewhat over-educated." Wilson was to leave Atlanta the following year without ever becoming a close friend of the editor.[39]   This today seems regrettable, for the future President could have profited from the warmth and understanding of Grady, just as the young journalist might have benefited from Wilson's depth of learning.

In the state election on October 4, Stephens polled 68 per cent of the votes. The Republicans had joined the Independents in supporting Grady's distant cousin, General Lucius J. Gartrell, but their hopes faded with the outbreak of an open fight between the Negro and "Lily White" elements. The ride of Stephens from Crawfordville to Atlanta was a triumphal march either for a "reunited Democracy" or for the "Atlanta ring," depending upon whether one read the *Constitution* or the Macon *Telegraph and Messenger*.

Interest now centered in the national election to be held in November. Georgia's two "doubtful districts" again were the scenes of bitter contests between Independents and regular Democrats for congressional seats. In the Seventh Dr. Felton was trying desperately to regain from Judson C. Clements the seat he had lost in 1880, while in the Ninth Allen D. Candler was campaigning against Emory Speer. Grady took no part in the campaign proper, but he realized that the outcome of these close races would make even bigger news than the almost certain victory of Stephens had been. He therefore turned his attention toward getting the election results for the *Constitution* as quickly as possible.

Both districts were made up largely of mountainous territory, much of it sparsely settled and with roads notoriously bad. In the past it had been days or weeks before final returns could be obtained. Grady determined to publish the complete results on the morning after the election. He chartered special engines, engaged telegraph operators to stay up all night, and established relays of horsemen in the mountains. One of the couriers rode forty-three miles in four hours and ten minutes over mountain roads, while seven others covered distances of more than twenty miles each. The arrangements cost the *Constitution* more than $1,000, but on the next day it had the news from every precinct. The two Independents were defeated, in accordance with Grady's predictions, and the Democrats once more had control of every congressional district in the state.

There was one more piece of unfinished business for the *Constitution* and its political friends. This was the election of Governor Colquitt to the United States Senate to take the place vacated by Hill's death. Many writers of the period have attributed Colquitt's success to Grady's skill in managing the Governor's campaign for votes in the legislature. Colquitt himself evidently thought Grady was responsible, for, upon leaving for Washington the following March, he presented his manager with a pair of handsome bays in appreciation.[40]

To celebrate Colquitt's victory, Grady invited the four senatorial candidates and the men making their nominating and seconding speeches to his home for what the invitations announced as "feeding at 6 and fiddling at 9." The "fiddling" was for the special benefit of Tom Watson, the young rebel who had seconded the nomination of Colquitt's chief opponent, Major J. C. C. Black of Augusta. After a dinner at which an abundance of champagne whetted the appetites of the guests for the merriment that followed, Watson engaged in his fiddling contest with Charles R. Pendleton, representative from Lowndes County and later to be editor of the *Macon Telegraph*. The unanimous verdict of those present gave Watson the prize — "a floral fiddle, with tuberose body and smilax strings."

"Let us bury all personal differences and have a general peace," Grady urged. "The elections are all over; good men are elected . . . and there is little cause for complaint, but much for congratulations." Well might he make such a conciliatory gesture, for, as the biographer of Watson points out, "with Brown and Colquitt in the Senate and Governor Ste-

[40] H. W. G. to Estelle Cuyler Smith, May 18, 1883, Grady Collection.

phens keeping step to the new music," there was little for the
Constitution and its favorites to ask that they did not have.[41]

6

Throughout political campaigns, the exposition, and all
his travels, there were few days when the *Constitution* did not
carry an article by "H. W. G." Wherever he might be, whatever he might be doing, whomever he might be talking to, he
always was on the alert for information and ideas that would
make the *Constitution* a better newspaper. With Howell and
Grady on the "inside" of virtually everything of significance
going on in Georgia, it was seldom that the paper was "beat"
on an important story.

While he was on the road, Grady's interpretative news articles, signed "H. W. G.," were printed regularly in the upper left-hand corner of the front page — the same position to
be made famous years later in the Hearst papers by Arthur
Brisbane's "Today" column. After his return to Atlanta in
1881, he continued to write many signed news articles and
also contributed, with varying degrees of regularity, a Sunday
column entitled "The Man About Town." This medley of
interviews, personality sketches, human-interest items, editorial comment, and gossip filled from one to three columns
on the first page. The prominent display Grady gave his own
writings was probably not so much an expression of egoism
as it was a shrewd and candid recognition of the feature of the
paper in which its readers were most interested.

"H. W. G. — the *nom de plume* of Henry W. Grady!" wrote
another Georgia editor in these months. "How often have we
eschewed the plethoric press dispatches, the sage wisdom of
the leader, the pointed pungency of the paragraph, the lurid
headlines of the last horrid sensation, to pounce with eager
avidity upon anything bearing that signature." [42] I. W. Avery, who had watched Grady with admiring interest ever
since his first letters from the University of Virginia, declared

[41] *Constitution,* November 15, 1882; Woodward, op. cit., p. 105.
[42] Clipping, Grady Scrapbooks.

in 1881 that there was "a vividness, an audacity and a velvety splendor about his articles . . . that no other man has approximated." After describing the *Constitution's* staff and asserting that no newspaper in the Union had "a better intellectual and literary equipment," Avery said: "His contemporaries on the journal will not consider it a derogation from their high claims to say that Mr. Grady is the genius of this powerful paper."

As managing editor, Grady had charge of both the news columns and the editorial page and wrote on any subject he chose. The *Constitution* itself explained that Howell, the editor-in-chief, contributed only on "special occasions," and that his contributions usually were "brief and on practical subjects." But the *Constitution* was far from being a one-man or even a two-man newspaper. The other two stockholders, W. A. Hemphill, the business manager, and N. P. T. Finch, the chief editorial-writer, also devoted full time to the paper. Finch, a former New York newspaperman, was credited by Avery with writing the "foreign or statistical editorials," while his associate, Harris, was said to be a "clincher" in dealing with new books, railroad rates, or the Negro question.[43]

Grady had been at the helm of the paper only a short time before he had a correspondent in every county of Georgia and in nearly every key city of the nation. Whenever Congress was in session he had a full-time correspondent on duty in Washington. In October 1881 the *Constitution* reported that it was spending more for telegraphic news than any other paper in the South.

The paper paid large tolls not only for general news but also for stories of sporting events, particularly baseball. One week Howell became alarmed at the size of the *Constitution's* bill for baseball news, in which he was much less interested than Grady. He warned his managing editor: "If you don't stop it, I'm going to charge it up to you."

"That's all right," replied Grady. "Charge it. I don't care. But I'm going to have the baseball news just the same."[44]

In October 1882 the *Constitution* announced that it could

43 Avery, op. cit., p. 614; *Constitution*, August 17, 1884.
44 "Bill Arp" in *Constitution*, December 29, 1889.

THE *CONSTITUTION*'S NEW BUILDING IN 1884

not print in its eight pages all the advertising that was being received, and that it was forced to limit street sales in order to accommodate its growing list of regular subscribers. The need for a larger paper and for more copies resulted, early in 1883, in the purchase of a new $25,000 perfecting press, "exactly like those of the *New York Herald.*" Soon afterward the paper announced plans for the erection, at the southeast corner of Forsyth and Alabama Streets, of a five-story brick building costing $100,000. This structure, occupied the following year, has been the *Constitution's* home down to the present day.

Grady realized that the field of a daily was limited, no matter how good a newspaper it might be. In 1883, therefore, he took personal charge of the *Weekly Constitution* in a determined effort to extend its circulation and influence. As was customary on most newspapers of that day, the weekly was made up principally of type held over from the daily, with the addition of special advertising and some special features. Grady personally selected every item that went into his weekly and soon added a popular woman columnist, "Betsy Hamilton" (Mrs. E. B. Ploughman), who wrote of country life in "hillbilly" style, to a list of featured writers that already included "Uncle Remus," "Bill Arp," and Dr. T. DeWitt Talmage. He increased the number of pages from eight to twelve and later to sixteen, and at the same time reduced the subscription price from $2.50 to $1.50 a year, with club prices ranging down as low as $1.00. Books, watches, pictures, and other merchandise were offered "at cost" along with subscriptions. After the weekly's circulation had increased in six months from 10,750 to 20,000, Grady jubilantly announced: "We are going right along to 50,000." [45]

In the first complete year of Grady's managing editorship, the Constitution Publishing Company paid total dividends of $31\frac{1}{2}$ per cent on its $100,000 capital stock. Although Grady's record for the following year shows that one 2 per cent dividend accrued from the company's outside investments and another 2 per cent from the state printing, which the *Constitution* handled either directly or through subcontract all

[45] *Weekly Constitution,* March 16, 1884.

through the eighties,[46] at least five-sixths of the profit clearly came from the newspaper itself. One reason for the high dividend rate is that the four stockholders — Howell, Grady, Hemphill, and Finch — paid themselves for full-time work only nominal salaries of $1,800 a year each. Later, after more of the paper's profits were being put into the new building and equipment, and after several persons outside the *"Constitution* family" had acquired shares of stock, the dividend rate was cut to an average of 10 to 12 per cent a year and the annual salaries of the four original stockholders were increased — Grady's to $6,000.

On December 27, 1881 Grady acquired an account book and inscribed on the first page his resolution to keep during 1882 a complete record of all the cash he received. "I am determined," he wrote, "that it shall go above $10,000 for the year." He kept the record only through October, by which time the dividends from the paper for ten months had reached $34\frac{1}{2}$ per cent. Perhaps Grady felt that he already had carried out his New Year's resolution, for his personal income in this same period had come to a total of $11,803. Of this amount, $1,500 represented salary, $2,713 profit on investments, and $7,590 dividends on his 220 shares of *Constitution* stock. By May 8, 1882 he was able with the aid of loans obtained in Atlanta to pay the remaining $10,000 due Cyrus W. Field.[47]

Even though Grady owned only a minority of the *Constitution's* stock, there seems to have been little conflict between his ideas on public questions and those of Howell, the editor-in-chief and principal stockholder. The two men were warm personal friends and usually saw eye-to-eye on matters of policy. In the only known instance where a serious difference of opinion did develop — on the prohibition question — they solved it amicably by taking no stand on the editorial page

46 The *Reports of the Comptroller General of the State of Georgia* disclose that the largest amount received by the Constitution Publishing Company from the state in any one year for printing and legal advertising was $10,557.17 during the twelve months ending September 30, 1882. The reports reveal that the Constitution Publishing Company was the "State Printer" from 1880 through 1883, and that from 1884 through 1889 the work was done in the Constitution Job Office "for the State Printer."

47 Account Book for 1882, Grady Collection; interview with Cyrus W. Field in Chicago *Daily Inter Ocean,* December 24, 1889.

and allowing each stockholder to express his own views in signed contributions to the news columns.

When Grady and Howell were teamed together, they formed an almost unbeatable combination. Equally energetic and courageous, the one possessed the business experience [48] that still was needed at times to balance the boyish enthusiasm of the other. Undoubtedly the shrewd judgment of the older man on political matters helped in no small measure to make the young "genius of the *Constitution*" also the "Warwick of Georgia politics."

[48] Howell was "a director in every railroad built into Atlanta during the eighties." He also took a leading role in such quasi-public enterprises as the First International Cotton Exposition and, later, the rebuilding of the Kimball House. It would be difficult to prove, however, that his financial interest in these undertakings was large enough to have been a primary factor in determining the editorial policies of the paper. Howell's dominant business interest and chief source of income, like Grady's, was the *Constitution* itself.

CHAPTER TEN

"*Warwick of Georgia Politics*"

So much a part of Georgia was the *Constitution* by 1883 that the establishment on February 24 in this year of a rival daily — the *Atlanta Evening Journal* — had no perceptible effect upon the older paper's growth. An earlier competitor, the *Post-Appeal,* had suspended publication several months before the appearance of the *Journal,* thus giving the *Constitution* another period to entrench itself. The *Evening Herald,* one of the ubiquitous Sam Small's numerous journalistic ventures, also had disappeared after a brief existence. The difficulties of the new *Evening Journal* in overcoming the *Constitution's* lead were augmented by the fact that it, like the old morning *Herald,* was forced at first to do without any regular press-association service. The *Journal* eventually became a success in spite of this handicap, but not until after two other brief-lived papers — the *Evening Star,* which shone for a while later in 1883, and the *Evening Capitol,* which lasted from 1885 into the early part of 1886 — had been eliminated from the Atlanta scene.

The growing number of short editorials and human-interest items on the editorial page of the *Constitution* from 1883 on showed unmistakably that Grady was giving more and more attention to this section of the paper. As a rule, however, he still preferred to express his views through his "Man About Town" column and in his signed, interpretative news stories. On the occasion of the Georgia Sesquicentennial at Savannah in February 1883, for example, he spread over the entire front page a feature article by "H. W. G." on the history of the state and its people.

The Sesquicentennial also was indirectly a means of bring-

ing Grady's powers as a Warwick back into play, for the trip
to Savannah proved to be too much for the invalid Governor
Stephens and led to his death on the night of Saturday, March
4. Inasmuch as it was impossible for the *Constitution* the next
morning to give all the details of the death and the funeral
plans, the paper came out for the first time with a Monday
morning edition. As secretary of the committee on arrangements for the funeral on Wednesday, Grady helped to manage a crowd of sixty thousand persons and to direct a vast procession in which a dozen bands played the "Dead March." He
then turned his attention to the selection of Stephens's successor — a task in which, the *Constitution* said, the chief aim
should be "Democratic harmony at all costs."

When the party convention met in Atlanta on April 10,
there were two leading candidates for the nomination. One
was James S. Boynton, who, as President of the state Senate,
automatically had succeeded to the governorship until the
special election could be held. The other was the Macon
leader Augustus O. Bacon, who had been Speaker of the House
of Representatives for eight of his twelve years in that body.
A third candidate, but not regarded seriously by many delegates, was Henry D. McDaniel, a banker, railroad director,
and member of the House from Walton County. In his ten
years in the legislature, McDaniel had sponsored the act tax-
ing railroads in the same manner as other property, and had
been co-author of the bill creating the state Railroad Commission.

The *Constitution* at first disclaimed supporting any candidate, but it clearly revealed its opposition to Bacon, whom
it accused of using "slander as a weapon for election." Bacon's
chief offense seems to have been his repeated references to the
Constitution as the "tool" of an "Atlanta ring," of which Senator Brown was the alleged head. The *Constitution* retaliated
by charging that Bacon was supported by "a small clique of
reformers," led by the Macon *Daily Telegraph and Messenger*. Similar accusations had been hurled back and forth by the
two papers during the campaign of 1882. Just what Bacon and
his friends proposed to "reform" is difficult to discover, for
there appears to have been little essential difference between

their policies and the *Constitution's* except a desire to put
an Atlanta hierarchy out and a Macon hierarchy in. In fact,
the *Constitution* later charged that, at the very time Bacon
was most loudly denouncing the "Atlanta ring," he was seeking an interview with Senator Brown with the desire of "making terms." [1]

At the opening of the 1883 convention each of the principal contenders possessed certain strategic advantages — Bacon
by virtue of having been in the field with a well-organized
machine for nearly two years, Boynton as the result of already
being in the governor's chair. Neither candidate, however,
had been able to muster a majority of delegates in the county
elections. The first ballot of the convention showed 139 votes
for Boynton, 136 for Bacon, 36 for McDaniel, and 20 for a
fourth candidate, Philip Cook. At the close of the second day
the delegates still were deadlocked, though Bacon had gained
more votes than Boynton and there was growing talk of a
Bacon victory the next morning.

As one of the behind-the-scenes manipulators of anti-Bacon
strength, Grady knew that the outcome of the contest probably would be decided at caucuses to be held during the night
at the Kimball House. The developments of the early evening
were discouraging. First Cook announced his withdrawal
from the race. Next McDaniel sent out word that he would
drop out at the next morning's session. Sixteen of the Mc-
Daniel delegates, led by Judge W. H. Erwin of Athens, were
reported ready to cast their votes for Bacon.

"I was struck squarely between the eyes — the hardest lick
I ever had in politics in my life," wrote Grady in explaining
to the Henry Hunter Smiths, who were his house guests, why
he did not return home that night from the hotel. "I was
astonished, sore at heart, and almost dismayed. It was the first
time I ever encountered treachery flagrant and unblushing.
. . . To have had Bacon elected by the *Tel. and Mess.* would
have disgraced me and hurt me. Almost everybody gave it up

[1] *Constitution*, June 20, 1886. Unless otherwise indicated, the account that
follows is based upon the reports of the *Constitution* and the Macon *Daily
Telegraph and Messenger* for April 1883, together with information obtained
in interviews with Judge John S. Candler, Judge Hugh M. Dorsey, and Judge
Richard B. Russell, Sr.

but me. But I determined to die with it if necessary. You both know how bad I wanted to be with you, and there I was at the hotel with the very ground slipping from under my very feet — fighting against odds and a hopeless fight. But I tell you now that if I had come home that night Bacon would have been Governor. . . ." [2]

What Grady had done was to persuade Judge Rufus T. Dorsey, leader of the Boynton forces, to throw the Boynton votes to McDaniel rather than to allow the McDaniel votes to go to Bacon. Under the strategy agreed upon for the next day, one of Grady's friends introduced a motion referring the question of the nomination to a committee of eighteen members, six to be appointed by Bacon, six by Boynton, four by McDaniel, and two by Cook. Despite the opposition of the Bacon leaders, who saw that this plan gave the McDaniel group the balance of power, the motion was adopted.

When the committee assembled, McDaniel requested that his name be withdrawn. The conferees thereupon decided to force a show-down between the two principal candidates. Nine votes had been cast for Bacon and only eight for Boynton when the anti-Baconites pulled their trump card. Realizing now that Boynton could not win, Judge Dorsey gained the floor to announce that the six Boynton men were switching their votes to McDaniel. With McDaniel's victory thus assured by a majority of ten to eight, his four members of the committee promptly put him back in the race, and he received the nomination.

In the special election ten days later, McDaniel was unopposed. He was praised by the *Constitution* as a "practical man" who would "administer the state's affairs as a skillful financier would handle the affairs of a great institution." McDaniel was indeed to be an able executive — so able, in fact, that no one would think it worth while to oppose him for re-election the following year. Woodrow Wilson, who watched the inaugural crowds from his office opposite the state Capitol, quoted a wag as saying that Georgia was "replacing a governor who could not walk with one who could not talk" — referring to the fact that Stephens was an invalid and Mc-

2 To Estelle Cuyler Smith, May 18, 1883, Grady Collection.

Daniel a stutterer. But the future President also regarded the new Governor as "sound, steady, sensible — not remarkable except for honesty — always remarkable in a latter day politician." [3]

Scarcely was the election over when Grady, in the company of Senator Brown, was off for south Georgia to write of the fortunes being made by farmers using modern methods in the raising of truck and fruit. The nature of his articles may be indicated by a few of the titles: "Treasure Truck," "Through Melon Land," "The Savings of Georgia Farmers," "The Largest Strawberry Farm in the State," "Berries and Politics," and "The LeConte Pear." Simultaneously the *Constitution* announced that it henceforth would publish daily telegraphic reports on the shipment of produce from Georgia, together with quotations from all the principal produce markets.

After the trip to the agricultural sections and a subsequent visit to Anniston, Alabama, to describe the progress of that thriving new town, Grady left with his family for another vacation at the seashore. So thoroughly had he enjoyed his outing at the coast in 1882 that he now interested a party of some sixty Atlantans in going to Cape May, New Jersey. Chartering two special Pullman cars, the Georgians went by way of Washington and Philadelphia and arrived on August 1 at the New Jersey resort. For the next two weeks Grady was the leader in every kind of boyish fun — at the dining table, in the ballroom, on the beach, and in the surf. One of the souvenir photographs shows him, clad in his bathing suit, holding the hands of two ladies similarly attired. Such a pose was quite unconventional for that day, but Grady had prearranged with the photographer to snap it while the entire party was in a beach studio for a group picture.

In the early morning hours of Sunday, August 12 — the day before Grady and his party left Cape May — the Kimball House, the center of Atlanta's political and social life, burned to the ground. The *Constitution* issued an extra on Sunday and came out with a special Monday edition giving further details. When Grady returned several days later, he applied

[3] Ray S. Baker: *Woodrow Wilson: Life and Letters* (New York, 1927), I, 155–6.

himself energetically to the campaign for stock subscriptions
to rebuild the hotel. Evan P. Howell was elected president of
the new Kimball House Company, and H. I. Kimball, the
promoter-builder extraordinary, was called back from Chicago to direct the undertaking. General Toombs was so delighted by this quick action that he greeted even Kimball
heartily and made the largest subscription — in excess of
$100,000 — to the $657,000 enterprise.[4] Soon a far more elaborate Kimball House than the old was rising skyward.

When the General Assembly convened in the fall, the members found themselves somewhat lost without the hotel that
had been the setting of so many political battles. But, catch-
ing the building fever themselves, the legislators appropriated
$1,000,000 for the erection of a new Capitol, something which
the *Constitution* had been advocating for more than two years.
Governor McDaniel became chairman and Howell a member
of the building commission, which was to go down in Georgia
history with the unusual distinction of completing its project
within the original appropriation.[5]

At the end of the year both the new Capitol and the Kimball House were listed by the *Constitution* as improvements
which it had been "first in promoting." Other civic accom-
plishments for which it took credit in 1883 were a comprehensive system of street improvement, organization of the Chamber of Commerce on a "business basis," and the beginning of
work on Atlanta's first city park. The new year dawned with
Grady using the columns of the paper in a cause even dearer
to his heart — the raising of funds to provide food, clothing,
and fuel for the city's poor, many of whom were suffering
acutely on account of a sudden spell of zero weather.

When the cold spell came on, Grady immediately divided
the city into districts and sent one member of the staff into
each district to find out exactly what cases needed relief. He
took one district himself and held a consultation with the
Mayor at midnight over the more serious cases. The next
morning the *Constitution* carried a news story on the results
of its reportorial survey and a stirring appeal for contribu-

---

[4] *Constitution*, July 15, 1884, January 31, 1889.
[5] Knight: *Reminiscences*, II, 534.

tions. But Grady did not depend upon printed appeals alone. With the aid of the energetic Kimball, he called throughout the night and morning upon merchants for definite gifts of coal, clothing, food, medicines, and other supplies. "Grady had a great way of deciding what his friends should give and he never begged for it," said a member of his staff. "Whenever he laid down his assessment, it was forthcoming without complaint or murmuring."

By eight o'clock the next morning the street in front of the *Constitution* office was piled "twenty feet high with the contributions for the needy, and every detail of transportation had been attended to. The setting sun that day found no case worthy of relief that had not been relieved." [6]

2

Although Grady ordinarily left the writing of editorials on national and international affairs to Finch and Harris, he reserved for himself the treatment of events in which he was particularly interested. A case in point was his editorial in the fall of 1883 commenting on the decision of the Supreme Court whereby the Civil Rights Act of 1875 was declared unconstitutional. Some extremists thought the overthrow of this act would bring about "a general retrogression on the race question," while other "fanatics" hoped the Constitution would be further amended to re-establish what the Court had wiped out. Declaring both of these views to be wrong, Grady reiterated his own ideas under the heading: "Where to Draw the Line" — one of the few editorials of these years that he regarded highly enough to save in his scrapbook:

The line has been drawn just where it should be. Just where nature drew it, and where justice commends. The negro is entitled to his freedom, his franchise, to full and equal legal rights, to his share in the privileges of the government and to such share in its administration as his integrity and intelligence will justify. This he ought to have and he must have. Social equality he can never

6 *Constitution*, January 6, 8, 1884; T. W. Reed, op. cit., p. 11; Harris, pp. 37-8.

have. He does not have it in the north, or in the east, or in the west. On one pretext or another he is kept out of hotels, theaters, schools and restaurants, north as well as south.

The truth is, the negro does not want social equality. He prefers his own hotels, his own societies, his own military companies, his own place in the theater. He is uncomfortable and ill at ease when he is forced anywhere else. Even on the railroads he prefers his own car, if he can be secure from the intrusion of disorderly persons. It is best, for his sake, as well as for general peace and harmony, that he should in all these things have separate accommodation.

Grady's later contribution to the *Century* magazine, entitled: "In Plain Black and White: A Reply to Mr. Cable," was simply an elaboration of these same views. George W. Cable, the Louisiana novelist, had come out in opposition to the racial segregation laws which were being enacted in the South following the overthrow of the Civil Rights Act. In his reply, Grady declared that Cable mistook the temper of the Southern people if he thought they ever would agree to the social intermingling of blacks and whites. "The intelligence of both races," he asserted, "is moving further away from that proposition every day."

Cable had attributed segregation to prejudice; Grady thought it was instinctive and "would assuredly develop" in any community where there were large numbers of both blacks and whites. But, "whether the race feeling is instinct or prejudice," he could reach "but one conclusion: the white and black races in the South must walk apart. Concurrent their courses may go — ought to go — will go — but separate. If instinct did not make this plain in a flash, reason would spell it out letter by letter."

Nevertheless, Grady agreed fully with Cable that it was "manifestly unfair to make a negro pay as much for a railroad ticket as a white man pays, and then force him to accept inferior accommodations," or to make him attend schools that did not afford "perfect equality in grade and opportunity." [7]

In accordance with this policy of "separate but equal" ac-

<hr/>

[7] Cable's article appeared in the *Century* for January 1885; Grady's reply was published in the April issue of the same year (XXIX, 909–17).

commodations for both races, which Grady consistently had advocated since his *Herald* days, the *Constitution* repeatedly urged federal aid for the improvement of Negro schools in the South. Lack of education, it contended, was causing the very conditions which were being cited by others as proof that the Negro was incapable of properly using education. "If education of the negro is not the chief problem that confronts the white people of the south," it declared, "then there is no other conceivable solution and there is nothing ahead but political chaos and demoralization." [8]

Another national issue frequently discussed by Grady both in signed articles and in editorials was the tariff. This was a matter of economic policy which bore a definite relation to his major interest: the economic rehabilitation of the South. The cotton economy of the old South had benefited by free trade, but Grady believed that the industries and many of the agricultural pursuits of the New South, such as the cultivation of rice along the Georgia coast, were profiting by protection. From a position which in 1880 had been even closer to free trade than the "tariff-for-revenue-only" plank of the Democratic Party in that year, the *Constitution* by 1884 had shifted gradually to the advocacy of a tariff "based on reason and common sense." The idea of free trade was "perfect so far as the argument went," the paper asserted, but conditions would "have to undergo a slow but complete revolution" before the tariff could be abolished.

Such a position naturally brought Grady into conflict with Henry Watterson of the Louisville *Courier-Journal*, the recognized proponent of free trade. In Watterson's eyes the *Constitution* had become a "Republican" paper.[9]

But the tariff was not yet the burning issue it was to be several years hence, and Grady's advocacy of "a happy medium between the two extremes of free-trade and ultra-protection" was thoroughly in accord with the complacent spirit of the eighties. The presidential campaign of 1884 was to be fought

[8] February 18, 1883. This and many other editorials on this same theme were written by Harris, according to Julia C. Harris: *Joel Chandler Harris: Editor and Essayist* (Chapel Hill, 1931), p. 103.

[9] Cited in *Constitution*, January 22, 1884.

not on the tariff issue, as both Grady and Watterson at first thought, but primarily on the question of the relative integrity of the two candidates.

Six months before the national conventions Grady predicted that James G. Blaine would be the Republican nominee. To combat Blaine, who faced violent opposition even in his own party because of his questionable dealings with the railroads and his unsatisfactory position on civil service, the *Constitution* regarded it essential that the Democrats nominate a man of the highest character. Whereas in 1880 the paper had urged Tilden to withdraw in order to bring about Democratic harmony in New York, it now praised him as the only man who could unite the party nationally. In the South especially Tilden was "a martyr awaiting vindication" who could command wide support.

It was obviously to prevent a mad scramble by other candidates for Southern votes that the paper persisted in backing Tilden, even after an interview by one of its own reporters revealed that he was too feeble to wage a campaign for the presidency. The interview was obtained by Evan P. Howell's twenty-year-old son, Clark, who, after graduating from the University of Georgia in 1883, had gone North to gain practical newspaper experience on the *New York Times* and the *Philadelphia Press*. Armed with letters of introduction from Senators Brown and Colquitt, young Howell called on Tilden and obtained his authorized statement that he was physically unable to run — a statement which the reporter found it easy to believe after seeing the old man's quivering and emaciated form. While glorying in its correspondent's scoop, the *Constitution* declared that it did not despair of Tilden's accepting the nomination, and that the election of delegates pledged to him was the only hope of uniting the party.

Behind the scenes, of course, feverish jockeying was going on among those who recognized the fact of Tilden's incapacity and who desired some particular candidate to be the beneficiary of his mounting strength in the convention. One of these was Cyrus W. Field, Tilden's neighbor and one-time partner. About the middle of May, General Gordon, then in New York, wired Grady to ask if he could come to that city, "your expenses being paid." Apparently Grady did not reply, for several days later Gordon wrote that the telegram had been sent at the request of Cyrus Field, who "asked me to get you to come to New York to see him." According to Gordon, Field had been opposed to his brother Stephen's again seeking the nomination for the presidency, but Roscoe Conkling, the New York Republican leader, now "had assured him that if Judge Field were nominated by the Democrats, he, Conkling, would take the stump for him." Cyrus Field also was quoted as saying that "three of the richest Republicans of the U. S. had agreed if Judge Field were nominated to furnish all the money necessary to give him an overwhelming election." [10]

Field's attempt to enlist the Atlanta editor's influence for his brother was in vain, for Grady did not accept the invitation to go to New York. Instead, immediately after Tilden's formal refusal to run, the *Constitution* endorsed Governor Grover Cleveland of New York, and a few days later the Tilden-pledged delegates to the Democratic state convention followed suit. The wisdom of Grady's judgment was to be demonstrated not only by Cleveland's subsequent record but also by the fact that the tactless "feast of the money kings," arranged by Field in support of Blaine, contributed to the Republican defeat. Justice Field's own allegiance to the "money kings" became so evident in later years that the *Constitution* referred to one manifestation of it as "a disgrace to the country and to the judiciary." [11]

Grady and Clark Howell went to Chicago for the Republican convention in June and the Democratic convention in July, covering both for the *Constitution* over a special leased wire. Later, while the Cleveland-Blaine campaign was at its height, the managing editor made a visit to New York City. Here he was joined for dinner one evening by a group of New England Democrats including Thomas M. Waller, Governor of Connecticut; John Boyle O'Reilly, poet, journalist, and soldier of fortune; and Patrick Collins, former Congressman and later Mayor of Boston. To these three men Grady an-

[10] John B. Gordon to H. W. G., May 17, 1884, Gordon Papers.
[11] Allan Nevins: *Grover Cleveland* (New York, 1934) , pp. 182–3; Felton, op. cit., p. 131.

nounced his intention of declaring a "sunshine holiday" in Atlanta when Cleveland was elected.[12]

Grady had little opportunity to do any active campaigning in Georgia, for it was a foregone conclusion that the Democrats would carry the South. A week before the election, however, he presided at a mass meeting of Atlanta Democrats. His introduction of Senator Brown as "one whose foresights were better than most men's hindsights" brought a tumultuous response which indicated that all factions were forgetting their differences in the flush of approaching national victory. The rally was a love feast which forecast Brown's easy re-election to the Senate a few weeks later.

Although the national election of Tuesday, November 4, actually remained in doubt for three days, the *Constitution* came out the next morning with headlines and news stories announcing "VICTORY! Cleveland is elected — the solid north is broken — the sectional lines are obliterated." Instead of relying on the press association reports, Grady had obtained estimates at five fifteen that morning from the leading New York newspapers, from the national committees, from the doubtful states, and from Cleveland himself. On the strength of these estimates, the *Constitution* asserted positively that the Democrats had won.

Each day and night until all doubt was removed, however, the *Constitution* kept open house at its new building, which recently had been occupied. The legislature was in session, and the legislators flocked into Grady's office, where the latest news was read aloud as it came over the wire.

Shortly before ten o'clock Friday morning, word was received that the Republicans had conceded defeat. The *Constitution's* brass cannon (a gift to Grady) boomed forth a signal to the city, and the excited Democrats gathered to celebrate. Elected "marshal of the day," Grady quickly appointed committees on music, bloody shirts, bonfires, and parade. In less than an hour several thousand persons were in line.

At the head of the procession were two volunteer drummers, following whom came Marshal Grady, his hat draped with a silk American flag. Behind him was the standard-

[12] Clipping, Grady Scrapbooks.

bearer, holding aloft another large flag. Next in line came the "bloody-shirt bearers" — men carrying red shirts stretched on cross poles with placards reading "We are going to burn this!" Following these were "about one thousand men bearing small flags," then fifty others bearing an immense flag stretched as a canopy. A brass band soon found a place in the parade, followed by "an endless line" of cheering men and boys.

Through Atlanta's main business streets the exultant procession moved until it reached the Capitol, where it "poured into the corridor like a torrent." When the marchers reached the door of the House of Representatives, Grady brushed by the doorkeeper, advanced down the main aisle, and with beaming face announced: "Mr. Speaker! A message from the American people." The House rose, and the column marched toward the Speaker's stand, with drums beating and colors flying. Mounting the rostrum, Grady seized the gavel from the hands of the presiding officer. He rapped for order, then proclaimed: "In the name of God and the American people, I declare this House adjourned to celebrate the election of Grover Cleveland, the first Democratic President in twenty-four years!"

The House paused before adjourning only long enough to adopt a resolution of congratulations to Cleveland and Hendricks. Loud calls then arose for Grady, but he already had gone to adjourn the Senate in the same Cromwellian manner and to escort Governor McDaniel to the capitol steps for a speech. While the bloody shirts were being burned, Atlanta orators waxed eloquent with phrases such as those of the "honey-tongued old war-horse" Tom Hardeman, who, referring to the carpetbaggers, exclaimed: "The Lord gave and the Lord hath taken away; blessed be the name of the Lord!"

That night the demonstration was intensified. "Never in the history of the city has there been seen anything that could compare with the outpouring of wildly enthusiastic democrats," reported the *Constitution*. Over a thousand torches were lighted and "the streets were filled with crackling bonfires, until the scene was like unto a view of the infernal regions. Everywhere was one shrieking mass, while shouts rent the air and horns shrieked and drums beat and bands played."

In front of the customs house Grady introduced Senators Brown and Colquitt and other dignitaries for speeches. When the last man had finished, there were again cries for Grady, but he "had escaped by the back door and was gone." Before he went home, however, he found time to send telegrams to his friends Waller, Collins, and O'Reilly in New England announcing that Georgia was taking a "sunshine holiday." [13]

Grady's action in "adjourning" the legislature was somewhat symbolic of the place he now held in the Democratic councils of Georgia and the nation. By using Tilden as a stalking-horse to hold the Southern votes in line, the editors of the *Constitution* had placed themselves in a most favorable light with the Cleveland administration, which definitely was seeking to distribute patronage in the South "in such a fashion as to discourage the Bourbon or unreconstructed element and bring forward younger men" like Grady. Consequently, when Atlanta was visited late in November by Samuel J. Randall, the Pennsylvania Congressman credited with "swinging the convention" to Cleveland, the three men serving as his hosts were Brown, Howell, and Grady. Two months later, when the new Vice President, Thomas A. Hendricks, came to the city, the person closest to his elbow at every turn was the *Constitution's* managing editor.[14]

Late in March 1885 Grady went to the White House for a conference with Cleveland himself. "I went in, feeling that at last the people had come together in peace and good will," he wrote. The new President impressed him as being "determined to give the country an efficient, economical, and honest government, administered on simple business principles — and above all to wipe out the last trace of sectional bitterness." [15]

3

Fully in keeping with the growing prestige of the *Constitution* was the new building, which was completed in August

13 *Constitution*, November 5–9, 1884; clippings, Grady Scrapbooks; Harris, pp. 610–11.
14 *Constitution*, November 28, 1884, February 5, 1885; Nevins: *Cleveland*, p. 323.
15 *Constitution*, April 5, 1885.

MEN WHO RULED GEORGIA IN THE EIGHTIES

The picture of Grady (upper right) is said by many of his friends to be the most lifelike in existence. This photograph was taken on the steps of Evan P. Howell's residence on the day the State Capitol Commission formally accepted the new building from the contractors. In the photograph are shown, from left to right, in first row: Henry D. McDaniel, Governor 1883-86; General Phil Cook; General John B. Gordon, Governor 1886-90. On second step: General E. P. Alexander. On third step, arms folded, W. W. Thomas. On fourth step, center, Evan P. Howell, editor-in-chief of the "Constitution," and right, Tom Glenn, Mayor of Atlanta 1888-89. On fifth step, W. H. ("Tip") Harrison (arm across breast) and A. L. Miller (hand in pocket). On sixth step, W. B. Miles, contractor for the capitol. At the upper left, with his hand on the watch chain, is George W. Adair. The bald-headed man with side whiskers, at top center, is W. A. Hemphill, business manager of the "Constitution." Others in the picture were connected with the building operations.

ASSOCIATES OF GRADY ON THE *CONSTITUTION*

This photograph, taken in the editorial rooms soon after Grady's death, shows five men who were thrown closely with him in the late eighties. From left to right, seated, are Clark Howell, who succeeded Grady as managing editor, and Joel Chandler Harris; standing are Wallace P. Reed, J. K. Ohl (city editor), and Frank L. Stanton. Later famous for his "Just from Georgia" column, Stanton was brought on the staff by Harris in the fall of 1889. Note the picture of Grady on Howell's desk.

From a photograph in the Joel Chandler Harris Collection

1884 at a cost of $100,000. Equipped with modern conveniences such as electric light, steam heat, and elevators, it was described as "the finest newspaper plant south of Ohio." Hardly was the staff settled when it put the new $27,500 perfecting press to a test by printing a "trade edition" of forty-four pages, which was acclaimed as the largest paper ever published in America. It also announced that it would "close the last gap between the *Constitution* and other metropolitan papers" by publishing a regular Monday morning edition. When Joseph Pulitzer's highly successful New York *World* thereupon greeted the *Constitution* as "the *World* of the South," Grady modestly replied by terming the *World* "the *Constitution* of the North."

On the first floor of the new building were the business quarters, where Howell's office was located. Grady's office was on the fourth floor. It opened on the one side into a reception hall leading into the general news room, and on the other into the library workshop of the two editorial-writers, Finch and Harris.

By April 1885 Grady's activities had increased to such an extent that it was necessary for him to employ a private secretary. Upon the recommendation of Clark Howell, who was now night editor, he gave the position to James R. Holliday, who not only knew shorthand but also had learned to manipulate one of the first typewriters in Atlanta. Grady's first dictated letter, Holliday recalls, was addressed to Frank H. Siddall, the Philadelphia soap millionaire, and sought an advertising contract. It ended with the phrase "While there's life there's soap."

Evidently the letter produced results, for the *Constitution* soon appeared with a full-page advertisement for Siddall's soap. The contract obtained by Grady totaled $12,000 — the largest in the paper's history.[16]

Grady's practice henceforth was to dictate his letters from nine to ten, the first hour of his working day, and then to throw open the door of his office to anyone who wished to see him. His own articles he preferred to write in longhand, although occasionally he did dictate a news story or editorial. In

16 Ibid., June 23, 1885.

spite of constant interruptions he turned out an amazing amount of copy. He had a remarkable facility for getting information out of his visitors, and it was rarely that anyone left his office without yielding an item for some part of the paper.[17]

In May 1885 the *Constitution* announced the opening of the formal campaign for funds to erect a new building for the Young Men's Christian Association, with Grady as chairman of the building committee. Within ten days more than $60,-000 had been subscribed, and at the end of two weeks the goal of $75,000 had been passed. The *Constitution* ran editorials daily on the value of the Y.M.C.A. and the need for the new building, but again it was the news columns and Grady's organizing skill that had the most telling effect. Under his Aladdin's touch, the homes of prominent Atlanta citizens — the Inmans, the Adairs, the Englishes, the Hemphills, the Hills — were thrown open to the public nightly for "parlor conferences" at which reports were made on the gifts received during the day. The *Constitution* printed the name of every subscriber with the amount of his gift, a special division of the subscription list being headed "Mothers, Wives, and Sisters." This latter group responded with particular enthusiasm to the frequent rendition by a visiting tenor of "Where Is My Wandering Boy Tonight?"

Another movement in which Grady was leader came to a climax in the summer of 1885 with the passage by the General Assembly of a bill authorizing the establishment of a state technological school. Since 1882 the *Constitution* had carried editorial upon editorial urging such a school; it was, in Grady's opinion, imperative to the industrial development of the state. Once the school had been authorized, Grady urged that the institution be located in Atlanta, close to the principal manufacturing enterprises, rather than in Athens or Macon. As a result of a meeting held in his office, more than $100,000 was raised as an inducement to locate the school in Atlanta. The city's case was presented to the legislative commission by Grady himself in a speech which, together with the greater amount of money provided, left no doubt that At-

17 Information from J. R. Holliday and Walter G. Cooper.

lanta would be the home of the new Georgia School of Technology.[18]

Following the death of General Grant in July, Grady once
more demonstrated his willingness to forgive a one-time foe
of the South. Overlooking Grant's shortcomings as President,
Grady based his tribute to the dead hero of the North upon
an incident which, he knew, would strike a chord of appreciation in the heart of every Southerner. Under the heading: "Atlanta's Silent Visitor," he described how Grant had
made a secret visit to Atlanta during his tour of the South in
the fall of 1865 and had returned to Washington with the report that the "mass of the thinking people of the South accept
the present situation in good faith." The "calm judgment" of
that report, declared Grady, "broke the full force of the cruel
legislation then in progress." [19]

Later in the year, when General Toombs died, Grady again
showed that he could make full allowance for the pathetic
failings of a great man, even one who had attacked him and
his newspaper more than once. His editorial paying respect to
the rugged virtues of Toombs has been admired perhaps as
much as any newspaper article he ever wrote:

The kingliest of Georgians is dead!
The rich life, riotous in affluence, is spent at last. The deeps
through which it swept in thunderous majesty and the shoals over
which it tumbled noisily are drained and bare.
Bob Toombs is no more!
Quenched is the imperious life. Stilled is the mighty heart.
Gone, the dauntless spirit. At rest, the turbulent emotions. Pulse-
less, the splendid form.
If God ever made the body of mortal man to shine with the hope
and inspiration of immortality, surely here it was. In the splendor
of his beauty, in the mightiness of his strength, in the vitality that
sparkled in his eyes and rushed through his veins, in the ease with
which he conquered and the heights to which he soared, in the
scope and freedom and boundless comprehension of his powers

[18] *Constitution*, July 30, 1885, October 1–21, 1886.
[19] Ibid., August 2, 1885. The editorial is reprinted in Allan Nevins: *American Press Opinion, Washington to Coolidge* (Boston, 1928) , pp. 383–5.

there was little suggestion of decay. Dazzled by his kingly beauty and majesty one might have said: "Surely he will conquer death!"

But the course of nature is unchangeable. Even the eagle's wings grow weary and are folded, and the strong man totters to the welcome grave. The glory fades from the cheek and the light dies in the eye. The majesty departs from the pallid brow, and the rich blood falters in the veins. The tongue that summoned forty million people to war babbles unmeaningly in its hollow cavern. The fingers that easily split this continent in two beat the air pitifully for support and guidance. The mighty spirit that bent senators to its will and that forged earth's bloodiest revolution, sicklied o'er at last with uplifting shadows, creeps aimlessly within the walls of memory, and weeps or laughs alike within itself.

Then God, in his wise and infinite mercy, comes and ends it all! His gentle hands clasp the wandering fingers. His kiss touches the maundering lips. There is peace at last. Georgia's glorious son sleeps. The unforgiven rebel awaits, in unbroken stillness, the final judgment of God. And death, touching the tranquil face with his unspeakable solemnity, revives therein something of the majesty and beauty of youth, that his people, gazing through the mist of tears, may see him last as they loved him best, when he stood among them in his kingly splendor.[20]

Far more characteristic than these eulogies of the dead, however, was Grady's zest for life, as manifested in his boyish love for sports. When John L. Sullivan came to Atlanta to give an exhibition of boxing, the Gradys, father and son, had ringside seats. In 1884 the *Constitution* helped to organize an Athletic Club to be "the patron of all manly sports" and to organize teams for competition with those of other cities. Declaring that his reporters were the greatest "leg artists" in the world, Grady personally promoted walking matches between representatives of the *Constitution* and its principal rivals, the *Evening Journal* and the Macon *Telegraph and Messenger*. Later he offered the prizes in a bicycle race from Atlanta to Fairburn, a distance of some twenty miles. The course of the race ran close to the railroad tracks, and a crowd of more than a thousand persons watched the event from a train of open cars. Finally, in the spring of 1885, Grady inspired the

[20] *Constitution,* December 16, 1885.

organization of Atlanta's first professional baseball club and became the first president of the Southern League, composed of teams in Atlanta and seven other Southern cities.[21]

Baseball fans in those early days of the game were willing to fight and bleed for the home club, according to a member of a Montgomery team that played Atlanta in the eighties. It was a matter of civic pride.

"There was a close decision against Atlanta at second base," recalled this player. "In a second the fans were all over the field. They weren't only after the umpire. They were after us. They looked on visiting players as their natural enemies. They were mad and had, not pop bottles, but sticks and knives and guns. The Montgomery team was scared stiff until Grady mounted a box, raised a hand, and began talking. He appealed to the sportsmanship of the mob and made the rioters feel ashamed of themselves. In two minutes the crowd had begun to file back to the grandstand." [22]

Grady personally covered the home games for the *Constitution*. He always took his secretary, Holliday, with him to the baseball park on North Avenue, just a short distance beyond his own home. After the game the two would return by the house and Grady would dictate the story that the secretary later transcribed at the *Constitution* office. "Once I became confused in my notes and wrote a story considerably different from the one he dictated," confesses Holliday. "But Mr. Grady had no words of criticism the next morning — only a curious smile and a hearty laugh."

4

As the election year of 1886 rolled around, Grady and his political friends found themselves without a candidate of sufficient strength to compete successfully with Augustus O. Bacon for the gubernatorial nomination. Still smarting under the McDaniel coup of 1883, the former Speaker of the House had been building up his organization continuously since that time. Consequently he had some fifteen hundred former

[21] Ibid., April 2, 1935 (article by Ralph McGill on the fiftieth anniversary of J. R. Holliday's connection with the paper).
[22] Interview with Bill Stickney in *Constitution*, May 25, 1921.

members of the legislature, scattered in every county of the state, working for him.

The county delegations to the Democratic state convention were selected in various ways — some by a county mass meeting or convention, some by a county executive committee, and only a very few by an actual vote of the people. Since each county acted "when and as" the controlling powers in that county decided, Bacon's following among the seasoned county politicians gave him a tremendous advantage. Two counties already had instructed their delegations to vote for the Macon candidate when Grady informed his intimate friends of his "sure-fire" plan to elect former Senator Gordon as governor.[23]

For several years the Confederate hero had had a checkered career in private business. In 1883 he had resigned the presidency of the Georgia Pacific Railroad and had sold his interest therein, presumably at a profit of some $200,000. Soon afterward, however, he had become involved in a Florida development scheme, the International Railroad & Steamship Company, which had gone on the rocks with disaster to the fortunes of the General as well as of his investors. In 1884 his reputation had suffered another blow from the publication of the Collis P. Huntington letters, which revealed that Gordon during his first term in the Senate had favored legislation sought by Huntington's Pacific railroad interests and hence had been mentioned by the promoter as "one of our men." Since the collapse of the Florida bubble the General had spent much of his time in New York, trying to recoup his losses, but he was known to be "somewhat out at the elbow" and eager to return to public life. The first step in Grady's program, therefore, was to put the General in a new suit and make him available as a candidate.

The spring of 1886 was a propitious time for such a move,

[23] Interview with H. W. G. in New York *Mail and Express*, [July 1886], Grady Scrapbooks; address by R. J. Guinn in *Editor's Forum*, VIII (July 1936), 7. The account that follows is based primarily upon the files of the *Constitution*, the *Macon Telegraph*, and the *Columbus Enquirer-Sun* for May–July, 1886, and upon interviews with Clark Howell, J. R. Holliday, Jack Spalding, and Judge John S. Candler. Cf. Woodward, op. cit., pp. 62–3, 120–1, and Felton, op. cit., pp. 507–14.

inasmuch as Gordon already was scheduled to deliver an address late in April at the laying of the cornerstone to a Confederate memorial in Montgomery, Alabama. Jefferson Davis, now gray and feeble, also had accepted an invitation to be present at this same ceremony. Probably no two living men could awaken more tender memories of the Lost Cause than these. Grady determined to bring them on to Atlanta.

The statue of Benjamin H. Hill was nearing completion, and the monument committee easily was persuaded to invite Davis to extend his trip from Montgomery to Atlanta for the unveiling. Although the correspondence [24] and advance publicity mentioned only that Davis would be the central figure on this occasion, Grady knew that he could arrange for Gordon to be in evidence whenever the strategy called for it. He was confident, too, that the thousands of veterans who would turn out to greet the former President could be depended upon to respond with enthusiasm to Gordon. Those veterans could determine the outcome of any political battle in Georgia.

By the time the *Constitution* came out with its special "Davis Issue" of April 25, the stage was set. Davis had accepted the invitation to come to Atlanta and to speak briefly at the unveiling. Grady had refused to be the principal speaker, arranging instead that this honor go to a leading Baconite, J. C. C. Black of Augusta. This gave the occasion an appropriate non-political atmosphere and hence assured a larger attendance. For himself Grady chose the post, far more important for his purposes, of master of ceremonies.

To cover the speeches of Davis and Gordon in Montgomery, Grady dispatched one of the *Constitution's* most colorful writers, P. J. ("Pea Jay") Moran. After "H. W. G." and a committee of Atlantans arrived in two private cars to escort Davis back to Georgia, "Pea Jay's" accounts were supplemented with sidelights by the managing editor himself. The receptions given Davis and Gordon at every stop between Montgomery and Atlanta were reported in detail on the front

[24] H. W. G. and R. D. Spalding to Davis, March 19–27, 1886, in *Jefferson Davis, Constitutionalist: His Letters, Papers and Speeches*, ed. by Dunbar Rowland (Jackson, Miss., 1923), IX, 409–13.

page of the *Constitution*. Urged by Gordon not to overtax himself by too many speeches, Davis placed his hand on the General's shoulder at Auburn, Alabama, and said: "This is my Aaron; let him speak for me." When the train reached Atlanta, therefore, it was Gordon who responded, at Davis's request, to the welcoming throng.

"In no other southern city was there ever such an overwhelming outpouring of the populace," reported the *Constitution* of the scenes surrounding the unveiling of the Hill monument on the next day. Most of Atlanta's 40,000 population turned out; in addition, trains brought an estimated 50,-000 persons from outside the city. Long columns of Confederate veterans, led by bands from various sections of the state, marched in almost endless procession to the site of the shrouded statue at the intersection of Peachtree, West Peachtree, and Baker Streets. School children scattered flowers in Davis's pathway as his carriage, drawn by four white horses, moved through the downtown district to the monument site.

The most dramatic moment in the long and tedious ceremony was not on the program — that is, not so far as the crowd had been informed. After the prayer, Grady introduced Dr. R. D. Spalding, chairman of the Hill Monument Committee, who presented the statue, and Governor McDaniel, who received it on behalf of the state. Then, just before Black was about to begin the main address, "a solitary horseman rode out of Peachtree Street toward the monument. He was mounted on a fine horse and wore the uniform of a lieutenant general of the Confederate Army." It was General Longstreet, whom Grady had befriended several years earlier by his articles explaining the General's course at Gettysburg. The General's alliance with the Republicans during Reconstruction had estranged him from Davis, but now he dismounted, climbed the steps of the platform, and walked straight toward his former chief. Davis rose, "threw his arms around the General's neck, and embraced him affectionately." Throughout Black's eulogy of Hill, the Confederate leaders sat side by side.[25]

Such was the setting when Grady, after the main speech, in-

25 Walter G. Cooper: *History of Fulton County* (Atlanta, 1934) , pp. 733–4.

troduced the "first and last president" of the Confederacy. "Other leaders have had their triumphs," he said, turning to Davis. "Conquerors have won crowns, and honors have been piled on the victors of earth's great battles, but never yet, sir, came man to more loving people. . . . This moment, in this blessed Easter week, witnessing the resurrection of these memories that for twenty years have been buried in our hearts, has given us the best Easter that we have seen since Christ was risen from the dead."

After Davis had finished his brief remarks and the unveiling was ended, there were many cries for Gordon, but "he could not be found." He had marched with his former soldiers in the procession and was "lost" somewhere in the vast audience.

Gordon's moment came later in the day. As the veterans milled through the Kimball House that afternoon, M. Dwinell, Grady's friend and former employer in Rome, jumped on a chair in the balcony overlooking the main lobby. Shouting for attention, he proposed a speech at eight o'clock that night by General Gordon. There were loud cries of "Aye! Aye!" Dwinell then raised his hat in the air and shouted: "Gordon! Gordon! Gordon!"

Soon Gordon appeared and mounted the chair vacated by Dwinell.

"My friends," he said. "This is the happiest day of my life. My heart is full and it is all yours." He declined, however, to speak that night.

Hardly had the General concluded his remarks when angry protests arose from certain Bacon supporters. One of the most vocal shook his fist at the crowd in the lobby and shouted that he had not come to Atlanta for a political demonstration. But Gordon's friends leaped to the defense, and the Baconite went down with a broken nose after passing the lie to a Gordon man who accused him of having served in the "commissary" rather than in the "fighting branch" of the Confederate Army. Excited conversation, spreading through the hotel and into the streets, quickly indicated that both sides now expected Gordon to be Bacon's opponent in the gubernatorial race.

Unable to restrain his enthusiasm any longer, Grady called to a friend, W. H. ("Tip") Harrison, in the hotel: "Tip, Confederate money will be good before midnight!" [26]

Whether Grady had anticipated it or not, this revival of Confederate spirit also brought repercussions from the North. A crowd in Albany, New York, sang "We'll hang Jeff Davis to a sour apple tree," while irate citizens in an Ohio town actually did hang the former Confederate President in effigy. The *New-York Tribune* attacked Davis as an "unrepentant old villain and Union-hater." Other Northern papers seized upon such incidents as Longstreet's appearance in Confederate uniform and Grady's reference to "the best Easter . . . since Christ was risen from the dead" as indications of a Southern desire to "strike for lost empire and revenge." [27] But as reprinted from day to day in the *Constitution,* these bitter comments of the Northern press only served to fan the fighting spirit of the Georgia Confederates into a white heat.

Meanwhile Davis and Gordon had gone on to Savannah for another great demonstration, the Chatham Artillery there having discovered conveniently that its centennial fell a few days after the unveiling ceremony in Atlanta. The *Constitution* denied that this joint tour of the two men through Georgia was merely a means of furthering Gordon's political claims. "If the revival of memories . . . has promoted General Gordon beyond other men," it declared, "then the cause is to be looked for further back than the proceedings of Saturday. If the popular heart kindled into applause wherever his scarred face was shown or his name mentioned, the cause is to be found in the popular heart. The people speak when they feel like speaking, and they are responsible to themselves for what they do."

On May 9 the *Constitution* printed Gordon's formal announcement of his candidacy for the governorship. This was accompanied by an open letter from Gordon to Bacon suggesting that both candidates request the Democratic state Executive Committee to recommend the holding of primary elections in every county. This was one of the most important

[26] Guyt McLendon in *Constitution,* May 23, 1921.
[27] Nevins: *Cleveland,* pp. 324–5.

phases of the Grady-Gordon strategy, for they knew that Bacon was no match for Gordon on the hustings.

Grady already had assumed personal command as Gordon's
manager. Taking Holliday and a corps of assistants with him,
he set up headquarters in a large storeroom near the *Constitution* office. The first undertaking was to send out a lithographed letter, bearing Gordon's signature, to every voter in
the state whose name and address could be obtained. Since
facsimile letters were uncommon in that day, many of the re-
cipients gained the impression that they had received a personal communication from the General himself. To key men
whom he knew from previous experience could be depended
upon, Grady dictated personal letters like this one to his
friend Harrison:

May 11, 1886

Col. W. H. Harrison,
Lumpkin, Ga.
My dear Tip:

Can you help out Gordon while you are in Stewart? I know that
you can do him a great deal of good if you will, and you may rest
assured it will not hurt you to do it. Our advices from all over the
state are overwhelming in his favor, and it looks to me like a cyclone. I have never yet been fooled very badly and I don't think
I am this time. Help him out in Stewart and the reward of the
just will be yours.

Very truly yours,
H. W. Grady [28]

Since Bacon refused to join Gordon in requesting primaries, it was necessary to work fast. Some counties were scheduled to select delegates before the end of May, and the remainder in June or the early part of July. Grady immediately
began dispatching his assistants where they were needed.

One of his field men was Frank O'Bryan, a young Atlanta
lawyer, who was assigned hurriedly to go to Elberton for the
Hart County convention. O'Bryan was supplied with two
notes — one to each of the leading politicians in the county.
"If you find that No. 1 is for Gordon, give him the note," di-

[28] State Archives, Atlanta.

rected Grady. "Otherwise, see No. 2. He's bound to be against No. 1."

The instructions to the sympathetic county politician were simple. He was to station *one-armed* or *one-legged* Confederate veterans at all crossroads to enlist the attendance of other veterans in the county at a caucus one hour before the convention opened. If it developed at this preliminary meeting that the convention was certain to go for Gordon, the veterans were to allow the delegates to be named immediately. If the sentiment was for Bacon, the veterans were to demand a primary and stall for time until Gordon could come into the county.

Whenever Gordon spoke in a county before the decision was reached, either in convention or at a primary, the effect usually was disastrous for his opponent. He "argued to the jury," while Bacon "argued to the court." Though Bacon also had served in the Confederate Army, his record lacked the glamour of the handsome, scar-faced General's. In addition, Grady arranged that crippled veterans, and the widows and orphans of veterans, always should be in conspicuous seats at Gordon's rallies. This created the impression that the former Confederates were unanimously behind their hero.

During a joint debate between the two men at Greensboro, Bacon produced one of the lithographed letters sent out over the General's signature and charged that by allowing them to be mailed Gordon had condoned "a gross deception." Voices in the audience immediately raised a cry for the letter to be read, but Bacon, apparently somewhat taken aback by this turn of events, tried to pass over the demand by ignoring it. When Gordon's turn came, he grasped the letter in his hand, raised it above his head, and said dramatically: "I don't wonder that my friend won't read it!" The letter, as read by Gordon, simply urged his friends to combat the efficiency of Bacon's political machine by demanding county primaries. By opposing primaries, Gordon shouted, Bacon and his supporters were trying to block the will of the people.

Young Clark Howell, covering the series of meetings for the *Constitution*, telegraphed such a glowing account of the reception given Gordon that even Grady became skeptical and sent his correspondent this message: "YOUR REPORT IS WONDERFUL PLEASE WIRE ME REAL FACTS."

The *Constitution* denounced Bacon's "underhanded tactics" in trying to obstruct an "expression of the popular will," and by June was devoting many columns of its editorial page to answering "slanderous insinuations" against its candidate. While admitting that Gordon as a public man might have made mistakes, and in private business affairs had been "unfortunate," the paper denied that he was corruptible. On his "perfect integrity," one editorial asserted, "we would put our life, our fortune, and our sacred honor."

By Sunday, June 13, Gordon had overcome Bacon's early lead in the number of instructed delegates to the convention. The race was still close, however, and Bacon's supporters were promised by the *Macon Daily Telegraph* that the trend would be reversed the following week. Evidently Gordon himself was none too sure that the *Telegraph* was wrong, for on the next Saturday, when a large number of county conventions were to be held, he and Howell came to headquarters early in the afternoon to follow the returns. Much to their surprise, Grady, to whom all the telegraphic reports of convention results were addressed, was not there. They waited several hours, and still no campaign manager and no telegrams appeared. "All sorts of rumors were afloat," and neither Gordon nor Howell knew what to expect.

Late in the afternoon Grady arrived. In reply to their words of reproof and inquiry, he gave them only one of his enigmatic smiles. But out of his pocket he pulled a bunch of telegrams, showing that Gordon had increased his lead so overwhelmingly that victory was certain.

The mystery as to why Grady had "deserted" the campaign at such a critical moment soon was cleared up. The Atlanta baseball team on the previous day had climbed to the top of the Southern League in an exciting game with Memphis. In order not to miss another game against the same opponents on Saturday afternoon, Grady had instructed the telegraph office to send all messages to him at the baseball park. Consequently he had yelled himself hoarse over Atlanta's pennant-clinching victory in baseball and over Gordon's victory in politics at one and the same time.[29]

When the convention met in Atlanta on July 28, Gordon had a first-ballot triumph of 252 votes to his opponent's 70. The victory was so sweeping that delegates from some of the most rabid Bacon territory, including Tom Watson's McDuffie County, did not even trouble to attend the convention. When the motion for a unanimous nomination was introduced, all but four counties acquiesced. The final vote by delegates was Bacon 10, Gordon 322.

5

Grady's successful management of this campaign was all the more remarkable in view of the fact that no daily paper in Georgia except the *Constitution* actively supported Gordon and that at least two-thirds of the weekly press opposed him. Moreover, the campaign was almost entirely defensive in its nature so far as Gordon was concerned. The Atlanta *Evening Capitol* expressed the opinion that Bacon had committed "a fatal blunder" by assaulting Gordon's character. "There is not a disinterested man in Georgia who knows Gordon who will believe that he is corrupt, or ever did a dishonest act," said the *Capitol*. "His whole life gives the denial to such a charge, and the accusation will continue to rally, as it has drawn to him, the masses of the people, in its indignant repudiation." [30]

Knowing that the indignation of the people, especially the veterans, could be aroused by these "slanderous insinuations" against their hero, Grady directed the campaign largely toward demanding primaries and getting out a full vote. The result was that "ten times as many primaries were held in this campaign . . . as in any campaign ever known in Georgia," and that more persons voted — "twice or three times over" — than in any previous Democratic contest. In many instances the vote in a county primary nearly equaled the white regis-

[29] Cooper: *History of Fulton County*, pp. 834–45.
[30] June 29, 1886.

tration, and in only three counties holding primaries did Bacon win. So crushing was this demonstration of popular support that Gordon entered the general election without any
opposition whatsoever.

A prominent Georgian who had witnessed every important
political campaign in the state for sixty years declared that he
never had known one that surpassed the Gordon campaign
"in brilliance of strategy." [31]

Journalistically, Grady's methods in this race differed from
his earlier campaigns in the greater use he made of the editorial page. The explanation is to be found not only in his increasing interest in this part of the paper but also in the nature of the attack waged against Gordon. It was largely an
attack on the man's personal integrity, based on charges growing out of his dealings with the railroads and his unfortunate
business ventures. All these insinuations were aired thoroughly on the hustings and in the opposition press, and Grady
took up each charge in detail on his editorial page and disposed of it to the satisfaction, at least, of a great majority of
the voters. [32]

Under Grady's influence the editorial page took on much
of the same sparkle and human interest that characterized his
news and feature stories. Instead of running only a few long
editorials every day, the managing editor covered the page
with bright paragraphs of repartee and with a large number
of short articles, none of them as a rule exceeding more than
five or six inches in length. So interested in the technique was
Charles A. Dana, editor of the New York *Sun* and a master of
the human-interest style, that he kept score on the *Constitution's* campaign editorials. One day he counted fifteen campaign items on the editorial page, on another day twenty-five,

[31] Guinn, loc. cit.

[32] Grady had discussed the Huntington letters, with reference to Gordon,
in the *Constitution* of January 3, 4, and 6, 1884, and again reviewed the charges
growing out of these letters in leading editorials on two Sundays during the
campaign — June 20 and 27, 1886. Gordon likewise, both in January 1884 and
during the campaign of 1886, answered the charge that he was "one of Huntington's men." The "unassailable fact" that Gordon "went into the Senate
poor, and came out poorer," was "absolutely irreconcilable" with the idea
that he would "barter his senatorial influence for money," said Grady. Cf.
Woodward, op. cit., p. 121.

and on still another thirty-eight, all "right to the point." Reprinting Dana's comment, Grady declared that editorials must be "brief and pointed" to be effective.[33]

It would be a mistake, however, to assume that Grady ordinarily devoted this much attention to the editorial page. Most of the *Constitution's* editorials in the eighties were written by two full-time editorial-writers — first by Finch and Harris, and then, after Finch's retirement in December 1885, by Harris and Wallace P. Reed. Grady wrote editorials when the occasion demanded, but he enjoyed most of all the activity and excitement associated with the covering of a big news story. The best example of this came soon after the Gordon campaign in his reporting of the Charleston earthquake — an exploit which served as a forerunner to the greatest speech of his career.

[33] *Constitution*, August 2, 1886.

CHAPTER ELEVEN

"The New South"

NEW flames of sectionalism began to flare up over the country with the approach of another congressional election in 1886. Thrown out of power in 1884 for the first time since the Civil War, many Republicans sought to get back into office through the time-proved expedients of "bloody-shirt waving" and "rebel-baiting." Others were convinced that, in order to regain national control, the Republican Party needed to carry some of the Southern states, and that it could do this only through the Negro vote. Hence they revived the agitation of earlier years for federal supervision of national elections in the South. Any such proposal inevitably was branded by Southerners as a "force bill."

Since the restoration of home rule in 1877 the Southern Democrats usually had been without opposition. As a result, the turbulence caused by widespread Negro voting, save in instances such as the Independent revolt in Georgia, had largely disappeared. The renewal of "force bill" discussion tended to make Northern investors uneasy about conditions in the South and threatened to retard the whole process of economic rehabilitation — a development which between 1882 and 1886 had resulted in an estimated increase of forty per cent in the region's wealth.

Grady's deep concern over the situation was revealed in October to Milton A. McRae, Cincinnati newspaperman, who spent a week-end in the Atlanta editor's home. The two men sat up until three o'clock Sunday morning discussing the efforts to eliminate sectionalism. McRae later recalled that, as Grady "talked with deepest emotion of the terrible misunderstanding and bitterness" between North and South, the tears frequently would course down their cheeks. "His voice was wonderful," the Northern visitor wrote, and "it seemed to me that I had never known so great a patriot." [1]

Of the Northerners who were investing heavily in the South, none had more reason to be alarmed over this new epidemic of sectionalism than John H. Inman of New York. Inman had done more than any other man in the North to assure the success of the International Cotton Exposition of 1881. He "is the leading southerner in New York and has sent not less than one hundred million dollars into this section," Grady wrote President Cleveland of Inman. "He is president of the largest iron and coal company in America with a capital of $22,000,000, and is active in the management of more than twelve thousand miles of southern railroad. . . . He is a leading director in every foot of railroad between Louisville and Atlanta, and . . . between Atlanta and Washington." [2]

As a director of the Richmond & Danville Railroad Company (a forerunner of the present Southern Railroad System), Inman was associated with two influential New York bankers — George F. Baker and H. C. Fahnestock — who were members of the historic New England Society in the City of New York. These two friends provided Inman a ready means of conveying to the officers of this society his suggestion that much good might be accomplished by having a progressive young Southerner bring a reassuring message to the North. [3] The society's annual dinner in December offered an ideal setting for such a message, for it always was attended by representative business and financial leaders and was reported widely in the press. Never before in the eighty-one-year history of the organization had a Southerner been invited to address it, and this fact alone would attract unusual attention to the occasion.

If Inman had not already suggested the Atlantan's name to his friends in the New England Society before the Charleston

---

[1] *Forty Years in Newspaperdom* (New York, 1924) , pp. 65–6.

[2] August 2, 1887, Cleveland Papers.

[3] Personal correspondence with Harry A. Cushing, secretary of the New England Society in the City of New York, and E. E. Norris, president of the Southern Railway System, Washington, D.C., based upon extensive examination of their records for the years 1885–7.

earthquake, then Grady's signed articles in the New York *World* could have reminded him to do so. Unquestionably the earthquake stories did build up the writer's prestige among the officers and members of the organization. Inman, however, had seen Grady frequently since the 1881 exposition. Moreover, his Atlanta brother, Samuel M. Inman, recently had bought half of N. P. T. Finch's quarter interest in the *Constitution*. John H. Inman, therefore, had ample opportunity to know that the paper's managing editor was as resourceful in making a speech as in covering an earthquake.

Grady was the logical man to sound the much-needed note of harmony and goodwill. He had grown up since the war and had no Confederate or Bourbon background to arouse Northern suspicions. Moreover, he was known as a journalist, not as a politician, and this fact would help to establish him in the eyes of the North as a disinterested spokesman. At that particular moment probably no man in public life could have inspired "confidence enough in the unselfishness of his objectives to make headway in the removal of distrust between the sections." [4] The business men of North and South, even in the darkest days of Reconstruction, had found a community of interests that politicians could never know; but their motives, too, were open to suspicion. Grady had "never held nor sought public office"; neither did he have any financial interests of consequence outside his newspaper. He combined an ideal background with the knowledge and the speaking skill necessary to rise to the occasion.

The telegram inviting Grady to appear in New York awaited him when he returned home on the night of November 6, after delivering an address of welcome to the National Prison Reform Convention in Atlanta. He called at least one member of the staff that night to tell him of the invitation. The next morning he came into the editorial room in an extremely thoughtful mood.

"Boys," he said, "I've been invited to respond to the toast to 'The New South' at the annual dinner of the New England Society in New York on December 22. Would you do it?"

Up to this time Grady never had spoken outside of Georgia,

4 Buck, op. cit., p. 130.

and none of his addresses had been published. But none knew his ability better than his staff. Harris, Wallace Reed, and the others who heard his question answered with one voice: "Go!"

"But," cautioned Grady, "you must remember that some of America's greatest orators have addressed that society."

"That's all right. Go!" [5]

Although the subject, "The New South," was by no means a new one to Grady,[6] he gave much thought to the preparation of his remarks in the six weeks remaining before the banquet. He had read the published proceedings of the New England Society and knew that many famous speakers, including one of his own idols, Daniel Webster, had addressed the organization. Moreover, he was aware that he would have a distinguished audience and that the printed reports would be examined critically in the South as well as in the North. He therefore studied carefully both the ideas to be discussed and the phraseology to be employed. The mistake of a word or of an insinuation might be fatal.

The seriousness of Grady's mood in these weeks was reflected in the fact that, ten days before the date of his New York speech, he again made a public profession of his religious faith. He was attending a regular Sunday morning service of the First Methodist Church, of which he and his wife were members. The pastor, Dr. Wilbur Fisk Glenn, preached from the text: "For the Lord's portion is his people." The minister developed the theme that a man occasionally should take inventory of his talents to see whether he is using them to the best advantage. At the conclusion of the sermon, when an invitation was extended to those who wished to apply for church membership, Grady went to the altar, shook the pastor's hand, and said: "Mr. Glenn, I want to take a new start." It was Dr. Glenn's last Sunday in the pastorate, but his suc-

[5] F. H. Richardson, op. cit., p. 17; Martin, op. cit., p. 653.

[6] Grady always gave Benjamin H. Hill the credit for "naming the New South" (Harris, p. 139). It is interesting to note, however, that Grady's first editorial entitled "The New South" (*Atlanta Daily Herald*, March 14, 1874) appeared soon after the beginning of a series of articles in *Harper's New Monthly Magazine* (January 1874) bearing the same title. *The New South* also was the name of a weekly industrial journal launched at Wilmington, N.C., in 1881 by Edward A. Oldham, to whom Grady once confided his desire to make a speech on the subject (Edward A. Oldham to author, August 20, 1942).

cessor, Dr. H. C. Morrison, promptly selected Grady for membership on the official board of the church.[7]

Grady's "reconsecration" might have been attributable to any one of several causes — a growing tension over his speech, a regret that the Jefferson Davis incident had contributed to the revival of sectionalism in the North, or other feelings caused by some inner turmoil of which even his friends had no inkling. But, whatever the cause, it is probable that his action on that Sunday morning did help to steady him emotionally for an occasion to which he attached unusual importance.

2

Grady was accompanied to New York by his Augusta friend Marion J. Verdery, who reported to the *Constitution* that the visiting speaker was "crowded with attentions." In the two days preceding the New England Society banquet he was given a reception by the Press Club and a dinner at the Union League Club. Asked by a reporter for the *Sun* what he intended to say in his approaching speech, Grady replied: "The Lord only knows. I have thought of a thousand things to say, five hundred of which if I say they will murder me when I get back home, and the other five hundred of which will get me murdered at the banquet." The *Tribune* quoted him as saying he was "loaded for bear," although the paper's representative thought he seemed "a trifle overcast with anxiety for the result." [8]

The dinner was held in the elaborate banquet hall of the famous Delmonico's Café, then located on the south side of Twenty-sixth Street, between Broadway and Fifth Avenue. All 360 seats had been sold long in advance, and several hundred persons had been unable to obtain tickets. "Never have so many of the members tried to get seats at the annual feast,"

[7] W. F. Glenn: "Henry Grady as I Knew Him," MS. in possession of Atlanta Historical Society; *Constitution*, December 14, 1886; *Life and Labors*, p. 422; information from church records and from Grady family.

[8] New York *Sun*, December 22, 1889; *New-York Tribune*, December 22, 23, 1889. Unless otherwise credited, the account that follows is based upon the report in the *Tribune* of December 23, which was adopted by the New England Society for its official proceedings.

reported the *Tribune*. "The unlucky junior members took
their courses outside and lined up along the walls and in the
doorways when the time for sentiment and oratory came."

The speakers' table extended across the south end of the
hall, while the six other tables ran the full length of the room.
At the center of the head table sat Horace Russell, the president of the society. On his right was Dr. De Witt Talmage, the
Brooklyn clergyman, and on the left was Grady. The other
guests of honor included General William T. Sherman, "griz-
zled and serious," and business and professional leaders such
as J. Pierpont Morgan, Lyman Abbott, Russell Sage, Seth
Thomas, Elihu Root, George H. Lincoln, H. M. Flagler, F.
Hopkinson Smith, and Grady's friend and sponsor, John H.
Inman.

Since the dinner celebrated the 266th anniversary of the
landing of the Pilgrims at Plymouth Rock, the first speaker,
Dr. Talmage, responded to the toast to "Forefathers' Day." In
a dignified and scholarly address he pictured the typical American yet to come: "Let us remember that the coming American is to be an admixture of all foreign bloods. In about
twenty-five or fifty years the model American will step forth.
He will have the strong brain of the German, the polished
manners of the French, the artistic taste of the Italian, the
staunch heart of the English, the steadfast piety of the Scotch,
the lightning wit of the Irish, and, when he steps forth, bone,
muscle, nerve, brain entwined with the fibres of all nationali-
ties, the nations will break out in the cry: 'Behold the American!' "

He then described the return of the victorious Northern
soldiers from the battlefields of the South — "side by side in
one great cause, consecrated through fire and storm and darkness, brothers in peril, on their way home from Chancellors-
ville and Kennesaw Mountain and Fredericksburg, in lines
that seemed infinite they passed on. . . ."

The next regular toast was to the President of the United
States, to which, in the absence of President Cleveland, the
reply was given by General Sherman. Sherman was saluted
when he rose to respond to the toast, and almost immediately
referred to the war — "I came from a bloody Civil War to

A NEW ENGLAND SOCIETY DINNER AT DELMONICO'S

The setting of Grady's "New South" speech, according to contemporary accounts, was similar to that shown in this drawing.

From *Frank Leslie's Illustrated Newspaper,* January 5, 1878.

New York twenty or twenty-one years ago, when a committee came to me in my room and dragged me unwillingly before the then New England Society of New York." In his address he quoted a conversation he had during his march through Georgia with a planter who had been amazed at the number of states represented in the Northern army and who supposedly had said: "We must have been a set of fools to throw down the gage of war to a country we didn't know the geography of!" When the General finished talking, the orchestra in the balcony burst into the strains of "Marching through Georgia."

It was in this atmosphere that the president of the society, introducing the next speaker, said: "We have with us tonight a man who has come from that country which General Sherman has just been telling us about — all the way from Georgia. Let us make him feel how glad we are to see him and how kind and affectionate is the feeling entertained by us towards the land from which he has come." As Grady rose, the audience stood and gave "three cheers and a tiger" for the New South.

"There was something in the scene that was inspiring," wrote Harris. "Near him sat . . . Sherman, who marched through Georgia with fire and sword, and all around him were the fat and jocund sons of New England, who had prospered by the results of the war while his own people had the direst poverty for their portion." In Grady's own words, "When I found myself on my feet, every nerve in my body was strung as tight as a fiddle-string, and all tingling. I knew then that I had a message for that assemblage, and as soon as I opened my mouth it came rushing out." [9]

Without any semblance of notes except a few scribbled words on the back of his menu card, Grady began by taking the "text" subsequently to become so familiar in the South:

"There was a South of slavery and secession — that South is dead. There is a South of union and freedom — that South, thank God, is living, breathing, growing every hour." These words, delivered from the immortal lips of Benjamin H. Hill,

9 Harris, pp. 15–16.

at Tammany Hall in 1866, true then, and truer now, I shall
make my text tonight.

Consciously or unconsciously, Grady had moved back the
date of Hill's first post-war address in New York by two years.
Likewise, he had paraphrased Hill's exact words into balanced sentences, which, with their rhythmic swing and judicious repetition of words, are much more characteristic of
Grady than of Hill.[10] But in this subtle way he had made his
first point: that in the first year after the war the South had
accepted its defeat in good faith, and that even in Reconstruction days one of the most gifted Southern statesmen had
brought a message of friendliness and goodwill to a New York
audience.

Having thus suggested that the South from the first had desired conciliation with the North, the speaker proceeded to
prepare his audience for an open-minded reception of his message. This he did by apt touches of humor and by symbolic
references designed to elicit a favorable response in the emotions of his hearers. So skillfully did he take his cue from the
two preceding speakers that he appeared to be improvising
entirely upon the inspiration of the moment. For example,
any feeling aroused by the singing of "Marching through
Georgia" he dismissed by referring to General Sherman as
one who was regarded in the South as "an able man," but
"kind of careless . . . about fire." He then "brought every
man to his feet" with his apparently spontaneous comment
upon Dr. Talmage's remark about the model American. Grady
used this as the springboard for a tribute to "the first typical
American, the first who comprehended within himself all the
strength and gentleness, all the majesty and grace of this republic, Abraham Lincoln."

It was chiefly through this device of identifying himself
with the sentiments of his Northern audience that Grady suc-

10 Benjamin H. Hill, Jr., op. cit., lists no speech given by his father "at
Tammany Hall in 1866," but refers to Hill's address before the Young Men's
Democratic Union in New York City during the presidential campaign of
1868 as "the first speech made in the North by a Southern man after the war."
Nowhere in the printed version of this speech do the exact words of Grady's
"text" appear, although the sentiments expressed are virtually the same.

ceeded in breaking down the "psychological resistance" of
his listeners and in freeing them from prejudice against what
he had to say. In thus appealing to the North, however, he
was careful to guard against an unfavorable reaction back
home. He added that he would not, if he could, dim the glory
won by the people of the South "in peace and war, or by word
or deed take aught from the splendor and grace of their civilization — never equalled and, perhaps, never to be equalled
in its chivalric strength and grace." There was "a New South,
not through protest against the old, but because of new conditions, new adjustments and, if you please, new ideas and
aspirations."

Grady's description of the return of the "footsore Confederate soldier," coming as it did in vivid contrast to Dr. Talmage's brilliant word picture of the return of the victorious
Northern armies, is regarded by most critics as "the finest expression of his career." [11] In mentioning Lincoln he touched
the sentiment of Northerners at its most responsive spot, but
in not naming any specific Confederate hero he avoided an-
tagonisms and provided his own people with a picture of brav-
ery and fortitude with which any Southerner who chose could
identify himself. James Buchanan Duke carried with him for
years a newspaper clipping of Grady's tribute to the "hero in
gray with a heart of gold," saying: "It reminds me a lot of
my own father," who "hustled and harvested like the man in
gray this fellow tells about." [12]

Then Grady went on to express the South's desire to let the
issues of the war be regarded as settled forever and to enter
upon a new era of peace and prosperity. Having won the sympathy of his listeners, as revealed by their frequent applause
and cheers, he devoted the last half of his twenty-minute address to demonstrating that there was, in the fullest sense, a
New South. In broad strokes he painted what was being accomplished in industry, agriculture, and education, and declared that his people were at work on the Negro problem

11 Marvin G. Bauer: "Henry W. Grady, Spokesman of the New South" (unpublished doctor's dissertation, University of Wisconsin, Madison, 1936), pp.
273-4.

12 John K. Winkler: *Tobacco Tycoon: The Story of James Buchanan Duke*
(New York, 1942), p. 183.

"in honor and equity." The South had "sowed towns and cities in the place of theories and put business above politics"; she had "found her jewel in the toad's head of defeat."

These were the points on which the conservative business man in his audience most desired reassurance. When Grady reached his dramatic peroration, in which he asked whether New England would "permit the prejudice of war to remain in the hearts of the conquerors, when it had died in the hearts of the conquered," he had his audience shouting: "No! No!" and cheering in a manner seldom witnessed in New York.[13]

Although it was midnight when the banquet ended, Charles R. Miller, editor of the *Times,* rushed back to the office to write for his editorial page of the next morning that Grady's was "the speech of the evening. . . . It was eloquent. It swept the whole range of emotion, of sentiment, and of patriotism. . . . In all its forescore years the society of Plymouth Rock worshippers never heard a speech that was better worth its while to hear and think about." The praise of other important New York papers a day later was equally unreserved. Said the Democratic *World:* "A speech as truly eloquent, in the highest meaning of that much misused word, has not been heard in this city for a long time past. . . . No one who heard Mr. Grady's fervent words could doubt the absolute sincerity of his declaration: 'I am glad that the omniscient God held the balance of battle in his Almighty hand, and that the American Union was saved from the wreck of war.' " The Republican *Tribune,* while criticizing the South for "prejudice and fraud" in the suppression of the Negro vote, thought that the speaker, in "spirit and purpose," as well as in "diction and logic," had "reached a high plane in contemporary oratory."

Since Grady's chief purpose in coming to New York was to reach the ear of those who had funds to invest, it is noteworthy that the New York *Commercial and Financial Chronicle,* in its issue of December 25, also carried a flattering review of the speech. The meaning of this becomes evident when one

[13] Bauer, op. cit., p. 2. The complete text of the speech, as corrected by Grady from the stenographic report of the *New-York Tribune,* is given in the Appendix. A more detailed rhetorical analysis may be found in the article by Bauer in *A History and Criticism of American Public Address* (New York, 1943).

looks through the files of the periodical and finds reference to so few other affairs of a "social" nature. As was remarked of another occasion on which a Southerner spoke in the North, "If it be said that the business men who thus mixed food with oratory were thinking of profits in the South, and that the speaker was interested in developing in the North an opinion favorable to the advancement of Southern ends, it can be answered that that is just what makes the episode significant." [14]

When Grady returned to Atlanta on Christmas Eve, he was met at the railroad station by a reception committee, a brass band, and "at least a thousand people," who escorted him to the Kimball House. Here the leading figures of Atlanta and Georgia passed through the parlors, partook of "a delicious champagne punch," and shook the hand of their rising national hero.

His triumph, the *Constitution* observed, was "the triumph of southern sentiment which has adjusted itself to new conditions, new hopes and new achievements."

3

Only one who has gone through the clippings from the newspapers and magazines that flooded the *Constitution* office in the days and weeks following "The New South" speech can appreciate fully the impression created by Grady in this one brief effort.[15] Although the speaker had prepared no advance manuscript to furnish to the press, a shorthand reporter for the *New-York Tribune* took down his remarks virtually verbatim. From this source most of the important dailies throughout the United States and a number in foreign countries obtained the address and reprinted it in whole or in part, with editorial comments. Perhaps the favorable impression previously created by Grady's refusal to run for Congress and by his earthquake stories helped to win him a favorable press, but

14 Buck, op. cit., p. 105.
15 The editorial comments on the speech are taken from the clippings in the Grady Scrapbooks, unless another source is indicated. All appeared in the days and weeks immediately following the address.

the fact remains that his fellow newspapermen gave him a "play" usually accorded only to men already prominent in public life. Even the arch-Republican *Chicago Tribune* eventually republished his talk in full, observing that "it is generally considered the speech of the year 1886 in the United States."

Leading magazines and reviews joined the chorus of praise. Richard Watson Gilder lauded the speech in the *Century* and wrote Grady for a corrected version to publish in the *Critic*. An even more significant comment was that of the *Nation,* edited by the able Edwin Lawrence Godkin, who wrote: "It was in every way a most notable address — full of an eloquence which stands the severe test of perusal in print the following morning . . . infused with the vital qualities of that oratory which touches the heart because there is sincere feeling behind the speaker's words." Godkin's sentiments were echoed by the popular *Frank Leslie's Illustrated Newspaper,* which thought that "the ready response from Maine to California is such a tribute to the orator's presentation of his cause as has not been paralleled of recent years."

The largest periodical display given the speech was that of *Harper's Weekly,* which carried a biographical sketch and a large pen drawing of the orator, in addition to an editorial. Pointing out that Grady had begun the work of bringing North and South together while writing for it and other Northern publications, the *Weekly* added: "How much of its somewhat more rapid strides forward in industrial prosperity than some of its neighboring states Georgia owes to Mr. Grady's excellent reports in the Northern press . . . could not well be over-estimated."

Grady had struck a note which was as popular in the South as in the North. One of the first Southerners to wire him congratulations was J. F. Hanson, owner of the *Macon Daily Telegraph* — the paper that usually had led the opposition to the *Constitution's* political candidates. Editorially the *Telegraph* remarked that Grady had "ably represented" both the Old South and the New South and had given "pleasure and satisfaction" not only to his hearers but to his fellow Southerners, who had "looked to the occasion not without apprehension."

In citing such comments, the *Atlanta Evening Journal* reported that only two newspapers among its hundreds of exchanges had objected to the speech or begrudged the speaker "his due meed of praise."

One of these dissenting papers was the Louisville *Courier-Journal,* which came out with some words of advice from Henry Watterson "To a Risen Young Man." While Watterson granted that Grady's talents fully entitled him to his newly won fame, he deplored the rise of a "school of thought" in the South whose motto, he said, was "get rich; honestly if you can; but get rich." Urging Grady and the *Constitution* to abandon their "protectionist" views in favor of his own "free-trade" policy, the Kentucky editor wrote:

> The argument runs somewhat thus: "The North has enriched herself robbing us; why should the stealing stop just as we are ready to go into business?" So all the old robber theories, which have amassed unequal and ill-gained fortunes in the East, are dinned into the ear of the honest, but impoverished, South. . . . Mr. Grady should throw himself across the bridle-path of this . . . fallacy. If he does not, it will presently become a thoroughfare, and if he lives long enough he will see the day when the best blood of the South will feed the factories which grind out squalor to millions and millions to masters as cruel and rapacious as ever trod New England soil. . . .

The only other Southern protest of consequence came from another "free-trade" paper, the Charleston *News and Courier,* which condemned both the speech and the speaker. "Nobody here has heard of Grady's speech," wrote the Charleston correspondent of the New York *Sun.* "The city newspapers did not publish it. The Charleston people have no love for the *Atlanta Constitution* or anybody connected with it since the earthquake." The *News and Courier* contended that Grady had so "belittled the disaster" as to discourage contributions for the relief of the earthquake sufferers — a charge hardly borne out by the articles in question. A much more plausible reason for the paper's unfriendly attitude was that Grady, in his final article on the quake, had referred to Charleston as "the last citadel of the old regime." Among other things he had quoted a "prominent Charlestonian" as saying that it was "strange the same section should hold and the same people inhabit two cities so dissimilar at every point as Charleston and Atlanta." To this the *News and Courier* now replied that it had been "preaching and practicing harmony and good-will" before Grady, "in a journalistic sense, was out of his swaddling clothes." Perhaps there was a touch of envy in this latter remark, for the Charleston paper's brilliant editor, D. W. Dawson, had been a pioneer in urging his people to "drop conceits and go to work" and in starting the movement to "bring the mills to the cotton." But that he now was out of tune with the trend of the times was indicated by the fact that, when he finally did get around to commenting on Grady's speech, he talked mainly of the "inextinguishable principle" of "self-government" which he said the Old South had fought to preserve.[16]

It was to be expected, of course, that some Republicans in the North would attack Grady as a trimmer. The *Chicago Tribune*, long before it deigned to print the talk, charged that the speaker's remarks in New York were inconsistent with those used in introducing Jefferson Davis in Atlanta the previous spring. An even more vitriolic attack of this kind came months later when Senator John J. Ingalls, described by Allan Nevins as "a waspish New Englander transplanted to Kansas," [17] delivered on the floor of the Senate a "long advertised speech." Ingalls branded as "sacrilege" and "blasphemy" Grady's references to Davis's giving Atlanta a "resurrection of memories" which had made "the best Easter . . . since Christ was risen from the dead."

"When was that orator sincere, Mr. President?" asked Ingalls. "When did he speak the sentiments, the feelings and convictions of the southern people, when he delivered that oration on the 1st day of May, 1886, in Atlanta, in the presence of applauding thousands, or when he went up to the New England dinner, in December of the same year, and spilled oil and wine all over the American people?"

16 Charleston *News and Courier*, December 30, 1886; Broadus Mitchell, op. cit., pp. 113–14.
17 Nevins: *Cleveland*, p. 339.

Replying in a two-column editorial, Grady reiterated that he was equally sincere in Atlanta and in New York. "Barring certain phrases in the first speech, the questionable taste of which the enthusiasm of the occasion may have excused," he said, "there is not a word of either, assuredly not a sentiment, or conviction, that I do not now deliberately repeat and re-affirm." The South would not deserve the respect of the world and could not maintain her own self-respect, he insisted, if she did not honor the men who had led her Lost Cause. At the same time the South accepted the results of the war, and "not one man in ten thousand of her people would reverse those results if they could." Those sentiments, he declared, could be delivered in sincerity on either side of the Mason and Dixon line.[18]

Grady must have been amused in reading over many of the newspaper clippings about his speech. He was termed "captain," "major," and, of course, "colonel." Few seemed to know what his middle initial stood for, the New York *Daily Star* and the *Montgomery Advertiser* recording it as "Walsingham." The New York *Sun* had it "Winchester," another paper had it "Witherspoon," and many printed it "Woodfen." But this hardly was disturbing, because Watterson many times had poked fun at Grady's middle name, insisting that the "W" stood for "Woodfire."

Nor could Grady have failed to be impressed by the many drawings of him that appeared in the newspapers and magazines, some of which bore little resemblance. Even the *Boston Herald* commented on the poor likenesses: "We are inclined to think that Mr. H. W. Grady . . . has good ground for rebellion in the portrait of him which was published in *Harper's Weekly*. Bro. Grady is really a handsome man, with an amiable, alert countenance and a remarkably bright and piercing eye — two of them, in fact — with which he manages to see what is going on, and to look into things deeper than the average of his fellow-beings." A Philadelphia writer, on seeing the same sketch, observed: "No man whose facial expression suggests that he had encountered a bad odor when a youth

[18] Ingalls spoke in the Senate on March 6, 1888. Both the speech and Grady's reply were printed in the *Constitution*, March 11, 1888.

and had never been able to forget it can ever rise to the upper
level of American statesmanship. . . ."

But these were only minor bits of flotsam on a huge tidal
wave of New South sentiment which now found Grady riding
at its crest. "Something great had indeed occurred." The historian Paul H. Buck finds it in Joel Chandler Harris's statement that Grady had become the very "embodiment of the
spirit of the New South." Buck likewise comments: "The
words that Grady uttered no longer seem important, even as
the cotton mills and iron furnaces built in the eighties appear
somewhat dwarfed by the growth of later years. . . . But
Grady's faith and Grady's optimism were a living fire peculiar
to the New South he served. He became the recognized apos-
tle of the new faith." [19]

Grady was not the first Southerner to plead for harmony
and trust between the sections. Lamar had said: "My countrymen, know one another, and you will love one another." Hill
repeatedly had urged North and South to "unite to repair the
evils that distract and oppress the country." And Watterson,
who up to this time had been even more prominent in Southern journalism than Grady, had proclaimed: "War or no war,
we are all countrymen, fellow-citizens." But Hill and Lamar
had spoken too soon, while Watterson was of much too con-
tentious a nature,[20] as well as too far apart from business interests on the tariff question, ever to be accepted as a "symbol
of peace and good will."

Grady was the right man speaking the right word at the
right time.

4

Almost immediately after Grady had delivered his stirring
address in New York, he was proposed as the logical running-

[19] Op. cit., pp. 193–4.

[20] As a member of Congress at the time of the Hayes-Tilden controversy,
Watterson had created alarm by asking for "a hundred thousand petitioners
. . . ten thousand unarmed Kentuckians" in Washington to prevent the Republicans from stealing the election. Though a leading Democrat, he eventually became a severe critic of both Cleveland and Wilson, the only two Democratic Presidents to hold office during his career. To those who remonstrated
with him he replied: "Things have come to a hell of a pass when a man can't
wallop his own jackass."

mate for Grover Cleveland in 1888. This vice-presidential
boom doubtless was stimulated by the death in 1885 of Vice
President Thomas A. Hendricks. The New York *Sun* early
nominated Grady for vice president, and added: "He may be
president." The *World* observed: "It is a dull day in the *Sun*
office when a new Presidential candidate is not discovered.
But in this case we are for Grady, and second the motion."

Once the motion had been made and seconded by two influential New York newspapers, other papers in the country
began to follow suit. The St. Louis *Republican* liked the idea
and quipped: "This is, apparently, the first recorded instance
in which an after-dinner oration, laid in between two volleys
of champagne corks, has been said to herald the way to the
White House. Still, there is no telling what a pushing Georgia
editor may not come to be through the judicious exercise of
fluent tongue and pen. . . ." *Harper's Weekly* reported that
Grady was being mentioned as a "proper candidate for the
Vice-Presidency," and that one enthusiastic Southern paper
had declared Cleveland and Grady "would sweep the South
like a whirlwind."

The vice-presidential boom was revived in May, when the
New York Herald printed a double-leaded editorial urging
Grady for the position, and the *World* again promptly seconded the nomination. Correspondents of the *Herald* in other
cities, obviously under instruction from the home office, began to gather comments, mostly very favorable to Grady. The
fun-loving Eugene Field of the *Chicago Daily News* caused a
little excitement by one of his typical fictitious biographies, in
which he asserted that Grady was ineligible for the vice-presidency because he was under the legal age, was a citizen of Ireland, and was still an "unpardoned rebel." James Gordon
Bennett probably knew better than to take Field seriously,
but nevertheless he wired Grady for a statement "settling the
date and place of his birth." When Bennett's paper came out
then with still another nominating editorial, even Grady's
few remaining newspaper critics in Georgia, such as the *Columbus Daily Enquirer-Sun,* began to register enthusiasm.[21]

21 *Columbus Daily Enquirer-Sun,* June 1, 1887.

Although the *Constitution* reprinted most of these comments, Grady gave no indication of his own feelings except to allow the paper to state editorially that it could not say whether the managing editor would accept the nomination if it was tendered to him. The editorial asked, however, somewhat significantly: "What do you democratic leaders think about it?"

The definite answer to this question was not to come until the following year, but two prominent Georgians registered immediate disapproval. One was Governor Gordon, and the other was Hoke Smith — both of them among Grady's closest friends for many years. But Gordon had grown cool, supposedly because many of the newspaper stories following "The New South" speech again had attributed his election as Governor to Grady. Smith, on the other hand, was a rising young lawyer only five years Grady's junior, politically ambitious for himself and probably envious of the national reputation Grady was acquiring. Smith had been a frequent visitor in Grady's home, had engaged in a real-estate investment with the editor in the early eighties, and undoubtedly had profited by the *Constitution's* many flattering references to himself. Yet both he and Gordon seemed fearful of the possibility that Grady, who heretofore had remained outside the political arena, might become a candidate for high office.

There was just one thing for an ambitious rival of so powerful a journalist to do, and that was to gain control of another newspaper.

Since its founding in 1883, the *Atlanta Evening Journal* had not been a serious competitor of the *Constitution*. Forced to do without Associated Press dispatches in its early years, it had featured local news, and subscribers who wanted complete state and national coverage had been compelled to take the *Constitution* also. The paper had changed hands after two years, but still could not pretend to offer either the news or the features afforded by its morning rival. Its editorial policy was so similar to the *Constitution's* that some persons suspected it of being owned or controlled by the older paper. Apparently no foundation existed for this suspicion, however, for when Hoke Smith made inquiries in the spring of 1887 about buying the paper, he found the owner quite willing to sell.

Forming a stock company consisting of himself and seven other Atlantans, Smith bought the *Journal* on June 1, 1887, for $12,000. He had no intention of giving up either his legal practice or his political ambitions, but he moved his law office into the newspaper building in order that he might be available for frequent consultation. He became president and publisher; H. H. Cabaniss, business manager; and Josiah Carter, former city editor of the *Constitution,* managing editor. At a later date Hoke Smith's brother, Burton, a son-in-law of Governor Gordon, also became a stockholder. Although the new publisher's announcement stated that the paper's policy would be solely "to promote the moral and financial growth of Atlanta and Georgia," the *Macon Telegraph* reported a "general impression" that the purchase was prompted by "political designs." [22]

There was no open break at this time between Grady and Smith, or between Grady and Gordon. In replying to the remark of the Athens *Banner-Watchman* at the time of the *Journal* purchase that the Governor had been "ungrateful" to Grady, the *Constitution* declared that it did "not need the governor. He is neither an editor, reporter, proof-reader, printer or pressman. We believe, however, that General Gordon is making an excellent governor. Let us express the hope that the boys who abused him as infamous and imbecile last summer and praise him as admirable now, will stand by their good opinions when he goes before the people again." Several weeks later, in following Gordon on the program of the Interstate Farmers' Convention in Atlanta, Grady spoke of "marching behind the blazing path of the Governor's eloquence, much as a one-armed woodchopper would follow the track of a South Georgia cyclone." And Gordon, surprisingly enough, referred to Grady as "more able to speak for the state than any man in Georgia." [23]

[22] Randolph L. Fort: "History of the Atlanta Journal" (unpublished master's thesis, Emory University, Atlanta, 1930), pp. 5–13; *Atlanta Evening Journal,* June 2, 1887; *Macon Daily Telegraph,* June 3, 1887.

[23] *Constitution,* August 16, 1887.

Neither did the rapid improvements in the *Journal* under Hoke Smith's ownership cause any decline in the rate at which the *Constitution* was growing. From a circulation of 95,000 in January 1887 the *Weekly Constitution* by midsummer had climbed past the 100,000 mark and was claiming the largest subscription list of any newspaper in the South. The *Journal* had no weekly edition as yet, and its daily circulation was only 4,100 as compared with its morning rival's 10,000 on week-days and 15,000 on Sundays. To improve its typographical appearance and to speed up production, the *Constitution* recently had installed stereotyping equipment and had bought a new $30,000 web perfecting press. "We have pretty well made up our minds," it announced, "to print right here in Atlanta the greatest American newspaper." A contemporary remarked that the New England dinner had given Grady and the *Constitution* "a boom the like of which has never before been known to any other publisher or journal in America." [24]

Undoubtedly Grady's growing fame as an orator had contributed to his newspaper's success, but his talents as a promoter were even more responsible so far as the *Weekly Constitution* was concerned. A friend from the Athens *Banner-Watchman* visited the *Constitution* office in March 1887 and obtained from Grady himself an account of the methods used in building up the weekly. The article must have been fairly accurate, for Grady allowed it to be reprinted in his own paper. The Athens visitor told how he checked carefully the mailing list of more than 100,000 names and found that the *Weekly Constitution* was being sent, as advertised, "to every post office in Georgia and to every state and territory in the Union."

Asked how this tremendous circulation — nearly twice as large as the population of Atlanta — had been achieved, Grady explained that the *Constitution* sent out "from ten to twenty thousand specimen copies" each week. It advertised widely in other newspapers; it had both traveling agents and volunteer solicitors; and it distributed by mail much promotion material, including a four-page premium list. To the books and watches which the weekly had offered at "wholesale

[24] Clipping, Grady Scrapbooks.

cash prices" when Grady first took it over in 1883, now were added clocks, shotguns, parlor organs, and many other articles of merchandise. A sewing machine which was sold for eighteen dollars with a one-year subscription would have cost forty-five dollars, the advertising declared, if bought through an agent. The *Constitution* was selling these machines in 1887 at the rate of more than two hundred a month.

But the most successful circulation-building device of all, according to Grady's secretary, was the annual drawing for $1,000 in Christmas presents. The names of all subscribers to the weekly were "placed in a hat" just before Christmas, and slips were drawn to determine the winners. The thirty-nine cash prizes totaled $1,050, the capital prize being $500 in gold. Agents sending in the most subscriptions received special prizes ranging up to $250.

It was methods like these, even more than the desire of potential subscribers to read the latest words of the "Spokesman of the New South," that brought the paid subscription list of the *Weekly Constitution* by 1888 up to 122,828 names — the largest circulation of any newspaper of its kind in the United States.[25]

5

But vice-presidential booms and mounting circulation were, after all, merely incidental by-products of Grady's speech before the New England Society. What of his major purpose — to allay sectional suspicions and thereby to encourage the economic development of the South?

In a series of articles on "The New South" for the *New York Ledger*,[26] Grady later summarized the more important aspects of the South's economic development from 1880 through 1887. In these eight years, he asserted, more than $260,000,000 had been invested in Southern manufacturing. While the South itself probably had furnished the greater portion of this money, a substantial part of it had come from the North. Indeed, the *Chattanooga Times* declared that, when

---

25 *American Newspaper Annual*, 1888 (Philadelphia: N. W. Ayer & Son).
26 November 16–December 21, 1889. The six articles later were published in book form under the title of *The New South* (New York, 1890).

investments in railroads were added to those in factories, three-fifths of the new capital had come from the North — a fact which the *Times* thought boded ill for the South. But Grady replied that the development had been "mainly engineered by Southern brains and enterprise," and that the future would show the South growing steadily richer and more independent. "When we learn the lesson of keeping at home the $400,000,000 we receive annually from our cotton crop," he wrote, "the South will be the richest section of this country." [27]

Grady thought that the South was learning this lesson. The number of cotton spindles in Southern factories, he pointed out, had trebled between 1880 and 1887. The lowly cottonseed, once thrown away, now was producing $60,000,000 a year in oil and $40,000,000 a year in cattle food and fertilizer. Reflecting economic growth generally, the amount of coal mined in the South had increased two and a half times, and the production of iron in 1887 had quadrupled that of 1880. The amount of timber taken from Southern forests had doubled, and several hundred furniture factories were helping to keep more of the wealth from this source at home. Census figures for the eighties were to reveal that Southern railroads had doubled their mileage by laying 20,000 miles of new track.[28]

Even the condition of agriculture offered some grounds for optimism. Although cotton prices still were depressed, the downward spiral appeared for the moment to have been checked, the farmer having received a half cent a pound more for his crop in 1887 than in 1886. Most of all, Grady was encouraged by the money which a small but growing minority of farmers were making from fruits, vegetables, and dairy products. The state already was realizing more than $1,000,000 a year from the shipping of watermelons to Northern markets — something which many persons had ridiculed as impractical when Grady advocated it in the early eighties.[29] And one Georgia county, which six years earlier had imported all

[27] *Constitution,* June 25, 1887.
[28] *Eleventh Census, 1890, Manufactures, Selected Industries.*
[29] Harris, p. 62.

its butter, now was shipping 90,000 pounds a year. The production of crops other than cotton was steadily increasing.

The psychological effect of this prosperity, particularly in the cities where it was most marked, was amazing. As Henry Watterson expressed it, "The South, having had its bellyful of blood, has gotten a taste of money, and is too busy trying to make more of it to quarrel with anybody." [30] And in that non-election year of 1887 Grady could detect the same feeling in the Northern business men whom he continually was entertaining in Atlanta.

If Grady's speech had indeed been a factor in stimulating this progress and in releasing the latent desire of the people of both sections for harmony, he had reason to be optimistic when he wrote:

What a pull it has been! Through the ashes and desolation of war — up the hill, a step at a time, nothing certain — not even the way! Hindered, misled, and yet always moving up a little, until — shall we say it? — the top has been reached, and the rest is easy! The desperate days of starvation — the doubtful days of experiment — these are over. And now the world will witness a change in the South, little less than magical. The ground has been prepared — the seed put in — the tiny shoots tended past the danger-point — and the day of the mighty harvest is here! [31]

[30] *New York Herald,* July 19, 1887.
[31] *The New South,* pp. 267–8.

CHAPTER TWELVE

"Incarnation of the Atlanta Spirit"

IT was in the months following "The New South" speech that the genius of Grady came to full flower — as journalist, showman, orator, and community leader. "There was a change in him from that time forth," Harris observed. "He put away some of his boyishness, and became, as it seemed, a trifle more thoughtful. His purpose developed into a mission, and grew in his mind, and shone in his eyes, and remained with him day and night." [1]

Grady must have felt that he could realize his purpose best by remaining in Atlanta, for he steadfastly refused offers which would have taken him elsewhere. First he declined a contract from a lyceum bureau for a series of fifty lectures at $250 each, although in this instance the *Augusta Evening News* declared that "Atlanta alone could afford to pay more than that and send him through the North if she were to consider the direct benefit that would result to her commercial enterprises." Next he rejected an offer — one report said "upon his own terms" and another at $10,000 a year — from "a well known New York journal," believed to have been Dana's *Sun*. He was equally indifferent when a group of Alabama capitalists tried to obtain him as editor of a paper in Birmingham. The "iron city" had enjoyed a phenomenal growth since its founding in 1871 and already had visions of supplanting Atlanta as the "capital of the New South." [2] But even a salary greatly in excess of the $6,000 a year he was now receiving from the *Constitution* could not induce Grady to

[1] Harris, p. 66.
[2] Clippings, Grady Scrapbooks; Edward A. Oldham to author, August 20, 1942.

leave the rapidly growing city of which he was so much a part and for whose future he held such high hopes.

Significant, because of President Cleveland's interest in it, is the fact that within a week after the New England Society talk an effort was made to place Grady at the head of a company to purchase the New York *Daily Star,* "the morning New York organ of the Democratic party." The negotiations were handled by James T. Woodward, president of the Hanover National Bank of New York, who was a close personal friend of the President and was frequently consulted by Cleveland's administration on financial matters. Associated with Grady in the proposed deal were E. A. Burke of the New Orleans *Times-Democrat* and A. H. Belo of the Galveston and Dallas *News* — both successful publishers. The trio took an option on the controlling shares of the *Star* in January and renewed it in April, but finally allowed it to expire. Although Grady had no intention of leaving Atlanta, he wrote with obvious relish of the *Constitution's* "establishing a branch office in New York and publishing a dual edition." [3]

The only new venture made by Grady at this time was one which might have been half anticipated because of the way in which he always tried to balance any encouragement of industrialization with some gesture toward agriculture. This was his purchase in April 1887 of a one-third interest in the monthly *Georgia Stock and Agricultural Journal,* the name of which he changed immediately to the *Southern Farm.* Grady became the nominal editor, but placed Dr. William Louis Jones, professor of agriculture at the University of Georgia, as managing editor in charge. Selling at one dollar a year, the fifty-two-page magazine soon amassed a circulation of 20,000, and the advice of Jones, "a clear-headed, practical farmer," was sought by agriculturalists all over the South. [4]

The *Southern Farm,* of course, was merely a side-line to Grady's main job of directing the news and editorial departments of the *Constitution.* So far as actual writing is con-

[3] H. W. G. to James T. Woodward, December 29, 1886, April 5, 11, 1887, Cleveland Papers; *Constitution,* March 20, 1887.

[4] *Constitution,* April 3, 1887; Hull: *Historical Sketch,* pp. 118–19. Apparently no copies of the *Southern Farm* have been preserved. After Grady's death it was merged with the *Southern Cultivator.*

cerned, he contributed fewer identifiable articles to the paper
now than before becoming nationally prominent. Signed stories by "H. W. G." no longer appeared on the first page, and
his "Man About Town" column ceased its occasional appear-
ances on Sundays. But Grady was the author of many of the
paragraphs appearing on the editorial page from time to time
under such titles as "Constitutionals," "Persons and Things,"
and "Notes by the Wayside." He frequently contributed the
leading editorial on week-days, and for Sunday often wrote
virtually the entire page by himself. Even though the majority of the editorials during the week ordinarily were written by Harris and his assistant, Wallace Reed, Grady probably was credited by most persons with being the author. Other
papers usually spoke of the *Constitution* and its managing editor interchangeably, so clearly did his personality dominate.

One must look beyond Grady's writing in the *Constitution*,
however, to find why he is today referred to by local historians
as the "incarnation of the Atlanta spirit." The secret will be
found in the many references in the news columns to his community activities. If a mass meeting was held to boom a new
factory or railroad, he usually was the main speaker; if a
committee was appointed, he became its generating force; if
prominent visitors were to be entertained, he was host. The
fact that he was Atlanta's first national figure made visitors
eager to meet him and Atlantans desirous of riding on his
coat tail. And Grady's coat tail was a mile long and almost
as wide.

"I believe Atlanta can achieve for herself the same prominence that we have worked in our business," Grady declared
to a group of Atlanta business men, after reminding them
that the weekly edition of the *Constitution* had outdistanced
every other newspaper in the country in circulation. "I do not
believe any place on earth offers as many advantages for everything that makes home desirable and makes the workshop
healthy and prosperous and enables you to distribute your
goods as does Atlanta." [5]

And since Grady had "arrived," since he unquestionably
had made a success of his newspaper, Atlantans listened to

[5] *Constitution*, December 12, 1888.

him and followed him. There is no better example of the magic his personality exerted than his leadership of the Piedmont Exposition of 1887.

2

The meeting that led to the Piedmont Exposition was held in the *Constitution* office at Grady's call.[6] When a group of twenty-six Atlantans had gathered one day in February, Grady explained that the purpose was to get fifty men who would subscribe $500 each toward the holding of a fair similar to the International Cotton Exposition of 1881. All those present became subscribers and Grady was elected vice president, after he had insisted with tact that a leading business man, Charles A. Collier, be president. The Piedmont Driving Association previously had been organized, with Grady as a director, and the two groups agreed to co-operate in selecting a park site which would be suitable both for the driving club and for the exposition grounds.

Determining to have a drawing card for a crowd that would surpass the results of his efforts for the 1881 exposition and the unveiling of the Hill monument, Grady set to work to induce President Cleveland and his bride of a year, the former Frances Folsom, to come to Atlanta. Most people in the South had never seen a president, to say nothing of the first Democratic President in twenty-four years, and Grady knew that this would arouse their enthusiasm as nothing else could. Georgia's invitation, engraved on sheets of Dahlonega gold and enclosed in a case of native hardwoods and precious stones, was delivered to the President by Senator Colquitt. On April 13 the *Constitution* announced Cleveland's acceptance.

With the aid of an appropriation from the City Council and a popular subscription conducted by the *Constitution*, the directors proceeded to lay out the exposition grounds and to erect the buildings in the new Piedmont Park. To all the

---

6 Unless other sources are credited, this account of the exposition is based upon the news stories appearing in the *Constitution* from February through October 1887.

multitudinous details — the planning of the park, the race track, the midway, the buildings, and the exhibits — Grady gave attention with the skill and enthusiasm of a master show-man. "When it seemed to him that he was taking too promi-nent a part in the management," said Harris, "he would send for other members of the fair committee, pour his sugges-tions into their ears, and thus evade the notoriety of introduc-ing them himself and prevent the possible friction that might be caused if he made himself too prominent." [7] One spectacu-lar entertainment feature scheduled was a sham battle cover-ing seventy acres and including four batteries of artillery, ten companies of cavalry, and "thousands of foot soldiers." Most of all, however, Grady was interested in the visit of the Presi-dent, which from a publicity standpoint was the headline attraction.

Grady's original plan, as confided to Cleveland's secretary, called for a special train carrying "a committee of perhaps six gentlemen, and six ladies," to go from Atlanta to Washington to bring the President to the exposition. As the train passed through each Southern state on the return trip, it was to pick up another car carrying the governor of that state and his staff. "The Senators from the southern states will also be invited," wrote Grady, "and it is my purpose to make this the largest gathering of representative southern men ever seen." This plan had to be abandoned, however, when the President de-cided to visit Georgia at the end of a rather extensive West-ern and Southern tour.[8]

Despite his desire to visit the South, Cleveland feared that some untoward incident might mar the trip. Late in August he wrote to Grady, enclosing a clipping of a dispatch from At-lanta stating that a movement was on foot to have Jefferson Davis there. "If any such business as that is indulged in," the President told L. Q. C. Lamar, "the people of Atlanta will find that one of their expected guests will not listen to their talk." Grady hastened to reply that there was "not the hint of truth" in the report. "You commended the discretion with

<hr />

[7] Harris, p. 56.

[8] H. W. G. to Daniel S. Lamont, July 15, August 2, 1887, Cleveland Papers.

which the Southern people met the flag episode," he reminded the President. "You shall have new reason to commend their good taste & discretion when your trip is over." [9]

The exposition opened on October 10 with an address by Congressman Samuel J. Randall, who was popular with Southern industrialists because of his tariff views and with Southerners generally because of his skillful handling of the Hayes-Tilden controversy while Speaker of the House. The exposition buildings, covering ten acres and representing an investment of more than $200,000, had been completed in less than four months and housed exhibits from every state in the Union. The advance publicity in national publications such as *Harper's Weekly* had been even better than that for the 1881 exposition. Correspondents were on hand, the *Constitution* said, "from every leading newspaper in America."

The weather for the first week was faultless, but shortly before the arrival of the presidential party on Monday night, October 17, it began to rain. The drizzle continued intermittently throughout Cleveland's entire stay. The program, however, was carried out fully in order not to disappoint a crowd described by the *Constitution* as the largest in the city's history. From every part of the South the visitors had come — on special passenger trains, in freight cars, in buggies and wagons, and even by ox cart. Unable to obtain hotel rooms, many slept either in their conveyances by the road or in churches and other public buildings thrown open for that purpose. Some paid a premium price for the privilege of spending the night in a barber's chair or on a billiard table.

Grady was with the President at every turn during the two-day visit. He escorted Mrs. Cleveland across the street from the railroad station to the Kimball House upon their arrival. He appeared on the balcony of the hotel a short time later to request the cheering thousands to disperse in order that the

[9] Cleveland to L. Q. C. Lamar, August 28, 1887; H. W. G. to Grover Cleveland, September 1887, Cleveland Papers. The "flag episode" refers to the furor created in the North earlier in the year by Cleveland's approval of a suggestion by the Secretary of War that the captured Confederate flags be returned to the Southern states. The order later was suspended by the President when it was discovered that he lacked the authority to make it. Grady wrote at the time (June 17, 1887) that the South would receive the flags gladly if sent "in a generous spirit," but if "given grudgingly" she would not accept.

COMMERCIAL CENTER OF ATLANTA IN 1887

Showing Kimball House at left and Union Station at right center.

From a drawing by Horace Bradley in *Harper's Weekly*, February 12, 1887.

President and his wife might rest from their journey. With President Collier of the exposition he took the distinguished guests the next morning on a carriage ride through the city's crowded streets to the exposition grounds. Here, in the rain and wind, Collier opened the exercises and Grady introduced the President, who spoke briefly to a throng estimated at 50,-000 persons.

Numerous social affairs were tendered President and Mrs. Cleveland in the moments not taken up by the exposition proper — a dinner at Governor Gordon's, a reception at the Capital City Club, a ladies' reception for Mrs. Cleveland at the Grady home, and a breakfast at Senator Colquitt's. When the presidential party left on Wednesday night it was still raining, but several thousand "young Democrats" turned out for a tumultuous torchlight demonstration. After Cleveland had spoken a few words of farewell from the station platform, there were loud calls for Grady, who replied: "My young countrymen, God knows I am proud of you tonight. I had the honor to call you out once before. That was to celebrate the first election of Grover Cleveland as President of the United States. I meet you again tonight to celebrate his coming among us. Let us adjourn now to go home to get dry, and wait until 1888, and then come out again to welcome his second election as President of the United States."

Thanks to Cleveland's visit, the two weeks' exposition made a profit of $58,000, all of which, the *Constitution* said, was to be invested in future expositions or returned to the subscribers on a pro rata basis. At first the directors planned to hold another fair in the fall of 1888, but finally they decided to give way to the city of Augusta, which was planning an exposition at that time. The Piedmont Park grounds and buildings thereupon were promised for the following year to Atlanta's Negro population for a "colored world exposition," and the next Piedmont Exposition was scheduled for 1889.

3

Scarcely had the exposition ended when Grady was drawn into one of the bitterest political battles of his career — and,

to him, perhaps the most distasteful. A referendum to determine the fate of Atlanta's two-year-old prohibition law had
been called for November 26, and Grady, to the surprise of
many persons, became the chief spokesman for the dry forces.

Although Grady for years had abstained from drinking anything stronger than an occasional glass of light sauterne "for
his stomach's sake," he served champagne at dinners and receptions in his own home and constantly was attending social
functions at which alcoholic beverages flowed freely. Indeed,
in entertaining prospective investors from the North, he
found rare old Southern whiskies a potent means of persuading the visitors to share his optimism for the future of Atlanta
and the New South. While always advocating temperance, he
deplored "fanaticism" in the temperance movement and once
had warned his own church against attempting to legislate its
members into total abstinence. When the chancellorship of
the University of Georgia later became vacant, Grady, as a
trustee, put his strength behind the movement to elect Professor H. C. White, who was opposed and finally defeated by
the more conservative majority on the grounds that he held
dances and served wine in his home.[10]

"In politics, and as a national movement, prohibition will
be a failure," the *Constitution* had contended. "As a non-
partisan, local matter regulated as the exigencies of the case
demand, by local option and high license, it will flourish and
do good." One of the "exigencies of the case" undoubtedly
was the fact that, whereas the slave could be controlled by his
owner in the use of liquor, the free Negro had as much right
as the white man to make himself drunk. "A drunken Negro
was looked upon as a greater menace than a drunken white
man, and both were considered objectionable for reasons economic as well as moral." [11]

It was doubtless for these latter reasons that the *Constitution* did not oppose the spread of the local-option movement
over the rural counties of Georgia in the early 1880's. By 1884
ninety counties were either totally dry or partly so. In the fol-

[10] Hull, *Historical Sketch*, pp. 124–25; *Minutes,* Board of Trustees, University of Georgia, 1888.
[11] Coulter: *Short History*, p. 396.

lowing year a state-wide local-option law was passed to permit
any county to hold an election on prohibition on petition of
one-tenth of the voters. When the first prohibition referendum was held in Atlanta and Fulton County in November
1885, the *Constitution* contented itself with urging an honest
election. After the drys had won by a majority of 228 out of
some 7,000 votes, the paper insisted that the law be given a
fair trial. Grady's principal concern, judging by his appeal
"To the People of Atlanta" on the eve of that election, was
that the city should remain united:

> Atlanta is built in the heart of a united people. Her glory is
> the comradeship of her sons. Her boast and her strength has been,
> that her name has had the power to fuse all factions, bury all dif-
> ferences, silence all bickerings. To this, more than to all other
> things combined, she owes her greatness. Sad will it be for her —
> and sadder still for her people — if the passion of the pending
> contest should outlive the counting of the lawful ballots, and de-
> stroy the unity of thought and sympathy and action that has made
> her invincible in the past, and given promise to her future. There
> is no reason why it should. . . . The result should be accepted in
> frankness and good spirit, and the divided factions should come
> together once more, shoulder to shoulder, for the glory and pros-
> perity of Atlanta.

Grady particularly feared that prohibition might split the
Democratic Party in the South or become a determining factor in the selection of candidates at the sacrifice of more important issues.

That, of course, is exactly what happened. The local anti-
prohibitionists organized, under the domination of Hoke
Smith, for the purpose of electing a wet mayor and city council. Grady, with his skill for conciliation, finally induced both
factions to come together and nominate a "fusion ticket."
However, the election of this ticket was only a temporary compromise. The antis, over Grady's protests, continued to work
for another referendum, even while the city was preparing for
the exposition. Thus, before the exhibits had been cleared
from the buildings, Grady found himself confronted with the
necessity of taking a stand in a controversy he had sought to

avoid. To make his choice more difficult, one of his partners, Howell, was aligned with the wets, while two others, Hemphill and Inman, were among the leading drys.

Grady refrained from taking any part in the organization meetings of either side, but, yielding to the importunities of his dry friends, he studied the matter and decided that he should speak in favor of giving prohibition in Atlanta a further trial. He indicated a reason for his decision when, in the first of two addresses for the prohibition forces, he said: "You must go down to the poorer classes to find out whether prohibition has been a blessing or an evil." He asserted that prohibition had not had a fair trial in Atlanta and that, even imperfectly tried, it had been an "unspeakable success." To support this latter contention, he cited a decrease in crime, an increase in school attendance, a substantial drop in the number of distress warrants, a virtual disappearance of the practice of garnisheeing wages, and a vast improvement in general business conditions throughout the city.[12]

Although the wets could and did reply with vehemence that all these conditions were not necessarily the result of prohibition, the drys thought Grady had made an extremely strong case. His speech was reprinted by the thousands of copies in temperance publications and special pamphlets.

Because of the conflicting views of the owners, the *Constitution* carried no editorials either for or against prohibition. Instead, it published in its news pages, under the label "Communicated," columns of speeches, letters, and statements from both sides. It later revealed, in answer to questions, that it received $1,676 for printing the contributions of the wets and $1,371 for printing those of the drys. The paper asserted, however, that Howell, Hemphill, Grady, and Inman had donated "much more than $3,047" to the two committees waging the campaign.[13]

"Grady is dry and Howell is wet, but all's fish that comes to Hemphill's net — you bet!" taunted the *Macon Telegraph* as

---

[12] The first prohibition speech was delivered on November 3. It was reported in the *Constitution* of November 4 and was published in its entirety on November 6.

[13] December 11, 1887.

it published a front-page cartoon which pictured a platform with Howell on one side, pouring Bourbon from a jug, and Grady on the other, pouring ice water from a pitcher. Between the two stood Hemphill, the business manager, giving both men his blessing because of the advertising dollars rolling into the *Constitution's* till.[14]

The climax of the campaign came on the night of November 17, when Grady was scheduled to address a rally of the drys at a big cotton warehouse while Howell spoke to a gathering of the wets at DeGive's Opera House. This situation gave Hoke Smith's *Evening Journal* on that day the opportunity to remark:

> Jack Spratt
> Could eat no fat,
>   His wife could eat no lean,
> Between them both
> They cleared the cloth
>   And licked the platter clean.

The reproduction of this ancient rhyme is not intended as an insinuation that Mr. Henry W. Grady, the silver-tongued prohibition orator of to-night, has any of the attributes of Jack Spratt, or that Colonel Evan P. Howell, the redoubtable champion of the antis, has any of the peculiarities of Jack Spratt's conjugal associate. The idea sought to be conveyed is that the fat and lean of prohibition will be energetically attacked by these gentlemen to-night at the same hour from opposite sides of the table.

It goes without saying that between them both the platter will be licked clean, and it is to be hoped that this hearty prohibition meal will be thoroughly digested and assimilated to Atlanta's system, that growth in her every tissue will be the result.

It would be hard to select two more effective speakers and two more entirely different.

"What is Colonel Howell's style of oratory?" said one newspaper man to another.

"Well," said he, "you have heard Grady? you know how he speaks?"

"Yes."

"Well, Grady makes you feel like you want to be an angel and

[14] *Macon Daily Telegraph,* November 13, 1887.

Howell   Hemphill   *Grady*

THE ATLANTA PROHIBITION CAMPAIGN OF 1887 AS SEEN BY THE "MACON TELEGRAPH"

with the angels stand, and Howell makes you feel as if he were the commander of an army, waving his sword and saying, 'Follow me,' and you would follow him to the death."

Both of these speakers will praise enthusiasm at the start. As Grady ascends the platform the band will play "Dixie" and the audience will be almost in a frenzy of delight. As Colonel Howell comes forward the band will be likely to play the "Marseillaise Hymn," — some air that stirs the sterner nature — and he will be received with thunders of applause.

.   .   .   .

Mr. Howell will doubtless deal in statistics; Mr. Grady will have figures, but they will not smell of the census. They will take on the pleasing shape that induced one of his reporters to plant a crop of Irish potatoes on a speculation. To-night Atlanta will be treated to a hopeful view of prohibition by the most eloquent optimist in the country. The contrast will be drawn with all the ruggedness of a strong, blunt man.

A crowd of some eight thousand persons — many times the number that could be packed into the Opera House — stood up in the cotton warehouse for more than two hours to hear Grady. The speaker began upon a humorous note, then shifted quickly to the serious: "I have been quoted as saying that I would give one thousand dollars if I had not spoken here two weeks ago. The statement is false. . . . If I have done or said anything in the thirty-seven years of my life that has my more perfect approval than that speech I do not remember it." He explained that he long had been a "high-license man" and for that reason had declined to take part in the 1885 campaign. But since the last election he had watched prohibition closely, and he was now convinced that "this experiment, imperfectly tried, has been wholly successful, and if it must be modified, that it can be modified better without barrooms than through them."

The body of this second address, like the first, consisted largely of figures and opinions from business men and city officials to show that Atlanta was a larger, wealthier, and happier city than it was before prohibition. As Grady approached the conclusion of the speech, he "pulled out all the stops" in a powerful emotional appeal that has been a classic in the repertoire of prohibitionists ever since:

My friends, hesitate before you vote liquor back into Atlanta, now that it is shut out. Don't trust it. It is powerful, aggressive and universal in its attacks. Tonight it enters an humble home to strike the roses from a woman's cheek, and tomorrow it challenges this republic in the halls of congress. Today it strikes a crust from the lips of a starving child, and tomorrow levies tribute from the government itself. There is no cottage in this city humble enough to escape it — no palace strong enough to shut it out. It defies the law when it cannot coerce suffrage. It is flexible to cajole, but merciless in victory. It is the mortal enemy of peace and order. The despoiler of men, the terror of women, the cloud that shadows the face of children, the demon that has dug more graves and sent more souls unsaved to judgment than all the pestilences that have wasted life since God sent the plagues to Egypt, and all the wars that have defeated since Joshua stood beyond Jericho. (Tumultuous applause for several minutes.) Oh, my countrymen, loving God and humanity, do not bring this grand old city again under the dominion of that power. (Cries of "We won't! we won't!") It can profit no man by its return. It can uplift no industry, revive no interest, remedy no wrong. You know that it cannot. It comes to destroy, and it shall profit mainly by the ruin of your sons or mine. It comes to mislead human souls and to crush human hearts under its rumbling wheels. It comes to bring gray haired mothers down in shame and sorrow to their graves. It comes to destroy the wife's love into despair, and her pride into shame. It comes to still the laughter on the lips of little children. It comes to stifle all the music of the home, and fill it with silence and desolation. It comes to ruin your body and mind, to wreck your home, and it knows that it must measure its prosperity by the swiftness and certainty with which it wreaks this work. Now, will you vote it back? (Applause, and cries of "We won't! we won't!") [15]

In spite of such oratory, the wets carried the election on November 26 by a majority of 1,112. One possible reason for Grady's defeat is that, for the first time in a political campaign, he was on the opposite side from the bulk of the money. Whereas the liquor dealers and distilleries had been "caught

[15] *Constitution*, November 20, 1887.

napping" in 1885, they now were thoroughly aroused and used every available means to win the fight for their continued existence. Money was spent freely by both sides, as the *Macon Telegraph* hinted in a cartoon showing both wets and drys paying obeisance to "Our Brother in Black in Atlanta," but the wets undoubtedly had the advantage in this respect.[16] There were numerous charges of illegal voting, and only an earnest plea by Grady prevented the dry leaders from contesting the results.

On the day after the referendum, the *Constitution* carried characteristic cards both from Howell and from Grady. After expressing his determination to do everything possible toward uniting Atlanta and keeping the sale of liquor within bounds, Howell declared: "I love Henry Grady as a brother, and no one appreciates more highly than I his noble and unselfish devotion to our city; no one knows better than I his earnestness and faithful attachment to her welfare." Grady expressed similar sentiments toward Howell, then added: "When everything else I have said or done is forgotten, I want the words I have spoken for prohibition in Atlanta to be remembered. I am prouder of my share in the campaign that has ended in its defeat than of my share in all other campaigns that have ended in victory. I espoused the cause deliberately, and I have worked for its success night and day, to the very best of my ability. My only regret is that my ability was not greater."

"This reunion of the owners of the *Constitution*," wrote a member of the staff, "was the prompt example which set a pattern for the community. Within a year from the close of the bitterest campaign in Atlanta's history, one in which many a house and many a family was divided against itself, the acrimony had almost entirely disappeared."[17] There were repercussions of it a year later, when the time came once more to select candidates for mayor and aldermen, but Grady again pleaded successfully for a "fusion ticket." The *Constitution's* platform for "Harmony in Atlanta" was to "keep prohibition

16 Coulter: *Short History*, pp. 397–8; *Macon Daily Telegraph*, November 20, 1887.
17 Harris, p. 617.

out of the race" and to "end permanently the division on this question."

But the prohibition campaign had left its marks on Grady. As a result of overtaxing his strength again so soon after his exertions in connection with the exposition, he was forced to take to bed. Two months later he still was so exhausted that, accompanied by his family and several friends, including Samuel M. Inman, he went to the Florida east coast for a vacation.

Taking the unpopular side of so controversial an issue as prohibition may have contributed also to the elimination of Grady from further consideration as a candidate for vice president in 1888. Whether any Southerner could have been nominated in this year is, of course, problematical. Even if Grady had never said a word on prohibition, his frequent pronouncements in favor of the tariff probably would have made him unacceptable to Cleveland as a running-mate. Soon after the President's message to Congress in December 1887, asking for a reduction in the tariff, the word went out from Washington that "no follower of Randall's need expect any patronage or other benefits." But in Georgia prohibition also was an issue that divided the Democrats, Walter B. Hill declaring in an open letter immediately before the national convention that both Grady and Senator Colquitt had been "notified by the liquor papers" that they must "give up their democracy or their prohibition." [18] Regardless of whether it was due to prohibition, the tariff, the section in which he lived, or a combination of all three, Grady must have known by the spring of 1888 that he was out of the picture as far as the vice-presidency was concerned.

Although Grady did not attend the convention at St. Louis in June, the *Constitution* remained loyal to Cleveland. "While we do not altogether agree with the policy outlined by the president on the matter of the tariff," the paper said, "we do not think that it will cause his defeat either for re-nomination or for re-election. There are other issues besides the tariff which guarantee the indorsement of Mr. Cleveland's administration by his election for another term." Grady's fail-

18 Nevins: *Cleveland*, p. 386; *Constitution*, April 18, May 21, 1888.

ure to attend the convention apparently was due, not to any
pique with the party or its leader, but rather to the fact that
by summer he was engrossed in another notable piece of showmanship and civic service — the Piedmont Chautauqua.

4

The Piedmont Chautauqua was patterned after the Chau-
tauqua Institution which had been founded on the shores of
Lake Chautauqua, New York, in 1874, to promote the train-
ing of Sunday-school teachers. Already some forty-two other
Chautauquas had sprung up over the country. After preliminary investigation and discussion, Grady called a meeting in
March 1888 to explain the movement to a group of Atlantans.
A plan was adopted for asking two hundred citizens to subscribe $100 each toward the undertaking. The Piedmont
Chautauqua was incorporated with M. C. Kiser, wealthy shoe-
manufacturer, as president, and Grady as vice president.
Kiser, then doing business estimated at one million dollars a
year, had started out "with little education and no money" in
the town of Salt Springs (now Powder Springs), twenty miles
west of Atlanta.[19] It was planned to develop the Chautauqua
at this point, where a spring-fed stream offered possibilities for
an artificial lake and other attractions.

Salt Springs already had one resort hotel, advertised as "the
most sumptuous summer hotel in the south." The promoters
of Chautauqua proposed to erect two smaller hotels and to
put up a classroom building, a restaurant accommodating
1,000 persons, and a tabernacle seating 7,000. Lots for summer cottages were staked out and offered for sale, space was
provided for various outdoor sports, and the stream was
dammed to provide boating and swimming facilities. The
Georgia Pacific Railroad promised to run special trains making the trip from the city to the grounds in thirty-five minutes.

In forming the faculty of the "Summer University," Grady
drew chiefly upon the staff of the University of Virginia, which
he still regarded as the strongest educational institution in the

[19] *Constitution*, March 28, May 25, 1888; sketch of Kiser in article by
H. W. G., August 15, 1880.

South. The Chautauqua announced that it would have instructors in Bible, English, foreign languages, the natural sciences, the fine arts, physical education, and "every chair of a first-class university." The entire curriculum was open to anyone upon payment of a ten-dollar fee, and any single department for a five-dollar fee.

Grady realized that the success of the enterprise depended, not upon the relatively small number registering for regular classes, but upon the size of the crowds coming out for the special attractions at night and for the sermons on Sunday. More than a score of celebrities were signed up for the program. Congressmen William McKinley and Roger Q. Mills came from Washington to give Georgians contrasting views on the tariff; Dr. Talmage delivered his lecture on "The Bright Side of Things"; and Thomas Nelson Page gave a reading of his "Unc' Edinburg's Drowndin'." There were sermons, chalk talks, and scientific demonstrations by many lesser personalities. A "Hungarian orchestra" gave daily concerts, and several larger bands appeared on special occasions. Four leading manufacturers of fireworks produced striking displays in competition for the "Chautauqua championship" and a $1,000 prize.

A barbecue formally opened the Chautauqua grounds on July 4. Henry W. Grady, Jr., and his friend, Eugene R. Black, who were "ticket-snatchers" on this occasion, recalled with particular relish one incident in connection with President Kiser's address of welcome. The speech had been written out in advance by Grady, but when Kiser rose he fumbled around in his pockets without being able to find the manuscript. Finally, he looked out upon the crowd and began hesitatingly by saying: "Right down thar is whar I used to hunt foxes." Not being able to think of any further extemporaneous remarks, he turned to those closest to him and asked: "Whar's Grady?" The *Constitution* of the next morning reported that "President Kiser's speech was a model of good sense and good humor, well and briefly expressed. It was just such a sensible talk as was to be expected from so sensible a man."

When the directors of the Chautauqua voted to invite Congressman McKinley to speak on the tariff, a mild furor was created. Senator Colquitt was requested to extend the invitation to the Ohio Congressman, but he refused to do so on the grounds that it was unwise for "a republican protectionist to go to Georgia and stir up strife in the democratic party." The *Constitution* deplored any attempt of the people's elected representatives in Washington to "censor freedom of thought, speech or action," declaring: "To say that our people, having ears to hear, should not hear, lest hearing they believe, is to admit the truth of the adversaries' position, the weakness of your own, or to cast a slur upon the intelligence of our people." The invitation finally was delivered by Senator Brown, who was arguing in Congress at this time that the proposed downward revision of the tariff would hurt the South more than New England.

On August 21 a crowd of several thousand persons listened for two hours to McKinley's speech. "Did it change the opinion of any?" asked the *Constitution* the next day. "That question can be answered only by the individuals themselves. But one thing is certain: Every man there, whether a protectionist or an advocate of a revenue tariff, left with the firm conviction that he had heard the grandest argument for protection ever made." Grady denied a report that the Chautauqua was trying to obtain James G. Blaine for an address, but added that he personally "would be glad to hear him or any other equally illustrious American."

The Chautauqua's largest crowd came out on August 28 to hear the closing address delivered by Grady himself on the subject of "Cranks, Croakers, and Creditors." The "cranks" were those who started the enterprise, the "croakers" those who were continually finding fault and predicting its failure, and the "creditors" those "whose patience and cooperation . . . enabled the Chautauqua to carry its season through and close it successfully." The Chautauqua's impresario paid his respects to the "original croaker . . . the frog . . . the meanest and unloveliest of created things. . . . God is not responsible for it," he continued, "for he made the tadpole — a very silent and sociable sort of fellow. The evolutionist made the frog." At the conclusion he spoke of the serious purpose which had prompted him to give so freely of his time to the enterprise:

More than ever in the world's history knowledge is power in this swiftly changing age. All the nations of the earth are in the race for mastery and if the South would hold her place she must hold it through knowledge. If she carves out a glorious destiny which lights her sons' ambition, knowledge is the chisel with which she must shape it out. The diffusion of knowledge is the prime object of Chautauqua. There is not a man or woman who has entered these gates and spent a day here observantly who has not left a better citizen — better equipped for his or her duty, with broadened lives, higher aspirations. As for me I have done some work but this I know is the best to which my hands have been given. We leave it poorer in pocket but richer in purpose.[20]

The earnestness of the speaker was indicated by the fact that Grady had given $5,000 out of his own pocket to complete the Chautauqua buildings, and $2,500 toward making up a deficit on the teachers' salaries.[21] The idea for a Chautauqua in Atlanta was sound, but the directors had made a grievous error in locating it so far away from the city — because some of the backers happened to own land there. In spite of this handicap, the Piedmont Chautauqua continued for many years to carry on the work Grady had started.

One prominent citizen, when asked after the Chautauqua whether he thought Atlanta would have a population of 100,-000 by 1900, replied yes, on one condition — "the settlement of this prohibition question in Atlanta. If we get this thing fixed, and Henry Grady gets two or three more attractions like the Piedmont Exposition and the Chautauqua, Atlanta will have 120,000 people in 1900. That man Grady has done more for Atlanta than any ten men in it, and nobody but the fools are down on him." [22]

5

In these same months Grady was engaged in scores of lesser public activities for Atlanta and Georgia. His reorgan-

20 MS., Grady Collection.
21 W. A. Hemphill in address at Piedmont Chautauqua, reported in *Constitution*, August 22, 1890.
22 Interview with Scott Thornton in *Constitution*, September 9, 1888.

ization of the languishing Atlanta Manufacturers' Association
in the fall of 1888 again demonstrated his skill at conciliation.
This association, founded in 1883, had claimed credit in one
year for bringing to Atlanta factories producing glass, excel-
sior, soap, furniture, hardware, spices, vinegar, bridges and
axles, and cottonseed oil. In 1888 the organization had become inactive. Grady called a meeting and in the opening talk
suggested that the association be expanded into a large civic
club, with several thousand members paying initiation fees of
ten dollars and annual dues of five dollars each. Hoke Smith,
however, thought that what was needed was a land company
to buy up factory sites and donate them or "sell them at bargain rates." Samuel M. Inman favored a manufacturers' loan
association to assist in financing new enterprises. When a
sharp division of opinion was threatened, Grady proposed
that all three plans be combined by forming a large membership organization to do the advertising and "get everybody
interested." There could be a real-estate department and a
loan department within the association, he suggested, to carry
out the ideas of Smith and Inman. Grady's compromise was
adopted. In another twelve months Atlanta had added to its
list of manufactures "double-concave razors," sewing machines, gold watches, and pianos.[23]

Besides its rapidly expanding list of industrial enterprises
Atlanta in these same months gained four new railroads, making eight in all. Noting that the city's population had grown
from 37,409 in 1880 to 60,000 in 1887, the *Constitution* campaigned editorially for paved streets, artesian water, and a
modern sewerage system to meet the expanding needs. In
1888 the paper announced plans for the building of the city's
first electric streetcar line, and the following year Grady was
one of the prominent citizens who took a turn running one of
the new cars.

In October 1888 the new Georgia School of Technology
opened in Atlanta, with Dr. Isaac S. Hopkins as its first president. Grady had encouraged Dr. Hopkins, while the latter was
president of Emory College, in his pioneer efforts to develop

[23] *Constitution*, December 12, 19, 1888; Henry W. Grady, *The New South*,
pp. 200–1.

technical education in Georgia. For example, the *Constitution* in 1887 had purchased for its job department, with considerable fanfare, a twenty-horsepower Corliss engine made by the Emory engineering students. As a trustee of the new state technological school, Grady now was partly responsible for selecting Dr. Hopkins to head the institution, as well as for raising the funds to bring Georgia Tech to Atlanta.

Presiding at the opening exercises was Nathaniel E. Harris, of Macon, a college-mate of Grady at the University of Georgia, and chairman of the legislative commission in charge of establishing the new school. Since Grady followed Harris on the program, the latter obviously had his editor-friend in mind when he referred to the place Atlanta now held in the life of Georgia. Said Harris:

Atlanta did not get on well at one time with the middle and southern portion of the state. Her people were not like our people, the push and energy of her citizens, the rapid strides which they made in wealth and progress, gave her more the appearance of one of our western or northern cities than of a southern metropolis. She had such a wonderful press to blow her own horn, and did it with such unceasing and inevitable persistance, that often when smarting under the sting of defeat we forgot she belonged to the state. "Get there somehow" was the motto on which she acted, and it went into everything she took a hand in, from a baseball game to a governor's election. . . . Yet she grew and distanced all her rivals, and made her influence felt in every hamlet and every neighborhood and in every gathering in this great state of Georgia. She purified her politics, she gathered the influence of the great around her, till by sheer force of will and energy she made the people recognize her as part of the commonwealth equally with Rome, with Macon and Savannah.[24]

For the moment it did appear that Atlanta's leadership in Georgia was being accepted as completely as was Grady's in Atlanta. Governor Gordon was re-elected without opposition in the fall of 1888. Mrs. Felton was praising McKinley and Senator Brown for their views on the tariff, and Dr. Felton, then in the legislature, was co-operating with the *Constitu-*

[24] *Constitution,* October 6, 1888.

tion in its stand for railroad-rate regulation and larger educational appropriations.[25] Most significant of all, Tom Watson,
later to be the very embodiment of the agrarian revolt, was in
1888 still a Democratic "elector at large," praying the "Good
Lord" to "keep the South solid," and fighting on the same
side as the *Constitution* in a successful battle against the "jute
trust" — a combination formed in the midsummer of 1888 to
control the price of the jute bagging used in baling cotton.
The nearest Watson came to an open break with Grady in
1888 was a speech poking fun at the "city orator's" idyllic
"dream farm," to which Grady sometimes said he had gone
when the pressure of scores of callers made it necessary for
him to lock his office door in order to finish a piece of work
before deadline.[26]

It may have been natural for a "city orator" to lay too much
stress on industrialization as a key to progress, and Grady, of
course, lacked the farm background of Watson. But he was
one "city fellow" who recognized repeatedly in his writings
and speeches that Georgia was fundamentally an agricultural
state and that even the cities could not attain a healthy prosperity so long as the farms remained impoverished. In a typical editorial he said:

That state is most prosperous in which town and country prosper alike, and in which all progress is equal and all growth sym-
metrical.

What Georgia needs is some force put at work that will uplift
and strengthen her villages and her country sites and bring them
up to the wonderful speed with which her towns and cities are
forging ahead.[27]

Grady earnestly believed, as he told the Atlanta Manufacturers' Association, that "what helps Atlanta helps Georgia."
But he never failed to add: "And what helps Georgia is bound
to help Atlanta."

25 Correspondence in Felton Papers.
26 Woodward, op. cit., pp. 114, 126–8, 140–2; Harris, pp. 19–20.
27 *Constitution*, August 25, 1889.

CHAPTER THIRTEEN

Statesman without Office

BECAUSE of his preoccupation with so many undertakings in Atlanta, Grady was forced throughout 1887 and the greater part of 1888 to decline the many invitations that came to him to make speeches outside his home city. From the date of "The New South" triumph until September 1888, except for the period of his illness, any time he could spare from the *Constitution* was taken up almost completely with the exposition, the prohibition campaign, or the Chautauqua. Now, with these ended, and with the national campaign between Cleveland and Benjamin Harrison under way, Grady the speaker swung into action again.

On October 9 Grady spoke at a fair in Rome. He was introduced by his friend John Temple Graves, editor of the *Rome Daily Tribune,* who, like Tom Watson, was one of Georgia's two "Democratic electors at large." Graves had edited the *Atlanta Evening Journal* under Hoke Smith for a few months in the latter part of 1887, but he always had been a friend and admirer of Grady. Of all those who had "labored with tongue or pen" to build up the South, Graves said, Grady was the first.[1]

This estimate of Grady's ability already had been endorsed by the managers of the Texas State Fair at Dallas, who had invited him to speak there October 27 on "The South and Its Problems." With the Republicans again agitating for a "force bill" and for representation in Congress based upon the number of votes actually cast, the views of the South's most prominent editor were of wide interest. Grady's friends persuaded him, therefore, to write out his speech so that proof-sheets

1 *Constitution,* October 10, 1888.

might be mailed in advance to newspapers throughout the country.

One morning Grady came into his office and announced that the speech was ready for delivery. When an audience composed of Howell, Harris, Holliday, and others of his associates had assembled, he delivered the hour-long address without referring to a note.

When he had finished, Harris said: "Grady, that speech is absolutely perfect. Do you suppose you can say it again?"

"Of course," replied Grady. "I can say it as often as I want to."

To prove this statement, he took Holliday into his office, dictated the speech exactly as he had delivered it, and had it set in type for release at the proper time. Later he refreshed his mind by having his secretary hold the proofs while he went through the address and recited the first sentence or two in each paragraph, "never missing a word." [2]

Grady left for Texas on Tuesday, October 23. Traveling in a private car, he was accompanied by fifteen Atlantans, including Holliday, Howell, Inman, and former Governor Mc-Daniel. Fifteen-year-old Henry Grady, Jr., and his chum Telamon Cuyler also made the trip, "after learning that it was to be in a private car and that a cook was going along." It was as a result of their conniving that Roscoe Anderson, the *Constitution's* office boy, was smuggled into a linen closet and carried along. Young Cuyler kept a diary, the manuscript of which is today the best original source of information about the journey.

The trip to Dallas was in the nature of an ovation. "He goes as the accredited immigration agent and boss talker of the Empire State," said the *Augusta Evening News*. At Memphis, Tennessee, where the party stopped for several hours, Grady was persuaded to make a brief impromptu talk to a group of business men at the Cotton Exchange. At Sherman, Texas, his train was met by "a solid acre of people," including a brass band and some fifteen hundred uniformed schoolgirls. Here and at the town of McKenny, where there was another large crowd, Grady made short speeches from the platform of his

[2] J. R. Holliday in *Constitution*, December 24, 1939.

car. There were expectant crowds at many other places along the route, but the train could not stop because of its schedule. By the time it pulled into Dallas at two o'clock Friday afternoon, the special car was filled with flowers.

Grady's speech at the Texas State Fair had been announced for eleven o'clock Saturday morning. By nine thirty the grandstand was "fairly well filled," and by the appointed hour between twenty and thirty thousand persons were seated or standing around the speakers' platform. Over the rostrum was extended an arch bearing a quotation from Grady's New England Society speech: "We have sowed cities in place of theories." A band was playing and a gala spirit prevailed.

As in "The New South" speech, Grady began by taking a "text" from his idol, Benjamin H. Hill. This time it was an inscription on the Hill monument in Atlanta: "Who saves his country, saves all things, and all things saved will bless him. Who lets his country die, lets all things die, and all things dying curse him." After identifying himself with his audience through local references, he launched into the development of his two main points: "first, the duty of the South in its relation to the race problem; second, the duty of the South in relation to its no less unique and important industrial problem."

Explaining why the South, despite its complete loyalty to the Union, must always be regarded as a distinctive region, Grady declared it was neither "provincialism" nor "sectionalism" that held the Southern states together, but "something deeper than these and essential to our system." It was the problem of how "to carry within her body politic two separate races, and nearly equal in numbers. She must carry these races in peace — for discord means ruin. She must carry them separately — for assimilation means disbasement. She must carry them in equal justice — for to this she is pledged in honor and in gratitude. She must carry them even unto the end, for in human probability she will never be quit of either." He pointed out that if the whites were divided, and the Negroes were skillfully led, the blacks would have the balance of power — "a thing not to be considered. If their vote was not compacted, it would invite the debauching bid of factions, and drift surely to that which was the most corrupt and cunning."

"The clear and unmistakable domination of the white race, dominating not through violence, not through party alliance, but through the integrity of its own vote and the largeness of its sympathy and justice through which it shall compel the support of the better classes of the colored race — that," he said, "is the hope and assurance of the South."

After deploring the "incendiary threats" of those who urged that the Negro be allowed to vote freely, regardless of the hazards, Grady pointed to the suspension of Chinese immigration in 1882 as a much more intelligent effort toward securing "the control of this republic" to "the homogeneous people that established and has maintained it." The next step would be taken, he said, "when some brave statesman, looking Demagogy in the face," would "demand that the standard of our citizenship be lifted and the right of acquiring our suffrage be abridged." Obviously he thought that eventually there should be restrictions to protect the ballot from the ignorant and unfit, irrespective of race or color. "When that day comes," he predicted, "the position of the South will be fully understood, and everywhere approved."

The speaker next took up the industrial prooiem. He described the tremendous progress already made by the New South, despite the "three billions of property" destroyed by the war, despite the "six hundred million dollars . . . given willingly of our poverty as pensions for Northern soldiers," and despite "the system of tariff taxes levied on the unmixed agriculture of these States" for the protection of Northern industries. He thought that the tariff should "be revised and its duties reduced," but he pointed out that the South now had "entered the industrial list" and should not blindly espouse either "free trade" or a "tariff for revenue only." Agriculture alone, he declared, "no matter how rich or varied its resources," could not "establish or maintain a people's prosperity."

Grady's peroration carried an emotional appeal such as he always used in making an important point. Pleading with "the young men of Texas" to have faith in themselves, he related the story of a soldier who lay wounded on a "hard-fought field" after the roar of the battle had died away. "Over the field flickered the lanterns of the surgeons with the litter bearers, searching that they might take away those whose lives could be saved. . . . This poor soldier watched, unable to turn or speak as the lantern grew near." The surgeon bent over the soldier, hesitated a moment, and left. Later he returned and again bent over the stricken man, saying: 'I believe if this poor fellow lives to sundown to-morrow he will get well.' . . . All night long these words fell into his heart as the dews fell from the stars upon his lips, 'if he but lives till sundown, he will get well.' " It was an entirely new feature of the address — one that Grady had introduced after hearing the incident related by Inman during the trip from Atlanta. But by urging the South to face its perplexing problems with a courage like that of the wounded soldier on the field, he made this anecdote the summation of his whole argument.[3]

When the speaker finished the story of the wounded soldier, "at least 1,000 people were in tears," wrote young Cuyler. But in changing to a more effective ending, Grady had wrecked six columns of type set in the *Constitution* office from the advance manuscript of his speech. Not only was the peroration new, but the remainder of the address given under the inspiration of the occasion was "at least fifty per cent different" from the version dictated in Atlanta. A telegram was sent at once to Clark Howell, night editor of the *Constitution:* "Suppress speech. It has been entirely changed. Notify other papers." The new portions then were written out from Holliday's notes and telegraphed to Atlanta.[4]

On Sunday the Atlantans went to Austin, where Grady was banqueted and called upon for three addresses — at the University of Texas, at the asylum for the blind, and before an assemblage of business men. On Monday the party visited the Alamo and other places of historical interest in San Antonio.

---

[3] *Constitution*, October 24–8, 1888. The text of the speech as given in the *Constitution*, October 28, is reprinted in Harris, pp. 94–120.

[4] Harris, p. 17; MS., Cuyler Diary, Grady Collection.

On Tuesday there were dinners and speeches in Houston and Galveston. The Georgians then headed home by way of New Orleans, reaching Atlanta on November 1.

"I do not believe any private citizen of this country ever received such an ovation so far from home and so long continued," said Inman upon their return. "It was simply a question of endurance — and in leaving Texas he had to decline many times more invitations than he accepted. At every town of any sort of prominence and at many stations immense crowds gathered with bands, and as the train rolled up there were calls for Mr. Grady that could not be resisted." [5]

Notwithstanding the acclaim given Grady in the South, the Dallas speech received relatively little attention in the North. The progress of the presidential campaign in the doubtful states was of much more concern to Northern papers than an address anywhere in a section already conceded to Cleveland. As soon as the election was over, however, the repercussions of Grady's Texas trip began to be heard more widely.

2

On the morning after Cleveland's defeat the *Constitution's* headlines reflected its managing editor's opinion that "The Tariff Question Did the Mischief." Grady did not try to lay the blame upon Cleveland or anyone else; he reaffirmed his loyalty to the Democratic Party and his belief in the necessity for a "solid South." The Republicans were determined, in his opinion, "to supervise Southern elections by federal machinery, and, if necessary, by federal bayonets," and "to base representation in the electoral college not on population, as at present, but on the average vote cast for a series of years in congressional elections." To combat these dangers, Grady issued another ringing cry to Southern Democrats:

The battle of 1892 must, therefore, be fought in the senate and in the house. . . . If in the senate or in the house these schemes can be arrested — these conspirators so denounced that they will falter in their work — if the people can be aroused to see the

[5] *Constitution*, November 2, 1888.

enormity of the outrage against liberty and the constitution involved in their schemes — then the democracy can and will be
restored to power in 1892. But everything depends on the ability
of the democratic minority in the senate and in the house. . . .[6]

At such a moment, when the possible consequences of the
Democratic defeat "engaged the thoughts of all and aroused
the fears of not a few," Georgians naturally looked to Grady
for leadership. He was the only Southern speaker of the late
eighties who had succeeded in gaining the attention and the
confidence of the North to any marked degree; he was one of
the few Southern editors whose writings had national circulation, both through his own paper and through frequent quotations in other publications. Almost overnight, therefore, a
"spontaneous movement" developed to send him to the
United States Senate in place of Senator Colquitt, who was to
come up for re-election by the Georgia legislature in about
two weeks. First to make the suggestion, apparently, was the
Augusta Evening News, but John Temple Graves's *Rome
Daily Tribune* promptly seconded it. The enthusiastic endorsement of many out-of-state papers showed the extent to
which Grady had become a national figure.

All this prompted the *Columbus Enquirer-Sun,* a political
opponent of the *Constitution,* to insinuate that "Grady's recent trip to Dallas was a preliminary intended as a kind of
boom" for the Senate race. The action of the Democratic
state convention the previous summer in endorsing Colquitt
was supposed to have "settled the affair," the Columbus paper said, but Grady's friends claimed that "the great Democratic defeat, chargeable to the tariff," made a change desirable.[7]

Since the Democratic defeat and the resultant threat of a
"force bill" were the reasons advanced for suggesting that
Grady replace Colquitt, it is doubtful whether Grady or his
friends had any immediate political designs in mind in making the Texas trip. The ovation he received, however, unquestionably did have the effect of centering attention upon

[6] Ibid., November 11, 1888.
[7] November 12, 1888.

him as a potential candidate. Moreover, Colquitt had indicated in a letter to a prominent Georgia politician just before the Democratic state convention in June that all was not well between him and Grady. Colquitt had desired a full endorsement of Cleveland's tariff message by the convention, whereas Grady and Senator Brown had maneuvered a resolution endorsing Cleveland's administration but not "descending to details." [8] The refusal of Colquitt to transmit the Piedmont Chautauqua's invitation to McKinley to come to Georgia for an address on the tariff had only aggravated this disagreement.

In an interview with the *Evening Journal* on November 12, Grady denied that he was a candidate, but the reports persisted. Although the *Constitution* at this time was ignoring the boom in its own editorials, it was carrying letters from "A Friend of Henry Grady" and news stories of "rousing Grady meetings," all of which gave every indication of being politically inspired. Finally, on Sunday, November 18, two days before the senatorial election, the *Constitution* published a two-column signed editorial in which Grady explained his position. He began with another denial, but one which was far from being as unequivocal as his refusal to run for Congress in 1882:

I am not a candidate for the United States Senatorship. This I have said positively to all who have approached me on the subject. I have never at any time been a candidate. I have never addressed a human being on the subject who did not first address me. I have not put foot in the capitol or hotels since the legislature assembled. Hundreds of friends all over the state will testify that I have declined their offers to come to Atlanta in my behalf. The strange and unexpected developments of the past week, as all concerned know, have been without my aid or suggestion — and rather in my despite.

The American Senate, he said, was "the ablest parliament on earth," and membership in it was "the highest honor . . . that any kingdom or republic can confer on any citizen." But

[8] Colquitt and Joseph E. Brown to L. N. Trammell, May 23, 1888, Trammell Papers.

he listed "three causes" as withholding him from the race: first, "my personal relations to Senator Colquitt"; second, "a reluctance to embarrass my friends who were complicated [*sic*], or to lay the burdens of a conflict on those who were busy with their own affairs"; and, third, "a determination to do nothing that could be construed into a criticism of the position of any democrat in the campaign of 1888. I have no desire to profit by the disaster of my party."

In the next paragraph he admitted that the opposition to Colquitt probably would not have developed if Cleveland had been re-elected. He then explained that certain of his friends believed "the changed relations of the parties at Washington" made desirable a change in the character of Georgia's representatives. "With a majority party it is a question of management," he said. "With the minority party it is a question of appeal. The majority administers, the minority protests. With the majority it is tact, it is diplomacy, it is compromise, to soothe and satisfy. With the minority it is agitation, it is outcry, it is to touch the public conscience."

Having thus indirectly set forth the principal argument for his candidacy, Grady proceeded to answer directly the complaint that he was a "protectionist":

How long is it to be asserted of every democrat who honestly differed with the majority on an economic issue, though he frankly and promptly accepted the party platform and fought its battle without flaw or failing, that he has no right to ask for democratic recognition, and that if the party should honor him it thereby dishonors itself? . . .

I am no "protectionist," and I never have been. I did believe and I do believe the tariff issue was imprudently forced in the last campaign. I believe firmly in the necessity of tariff revision. I have said this in every speech I have made on the subject. Tariff reform can be effected only through the democratic party.

The editorial closed with a reaffirmation that "whether my lot be cast in high or humble place, I shall have but one ambition — and that — when Georgia calls, to stand side by side with those who are first at her feet and last in her service."

Grady did *not* say that he would refuse the senatorship, but merely that he was not a candidate. One cannot avoid concluding with the *Macon Telegraph* and the *Columbus Enquirer-Sun*, therefore, that Grady would have welcomed the call to serve, if it could have come without an acrimonious controversy. Indeed, Grady most likely would have preferred the senatorship to the vice-presidency, for, as the *Boston Herald* pointed out, the latter office was one place in which he would have to keep silent, or, if he spoke, "nobody would pay any attention." The best evidence that he did wish to go to the Senate is to be found in the fact that the failure of Governor Gordon and Hoke Smith to lend any aid to the boom led to Grady's final and definite estrangement from these one-time close friends — the only lasting personal quarrel, perhaps, of his whole life.

At the time of Colquitt's re-election the word went out merely that Grady had refused to allow his name to go before the legislature, which was true. But in 1890, when Gordon himself was a candidate for the Senate, Clark Howell referred to the Governor's treatment of Grady in 1888 as an instance of "ingratitude which has not its parallel in the history of Georgia politics." While the senatorial boom for Grady was under way, Howell said, Gordon not only refused to give "an encouraging word," but his office was "the headquarters of the opposition." Howell asserted that more than seventy members of the legislature had agreed to support Grady and that his election would have been assured if Gordon's assistance had not been withheld.

Howell also referred to an occasion in January 1887 when Senator Brown had been expected to retire on account of illness and speculation was rife as to whether the Governor would appoint Grady to fill the anticipated vacancy. At that time, said Howell, Gordon wrote Grady a letter referring to him "in language that would make the friends of Governor Gordon blush." Grady's reply to the Governor closed with this striking paragraph:

In your letter you say that I have for years "professed" a sincere friendship for you. You will pardon me for saying, my dear general, that this word is a poor summing up of our relations for the past fifteen years. However, I shall enter no defense to the doubt and discourtesy it carries. To the sincerity of my friendship for you, I prefer to let the record of those fifteen years bear testimony. The open record to the public; the open and sealed record to you.

Commenting on these revelations, Grady's secretary, Holliday, said: "Governor Gordon's conduct hurt him more than the outside world ever knew." [9]

As for Hoke Smith, the *Athens Banner* said immediately after the election of Colquitt that no paper in the state had treated Grady "so ungenerously" as the *Atlanta Evening Journal* and its proprietor. This probably was what Grady had in mind when he referred in his signed editorial to "the studied attempt of one newspaper to decry the number and sincerity of my friends." Smith had declared that the *Constitution's* managing editor had "no support whatever" — a remark which could have offended a political Warwick like Grady far more than the *Journal's* charges that he was a "protectionist" and stood "on the republican platform."

But Grady refrained from any personal retaliation upon Smith, as well as upon Gordon. So far as the public knew, he harbored no ill feelings. Not until after his death did his family and friends realize fully the depth of the wound that Smith had left. Then, in a book containing instructions for his family, was found a page where once he had written that, in the event of his death, his wife should go for advice to "my friend, Hoke Smith." Some time before he died those instructions had been carefully changed.[10]

Although this break between Grady and the Smith-Gordon combination marked the beginnings of factional alignments in Georgia politics which were to last for many years,[11] it

[9] *Constitution*, November 16, 1890.
[10] Information from Henry W. Grady, Jr., and Clark Howell.
[11] From 1887 to 1936 the *Atlanta Constitution* and the *Atlanta Journal* usually were on opposite sides of the fence in state politics, although like most other Southern newspapers they have an unbroken record of loyalty to the Democratic Party in national campaigns. One will look in vain, however, for any consistent division along liberal-conservative lines between the two papers or the factions with which they have been identified. Factional politics under the one-party system of the South usually revolves around personalities who merely seize upon the issue which at the moment gives the most promise of

should be emphasized that Grady did not allow his personal disappointment to become the basis of a public controversy while he lived. He had no taste for quarrels, and he usually passed by in good-natured indifference allusions to himself which would have brought an indignant response from a person of different temperament. Others later might condemn Smith and Gordon as having kept up their friendship with Grady only "as long as they could use him," but the man most affected by their conduct simply said in private: "Some day they'll get what's coming to them," and let the matter drop.

In his next important speech — that at the Augusta National Exposition on Thanksgiving Day — Grady made the statement which was the closest he ever came to revealing publicly his feelings about the senatorial race:

I know not what the future may hold for the life that recent events have jostled from its accustomed path. It would be affectation to say that I am careless — for, in touching it with your confidence, you have kindled inspirations that, cherished without guile, may be confessed in frankness. But if it be given to man to reach the human heart, and plumb the quicksands of human ambition, I know that I speak the truth when I say that if ever I hold in my grasp any honor, in the winning or wearing of which my State is disadvantaged, and my hand refuses to surrender it, I pray God that in remembrance of this hour He will strike it from me forever. . . .[12]

---

unseating the group in power. For example, Hoke Smith, who as Secretary of the Interior in Cleveland's second Cabinet warmly defended the President's conservative monetary policies, later resigned because of the pressure of "free silver" sentiment which the *Constitution* was supporting. Yet in his successful campaign against Clark Howell for the governorship in 1906, Smith was aligned with Tom Watson and the Populist faction. The most ironical twist of all in the growing progressivism of Grady's one-time rival is that in 1907, as Governor, Smith, the one-time leader of Atlanta's anti-prohibition forces, signed the bill making Georgia a dry state.

Since 1936 the *Journal* and the *Constitution* have agreed much more often than they have disagreed in state affairs. In 1942 they fought side by side for the election of Governor Ellis Arnall, whose pronouncements on Southern problems up to this writing (July 1943) have been in many respects like Grady's.

[12] This and the subsequent excerpts from the Augusta speech are taken from the version in Harris, pp. 121–41, which is the same as that appearing in the *Constitution* of November 30, 1888.

3

Grady spoke at the Augusta Exposition on "Carolina Day," with the governors and legislatures of both Georgia and South Carolina as honor guests in the audience. The *Augusta Chronicle* reported that he was "given an ovation as he mounted the stage, and many who had never seen him, but had read his wonderful speeches made on other occasions, marvelled at the youthful appearance of the beardless orator."

The Augusta speech was similar to the one delivered at Dallas; its special significance lay mainly in the fact that it revealed Grady's views on the race problem at a time when no election was imminent. In this address he recognized frankly that every day the South remained solid, the drift toward a solid North was deepening. He also acknowledged the disadvantages inherent in the lack of a normal two-party system in the South. But these penalties, he thought, were insignificant compared with the fact that a division of the whites would "put the balance of power in the hands of an ignorant and dangerous class."

"The fact that thoughtful Southerners fully appreciated the price they were paying is proof, perhaps, that the new discipline grew out of necessity and was not a reflection of an inhuman spirit," says the historian Buck.[18] That Grady not only sensed the price, but also understood that the South was faced by what seemed to be a "basically insoluble" problem, was indicated by these words:

I know the ideal status is that every State should vote without regard to sectional lines. The reconciliation of the people will never be complete until Iowa and Georgia, Texas and Massachusetts may stand side by side without surprise. I would to God that status could be reached! If any man can define a path on which the whites of the South, though divided, can walk in honor and peace, I shall take that path, though I walk down it alone — for at the end of that path, and nowhere else, lies the full emancipation of my section and the full restoration of this Union.

[18] Op. cit., p. 289.

Grady offered no single panacea for the problem, because he knew there was none. He simply urged the South to treat the Negro fairly while educating him for better things, "to maintain the political as well as the social integrity of her white race, and to appeal to the world for patience and justice":

Let us show that it is not sectional prejudice, but a sectional problem that keeps us compacted; that it is not the hope of dominion or power, but an abiding necessity — not spoils or patronage, but plain self-preservation that holds the white race together in the South. Let us make this so plain that a community anywhere, searching its own heart, would say: "The necessity that binds our brothers in the South would bind us as closely were the necessity here."

The speaker pointed out to "the fair-minded Republicans of the North" the "intimacy and friendliness" that were generally characteristic of relations between Negroes and whites in the South when they were left free from outside interference. He made his most impassioned utterance, however, in pleading with Southerners themselves to meet the problem by demonstrating to the Negro that "his best friends are the people among whom he lives":

Let us give him his uttermost rights, and measure out justice to him in that fullness the strong should always give to the weak. Let us educate him that he may be a better, broader, and more enlightened man. . . . Let us strike hands with him as friends — and as in slavery we led him to heights which his race in Africa has never reached, so in freedom let us lead him to a prosperity of which his friends in the North have not dreamed. . . . And let us remember this — that whatever wrong we put on him shall return to punish us. Whatever we take from him in violence, that is unworthy and shall not endure. What we steal from him in fraud, that is worse. But what we win from him in sympathy and affection, what we gain in his confiding alliance and confirm in his awakening judgment, that is precious and shall endure — and out of it shall come healing and peace.

This was no maudlin sentimentality, but an expression of the attitudes that Grady had displayed consistently in his dealings with the Negro, not only in his writings and speeches but in his personal affairs. His feelings toward the less fortunate race were characterized by that same broad sympathy which included every human being in its scope. "If the South is to be elevated," the *Constitution* declared, the Negro "must be elevated along with it."

Grady knew from first-hand investigation the part played by Republican-controlled Negroes in the theft of the presidency and other crimes of Reconstruction days; he had seen both Democrats and Independents bandying for Negro votes in the Georgia elections of the early 1880's; he realized that such votes had been purchased by both sides in the Atlanta prohibition referendum. Although he admitted and deplored instances in which Negro votes had been "suppressed by violence, or miscounted by fraud," he knew that conditions had improved immeasurably since Southern whites had gained control of their own affairs. He was quite certain that any form of "force bill," such as many Republicans were advocating, could lead only to disaster — for blacks as well as whites. The whole matter, he believed, must be left with "that people most interested in its honorable settlement."

Unless the North recognized the necessity for dealing with the problem by evolutionary rather than by revolutionary means, he feared that the South would be led through terrors compared to which the horrors of Reconstruction would be "as the fading dews of morning to the roaring floods."

4

The acclaim accorded Grady's Augusta speech seemed to bear out the contention of those observers who denied that his withdrawal from the Senate race had constituted in any sense a "repudiation" of his leadership. In fact, said one Colquitt editor, Grady's attitude merely showed anew his loyalty to the party and his kind feelings for Senator Colquitt personally:

If any one thinks that Henry W. Grady has been repudiated by the Democracy of Georgia, they have only to set him before the people with a clear field and on his own merits, and the scale of prejudice will soon fall from their eyes. Turn him loose in the State — let him meet the people face to face — and we do not believe there is a man in Georgia who can defeat him for any office within the gift of the people.

Henry Grady is not only the brightest intellect in our State, but the brainiest man in the South; and besides, he has about him a personal magnetism that will sway the masses to his will.

This same editor declared that Grady's signed editorial in the *Constitution* had removed "the only bar between him and his people — the question of tariff reform." It made no difference now what position the *Constitution* took, the editor continued; the people knew that Grady was with them "in their fight against the monopolists." Grady never had asked anything from his native state, but when he did, the writer affirmed, the people would "not turn to him a deaf ear." [14]

Judged by all barometers except the Senate race, Grady's popularity did appear to be at a new high. A letter to his mother soon after his Augusta appearance revealed that he had far more invitations for speeches than he could fill. The volume of his correspondence was tremendous — so huge, in fact, that he instructed Ann Grady to address him in care of the *Southern Farm* in order that he might receive her letters promptly. He had bought a home for his mother the previous year in Athens, where she and Mattie had moved shortly before he obtained a position for his brother, Will, with the Department of the Interior on an Indian reservation in North Dakota. These changes had given Henry and Julia more room in their own home for the increasing amount of entertaining they were being called upon to do. "I went out for a half-hour today — the first time I had been on Whitehall in six months," Grady wrote to his mother on December 24, 1888, in telling of these many demands upon his time.

This same Christmas Eve letter also revealed that Grady was passing through one of those periods of melancholy such as he had experienced following his political defeat at Virginia, and such as he had undergone in 1878 at the time he

[14] Clipping from *Elberton Star* in Grady Scrapbooks.

THE GRADY FAMILY IN 1888

THE GRADY HOME IN ATLANTA, 1881–9

Long since razed to make way for a business structure, the residence stood at No. 353 (now 529-33) Peachtree Street.

*Living-Room, with Grady's
favorite chair
in center*

Parlor and Hall   *Study*

INTERIORS OF THE GRADY HOME AS IT APPEARED IN THE
LATE EIGHTIES

From the photographs by Telamon Cuyler

wrote in his diary of "snuffing out" his life. After declaring that Gussie was "the sweetest child that ever lived" and the comfort of his life, he made this reference to Christmas: "I haven't bought a present for a soul, not even for Gussie. I haven't had the heart somehow to do it." [15]

Grady's depressed feelings may not have been due entirely to political disappointment or even to his genuine concern over what the new Republican administration might do about the Negro problem, for a number of personal matters were worrying him at this same time. For one thing, Julia recently had suffered a miscarriage and had been led by their physician to believe that she might be facing a serious illness. And earlier in 1888, upon receiving a tip from Samuel M. Inman on their Florida trip that June cotton would soon go up to fourteen cents a pound, Grady had bought 500 bales of cotton on margin at 10.85. His secretary, Holliday, acting upon his advice, had bought fifty bales. When cotton went steadily down instead of up, Grady lost $5,000 on the deal and Holliday $500 — the latter being a loss which the editor insisted on paying, although his secretary refused to let him. But this unfortunate speculation, together with the $7,500 he had contributed toward the Chautauqua deficit, had prevented Grady from paying all his debts in 1888, as he had hoped, and had caused his letters to members of his family to take on a more serious tone than they had displayed in his "flush days" of 1887.[16]

The readers of the *Constitution* would never have guessed Grady's despondency, however, for on the day after writing his mother he composed one of the most beautiful word pictures of his career — his editorial on "A Perfect Christmas Day":

No man or woman now living will see again such a Christmas Day as the one which closed yesterday when the dying sun piled the western skies with gold and purple!

A winter day it was, shot to the core with sunshine! It was enchanting to walk abroad in its prodigal beauty, to breathe its elixir, to reach out the hands and plunge them open-fingered

[15] Grady Collection.
[16] Correspondence, Grady Collection; information from J. R. Holliday and Mrs. Augusta Grady Black.

through its pulsing waves of warmth and freshness. It was June and November welded and fused into a perfect glory that held the sunshine and snow beneath tender and splendid skies. To have winnowed such a day from the teeming winter was to have found an odorous peach on a bough whipped in the storms of winter. One caught the musk of yellow grain, the flavor of ripened nuts, the fragrance of strawberries, the exquisite odor of violets — the aroma of all seasons in the wonderful day. The hum of bees under-rode the whistling wings of wild geese flying southward. The fires slept in drowsing grates, while the people, marveling outdoors, watched the soft winds woo the roses and the lilies.

Truly it was a day of days! Amid its riotous luxury surely life was worth living. Worth living to hold up the head and breathe it in as thirsting men drink water; to put every sense on its gracious excellence; to throw the hands wide apart and hug whole armfuls of the day close to the heart, till the heart itself is enraptured and illumined. God's benediction came down with the day, slow dropping from the skies. God's smile was its light, and all through and through its supernal beauty and stillness, unspoken but appealing to every heart and sanctifying every soul, was His invocation and promise, "Peace on Earth, Good Will to Men." [17]

But Grady's melancholy called for more comfort than the outpouring of his soul in letters and editorials could give him. Consequently he took the train for Athens and spent the week-end with his mother. Upon his return to the office he told Mrs. J. K. Ohl, the wife of his city editor, that he never "felt happier" than on that visit:

I got there at night. She had saved supper for me and she had remembered all the things I liked: She toasted me some cheese over the fire. Why I hadn't tasted anything like it since I put off my round jackets. And then she had some home-made candy, she knew I used to love. . . . I just felt sixteen again as we sat and talked, and she told me how she prayed for me and thought of me always, and what a brightness I had been to her life, and how she heard me coming home in every boy that whistled along the street. When I went to bed she came and tucked the covers all around me in the dear old way that none but a mother's hands know, and I felt so happy and so peaceful and so full of tender memories that I cried happy, grateful tears until I went to sleep.[18]

The sympathy of his mother was needed all the more by Grady at this moment because Julia, to whom he usually looked for comfort, had steadfastly opposed any change in his earlier decision not to run for political office. The wife probably was too much relieved over the outcome of the Senate boom to understand fully the husband's deeper feelings, but in Ann Grady's eyes Henry was still the boy who had suffered so bitterly from a political disappointment in his year at the University of Virginia.

5

Journalism, as always, provided the greatest compensations. Within six weeks after that melancholy Christmas Grady was again directing the news staff of the *Constitution* in one of the reportorial feats in which he so much delighted. A sensational murder story in Alabama had come to a climax late one Saturday night with a dispatch from the *Birmingham Age-Herald* announcing that it had an exclusive story on the latest developments in the case. The *Constitution* offered to buy the story but was refused. Instead Grady was requested to run an advertisement stating that a special train bringing a supply of *Age-Heralds* and a corps of newsboys would reach Atlanta at eight fifteen Sunday morning. The managing editor agreed to run the notice without charge and even wrote an editorial commending the Birmingham paper upon its enterprise; he determined, however, that he would not be scooped if he could help it.

The night train for Birmingham was to leave in about ten minutes. Hurriedly rounding up Holliday, a reporter, and two telegraph operators, Grady rushed them to the station. Just as he anticipated in his instructions to them, they reached Anniston, Alabama, some minutes ahead of the *Age-Herald's* special. Since the identity of the *Constitution* men was un-

[18] Harris, p. 46.

known, they easily obtained a copy of the *Age-Herald* when the train from Birmingham passed through. The reporter and the telegraph operators attended to wiring the story to the *Constitution* while Holliday, still unrecognized, had the audacity to ride back to Atlanta on the *Age-Herald's* own train.

Meanwhile the *Constitution* staff in Atlanta was busy. As the story was received from the operators in Anniston, it was sent paragraph by paragraph to the composing room. By seven thirty o'clock Sunday morning the story was in type, and the forms were rumbling toward the press room. Fifteen minutes later the *Constitution* was on the street with an extra giving the complete story of the murder. Nearly eleven thousand copies of the extra had been sold by eleven o'clock, when the *Age-Herald's* special train finally arrived.

The *Age-Herald* also did a good business in Atlanta because the report of the *Constitution's* feat had spread rapidly and many people were eager to compare the stories of the two papers. In a front-page article the next day Grady congratulated the Birmingham paper on its enterprise, but added that "of course it ought not to think of getting to Atlanta with the news before the *Constitution* has it. That is a thing that we don't allow, and a less enterprising paper than the *Age-Herald* would never try it." [19]

Some months later Grady demonstrated that the *Constitution* could succeed where the *Age-Herald* had failed. E. W. Barrett, who was now the *Constitution's* Washington correspondent, had obtained for the Sunday paper an exclusive interview with Rube Burrow, a notorious train-robber and murderer. Arranging for a special car on the night train, Grady sent Barrett, two circulation clerks, nineteen newsboys, and 9,000 copies of the *Constitution* to Birmingham. He wired the *Age-Herald* that the *Constitutions* were coming, precisely as the Birmingham paper had notified him.

The *Age-Herald* rushed out a special engine and one coach to meet the *Constitution* train at Tallapoosa, Georgia. For several minutes the two trains were stopped alongside each other and not more than six feet apart. But Grady had ordered that the doors and windows of the *Constitution* car be locked

[19] February 4, 1889.

fast and that not a single paper be let out until the train reached Birmingham. The *Age-Herald* representatives thus were forced to wire back that they could not obtain the story.[20]

Soon after the first brush with the *Age-Herald*, Grady achieved an equally brilliant piece of editorial leadership — the raising of funds for the building of the Confederate Soldiers' Home in Atlanta. A committee of Texas citizens, headed by Major Joe Stewart, had been soliciting in New York City for such a home and after a month had received only $1,500. This news stirred Grady's Southern pride and humanitarian impulses into action.

"Come home, Major Joe Stewart!" he cried out in a double-leaded editorial. "The people of Georgia pay annually over $3,000,000 as their share of the taxes from which the soldiers of the union army are pensioned, and they do not complain." After describing the needs of Southern veterans, he then declared: "We must build a Confederate Home in Georgia! We must build it at once! . . . We start the subscription list for the 'Georgia Confederate Home' as follows: *The Constitution Publishing Co.* — $1,000. And we shall not rest, night or day, until the list is finished, the money raised, the Home started, and established in the love of our people! Every morning we shall print the list of subscribers. Who will be the first to subscribe?"

Within a week the *Constitution* had received nearly $50,000 in subscriptions, and Grady, over his protests, was elected president of a board to supervise the building of the home.[21]

Through such exploits Grady proved repeatedly that he could arouse the interest of the people and stimulate them to action as no other man in Georgia could do. After all, a senator or governor could represent only one state, but the directing genius of the most widely circulated paper in the South could and did speak for an entire section, irrespective of state lines.

The politicians in Washington seemed to sense this fact. For example, in January Senator William E. Chandler of New Hampshire publicly asked "what Mr. Grady thought" a Re-

20 *Constitution*, November 10, 11, 1889.
21 Ibid., April 6–10, 19, 1889.

publican President, House, and Senate "for the first time in twelve years" should do about the Fifteenth Amendment. Grady immediately replied that, in his "honest opinion," the Republican Party now realized that the Fifteenth Amendment was "an awful blunder . . . conceived in passion and passed in haste." He again compared the sudden enfranchisement of the unprepared Negroes in Reconstruction days with the gradual enfranchisement of the Indians and the exclusion of the Chinese. Identifying Chandler devastatingly with the Florida election frauds of 1876, Grady said that the Senator's concern over the enforcement of the Fifteenth Amendment might well be likened to that of a burglar rushing down the streets with his pockets full of booty and crying: "Stop thief!" "The dominance of the white race," he said, "is simply the domination of intelligence and property, and it will continue to dominate here, in spite of statutes or force, just as it would dominate in New Hampshire under the same circumstances." [22]

Since the Fifteenth Amendment obviously could not be repealed, the clear implication of Grady's statement was that the Southern states should be allowed to find a way out of their dilemma as best they could, so long as they did not violate the purely negative language of the amendment by restricting the franchise on the basis of color.

[22] Ibid., January 28, 29, 1889.

CHAPTER FOURTEEN

National Pacificator

Since Grady was essentially a pacificator, he took great care throughout 1889 to avoid saying anything in his newspaper articles or in his speeches which might have fanned the flames of "force bill" agitation. Whenever a clash occurred between whites and blacks in the North, he would draw the editorial moral that racial prejudice was just as strong in one section as in another — a position which was to be supported conclusively in later years by the findings of the Negro historian-sociologist W. E. B. Du Bois.[1] But unless some news event or a Republican inquiry such as Chandler's made editorial comment desirable, Grady preferred to ignore the threatened federal election law and to concentrate upon matters of more immediate regional concern. Foremost among these was the growing friction between agriculture and industry — a conflict which cried for a master conciliator no less than did the recurring antagonism between the sections.

With cotton prices still as depressed as they were in 1887, the deplorable credit and lien system described by Grady in his *Harper's Magazine* article of 1881 was driving more and more small farmers to the brink of serfdom. True, the farmers themselves had contributed to their difficulties by failing to raise their own supplies and stock, as Grady and others repeatedly had urged them to do. The farmers were not always to blame for this, however, since their landlords and commission merchants required them to raise a money crop — cotton. Now, in the face of mounting taxes, the average price paid for that cotton had hovered for three years around eight and a half cents, and no relief was in sight.

[1] Buck, op. cit., p. 293.

Just as they had sought help in the seventies through the Granger movement, Georgia farmers now were flocking by the thousands into the Farmers' Alliance. This organization had made its appearance at the Interstate Farmers' Convention, which Grady had addressed in 1887. As indicated by his speech at that time, Grady was among the first to comprehend the meaning of the movement. He was the publisher of a farm journal; he had traveled frequently in the rural sections and had written many articles on farming. Following the organization of the Alliance he had written sympathetic interviews with its leaders explaining how they hoped to help themselves through organization and co-operation. Beginning in December 1888 and continuing throughout the early months of 1889 he personally supervised a page in the Sunday *Constitution* in which farmers were invited to discuss their problems and to advance solutions. "It is a period of organization and development," Grady wrote, "and there is no reason why the Alliance should not prove beneficial not only to the individual farmer, but to farmers as a class."

Except for a brief talk before the Southern Society of New York in April, Grady turned down every invitation from the North and West during the spring and summer of 1889 in order to have time for speeches in Georgia on this problem. In his talk before the Alliance men in 1887, he had proposed a compact "that if it be true that we are losing ground we will search for the mistakes and errors in our system and cast them out forever." [2] He was continually searching for these "mistakes and errors" in his news articles and editorials, and the crescendo of his convictions found expression in a series of three addresses — at the Albany (Georgia) Chautauqua in March, at the University of Virginia in June, and at Elberton, Georgia, in July.

At Albany a public holiday was declared and more than three thousand persons jammed into a tent seating two thousand to hear Grady. After picturing the declining wealth of the agrarian counties, the speaker emphasized that the Civil War no longer could be blamed for the plight of the farmers. The total taxable wealth of Georgia was now, for the first time

2 *Constitution,* August 17, 1887.

since 1860, equal to that with which, excluding slaves, the state had entered the war. He reaffirmed that when the slaves were freed, the South had gained far more in moral power than it had lost in production. But the tax-books showed that the cities and towns had gained $60,000,000 in property values since 1860, while the country was $50,000,000 poorer. This, he affirmed, was "the secret of the trouble":

To garner wealth in the crowded markets by stripping the farmer and the field; to pile up fortunes while our country-sides languish under mortgage and poverty — that is to endanger the commonwealth. . . . Now the farmer realizes that at last. He realizes that while he has dug from the soil the wealth that is building up the cities and making great fortunes, he has held but little of it to himself. . . . He realizes that he has made the wealth h⸱ witnesses, but is not permitted to share, and it is against this th⸱t the present farmers' organization — the most serious that we have ever seen — is the natural, nay more, the proper, inevitable and logical protest.

.   .   .   .

I tell you, my countrymen, I do not talk for buncombe. I a⸱ not care for the opinion of this man or that man, but I tell you that the secret of the trouble in Georgia is found in the figures I have given you; that while the cities have grown $60,000,000 richer, the farmers have grown $50,000,000 poorer. There is no getting around it. Now, if our laws are unjust to the farmer, let us change them. If our business systems are wrong, let us modify them. Let us join hands with him, not in contention, but in sympathy and do that which is best for the diffusion of wealth alike among the towns and the country.[3]

"Against Centralization" was the subject of Grady's next important address, which was delivered before the literary societies of the University of Virginia during Commencement Week. The editor made it plain that he was not seeking to revive the "dead issue" of state's rights. He was glad that the right of a state to leave the Union had been denied by the war, and that the Republic was "an indissoluble union of indestructible states." But he decried "the increasing tendency

3 Ibid., March 28, 29, 1889.

to concentrate in the federal government powers and privileges that should be left with the states, and to create powers that neither the state nor federal government should have."

What Grady attacked most vigorously was not centralization in government, but "the consolidation of capital," which he saw taking place under a "paternalism run mad." He saw "the centralist and the monopolist" walking hand in hand — "the strong government protecting the money power, and the money power the political standing army of the government." Predicting that "the time is approaching when the issue between plutocracy and the people will be forced to trial," he declared:

We have read of the robber barons of the Rhine who from their castles sent a shot across the bow of every passing craft, and descending as hawks from the crags, tore and robbed and plundered the voyagers until their greed was glutted, or the strength of their victims spent. Shall this shame of Europe against which the world revolted, shall it be repeated in this free country? And yet, when a syndicate or a trust can arbitrarily add twenty-five per cent to the cost of a single article of common use, and safely gather forced tribute from the people, until from its surplus it could buy every castle on the Rhine . . . where is the difference? . . . I do not overstate the case. Economists have held that wheat, grown everywhere, could never be cornered by capital. And yet one man in Chicago tied the wheat crop in his handkerchief, and held it until a sewing-woman in my city, working for ninety cents a week, had to pay him twenty cents tax on the sack of flour she bore home in her famished hands. Three men held the cotton crop until the English spindles were stopped and the lights went out in 3,000,000 English homes. Last summer one man cornered pork until he had levied a tax of $3 per barrel on every consumer, and pocketed a profit of millions. The Czar of Russia would not have dared to do these things. And yet they are no secrets in this free government of ours! . . .

The address ended, however, on an optimistic note. "I always bet on sunshine in America," said Grady. "Centralism will be checked, and liberty saved — plutocracy overthrown and equality restored. The struggle for human rights never

goes backward among English-speaking peoples." His peroration was almost prophetic in its fervor:

I catch the vision of this Republic — its mighty forces in balance,
and its unspeakable glory falling on all its children — chief among
the federation of English-speaking people — plenty streaming from
its borders, and light from its mountain tops — working out its
mission under God's approving eye, until the dark continents are
opened — and the highways of earth established, and the shadows
lifted — and the jargon of the nations stilled and the perplexities
of Babel straightened — and under one language, one liberty,
and one God, all the nations of the world hearkening to the
American drum-beat and girding up their loins, shall march amid
the breaking of the millennial dawn into the paths of righteous-
ness and of peace! [4]

Grady's attitude toward a strong central government dedi-
cated to the interests of the many rather than the few was
made clear by his speech on "The Farmer and the Cities," delivered on July 23 at Elberton. Before a rural audience gathered in the open for a barbecue he again reviewed the tenden-
cies that were "bringing villages and country under mortgage
to the city." What was needed to relieve the most menacing
form of centralization, "the consolidation of capital," he said,
was "the leveling of our colossal fortunes and the diffusion of
our garnered wealth amid the great middle classes of people."
In elaborating upon this point he gave approval to the general
direction of much of the progressive legislation of later years:

The government can protect its citizens. It is of the people, and
it shall not perish from the face of the earth. It can top off these
colossal fortunes and, by an income tax, retard their growth. It
can set a limit to personal and corporate wealth. It can take trusts
and syndicates by the throat. It can shatter monopoly; it can
equalize the burden of taxation; it can distribute its privileges
impartially; it can clothe with credit its lands now discredited at
its banks; it can lift the burdens from the farmer's shoulders, give
him equal strength to bear them — it can trust the people in
whose name this Republic was founded; in whose courage it was

[4] Ibid., June 26, 1889.

defended; in whose wisdom it has been administered, and whose stricken love and confidence it can not survive.

Even so, the speaker was careful to remind the listener of his own individual responsibility. He emphasized that the government, no matter what it might do, "does not do all that is needed, nor the most." Once more he urged diversified farming: "To mortgage our farms in Boston for money with which to buy meat and bread from Western cribs and smokehouses is folly unspeakable." And since he believed that "all true reform must begin with the people," he drew in his peroration a picture of an ideal farmer's home — a passage which in "effectiveness and pathos" was declared by Harris to be "unequaled in modern literature." [5]

Grady's address at Elberton formed the pattern for a dozen talks which he made over a period of two months before audiences composed largely of farmers. From Elberton he went to Anderson, South Carolina, for a speech, and thence on a trip down the Savannah River. Later he accompanied Harris to Eatonton, the latter's boyhood home, for an address.

His conversation with Harris on the train to Eatonton revealed his concern lest his motives in making these talks in the agricultural districts be misunderstood. "There are people who will say that I am making a campaign in my own behalf," he said, "and you will hear it hinted that I am going about the state drumming up popularity for the sake of running for some office." [6] There is always the possibility, of course, that even the most high-minded leader may be rationalizing desires that lurk in the unconscious, but any ambition that Grady had for public office seems to have been subordinate to his earnest wish to prevent the impending industrial-agrarian conflict. That he was more interested in bringing about peace than in being himself the beneficiary of it was indicated by his "Strictly Confidential" note to W. J. Northen, president of the State Agricultural Society:

Let me give you an idea. Put yourself in line with the movement to bring about peace between the agricultural and commercial in-

[5] Harris, pp. 18–19, 158–79.
[6] Ibid., p. 13.

terest of the state which is now threatened by the Alliance. The
farmers have the sympathy of the commercial community in their
efforts to organize and cooperate, but there is a danger that these
two interests will find themselves in hopeless opposition unless
somebody smooths the friction. The man who does it will be master of the situation. H. W. G.[7]

Grady was no wild-eyed reformer; neither was he a blind
conservative. He saw many evils that needed to be corrected,
both in agriculture and in industry. But he did not seek to
remedy the ills of the one simply by a blanket attack upon the
other: his humanitarianism was broad enough for him to recognize good in a banker as well as in a farmer. In condemning
the "whole infamous system of trusts," for example, he warned
Constitution readers both against "relaxing their vigilance or
abating their indignation" and against being "misled by dem-
agogues into positions not based upon justice and common
sense." At Elberton he declared that if he had "the disposal
of 100,000 immigrants at Georgia's gates," only 5,000 would
enter Atlanta, while 75,000 would go to the shops and factories of the towns and villages, and 20,000 to the farms. His
program called for a balanced development between agriculture and industry — an ideal extremely difficult to attain, as
the economic perplexities of more recent years well prove.

Like most "middle-of-the-road" leaders, Grady drew fire
from extremists on both sides. On the one hand he continued
to be attacked by conservatives of the Old South school, like
Charles Colcock Jones, who accused him of belittling "the
characteristics of yesterday." On the other he was being denounced with increasing bitterness by agrarian radicals like
Tom Watson, who questioned Grady's sincerity by insinuating that he was "the known champion of Rail Road Kings, &
R. R. combinations" and "cheek by jowl" with the influences

[7] March 4, 1889, Northen Papers. Northen followed Grady's advice well
enough to be elected Governor in 1890. In that same year the Farmers' Alliance gained control of the Georgia legislature and passed much constructive
social legislation. The more radical "wool hat boys" soon became dissatisfied
with the "silk stocking" faction, however, and joined the Populist movement
of the nineties. Just as Grady predicted, this division of the Southern whites
caused both sides again to court the Negro vote, and "some of the turbulence
of Reconstruction came back again." — Coulter: *Short History,* pp. 371–4.

responsible for "the curse of High Tariff." [8] But the Old South was gone, whether Jones was willing to admit it or not. As for Watson, even he was to revise his estimate of Grady's motives, when the heat of battle was over, by saying: "Some of the greatest editorials ever published were written by Henry Grady, some of the most brilliant reporting ever done was the work of Henry Grady, the most enthralling speech I ever heard was made by Henry Grady. I am sure that America never produced a truer patriot than Henry Grady." [9]

2

During this same summer Grady again gave considerable attention to the Piedmont Chautauqua, of which he still was vice-president, although his out-of-town engagements prevented him from devoting as much time to it as in the previous year. His principal contributions to the program consisted of an address on Veterans' Day and another on the closing night.

In August, traveling with a large delegation of Atlanta veterans, Grady went to Americus to speak at the annual Confederate reunion. Before the train left the station, he breezed through the coaches and gathered up all the tickets, which he took to the ticket office for a refund to be made upon his own responsibility. Laughing like a schoolboy, he then marched back through the cars and returned the price of a ticket to every veteran.[10]

In September occurred an event which undoubtedly contributed to Grady's tension over the race question. Following the lynching of a Negro for an assault upon a white girl at East Point, a suburb of Atlanta, a mob of white men went about dragging innocent blacks from their homes and whipping them. Grady came out the next morning with an editorial strongly condemning the outrages. Two days later, in reply to an anonymous letter stating that "your political aspiration is gone to hell on account of your article on the whipping of

[8] Woodward, op. cit., pp. 124, 128.
[9] Letter from Thomas E. Watson to *Constitution,* May 25, 1921.
[10] Clipping, Grady Scrapbooks.

the niggers," he published a two-column editorial expressing
his views even more vigorously. "We cannot conceive of a political aspiration so earnest as to interfere with our slightest
duty as an editor," he wrote. "We cannot expect, and we will
not deserve, the confidence of the North, if such outrages . . .
go unrebuked and unpunished. Worse than that, we cannot
hold our self-respect." [11] By discharging a *Constitution* em-
ployee who had taken part in the whippings, Grady showed
that these were no idle words. He stuck by his guns in demanding punishment for the offenders, even after a "packed meeting" of the Young Men's Democratic Club adopted resolutions
condemning "Henry W. Grady of the *Atlanta Constitution*"
for his attitude.

By October, however, the attention of Grady and most Atlantans was diverted from the race question by the second
Piedmont Exposition. The *Constitution* celebrated the opening of the fair by bringing out the largest paper in its history
— an edition of fifty-six pages, as contrasted with only forty
pages for the 1887 opening. During the three weeks' program
Grady served as impresario for the two biggest drawing cards
— Farmers' Alliance Day and an address by Governor David
B. Hill of New York. It was in opening the Alliance Day ceremonies that the editor struck the keynote of so much of his
writing and speaking in these months: "There is no place for
divided hearts in the South. . . . That man is a patriot who
brings together the classes that are estranged and, uniting them
in common purpose, enlists them in a common cause." [12]

Grady acted as master of ceremonies on Alliance Day, but
on the day Hill spoke he remained in the background, leaving
the task of introducing the New York Governor to Senator
Colquitt. Moreover, in answering the loud and repeated calls
for himself, following Hill's address, Grady meticulously
avoided any reference to the preceding speaker. There are
two possible interpretations of this: one, that he simply
thought it good political strategy to identify himself with the

[11] September 8, 1889. Many sentences and phrases of this editorial are
the same as those in his Dallas and Augusta speeches; others bear a striking
similarity to the address he was to give a few months later at Boston.
[12] *Constitution,* October 25, 1889.

farmers' movement but not with Hill; the other, that he had doubts in his own mind about Hill's qualifications for the presidency and did not wish to be placed in the position of endorsing a potential candidate of somewhat dubious integrity. Certain of the "tariff Democrats" in Georgia already were beginning to look with favor upon Hill's aspirations to be the next nominee, but Grady, from all indications, was still inclined personally toward renominating Cleveland.[13]

Supporting this latter interpretation is the fact that another honor guest at the exposition, and one whom Grady did introduce, was his Boston friend Patrick Collins, who had presided over the convention that renominated Cleveland in 1888 and who was to help in the former President's renomination and re-election in 1892. Collins was the emissary who brought Grady an invitation to address the Boston Merchants Association at its annual banquet on December 12. The other principal speaker on this occasion was to be Grover Cleveland! As the *Washington Post* so sagely observed, "The coincidences which couple these illustrious names are of the sort that are carefully thought over a long time in advance."

Collins was quite certain, at least, that his Atlanta friend had an "illustrious name." Once while they were together Grady was holding forth with typical enthusiasm about the widening fame of Atlanta. As evidence he declared that he recently had received a card from a remote part of Europe addressed simply to "Henry W. Grady, Atlanta" — no state, no U. S. A. Collins quickly commented: "But why Atlanta? That was superfluous." [14]

3

The topic of Grady's Boston speech, "The Race Problem in the South," probably was decided upon by agreement with

[13] Ibid., October 17, 1889; Nevins: *Cleveland*, pp. 475–6. The *Constitution* after Grady's death actively supported Hill's pre-convention campaign for the nomination, and the New York Governor spoke at the unveiling of the Grady monument in Atlanta on October 21, 1891, obviously for the purpose of enlisting Southern votes.

[14] Clipping, Grady Scrapbooks; M. E. Hennessy and James Morgan of *Boston Globe* to author, August 14, 1942. Mr. Morgan was a close friend of Patrick Collins.

Collins after it became known that Congressman Henry Cabot Lodge of Massachusetts was determined to press for the enactment by the new Republican Congress of a law establishing federal supervision over all polling places in national elections. In the discussion that had taken place since the 1888 election many moderate Republicans had united with Democrats in expressing the view that such legislation would prove disastrous to peaceful relations between the sections. Collins and other Democratic leaders in Massachusetts were eager, therefore, for the members of the Boston Merchants Association to hear the viewpoint of the South presented by that section's most persuasive spokesman.

After President Harrison, in his message to Congress on December 3, urged the adoption of a "force bill" such as Lodge had proposed, Grady realized that the die was cast. Thoroughly alarmed by the possible consequences of such a law, he prepared as never before for his Boston address. He locked himself in a room at his home "for hours at a time" to work upon it.

This strain evidently was too much for a man who only recently had written his mother: "If only I could let my mind rest a little!" Several weeks before the time to leave for Boston, Grady suffered from an attack of dizziness. He was standing at the telephone in his home when he reeled and fell. Although he was confined to his bed for only a few days, he still was weak from this attack and, in addition, suffering from a cold as the date of his departure approached. Both his wife and his physician, Dr. F. H. Orme, urged him to cancel the engagement, but he replied that "to stay now is out of the question." He did promise to keep as quiet as possible and to come back to Atlanta immediately after the speech.

The doctor's advice to "keep quiet" apparently was forgotten in the excitement of the events that followed. A group of fifteen Atlantans made the trip to Boston with Grady in a private car. His naturally nervous temperament was stimulated both by his illness and by the importance of the impending speech, and he talked more than usual on the train. During a stop-over in Washington, he spent considerable time chatting with his friends among newspapermen and politicians. Amos

Cummings, managing editor of the New York *Sun,* reported that in a visit to his room Grady "talked earnestly for two hours." A Chicago correspondent was impressed by the Atlanta editor's grave concern over the race problem, saying that he seemed to fear "a spark that would create a disturbance which might shake the entire South." [15]

In Washington Grady also had "a very instructive debate" with former Governor George S. Boutwell of Massachusetts, who, as a member of Congress in Reconstruction days, had helped to frame the Fourteenth Amendment and had advocated the Fifteenth Amendment. "He was hard to convince at first, but I evidently impressed him, and left him very much mollified and softened," Grady wrote a friend in Atlanta. "By this token I hope to soften them all, for I gave him only a part of my speech. He gave me some very interesting facts and suggestions, and I really find myself strengthened in my position more than ever. I feel that I will win justice for my people, for our people. God grant that I may. I have no other purpose in going. . . . I've had an easier time today, the growing excitement of my speech nerves the cold and trouble. In every way I am better now, even than I was this morning." [16]

During a stop-over in New York City the next day and night, however, Grady confided in a letter to his wife that "I have been so sick I haven't had the heart to write. . . . I am so *tired.* That's just the feeling. If I don't brace up in Boston I'll 'bust.' " He stayed close to his hotel room in New York and received treatment from a homeopathic physician, but by the time the Atlantans reached Boston on December 11, the day before the banquet, he was much worse. "I haven't left my room since I reached Boston and don't think I can," he wrote Julia. "The crowd is out at various lunches, 2 dinners, &c, & I am locked up with Dr. Wesaloff, who is doctoring me constantly. . . . They certainly expect a great deal from me, & I will justify them, if my voice is good." He went on to say that "I have never had such a reception as I have here — a suite of rooms, private dining room, &c — everything exqui-

[15] Clipping, Nicholson Scrapbooks; Chicago *Daily Inter Ocean,* December 24, 1889.
[16] To Walter A. Taylor, reprinted in *Constitution,* December 31, 1889.

site. They make as much of me as of Mr. Cleveland & we have a public reception at 5 to 6:30 when I expect to take more cold." [17]

But Grady's spirits rose to the occasion and carried him through the reception and the banquet that followed. Both functions were held at the Hotel Vendome, where he was stopping. It was described as "the only hotel in Boston with a dining room large enough to accommodate the crowd." More than four hundred persons were packed into the dining-room, and "hundreds of others would have paid double or treble price for tickets" if they had been available. "As a gathering of representative brains, capital, business and social eminence," reported the *Boston Daily Globe*, "it has not been surpassed in Boston in recent years."

The banquet hall was decorated with cut flowers and patriotic colors, a large American flag being hung just behind the speakers' table. At this table sat "fourteen famous men" — Jonathan A. Lane, president of the Merchants Association, in the center, with Grady at his right and Cleveland at his left; and then, ranged on either side, Governor Oliver Ames of Massachusetts, Andrew Carnegie, William L. Putnam, General Clinton B. Fisk, Patrick Collins, Leverett Saltonstall, William E. Russell, John Lowell, Homer Rogers, Leopold Morse, and Francis Lynde Stevens. In the party of Southerners accompanying Grady were Howell, Holliday, former Governor Rufus B. Bullock, Dr. J. W. Rankin, Clarence Knowles, S. M. Inman, Dr. R. D. Spalding, Thomas D. Meador, W. A. Hemphill, Judge George Hillyer, John H. Inman, Marion J. Verdery, Patrick Calhoun, President Norton of the Louisville & Nashville Railroad, and a *Constitution* reporter.

President Lane started the program shortly after eight o'clock by reading a letter from James Russell Lowell, who expressed his regrets at being unable to attend "a dinner where distinctions of party are sunk in that common interest of patriotism which we all share together." Former President

[17] From New York and Boston [December 10, 12, 1889], Grady Collection. Julia's father, Dr. William King, had been a homeopathic physician, which probably accounts for the fact that Grady always called a homeopath rather than an allopath.

Cleveland, the first speaker, then spoke on the subject "Political Selfishness." Cleveland deplored the purchase of votes by "selfish interests" and the intimidation of employees by employers — evils which at that time probably were far more prevalent in the industrial centers of the North than in the South. By stressing the responsibility of the Northern business man for these conditions, the former President indirectly helped to prepare his listeners for an open-minded hearing of Grady's presentation of the Southern viewpoint on the question of Negro voting.

When Grady was introduced, the cheering and applause lasted for "several minutes." He thanked his audience for the ovation, referring to it as evidence that "a citizen of this republic, no matter from what section he may come, if he carry the American spirit in his heart, can find nowhere in this broad land . . . strangers or estrangement, but everywhere friends and comradeship." He then came quickly to the body of his address, which was to be described by the *New-York Tribune's* correspondent as "one of the most eloquent speeches heard in Boston in many a day," and by still another auditor as "a cannon ball in full flight, fringed with flowers." [18]

Grady began by saying that the task assigned to him of discussing the race problem "without making a political speech" was as perplexing as the dilemma of the little girl whose mother permitted her to go out to swim but forbade her to go near the water. After this touch of humor he proceeded to establish common ground with his audience by paying a glowing tribute to the spirit of New England. Then he launched into his main theme by describing the abundant resources of the South — its farms, timber lands, and mines — and contrasting its scanty population with that of overcrowded New England. But the South had fewer Northern-born citizens in 1880 than in 1870, and fewer in 1870 than in 1860. There could be "but one answer" to this: "It is the very problem we are now to consider. I thank God as heartily as you do that human slavery is gone forever from American soil. But the

[18] *Constitution, New-York Tribune*, December 13, 1889. The quotations from the speech are based upon the versions appearing in the *Constitution* of December 15 and Harris, pp. 180–99.

freeman remains. With him a problem without precedent or parallel."

Grady declared that the men of the South, who felt that their prosperity depended upon a satisfactory solution of the race problem, were "resolute, clear-minded, and broad-minded." He was most emphatic on this point: "Mr. President, we need not go one step further unless you concede right here that the people I speak for are as honest, as sensible, and as just as your people, seeking as earnestly as you would in their place, rightly to solve the problem that touches them at every vital point. . . . Admit this, and we may reach an understanding tonight."

He knew that Northern newspapers frequently had played up stories of disorder and violence in the South. This unfavorable publicity, indeed, was one of the main reasons for the hesitancy of capitalists in investing more heavily in the region. Grady therefore proceeded to suggest, as he had done frequently in his editorials, that violent outbursts in the South were no more "significant and representative" than similar incidents in the North:

Lawless men may ravage a county in Iowa and it is accepted as an incident — in the South a drunken row is declared to be the fixed habit of the community. Regulators may whip vagabonds in Indiana by platoons, and it scarcely arrests attention — a chance collision in the South among relatively the same classes is gravely accepted as evidence that one race is destroying the other. We might as well claim that the Union was ungrateful to the colored soldiers who followed its flag, because a Grand Army post in Connecticut closed its doors to a negro veteran, as for you to give racial significance to every incident in the South, or to accept exceptional grounds as the rule of our society.

Asserting that the $450,000,000 worth of cotton raised in the South that year was not due to the labor of an "oppressed race," he presented statistics to show that the Negro in the South was as well off as his Northern brother in respect to character, prosperity, and legal protection. The small vote cast in the South, he said, was matched in many Northern cities, as illustrated by the fact that in the recent election Virginia had cast 69 per cent of her vote, while Massachusetts had cast only 49 per cent of hers. Surely, he said, the American people would not "see one section condemned for what another section is excused!" Time and patience alone, he insisted, could solve the problem.

In his New England Society speech Grady had picked his way rather daintily around the Negro problem; now he realized the time had come to speak frankly. "You may pass force bills," he told his Boston audience, "but they will not avail. . . . We wrested our State government from negro supremacy when the Federal drumbeat rolled closer to the ballot-box and Federal bayonets hedged it deeper about than will ever again be permitted in this free government. But, sir, though the cannon of this Republic thundered in every voting district of the South, we still should find in the mercy of God the means and the courage to prevent its re-establishment!"

After challenging the North's understanding of the Southern attitude toward the Negro by declaring that "the love we feel for that race you cannot measure or comprehend," the speaker rose to an emotional height in his description of the slave who was with William S. Grady when the latter was mortally wounded at Petersburg:

I catch another vision. The crisis of battle — a soldier struck, staggering, fallen. I see a slave, scuffling through the smoke, winding his black arms about the fallen form, reckless of the hurtling death — bending his trusty face to catch the words that tremble on the stricken lips, so wrestling meantime with agony that he would lay down his life in his master's stead. I see him by the weary bedside, ministering with uncomplaining patience, praying with all his humble heart that God will lift his master up, until death comes in mercy and in honor to still the soldier's agony and seal the soldier's life. I see him by the open grave, mute, motionless, uncovered, suffering for the death of him who in life fought against his freedom. I see him when the mound is heaped and the great drama of his life is closed, turn away and with downcast eyes and uncertain step start out into new and strange fields, faltering, struggling, but moving on, until his shambling figure is lost in the light of this better and brighter day. And from the grave comes a voice saying: "Follow him! Put your arms about him in his need, even as he put his about me. Be his friend as he was mine." And out into this new world — strange to me as to him, dazzling, bewildering both — I follow! And may God forget my people — when they forget these! [19]

Following a climax such as this, there was little left for Grady to do but to make his final appeal for sympathetic understanding and a truly national patriotism:

Such, Mr. President, is this problem as we see it; such is the temper in which we approach it; such is the progress made. What do we ask of you? First, patience; out of this alone can come perfect work. Second, confidence; in this alone can you judge fairly. Third, sympathy; in this you can help us best. Fourth, loyalty to the republic — for there is sectionalism in loyalty as in estrangement. This hour little needs the loyalty that is loyal to one section and yet holds the other in enduring suspicion and estrangement. Give us the broad and perfect loyalty that loves and trusts Georgia alike with Massachusetts — that knows no south, no north, no east, no west, but endears with equal and patriotic love every foot of our soil, every State in our Union.

During an hour of speaking Grady was interrupted twenty-nine times by "applause," "great applause," "cries of good," "applause and cheers," and "cheers." The *Boston Herald* reported the next morning that "the eyes of many in the great company were dimmed with tears as the last words of the glowing peroration fell from the lips of the speaker, and hardly had he finished when the audience rose en masse and joined in one great cheer. So long was it continued that President Lane's remarks in introducing the next speaker [Andrew Carnegie] were almost inaudible." When it is considered that

[19] This is the passage to which Mrs. William Lawson Peel, Grady's next-door neighbor, referred in the *Constitution*, May 24, 1921. When Grady had finished the speech, wrote Mrs. Peel, he sent for her and, ushering her into his study, said: "Here, read this." He then left the portion of the manuscript containing this tribute in her hands. A few minutes later he peeped in, and seeing his neighbor in tears over the passage, "he screamed with laughter and cut up like a boy, saying: 'I've got her crying; it's all right.'"

the audience was predominantly Republican, and that Boston was the very heart of "force bill" sentiment, this response seems all the more remarkable. All the Republican newspapers in Boston differed editorially with Grady's views, but their news reports of the speech were uniformly glowing.

The New York newspapers of the next day also carried extensive accounts of the speech. Said the *Herald:*

Before he had gotten half through his address two-thirds of his hearers were in tears. No orator ever "carried an audience off its feet" more easily or more completely.

"It was the most wonderful thing I ever heard," exclaimed a veteran Washington correspondent as he left the dining hall, and so said every one else. He played upon the sensibilities as the master hand sweeps the harp, evoking now laughter, now wild applause, now tears. The scene during the hour which he occupied has rarely if ever been witnessed in Boston. It was an oratorical triumph of the first magnitude.

Since Grady was a sick man, the description of the speaker as given by the *Boston Daily Globe* was enlightening: "He speaks with that manner few orators have; he puts into his words all the energy of gesture and well-toned voice and with a perfect command of his words, and every word in its right place. When speaking in a room as warm as was the one wherein he spoke last night he keéps in one hand a big silk handkerchief with which he brushes back his drooping hair from his forehead. . . . He seemed impatient sometimes when rounds of applause interrupted him, and spoke rapidly at all times." [20] After learning that the orator was quite ill when he was speaking, the editorial-writer of the *Boston Herald* declared that "a man of less rugged strength would have yielded before the trial was half over, but Grady's physique carried him through." [21]

Grady evidently felt that the effort had been worth while, for he wrote the next day that "literally hundreds of men" had told him that Republicans and Democrats alike were enthusiastic over the speech. "It has put our people right and

20 December 13, 1889.
21 December 24, 1889.

will stand to their credit," he said. "That is something to live
for, isn't it?" [22]

The weather had been mild when the party of Georgians
reached Boston, but by the next morning, Friday the 13th,
a wintry blast had enveloped the city. Regardless of both
weather and illness, however, Grady kept an engagement to
make a pilgrimage to Plymouth Rock, where with head bared
he made a few impromptu remarks. That afternoon the Bay
State Club, a Democratic organization, gave a luncheon at
the Parker House in honor of Cleveland and the Southern
visitors. Charles H. Taylor, publisher of the *Globe*, presided
and introduced "the matchless orator of Georgia." Although
Grady now was "so hoarse that he could hardly talk," he made
a bright speech on the progress of the South. In it he used as
an illustration his now famous story of the "Pickens County
funeral." After describing a South that "didn't furnish a thing
for that funeral but the corpse and the hole in the ground,"
the speaker said:

Now we have improved on that. We have got the biggest marble-
cutting establishment on earth within a hundred yards of that
grave. We have got a half-dozen woolen mills right around it,
and iron mines, and iron furnaces, and iron factories. We are
coming to meet you. We are going to take a noble revenge, as my
friend, Mr. Carnegie, said last night, by invading every inch of
your territory with iron, as you invaded ours twenty-nine years
ago.

At this point occurred perhaps the most significant incident
of the speech — Grady's reply to "a voice" which asked: "I
want to know if the tariff built up these industries down
there?" The speaker replied: "The tariff? Well, to be perfectly
frank with you, I think it helped some; but you can bet your
bottom dollar that we are Democrats straight through from
the soles of our feet to the top of our heads, and Mr. Cleveland will not have if he runs again, which I am inclined to
think he ought to do, a stronger following." This spontaneous statement carried the same implication as his deliberate
avoidance of mentioning Governor Hill's name at the Pied-

[22] To Walter A. Taylor, reprinted in *Constitution*, December 31, 1889.

mont Exposition: namely, that in the impending contest for the Democratic nomination Grady's sympathies still were with Cleveland. If one is looking for a political motive behind Patrick Collins's activity in bringing Grady to Boston, he may find it in the question asked the next morning by the *Globe:* "How would 'Cleveland and Grady' sound for 1892?" [23]

When the Atlantans left Boston late Friday night, Grady's cold was worse. Complaining of feeling feverish, he walked briskly up and down the platform as he waited for the train to depart. In New York the next day, after suffering a severe chill, he called a physician to his room at the Fifth Avenue Hotel. The doctor told him that he had had a narrow escape from pneumonia and that it might be dangerous for him to continue the journey to Atlanta. He replied, however, that if he was facing a serious illness he desired to be at home with his family.

Grady obeyed the physician's instructions to the extent of remaining away from the breakfast given in his honor by the Southern Society and from a dinner tendered him by John H. Inman. He also canceled an appointment with Robert Bonner, whose *New York Ledger* had paid him $1,000 for the series of six articles it was then running on "The New South." But at noon he got out of bed and rode in a closed carriage to a private luncheon with former President Cleveland. That was one engagement he evidently regarded as too important to miss. [24]

After his return to the hotel Grady was interviewed by a reporter for the *World,* who showed him the comments of the leading newspapers on his Boston address. With the exception of a few moderate papers like the *Springfield Republican,* the Republican press was quite critical. The *World,* a Democratic paper which had praised the speech, sought a reply for publication. Grady took the questions that the correspondent had prepared and promised to dictate a reply on the way home, if he was able.

[23] *Boston Daily Globe,* December 14, 1889; Harris, pp. 204–5.
[24] *New York Herald,* December 15, 16, 1889; *Constitution,* December 14, 31, 1889.

"I am not well," he explained, "and somehow I fear a protracted spell of sickness. But even if my critics remain unanswered, I shall have no fear of my case as it stands. My figures cannot be put aside or disproved. I do not say it boastingly, but the South's position is precisely as I stated it in Boston. Indeed, I should not have been at greater pains to be correct if I had felt that it was to be my last speech, and my reputation as a fair man and a loyal son of the South would rest on my utterances on that occasion." [25]

Shortly after the reporter left, Grady wrote one more letter to his friend Walter A. Taylor in Atlanta. "I am a prisoner, my eyes running with cold till I can't see," he related. "I have had company all day, but it has been mighty dreary. I am afraid now I will not be able to travel tomorrow night, but I am coming home if I die." [26]

The Georgians left New York at midnight Sunday. Grady grew steadily worse as the trip progressed, and by the time the train reached Atlanta he was unable to walk without assistance.

[25] New York *World*, December 23, 1889.

[26] "Saturday night" [December 14], reprinted in *Constitution*, December 31, 1889.

CHAPTER FIFTEEN

Sunset at Noon

GRADY returned to a South that was thrilling with pride for a brilliant son. So clearly had he voiced the views of his own people in his Boston speech that in the mass of clippings preserved from Southern newspapers not a single unfavorable comment can be found. Even the usually critical Charleston *News and Courier* joined in the acclaim by printing the address in full and by referring to the speaker as the "Demosthenes of the South." [1] Atlanta's Negro newspaper, recognizing in his remarks the wisdom of a proved friend, added its praise in an editorial on "Our Matchless Grady." And that best of all popularity barometers, the *Weekly Constitution,* registered a new high by receiving 2,043 subscriptions on the day before its managing editor reached Atlanta. Grady once had said that when the names began coming in at the rate of 2,000 a day he would be ready to die. [2]

Advised in a telegram from the Southerners accompanying him that Grady had made "the grandest speech of his life" and had "captured this whole people," the Mayor and the presidents of various civic organizations in Atlanta arranged for a public reception immediately following his return on Tuesday, December 17. Shortly before time for the train to arrive, however, Grady's physician received a telegram stating that he was too ill for the demonstration. Several hundred persons who had gathered for the reception at the Chamber of Commerce Hall therefore joined the other hundreds already waiting at the railroad station. When Grady was assisted from the car, he was cheered loudly and a garland of flowers

[1] December 14, 1889.
[2] *Constitution,* December 17, 1889; *Life and Labors,* p. 77; Harris, p. 66.

was thrown over his shoulders, but he was too ill to respond. Flushed with fever and coughing violently, he was led on the arms of Dr. Orme and Donald M. Bain to the physician's carriage and hurried directly to his home.

Each day his condition grew steadily worse. On Thursday his son spoke to him of something to be done when he got well. "Your father will never get well," was the answer. That night he became delirious, and the next day pleuropneumonia developed.

When his mother arrived from Athens, in answer to telegraphic summons, a friend told her: "I cannot believe that Mr. Grady will die. He has work yet to do."

"Perhaps his work is finished," the mother replied.

Grady's own words to his mother in one of his last conscious moments were: "If I die, I die serving the South, the land I love so well. Father fell in battle for it. I am proud to die talking for it." [3]

It was not until Sunday that most Atlantans began to realize that Grady's illness might prove fatal. The *Constitution* each morning carried brief reports on his condition, but simply stated that he was too ill to transact business or to receive visitors. By the week-end, however, three other doctors had been called into consultation,[4] and it became known generally that his condition was serious.

On Sunday morning Mrs. Grady asked Mrs. William Lawson Peel, their next-door neighbor, to sit by the bed and read to the patient. She told him jokes but met with no response. Finally she mentioned the Jefferson Davis memorial service [5] held in Atlanta during his absence. He was interested and wished to hear more about it. Mrs. Peel read him the oration

[3] *Constitution*, December 17–23, 1889.

[4] After Grady's death there were rumors that his illness might not have been fatal if his physician, a homeopath, had been willing to follow a different method of treatment. However, Dr. W. S. Elkin, dean emeritus of the Emory University School of Medicine, who was a practicing physician in Atlanta at the time, says Grady's doctor was "a sensible old fellow" who would not have objected to another mode of treatment if the allopaths called into consultation had wished. The patient was in such a state of nervous exhaustion and had been subjected to such repeated exposure that it probably was too late for any treatment known at that time to do him any good.

[5] Davis died December 6, two days before Grady's departure for Boston.

of Bishop Haygood, closing with the words: "And the little children cried in the streets." Grady wept softly. After a few minutes he repeated the words: "And the little children cried in the streets," and lapsed into unconsciousness.[6] At three forty o'clock Monday morning, December 23, he died.

On Christmas Day the final rites were held. The body lay in state at the First Methodist Church from eleven o'clock in the morning until two in the afternoon. Members of the Chi Phi fraternity acted as ushers and served as a guard of honor. More than 7,000 persons — high and low, rich and poor, old and young, black and white — passed by the flower-banked casket. Other hundreds were standing in line outside the church when the auditorium was cleared for the services. Because of the limited seating capacity of the church, only the family, the intimate friends, the *Constitution* employees, and the numerous other honorary escorts could be admitted.

At Mrs. Grady's request, the services were simple. Six ministers, all friends of the editor, took part, but there were no eulogies of any kind. Assisting the pastor, Dr. H. C. Morrison, who gave the opening prayer, were Dr. W. F. Glenn, Dr. J. W. Lee, and General Clement A. Evans, all of whom read brief Scripture lessons; Dr. H. C. Barnett, pastor of the First Presbyterian Church, who also offered a prayer; and Dr. I. S. Hopkins, who pronounced the benediction. The choir sang four hymns, including Grady's favorite, "Shall We Gather at the River?"

The funeral procession was one of the largest ever seen in Atlanta, but that, too, without any pomp or display. The day was bright and beautiful, full of the sunshine Grady loved so well. But all the gay Christmas colors in the business section had changed overnight to somber black and white. For the distance of a mile or more to Oakland Cemetery the streets were lined with silent, sorrowful people. The only noise breaking the stillness as the long procession moved on its way came from the tolling of the bells on churches, schools, and public buildings.

At Oakland the burial service of the church was read by

[6] Mrs. Peel in *Constitution*, May 24, 1921.

Dr. Morrison. The casket then was placed in the Grant family mausoleum, where it was to remain until the Grady vault could be built in the new Westview Cemetery. As the doors thus closed upon a career cut off at its zenith, the most appropriate words spoken seemed to be those of the minister when he said: "The sun has gone down at noon today." [7]

2

"It is doubtful if any man in the history of this people, any private citizen at least, has been as universally mourned as Henry W. Grady," commented the *New-York Tribune*. The circumstances leading up to his fatal illness gave rise to the feeling that he had sacrificed his life to bring about peace and goodwill between the two sections, and a wave of sympathy swept over the nation. Just as the people of both sections had experienced in the death of Horace Greeley in 1872 "a common heart throb" that facilitated the processes of reconciliation, so their grief now revealed a union of hearts that knew "no South, no North, no East, no West." In this general recognition that his untimely passing constituted "a loss to the whole country" was the only consolation of the hour, the *Tribune* thought.[8] John Temple Graves caught the keynote of popular feeling and placed his own feet on the ladder of oratorical fame when he declared at Atlanta's memorial service, on the day after the funeral, that Grady had died "literally loving a nation into peace." [9]

In the judgment of his contemporaries, Grady unquestionably ranked as a national leader of extraordinary promise. Patrick Collins — he who apparently had such significant hopes for the Atlantan's political future — considered him without doubt "the most brilliant son of the Republic." [10] Another New England friend, John Boyle O'Reilly, wrote in the *Boston Pilot* that he had "leaped from the position of a modest Georgia editor to the best known and the greatest

[7] *Constitution*, December 26, 1889.
[8] December 24, 1889.
[9] *Constitution*, December 27, 1889.
[10] Harris, p. 378.

orator on the continent." [11] And Andrew Carnegie wired the
people of Atlanta: "Only those who stood at his side and heard
him at Boston can estimate the extent of the nation's loss in
his death. It seemed reserved for him to perform a service to
his country which no other could perform so well." [12]

When the economic and social forces of his time are placed
in proper perspective, it is too much to say, as did the *New
York Times*,[13] that Grady was "the creator of the spirit" which
animated the New South. But the flood of comments from the
American press does reveal that in the eyes of his fellow journalists he met fully the test of a great man as one who "ex-
presses more successfully than others the real spirit of the age
of which he is the supreme embodiment." [14] Consequently he
was recognized generally as the symbol of the New South — a
term which had come to imply both economic regeneration
and national reconciliation. With this movement his name
was to be as inseparable as is Webster's with Union, Davis's
with Secession, or Lincoln's with Emancipation.

Godkin, writing in the *Nation*,[15] thought that Grady's death
removed "the most conspicuous journalist in the South, for
although not yet forty years of age, his name was better known
than that of any other editor in that part of the country."
And more than any other man of his section, observed the
New York *World*, "he had the ear of the people of the North.
They believed the patriotic assurances which he made in behalf of his people, because they knew him to be honest and
sincere and thoroughly devoted to all that makes for the best
in public affairs." [16] The main reason he was so effective, in
the opinion of the *New York Herald,* was that "when he spoke
he had something to say, and that he was of so cheerful and
hopeful a spirit that he was able to affect his hearers with his
own optimism." [17] The *New York Ledger* asserted that, in

[11] Cited in *Constitution*, December 30, 1889.
[12] Undated telegram, Grady Collection.
[13] December 24, 1889.
[14] Edwin R. A. Seligman: *The Economic Interpretation of History* (New
York, 1924) , p. 98.
[15] December 26, 1889.
[16] December 24, 1889.
[17] December 24, 1889.

"HIS GREAT WORK UNFINISHED"

From the two-page color lithograph by Victor in Judge magazine, January 11, 1890

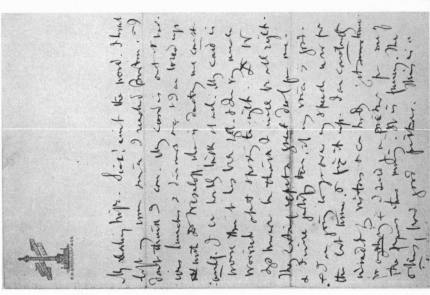

GRADY'S LAST LETTER TO HIS WIFE

Considerably reduced in size. From the original in the Grady Collection.

bringing North and South into a clearer understanding of each other, his career stood "unequalled in the history of the past quarter of a century." [18]

Many Republicans now agreed with the Chicago *Inter Ocean* that Grady had taken as advanced a position as he could on the race question "without cutting himself off from all influence over his own people." [19] This was the view expressed by Chauncey M. Depew, who told the New England Society of New York a few hours after the Atlantan's death that Grady's attitudes, as compared with those of Old South statesmen like Toombs, were so liberal that Toombs would have held him "an enemy to the state." [20] It was his understanding of "what the public will stand," in the opinion of the *Philadelphia Press*, that made him pre-eminently a great leader: "Ability as a writer, keen appreciation of 'news,' and tireless industry, which he had, must all be held second to the power he possessed in an eminent degree of divining the drift and tendency of public feeling, being neither too early to lead it nor too late to control it." [21]

That he ranked as the outstanding Southern orator at the time of his death there seems to have been no doubt. This is a judgment borne out by the wide extent to which his New England Society speech later was reprinted as a specimen of American eloquence. It is confirmed further by the recently published *History and Criticism of American Public Address*,[22] which includes Grady among the twenty-eight men selected by teachers of speech as the nation's most representative public speakers. Grady is treated not primarily as a great thinker but as a great personality — one whose orations were powerful because of their clarity, vividness, and rich imagery, and, most of all, because of their strong emotional quality.

That he was the leading Southern journalist of the late eighties also was the general opinion. Some commentators ranked him second in influence to Henry Watterson, but the Louisville editor, ignoring for the moment their differences

[18] December 28, 1889.
[19] December 24, 1889.
[20] *New York Herald*, December 24, 1889.
[21] Cited in Harris, p. 453.
[22] New York: McGraw-Hill Company; 1943.

on the tariff, hailed him as "the one publicist of the New South, who, inheriting the spirit of the old, yet had realized the present, and looked into the future with the eyes of a statesman and the heart of a patriot." [23] Watterson was to cut a much longer swath across the field of public affairs, yet probably in no three-year period of his career was he to leave as wide or as deep a mark as did his Atlanta contemporary in the years from 1886 to 1889.

In retrospect, "Marse Henry" seems to belong to an earlier era of personal journalism, while Grady, with his emphasis upon news-gathering, promotion, and avoidance of editorial abuse, appears amazingly modern. Grady made no startling innovations in his chosen profession, but probably no other Southern editor of his time combined in such a large measure the reportorial enterprise of James Gordon Bennett, the editorial purposefulness of Samuel Bowles, the promotive skill of Joseph Pulitzer, and the human-interest instinct of Charles A. Dana — the four men who successively influenced him most in his ideas about journalism. In the opinion of the *Journalist*, a trade publication, he had made the *Atlanta Constitution* of 1889 "the model newspaper of the Southern states." Within a year after his death the paper began calling itself, with some justification, "The South's Standard Newspaper." And in its own state it was to be known popularly for a generation to come as the "Georgia Bible." A youngster who grew up in a small Alabama community during the Grady era said the *Constitution* was such an accepted institution in his town that he "thought it was started by a convention in 1787." [24]

No finer tribute has been paid Grady by a journalist than by Henry H. Cabaniss, who was a member of the Hoke Smith company that bought the *Atlanta Journal* in 1887, and who remained with the *Constitution's* chief competitor for nearly half a century. In an interview shortly before his own death Cabaniss said: "I have known and worked with some of the towering figures of the profession — Victor F. Lawson, Melville E. Stone, Frank B. Noyes, Adolph S. Ochs, and many oth-

23 Harris, p. 5.
24 H. C. Nixon, op. cit., p. 36; Mott, op. cit., p. 456n.

ers, but to my mind the greatest of all was my rival, Henry W. Grady. He was more keenly alive to newspaper opportunities, both editorial and business, than any other man who ever lived."

Even his enemies recognized "his sincerity and manliness," wrote Dr. Henry M. Field in the *New York Evangelist*.[25] This was true in his own state, where the *Macon Telegraph*, with which Grady had crossed so many political lances, declared that "Georgia had no more famous citizen and perhaps there never was a man in this state in private station who was so much admired." [26] It was true also throughout the South and the nation, as illustrated by the Charleston *News and Courier's* glowing tribute,[27] which quoted the once antagonistic *Boston Herald* as now conceding that "if Massachusetts and Ohio had a colored population as large in proportion to the white as have South Carolina and Louisiana, the political conditions, so far as the race question is concerned, would be exactly the same in the two Northern and in the two Southern states." The Republican *Indianapolis Journal*, which had condemned Grady after the Boston speech as an "Orator Jekyll, Editor Hyde," acknowledged following his death that his attitudes were based on a sincere love not only for the South but for the whole country.[28]

The widespread belief in his disinterestedness was strengthened by the announcement that he had died a relatively poor man. His estate was appraised for administrative purposes at $122,423.33, all of which except $15,090 represented the market value of his stock in the Constitution Publishing Company. Shares with a par value of $100, which he had bought at $80 in 1880, were selling for $500 in 1889 — an increase of more than 500 per cent in the nine years of his managing editorship. Even so, there was a mortgage upon his home at the time of his death, principally as the result of his over-optimism concerning the cotton market and his insistence upon paying far more than his just share of the 1888 Chautauqua deficit.

[25] Cited in *Constitution*, December 30, 1889.
[26] December 24, 1889.
[27] December 24, 1889.
[28] December 24, 1889.

Be it said to the credit of his capitalist friends that a group of them, under the inspiration of Samuel M. Inman, quickly paid off the mortgage and presented Mrs. Grady with a clear title to the house. Since Grady had died without a will, the remainder of his estate was divided equally among the widow, the son, and the daughter.[29]

"The memory of his brilliant but brief career will become dearer to the people when they realize that his genius was never swayed by an unworthy motive nor employed in an unworthy cause," said the *Constitution* editorially. During the last ten years of his life, wrote Harris, "there was not a day . . . that he could not have made thousands of dollars by placing his pen at the disposal of men interested in speculative schemes. . . . He had hundreds of opportunities to write himself rich. . . . Had he served his own interests one-half as earnestly as he served those of the people, he would have been a millionaire." To this Clark Howell, his successor on the *Constitution,* later added: "He was the least selfish man that I have ever known; his thoughts were always of somebody else." [30]

Feelings like these, multiplied a thousandfold, prompted people in all parts of the country to send in contributions for the monument which was unveiled on October 21, 1891, at Forsyth and Marietta Streets, the intersection now known as Henry Grady Square. The heroic statue of Grady and the draped female figures representing "History" and "Memory" were the work of Alexander Doyle, a New York sculptor. A year later the Grady Hospital, also built by public subscription, was presented to the city of Atlanta to be operated as a municipal charity hospital — an enterprise which Grady had been advocating in the *Constitution* preceding his death. Of

---

[29] Records of the Ordinary, Fulton County. Most of Grady's *Constitution* stock still remains in the family. His son, Henry W. Grady, Jr., later joined the *Constitution* organization and at the time of his death in 1942 was president of the Southern Engraving Company, a *Constitution* subsidiary.

[30] Harris, pp. 60, 65; Clark Howell: "Henry W. Grady," in *Chautauquan,* V (September 1895) , 703. Howell succeeded Grady as managing editor and in 1897, upon Evan P. Howell's retirement, became editor-in-chief. Upon Clark Howell's death in 1936 he was succeeded by Clark Howell, Jr., who in September 1942 took the title of "president and publisher" and promoted Ralph McGill, then executive editor, to the position of editor.

lesser memorials — a national highway, a Georgia county, a school of journalism, a great hotel, to say nothing of namesakes by the hundreds into the third and fourth generations, there are no end. A national magazine once said that "every skyscraper which arises in these astonishing cities of the New South is in a real sense a monument to Grady and his genius." [31]

3

Despite the general recognition of Grady's power and promise as a leader, a number of comments implied that in death he might be doing more to "bridge the bloody chasm" than he could have done in life. Godkin suggested this in the *Nation* when he observed that the Boston speech had been made "more impressive" by Grady's death and "was by far the most effective of all his appeals to the public." [32] The *Southern Cultivator,* a farm journal published in Atlanta, expressed the same idea in commenting upon the words of Grady's mother that "perhaps his work is finished":

His work was finished. . . . No subsequent act of his could have fixed him more firmly, or more deeply, in the affections of his people. . . . He died at the opportune moment for himself and his country. His noble speech in Boston, so happily blending truthfulness, boldness, and tenderness, has been wonderfully emphasized by his death.[33]

Possibly Grady's final appeal to the North, reinforced as it was so dramatically by his death, did contribute to the defeat of the federal election law [34] and thus to the definite acceptance by the North of the attitude that the Negro question should be left to the South to solve. "Emotion," as was said of the feelings aroused by Greeley's death, "is an elusive

[31] Cited by Rupert B. Vance: *Human Geography of the South* (Chapel Hill, 1932), p. 275.

[32] December 26, 1889.

[33] January 1890.

[34] The federal election law or "force bill" was passed by the House on July 2, 1890, by a majority of six, but was defeated by the Senate in January 1891.

thing, often impossible to analyze." The final collapse of the "force bill" movement was attributed at the time by both sides to the opposition of Northern business leaders. These were the very groups to whom Grady, with his keen insight into the relation between economics and politics, had addressed his speeches in the North, both in 1886 and in 1889. The best and most recent history of the reconciliation movement concludes that the "force bill" actually was killed by "the hostility of public opinion." [35] Modern polls of public opinion, however, reveal that the attitudes of the masses are affected more profoundly by events touching the emotions than by any other factors. Perhaps the death of Grady did soften the hearts of the North toward the views he expressed.

Unless one is willing, however, to ascribe to a wave of popular sympathy far more influence than is justified by our knowledge of the facts, it is difficult to see in the death of Grady, at the age of only thirty-nine, anything but a calamity for the South. Once he was removed from the scene, there seemed to be no Southern leader with a vision and an influence comprehensive enough to unite both business and agriculture in a broad progressive program. Thus the opportunities for constructive leadership offered by the mounting agrarian distress — a problem to which Grady was giving increased attention in the year of his death — were left in the nineties to the "narrow-minded Tom Watsons and Ben Tillmans." [36] Grady not only possessed the confidence of the overwhelming majority of all classes in the South, but combined an attitude of liberalism with an enlightened and entirely practical approach to the difficult race problem. Men of the Watson stripe, on the other hand, eventually caused the public to identify the demand for progressive reforms with the lowest type of Negro-baiting, Jew-baiting, and Catholic-baiting — an identification "heavy with tragic consequences for the South." [37]

35 Buck, op. cit., p. 280.
36 H. C. Nixon in "Twelve Southerners," *I'll Take My Stand* (New York, 1930) , pp. 193–4. Dr. Nixon, an agrarian who really knows the feel of the plow, says: "The agrarian protest in the South would have had a wiser leadership if Grady had lived."
37 C. Vann Woodward: "The South in Search of a Philosophy" (Phi Beta Kappa Series, University of Florida, No. 1) , p. 14.

Not the least tragic of these consequences was the fact that certain interests found it all too easy at times to make the "New South" slogan a shield for unbridled industrial exploitation rather than the symbol of general economic betterment and national goodwill which Grady intended it should be.

Of course Grady might have been out of place in the stormy nineties, just as he was thoroughly at home in the relatively placid eighties. The problems then coming to the fore — the agrarian problem, the labor problem, the trust problem — were common to the nation at large and hence much too broad and too complex to be solved completely by the methods that he found so successful in his personal contacts. But the way in which Grady had responded to every major economic and political trend of his lifetime — Reconstruction, the New Departure, the restoration of home rule, industrialization, and the incipient agrarian revolt — leads to the conclusion that, had he lived, he would have continued to utilize his talents for what he honestly conceived to be best — not for the South alone, but for the North as well; not simply for the whites, but also for the blacks; not for one class, but for all classes.

Good journalist that he was, he always kept an ear to the ground. But his eyes were upon the stars.

The New South

By HENRY W. GRADY [1]

"THERE was a South of slavery and secession — that South is dead. There is a South of union and freedom — that South, thank God, is living, breathing, growing every hour." These words, delivered from the immortal lips of Benjamin H. Hill, at Tammany Hall in 1866,[2] true then, and truer now, I shall make my text to-night.

Mr. President and Gentlemen: Let me express to you my appreciation of the kindness by which I am permitted to address you. I make this abrupt acknowledgment advisedly, for I feel that if, when I raise my provincial voice in this ancient and august presence, I could find courage for no more than the opening sentence, it would be well if, in that sentence, I had met in a rough sense my obligation as a guest, and had perished, so to speak, with courtesy on my lips and grace in my heart. (Laughter.) Permitted through your kindness to catch my second wind, let me say that I appreciate the significance of being the first Southerner to speak at this board, which bears the substance, if it surpasses the semblance, of original New England hospitality (applause), and honors a sentiment that in turn honors you, but in which my personality is lost, and the compliment to my people made plain. (Laughter.)

I bespeak the utmost stretch of your courtesy to-night. I am not troubled about those from whom I come. You remember

[1] As reported by the *New-York Tribune*, December 23, 1886, and subsequently corrected by Grady for the published proceedings of the Eighty-first Anniversary Celebration of the New England Society in the City of New York.

[2] See above. p. 245.

the man whose wife sent him to a neighbor with a pitcher of milk, and who, tripping on the top step, fell, with such casual interruptions as the landings afforded, into the basement; and while picking himself up had the pleasure of hearing his wife call out: "John, did you break the pitcher?"

"No, I didn't," said John, "but I be dinged if I don't." (Loud laughter.)

So, while those who call to me from behind may inspire me with energy if not with courage, I ask an indulgent hearing from you. I beg that you will bring your full faith in American fairness and frankness to judgment upon what I shall say. There was an old preacher once who told some boys of the Bible lesson he was going to read in the morning. The boys, finding the place, glued together the connecting pages. (Laughter.) The next morning he read on the bottom of one page: "When Noah was one hundred and twenty years old he took unto himself a wife, who was" — then turning the page — "140 cubits long (laughter), 40 cubits wide, built of gopher wood (laughter), and covered with pitch inside and out." (Loud and continued laughter.) He was naturally puzzled at this. He read it again, verified it, and then said: "My friends, this is the first time I ever met this in the Bible, but I accept it as an evidence of the assertion that we are fearfully and wonderfully made." (Immense laughter.) If I could get you to hold such faith to-night I could proceed cheerfully to the task I otherwise approach with a sense of consecration.

Pardon me one word, Mr. President, spoken for the sole purpose of getting into the volumes that go out annually freighted with the rich eloquence of your speakers — the fact that the Cavalier as well as the Puritan was on the Continent in its early days, and that he was "up and able to be about." (Laughter.) I have read your books carefully and I find no mention of that fact, which seems to me an important one for preserving a sort of historical equilibrium if for nothing else.

Let me remind you that the Virginia Cavalier first challenged France on this continent — that Cavalier John Smith gave New England its very name, and was so pleased with the job that he has been handing his own name around ever since

— and that while Miles Standish was cutting off men's ears for courting a girl without her parents' consent, and forbade men to kiss their wives on Sunday, the Cavalier was courting everything in sight, and that the Almighty had vouchsafed great increase to the Cavalier colonies, the huts in the wilderness being as full as the nests in the woods.

But having incorporated the Cavalier as a fact in your charming little books I shall let him work out his own salvation, as he has always done with engaging gallantry, and we will hold no controversy as to his merits. Why should we? Neither Puritan nor Cavalier long survived as such. The virtues and traditions of both happily still live for the inspiration of their sons and the saving of the old fashion. (Applause.) But both Puritan and Cavalier were lost in the storm of the first Revolution; and the American citizen, supplanting both and stronger than either, took possession of the Republic bought by their common blood and fashioned to wisdom, and charged himself with teaching men government and establishing the voice of the people as the voice of God. (Applause.)

My friends, Dr. Talmage has told you that the typical American has yet to come. Let me tell you that he has already come. (Applause.) Great types like valuable plants are slow to flower and fruit. But from the union of these colonist Puritans and Cavaliers, from the straightening of their purposes and the crossing of their blood, slow perfecting through a century, came he who stands as the first typical American, the first who comprehended within himself all the strength and gentleness, all the majesty and grace of this republic — Abraham Lincoln. (Loud and long continued applause.) He was the sum of Puritan and Cavalier, for in his ardent nature were fused the virtues of both, and in the depths of his great soul the faults of both were lost. (Renewed applause.) He was greater than Puritan, greater than Cavalier, in that he was American (renewed applause) , and that in his homely form were first gathered the vast and thrilling forces of his ideal government — charging it with such tremendous meaning and so elevating it above human suffering that martyrdom, though infamously aimed, came as a fitting crown to a life consecrated from the cradle to human liberty. (Loud and prolonged cheering.) Let us, each cherishing the traditions and honoring his fathers, build with reverent hands to the type of this simple but sublime life, in which all types are honored; and in our common glory as Americans there will be plenty and to spare for your forefathers and for mine. (Renewed cheering.)

In speaking to the toast with which you have honored me, I accept the term, "The New South," as in no sense disparaging to the old. Dear to me, sir, is the home of my childhood and the traditions of my people. I would not, if I could, dim the glory they won in peace and war, or by word or deed take aught from the splendor and grace of their civilization,— never equalled and, perhaps, never to be equalled in its chivalric strength and grace. There is a New South, not through protest against the old, but because of new conditions, new adjustments and, if you please, new ideas and aspirations. It is to this that I address myself, and to the consideration of which I hasten lest it become the Old South before I get to it. Age does not endow all things with strength and virtue, nor are all new things to be despised. The shoemaker who put over his door "John Smith's shop. Founded in 1760," was more than matched by his young rival across the street who hung out this sign: "Bill Jones. Established 1886. No old stock kept in this shop."

Dr. Talmage has drawn for you, with a master's hand, the picture of your returning armies. He has told you how, in the pomp and circumstance of war, they came back to you, marching with proud and victorious tread, reading their glory in a nation's eyes! Will you bear with me while I tell you of another army that sought its home at the close of the late war — an army that marched home in defeat and not in victory — in pathos and not in splendor, but in glory that equalled yours, and to hearts as loving as ever welcomed heroes home. Let me picture to you the footsore Confederate soldier, as, buttoning up in his faded gray jacket the parole which was to bear testimony to his children of his fidelity and faith, he turned his face southward from Appomattox in April, 1865. Think of him as ragged, half-starved, heavy-hearted, enfeebled by want and wounds; having fought to exhaustion, he surrenders his gun, wrings the hands of his comrades in silence, and lifting his

tear-stained and pallid face for the last time to the graves that
dot the old Virginia hills, pulls his gray cap over his brow and
begins the slow and painful journey. What does he find — let
me ask you, who went to your homes eager to find in the welcome you had justly earned, full payment for four years' sacrifice — what does he find when, having followed the battle-
stained cross against overwhelming odds, dreading death not
half so much as surrender, he reaches the home he left so prosperous and beautiful? He finds his house in ruins, his farm
devastated, his slaves free, his stock killed, his barns empty,
his trade destroyed, his money worthless; his social system,
feudal in its magnificence, swept away; his people without
law or legal status, his comrades slain, and the burdens of others heavy on his shoulders. Crushed by defeat, his very traditions are gone: without money, credit, employment, material
or training; and beside all this, confronted with the gravest
problem that ever met human intelligence — the establishing
of a status for the vast body of his liberated slaves.

What does he do — this hero in gray with a heart of gold?
Does he sit down in sullenness and despair? Not for a day.
Surely God, who had stripped him of his prosperity, inspired
him in his adversity. As ruin was never before so overwhelming, never was restoration swifter. The soldier stepped from
the trenches into the furrow; horses that had charged Federal
guns marched before the plow, and fields that ran red with human blood in April were green with the harvest in June;
women reared in luxury cut up their dresses and made
breeches for their husbands, and, with a patience and heroism
that fit women always as a garment, gave their hands to work.
There was little bitterness in all this. Cheerfulness and frankness prevailed. "Bill Arp" struck the keynote when he said:
"Well, I killed as many of them as they did of me, and now I
am going to work." (Laughter and applause.) Or the soldier
returning home after defeat and roasting some corn on the
roadside, who made the remark to his comrades: "You may
leave the South if you want to, but I am going to Sandersville,
kiss my wife and raise a crop, and if the Yankees fool with me
any more I will whip 'em again." (Renewed applause.) I
want to say to General Sherman — who is considered an able

man in our parts, though some people think he is a kind of careless man about fire — that from the ashes he left us in 1864 we have raised a brave and beautiful city; that somehow or other we have caught the sunshine in the bricks and mortar of our homes, and have builded therein not one ignoble prejudice or memory. (Applause.)

But in all this what have we accomplished? What is the sum of our work? We have found out that in the general summary the free negro counts more than he did as a slave. We have planted the schoolhouse on the hilltop and made it free to white and black. We have sowed towns and cities in the place of theories and put business above politics. (Applause.) We have challenged your spinners in Massachusetts and your iron-makers in Pennsylvania. We have learned that the $400,000,-000 annually received from our cotton crop will make us rich, when the supplies that make it are home-raised. We have reduced the commercial rate of interest from 24 to 6 per cent., and are floating 4 per cent. bonds. We have learned that one northern immigrant is worth fifty foreigners, and have smoothed the path to southward, wiped out the place where Mason and Dixon's line used to be, and hung our latch-string to you and yours. (Prolonged cheers.) We have reached the point that marks perfect harmony in every household, when the husband confesses that the pies which his wife cooks are as good as those his mother used to bake; and we admit that the sun shines as brightly and the moon as softly as it did "before the war." (Laughter.) We have established thrift in city and country. We have fallen in love with work. We have restored comfort to homes from which culture and elegance never departed. We have let economy take root and spread among us as rank as the crab grass which sprung from Sherman's cavalry camps, until we are ready to lay odds on the Georgia Yankee, as he manufactures relics of the battlefield in a one-story shanty and squeezes pure olive oil out of his cotton seed, against any Down-easter that ever swapped wooden nutmegs for flannel sausages in the valleys of Vermont. (Loud and continuous laughter.) Above all, we know that we have achieved in these "piping times of peace" a fuller independence for the South than that which our fathers sought to **win** in the forum by their eloquence or compel on the field by their swords. (Loud applause.)

It is a rare privilege, sir, to have had part, however humble, in this work. Never was nobler duty confided to human hands than the uplifting and upbuilding of the prostrate and bleeding South, misguided, perhaps, but beautiful in her suffering, and honest, brave and generous always. (Applause.) In the record of her social, industrial and political illustration we await with confidence the verdict of the world.

But what of the negro? Have we solved the problem he presents or progressed in honor and equity towards the solution? Let the record speak to the point. No section shows a more prosperous laboring population than the negroes of the South; none in fuller sympathy with the employing and land-owning class. He shares our school fund, has the fullest protection of our laws and the friendship of our people. Self-interest, as well as honor, demand that he should have this. Our future, our very existence depend upon our working out this problem in full and exact justice. We understand that when Lincoln signed the Emancipation Proclamation, your victory was assured; for he then committed you to the cause of human liberty, against which the arms of man cannot prevail (applause) ; while those of our statesmen who trusted to make slavery the corner-stone of the Confederacy doomed us to defeat as far as they could, committing us to a cause that reason could not defend or the sword maintain in the light of advancing civilization. (Renewed applause.) Had Mr. Toombs said, which he did not say, that he would call the roll of his slaves at the foot of Bunker Hill, he would have been foolish, for he might have known that whenever slavery became entangled in war it must perish, and that the chattel in human flesh ended forever in New England when your fathers — not to be blamed for parting with what didn't pay — sold their slaves to our fathers — not to be praised for knowing a paying thing when they saw it. (Laughter.) The relations of the southern people with the negro are close and cordial. We remember with what fidelity for four years he guarded our defenseless women and children, whose husbands and fathers were fighting against his freedom. To his eternal credit be it said that whenever he struck a blow for his own liberty he fought in open battle, and when at last he raised his black and humble hands that the shackles might be struck off, those hands were innocent of wrong against his helpless charges, and worthy to be taken in loving grasp by every man who honors loyalty and devotion. (Applause.) Ruffians have maltreated him, rascals have misled him, philanthropists established a bank for him, but the South, with the North, protests against injustice to this simple and sincere people. To liberty and enfranchisement is as far as law can carry the negro. The rest must be left to conscience and common sense. It should be left to those among whom his lot is cast, with whom he is indissolubly connected and whose prosperity depends upon their possessing his intelligent sympathy and confidence. Faith has been kept with him in spite of calumnious assertions to the contrary by those who assume to speak for us or by frank opponents. Faith will be kept with him in the future, if the South holds her reason and integrity. (Applause.)

But have we kept faith with you? In the fullest sense, yes. When Lee surrendered — I don't say when Johnson surrendered, because I understand he still alludes to the time when he met General Sherman last as the time when he "determined to abandon any further prosecution of the struggle" — when Lee surrendered, I say, and Johnson quit, the South became, and has since been, loyal to this union. We fought hard enough to know that we were whipped, and in perfect frankness accepted as final the arbitrament of the sword to which we had appealed. The South found her jewel in the toad's head of defeat. The shackles that had held her in narrow limitations fell forever when the shackles of the negro slave were broken. (Applause.) Under the old regime the negroes were slaves to the South, the South was a slave to the system. The old plantation, with its simple police regulation and its feudal habit, was the only type possible under slavery. Thus was gathered in the hands of a splendid and chivalric oligarchy the substance that should have been diffused among the people, as the rich blood, under certain artificial conditions, is gathered at the heart, filling that with affluent rapture, but leaving the body chill and colorless. (Applause.)

The old South rested everything on slavery and agriculture, unconscious that these could neither give nor maintain healthy growth. The new South presents a perfect Democracy, the oligarchs leading in the popular movement — a social system compact and closely knitted, less splendid on the surface but stronger at the core — a hundred farms for every plantation, fifty homes for every palace, and a diversified industry that meets the complex needs of this complex age.

The new South is enamored of her new work. Her soul is stirred with the breath of a new life. The light of a grander day is falling fair on her face. She is thrilling with the consciousness of growing power and prosperity. As she stands upright, full-statured and equal among the people of the earth, breathing the keen air and looking out upon the expanding horizon, she understands that her emancipation came because in the inscrutable wisdom of God her honest purpose was crossed and her brave armies were beaten. (Applause.)

This is said in no spirit of time-serving or apology. The South has nothing for which to apologize. She believes that the late struggle between the States was war and not rebellion, revolution and not conspiracy, and that her convictions were as honest as yours. I should be unjust to the dauntless spirit of the South and to my own convictions if I did not make this plain in this presence. The South has nothing to take back. In my native town of Athens is a monument that crowns its central hill — a plain, white shaft. Deep cut into its shining side is a name dear to me above the names of men, that of a brave and simple man who died in brave and simple faith. Not for all the glories of New England — from Plymouth Rock all the way — would I exchange the heritage he left me in his soldier's death. To the foot of that shaft I shall send my children's children to reverence him who ennobled their name with his heroic blood. But, sir, speaking from the shadow of that memory, which I honor as I do nothing else on earth, I say that the cause in which he suffered and for which he gave his life was adjudged by higher and fuller wisdom than his or mine, and I am glad that the omniscient God held the balance of battle in His Almighty hand, and that human slavery was swept forever from American soil — the American Union saved from the wreck of war. (Loud applause.)

This message, Mr. President, comes to you from consecrated ground. Every foot of the soil about the city in which I live is as sacred as a battle-ground of the republic. Every hill that invests it is hallowed to you by the blood of your brothers, who died for your victory, and doubly hallowed to us by the blow of those who died hopeless, but undaunted, in defeat — sacred soil to all of us, rich with memories that make us purer and stronger and better, silent but staunch witnesses in its red desolation of the matchless valor of American hearts and the deathless glory of American arms — speaking an eloquent witness in its white peace and prosperity to the indissoluble union of American States and the imperishable brotherhood of the American people. (Immense cheering.)

Now, what answer has New England to this message? Will she permit the prejudice of war to remain in the hearts of the conquerors, when it has died in the hearts of the conquered? (Cries of "No! No!") Will she transmit this prejudice to the next generation, that in their hearts, which never felt the generous ardor of conflict, it may perpetuate itself? ("No! No!") Will she withhold, save in strained courtesy, the hand which straight from his soldier's heart Grant offered to Lee at Appomattox? Will she make the vision of a restored and happy people, which gathered above the couch of your dying captain, filling his heart with grace, touching his lips with praise and glorifying his path to the grave; will she make this vision on which the last sigh of his expiring soul breathed a benediction, a cheat and a delusion? (Tumultuous cheering and shouts of "No! No!") If she does, the South, never abject in asking for comradeship, must accept with dignity its refusal; but if she does not; if she accepts in frankness and sincerity this message of good-will and friendship, then will the prophecy of Webster, delivered in this very Society forty years ago amid tremendous applause, be verified in its fullest and final sense, when he said: "Standing hand to hand and clasping hands, we should remain united as we have been for sixty years, citizens of the same country, members of the same government, united, all united now and united forever. There have been difficulties, contentions, and controversies, but I tell you that in my judgment

> "Those opposed eyes,
> Which like the meteors of a troubled heaven,
> All of one nature, of one substance bred,
> Did lately meet in th'intestine shock,
> Shall now, in mutual well beseeming ranks,
> March all one way."

(Prolonged applause.)

Bibliography

PRIVATE PAPERS AND MANUSCRIPTS

GROVER CLEVELAND PAPERS. Library of Congress. Contain eight letters and two telegrams from Grady to Cleveland, as well as other correspondence bearing upon the relations between the two men.

REBECCA L. FELTON PAPERS. University of Georgia Library. Contain letters to Mrs. Felton and her husband, Dr. William H. Felton, from many political leaders of the eighties. One of them, William H. Hidell, a former secretary to Alexander H. Stephens, makes uncomplimentary references to Grady and other Democrats who opposed the Independent movement.

JOHN B. GORDON PAPERS. State Archives, Atlanta. Contain one significant MS. letter from Gordon to Grady.

HENRY W. GRADY COLLECTION. Emory University Library, Atlanta. The largest and most useful source of biographical material, much of it heretofore inaccessible. Contains more than one hundred letters, mostly from Grady to members of his family; twelve scrapbooks, covering nearly his entire newspaper career; manuscripts of two unpublished speeches; diaries for the years 1878 and 1879; Grady's account book for 1882; fragments of various writings; many photographs; and miscellaneous memorabilia such as Grady's menu card at the New England Society dinner.

JOEL CHANDLER HARRIS COLLECTION. Emory University Library, Atlanta. Contains, among a wealth of other items, scrapbooks with clippings from the Atlanta *Sunday Gazette,* published jointly by Grady and Harris in 1878-9.

NICHOLSON SCRAPBOOKS. University of Georgia Library. Contain a few clippings not duplicated in the Grady Collection.

WILLIAM J. NORTHEN SCRAPBOOKS. State Archives, Atlanta. Contain several MS. letters from Grady.

ALEXANDER H. STEPHENS PAPERS. Library of Congress. Contain a small amount of correspondence between Grady and Stephens.

L. N. TRAMMELL PAPERS. Emory University Library, Atlanta. Letters to Trammell from other Georgia political leaders contain occasional references to Grady.

HENRY WATTERSON PAPERS. Library of Congress. Contain no Grady correspondence, but are useful for light thrown upon characters of Watterson, Victor Newcomb, and other associates of Grady.

NEWSPAPERS AND OTHER PERIODICALS

Athens (Georgia) *Southern Watchman*, 1854–69.

Atlanta Constitution, 1868–1943. Issues of particular usefulness after the Grady period are those of September 26, 1917 (Golden Jubilee Edition) ; May 22, 1921 (Grady Memorial Edition) ; June 14, 1928 (Sixtieth Anniversary Edition) ; December 24, 1939 (Grady Memorial Edition) ; September 1, 1942 (Seventy-fifth Anniversary Edition).

Atlanta Daily Herald, 1872–6.

Atlanta *Daily News*, 1874–5.

Atlanta Daily News, 1900–1.

Atlanta *Evening Capitol*, 1885–6.

Atlanta *Evening Star*, 1883.

Atlanta Journal, February 24, 1883–June 30, 1887. Apparently no files exist for the remainder of the Grady period.

Columbus (Georgia) *Daily Enquirer-Sun*, 1879–90.

Frank Leslie's Illustrated Newspaper, 1878–90.

Harper's Weekly, 1881–9.

Macon Daily Telegraph, 1880–90. Title prior to January 1, 1885: *Daily Telegraph and Messenger*.

Nation, The, 1886–9.

New York Herald, 1876–89.

New York *World*, 1886–9.

Public Opinion, 1886–90.

Rome (Georgia) *Daily Commercial*, May 16, 1871; September 4, 1872. These are the only complete issues available for the Grady period. Numerous clippings, however, are preserved in the scrapbooks of the Grady Collection.

Rome (Georgia) *Tri-Weekly Courier*, 1869–72.

Rome (Georgia) *Weekly Courier*, 1869–72.

Savannah Morning News, 1880–9.

In addition to these files, which were used extensively, reference was made as indicated to many other newspapers and magazines found in the libraries of Emory University and the University of Minnesota, the Wisconsin State Historical Library, the New York Public Library, the Boston Public Library, the Carnegie Library of Atlanta, and the Library of Congress.

BOOKS AND ARTICLES BY GRADY

Addresses Delivered at the Annual Banquet of the Boston Merchants Association, December 12, 1889. Published by the Association.

Anniversary Celebration of the New England Society in the City of New York, December 22, 1886. Published by the Society.

Complete Orations and Speeches of Henry W. Grady, The. Edited by Edwin DuBois Shurter. New York, 1910. Contains only the more important speeches.

"Cotton and Its Kingdom," in *Harper's New Monthly Magazine,* LXIII (October 1881), 719–34.

"Early Journalistic Writings" (1869–83), in *A Study of the Early Journalistic Writings of Henry W. Grady,* by Russell F. Terrell, pp. 93–176. Nashville, Tennessee, 1927.

"In Plain Black and White," in *The Century,* XXIX (April 1885), 909–17. A reply to George W. Cable.

New South, The, with a character sketch of Henry W. Grady by Oliver Dyer of the New York *Sun.* New York, 1890. This is not the lecture "The New South" but a series of six articles published in the weekly *New York Ledger,* November 16–December 21, 1889.

New South and Other Addresses, The, with a biography of Henry W. Grady by Edna H. L. Turpin. New York, 1904.

Speeches of Henry W. Grady, The, with a short biographical sketch of his life. Atlanta, 1895.

"Writings and Speeches," in Harris, J. C.: *Life of Henry W. Grady,* pp. 83–310. New York, 1890.

BOOKS AND ARTICLES ABOUT GRADY

CRAWFORD, T. R. "Early Home of Henry W. Grady," in *New England Magazine,* II (June 1890), 425–36. Author, a former resident of Athens, joined staff of *Constitution* after Grady's death.

DUGAT, GENTRY. *Life of Henry W. Grady.* Edinburg, Texas, 1927. A non-critical sketch based on secondary sources.

DYER, OLIVER. "A Character Sketch of Henry Woodfin Grady," in Grady, H. W.: *The New South.* New York, 1890. A tribute from an admirer on the staff of the New York *Sun.*

GRAVES, JOHN TEMPLE. "Eulogy of Henry W. Grady," in Knight, Lucian L.: *Georgia's Bi-Centennial Memoirs and Memories,* II,

352–7. Atlanta, 1931. The speech made famous by the words: "When he died he was literally loving a nation into peace."

GRAVES, JOHN TEMPLE, II. "Henry W. Grady," in *Atlanta Historical Bulletin*, V (January 1940), 23–31. An interpretation of Grady's present-day significance.

HARRIS, J. C. *Life of Henry W. Grady, Including His Writings and Speeches*. New York, 1890. (Referred to in the text as Harris.) A "labor of love," put together hastily following Grady's death and containing many errors.

HOWELL, CLARK. "Henry W. Grady," in *Chautauquan*, V (September 1895), 703–6. A tribute from the man who succeeded Grady on the *Constitution*.

LEE, JAMES W. *Henry W. Grady, the Editor, the Orator, the Man*. St. Louis, 1896. Eulogistic character sketch by a Methodist minister.

———. "Henry W. Grady, Editor, Orator, Man," in *Arena*, II (June 1890), 9–23.

Life and Labors of Henry W. Grady. Published by H. C. Hudgins & Co. Atlanta, 1890. A volume brought out to compete with the "official" life by Harris; published under several different imprints, including Dallas, New York, and Richmond.

LINDSLEY, C. F. "Henry Woodfin Grady, Orator," in *Quarterly Journal of Speech Education*, VI (April 1920), 28–42. A brief analysis of Grady's techniques as an orator.

NIXON, RAYMOND B. "Henry W. Grady, Reporter," in *Journalism Quarterly*, XII (December 1935), 341–56.

REED, T. W. *Henry W. Grady*, an address before the Georgia Press Institute at the University of Georgia, February 21, 1931. Athens, 1936. Mr. Reed worked under Grady on the *Constitution* for several months and later lived in the home of Grady's mother in Athens.

RICHARDSON, F. H. *A Fruitful Life*. An address before the Georgia Chautauqua at Albany, Georgia, March 30, 1890. Albany, 1890. Mr. Richardson was an associate of Grady on the *Constitution* staff.

SPALDING, JACK J. "Henry W. Grady," in *Atlanta Historical Bulletin*, II (September 1937), 67. Brief remarks by a close friend.

TERRELL, RUSSELL F. *A Study of the Early Journalistic Writings of Henry W. Grady*. George Peabody College Contributions to Education, No. 39. Nashville, Tennessee, 1927. Analyzes selections from Grady's early writings (1869–83) as literature.

WADE, JOHN DONALD. "Henry W. Grady," in *Southern Review*, III (Winter 1938), 479–509. A clever but cynical treatment of Grady and the New South philosophy.

BIOGRAPHIES, REMINISCENCES, AND PUBLISHED CORRESPONDENCE OF CONTEMPORARIES

BAKER, RAY S. *Woodrow Wilson: Life and Letters.* 5 vols. New York, 1927–35.

BARNUM, P. T. *Struggles and Triumphs: or Forty Years' Recollections of P. T. Barnum.* Written by Himself. Buffalo, New York, 1872.

CATE, WIRT A. *Lucius Q. C. Lamar: Secession and Reunion.* Chapel Hill, North Carolina, 1935.

CLARK, CHAMP. *My Quarter Century of American Politics.* New York, 1920.

DANIELS, JOSEPHUS. *Tar Heel Editor.* Chapel Hill, North Carolina, 1939.

Davis, Jefferson, Constitutionalist: His Letters, Papers, and Speeches. Edited by Dunbar Rowland. 10 vols. Jackson, Mississippi, 1923.

DEMPSEY, ELAM F. *Atticus Green Haygood.* Nashville, Tennessee, 1940.

ECKENRODE, H. J. *Rutherford B. Hayes: Statesman of Reunion.* New York, 1930.

FELTON, REBECCA LATIMER (Mrs. William H.). *My Memoirs of Georgia Politics.* Atlanta, 1911.

FIELDER, HERBERT. *Life and Times of Joseph E. Brown.* Springfield, Massachusetts, 1883.

HARRIS, JULIA COLLIER. *Joel Chandler Harris, Editor and Essayist.* Chapel Hill, North Carolina, 1931.

———. *The Life and Letters of Joel Chandler Harris.* Boston, 1918.

HARRIS, NAT E. *Autobiography: The Story of an Old Man's Life with Reminiscences of Seventy-Five Years.* Macon, Georgia, 1925.

HENDRICK, BURTON J. *The Life and Letters of Walter Hines Page.* 2 vols. New York, 1924–5.

HILL, BENJAMIN H., JR. *Senator Benjamin H. Hill: His Life, Speeches and Writings.* Atlanta, 1891.

"Howell, Evan P.," Anonymous sketch of, in *Georgia Historical Quarterly,* I (March 1917), 52–7.

KNIGHT, LUCIAN LAMAR. *Reminiscences of Famous Georgians.* 2 vols. Atlanta, 1908.

MCRAE, MILTON A. *Forty Years in Newspaperdom.* New York, 1924.

MITCHELL, EUGENE MUSE. "H. I. Kimball: His Career and Defense," in *Atlanta Historical Bulletin,* III (October 1938), 349–83.

NEVINS, ALLAN. *Grover Cleveland: A Study in Courage.* New York, 1932.

——. *Letters of Grover Cleveland, 1850–1908.* Boston, 1933.

"Newcomb, Victor," in Johnston, J. Stoddard: *Memorial History of Louisville, Ky.* (Chicago, 1896), I, 474–5.

PEARCE, HAYWOOD JEFFERSON, JR. *Benjamin H. Hill: Secession and Reconstruction.* Chicago, 1928.

PENDLETON, LOUIS. *Alexander H. Stephens.* Philadelphia, 1907.

PHILIPS, ULRICH B. *The Life of Robert Toombs.* New York, 1913.

RICHARDSON, E. RAMSAY. *Little Aleck: A Life of Alexander H. Stephens.* Indianapolis, 1932.

SEITZ, DON C. *Horace Greeley.* Indianapolis, 1926.

——. *The James Gordon Bennetts.* Indianapolis, 1928.

——. *Joseph Pulitzer.* New York, 1924.

STOVALL, PLEASANT A. *Robert Toombs.* New York, 1892.

STREET, JULIAN. *American Adventures.* New York, 1917.

WATTERSON, HENRY. *"Marse Henry": An Autobiography.* New York, 1919.

WERNER, M. R. *Barnum.* New York, 1923.

WINKLER, JOHN R. *Tobacco Tycoon: The Story of James Buchanan Duke.* New York, 1942.

WOODWARD, C. VANN. *Tom Watson: Agrarian Rebel.* New York, 1938.

BOOKS AND ARTICLES FOR GENERAL BACKGROUND

American Newspaper Annual, 1881–95. Published by N. W. Ayer & Son, Philadelphia.

American Newspaper Directory, 1869–80. Published by George P. Rowell & Co., New York.

ARNETT, ALEX MATHEWS. *The Populist Movement in Georgia.* New York, 1922.

ARTHUR, JOHN PRESTON. *Western North Carolina: A History from 1730 to 1913.* Raleigh, North Carolina, 1914.

AVERY, ISAAC W. *History of the State of Georgia from 1850 to 1881*. New York, 1881.

BATTEY, GEORGE MAGRUDER, JR. *A History of Rome and Floyd County, Georgia*. Atlanta, 1922.

BLEYER, WILLARD G. *Main Currents in the History of American Journalism*. Boston, 1927.

BOWERS, CLAUDE G. *The Tragic Era*. Cambridge, 1929.

BUCK, PAUL H. *The Road to Reunion*. Boston, 1937.

CAIN, ANDREW W. *History of Lumpkin County, 1832–1932*. Atlanta, 1932.

CASH, W. J. *The Mind of the South*. New York, 1941.

COOPER, WALTER G. *Official History of Fulton County*. Atlanta, 1934.

——. *The Story of Georgia*. 4 vols. New York, 1938.

COULTER, E. MERTON. *College Life in the Old South*. New York, 1928.

——. *A Short History of Georgia*. Chapel Hill, North Carolina, 1933.

CULBRETH, DAVID M. R. *The University of Virginia*. New York, 1908.

DABNEY, VIRGINIUS. *Liberalism in the South*. Chapel Hill, North Carolina, 1932.

DAVIDSON, GRACE GILLAM. *Early Records of Georgia:* Vols. I–II, Wilkes County. Macon, 1932.

DAVIS, JEFFERSON. *Rise and Fall of the Confederate Government*. 2 vols. New York, 1881.

DUNNING, WILLIAM A. *Reconstruction, Political and Economic, 1865–1877*. New York, 1907.

EDENS, A. HOLLIS. "The Founding of Atlanta," Part Three, in *Atlanta Historical Bulletin*, V (January 1940), 65–85.

GRADY, BENJAMIN. *John Grady of Dobbs and Duplin, with Some of His Descendants*. Washington, 1930.

GRAVES, JOHN TEMPLE, II. *The Fighting South*. New York, 1943.

GUINN, R. J. Address at Golden Anniversary Meeting of Georgia Press Association, in *Editor's Forum*, VIII (July 1936), 7–9.

HAWK, EMORY Q. *Economic History of the South*. New York, 1934.

HESSELTINE, WILLIAM B. *A History of the South, 1607–1936*. New York, 1936.

History and Criticism of American Public Address, A. 2 vols. New York, 1943.

HORN, STANLEY F. *Invisible Empire: The Story of the Ku Klux Klan*. Boston, 1939.

HOWELL, CLARK. *History of Georgia.* 4 vols. Atlanta, 1926.

HULL, AUGUSTUS L. *Annals of Athens, Ga., 1801–1901.* Athens, 1906.

——. *A Historical Sketch of the University of Georgia.* Atlanta, 1894.

JONES, CHARLES C., and GORDON, JOHN B. *The Old South: Addresses before the Confederate Survivors Association.* Augusta, 1887.

JOSEPHSON, MATTHEW. *The Robber Barons.* New York, 1934.

KELLEY, WILLIAM D. *The Old South and the New.* New York, 1888.

KENDRICK, B. B., and ARNETT, A. M. *The South Looks at Its Past.* Chapel Hill, North Carolina, 1935.

KENT, FRANK R. *The Democratic Party.* New York, 1928.

LEE, ALFRED M. *The Daily Newspaper in America.* New York, 1937.

LEWINSON, PAUL. *Race, Class, and Party.* New York, 1932.

McCLURE, A. K. *The South: Industrial, Financial, Political.* Philadelphia, 1886.

MARTIN, THOMAS H. *Atlanta and Its Builders.* 2 vols. New York, 1902.

MILTON, GEORGE FORT. *The Age of Hate: Andrew Johnson and the Radicals.* New York, 1930.

MIMS, EDWIN. *The Advancing South.* New York, 1926.

MITCHELL, BROADUS. *The Rise of Cotton Mills in the South.* Baltimore, 1921.

MOTT, FRANK L. *American Journalism: A History.* New York, 1941.

NEVINS, ALLAN. *American Press Opinion, Washington to Coolidge.* Boston, 1928.

——. *The Emergence of Modern America, 1865–1878.* Volume VIII in *A History of American Life,* edited by Arthur M. Schlesinger and Dixon Ryan Fox. New York, 1927.

NIXON, H. C. *Possum Trot.* Norman, Oklahoma, 1941.

NORTHEN, WILLIAM J. *Men of Mark in Georgia.* 3 vols. Atlanta, 1911.

ODUM, HOWARD W. *Southern Regions.* Chapel Hill, North Carolina, 1936.

PARK, ORVILLE A. "The Georgia Scotch-Irish," in *Georgia Historical Quarterly,* XII (June 1928), 115–35.

PATTEE, FRED LEWIS. *A History of American Literature since 1870.* New York, 1915.

PHILLIPS, U. B. *A History of Transportation in the Eastern Cotton Belt to 1860.* New York, 1908.

REED, WALLACE P. *History of Atlanta, Georgia.* Syracuse, 1889.

RHODES, JAMES F. *History of the United States.* 8 vols. New York, 1893–1919.

ROWE, H. J., publisher. *History of Athens and Clarke County.* Athens, 1923.

SELIGMAN, EDWIN R. A. *The Economic Interpretation of History.* Second edition, revised. New York, 1924.

SKAGGS, WILLIAM H. *The Southern Oligarchy.* New York, 1924.

STEED, HAL. *Georgia: Unfinished State.* New York, 1941.

STEPHENSON, GEORGE M. *American History since 1865.* New York, 1939.

THOMPSON, C. MILDRED. *Reconstruction in Georgia — Economic, Social, Political, 1865–1872.* (Studies in History, Economics and Public Law, No. 154, Columbia University Press.) New York, 1915.

THOMPSON, HOLLAND. *The New South.* New Haven, Connecticut, 1921.

TRAMMELL, WILLIAM DUGAS. *Ça Ira: A Novel.* New York, 1874. The character Malcomb has been identified as Joseph E. Brown.

"TWELVE SOUTHERNERS." *I'll Take My Stand.* New York, 1930.

United States Congress, Testimony Taken by Joint Select Committee on Condition of Affairs in the Late Insurrectionary States, VI–VII (Testimony taken by the Committee in Georgia, July 7–November 8, 1871). 13 vols. Washington, 1872.

VANCE, RUPERT B. *Human Geography of the South.* Chapel Hill, North Carolina, 1932.

WADE, JOHN DONALD. "Old Wine in a New Bottle," in *Virginia Quarterly Review,* XI (April 1935), 239–52.

WOODWARD, C. VANN. "The South in Search of a Philosophy." (Phi Beta Kappa Series, University of Florida, No. 1.) Gainesville, Florida, 1938.

UNPUBLISHED MONOGRAPHS

BAUER, MARVIN G. "Henry W. Grady, Spokesman of the New South." Unpublished doctor's dissertation, University of Wisconsin, Madison, 1936. A "rhetorical and analytical" study of Grady as an orator. The most significant parts are included in Dr. Bauer's article on Grady in *A History and Criticism of American Public Address.*

FORT, RANDOLPH L. "History of the *Atlanta Journal.*" Unpublished master's thesis, Emory University, Atlanta, 1930.

GLENN, W. F. "Henry Grady as I Knew Him." MS. in possession of Atlanta Historical Society.

PLUMMER, LEONARD NIEL. "Political Leadership of Henry Watterson." Unpublished doctor's dissertation, University of Wisconsin, Madison, 1940.

TURNBULL, W. T. "Grady as an Orator." MS. in the Joel Chandler Harris Collection, Emory University, Atlanta. A paper written in 1890 by a jurist who heard Grady's speech at Emory College in 1878.

WARD, G. G. "History of Gilmer County." MS. in possession of its author, Atlanta.

Index